Running for President

A Journal of the Carter Campaign

by Martin Schram

Published in hardcover as:
*Running for President 1976:
The Carter Campaign*

A KANGAROO BOOK
PUBLISHED BY POCKET BOOKS NEW YORK

POCKET BOOKS, a Simon & Schuster division of
GULF & WESTERN CORPORATION
1230 Avenue of the Americas, New York, N.Y. 10020

FOR PAT
AND KENNETH AND DAVID

Acknowledgments

The story of Jimmy Carter's rise from semi-obscurity as an ex-governor of Georgia to the forefront of American politics is also, in part, the story of the many others who sought the presidency in 1976 and failed. How and why Jimmy Carter made it must be understood in the context of how and why Scoop Jackson and Mo Udall and Birch Bayh and George Wallace and Frank Church and Jerry Brown and Hubert Humphrey . . . and, finally, Gerald Ford did *not* make it. The story unfolded over many months, in events that occurred in many places across the country; and it could not have been covered fully by one person alone. Most of the major newspapers began covering the 1976 presidential campaign well before the first vote was counted in the caucuses in Iowa in January and *Newsday* was no exception.

Newsday Washington correspondent Myron S. Waldman, one of the capital's most aggressive political reporters, is known not only for being savvy, but also for being well prepared. So it was that before leaving to report on the Iowa caucuses, he moved to fortify himself against the blizzards that often grip the heartland and discourage reporters from attempting farm-to-farm interviews. He stopped off at a discount warehouse in Washington, D.C. and bought a surplus World War II coat last worn by a British civil-disaster warden during the blitz. It was dark blue and double-breasted, with blue plastic buttons stamped with an anchor; it fell to nearly floor-length, was as thick as an Army-issue mattress, and cost thirty-nine dollars. Thus prepared, Waldman went to the Midwest and covered the year's first political contest with his usual dedication, clarity, and attention to detail, undaunted by the fact that Iowa was experiencing an often snowless January. Throughout the campaign of 1976, Waldman kept aggressive and insightful watch over the efforts of a number of Democrats who sought the nomination that eventually went to Carter. His reporting contributions were invaluable to the early chapters of this book.

Jean Heller is an award-winning investigative reporter who, over the years, has exposed inhuman syphilis experimentation on black men in Alabama and has recorded the dealings of major oil companies during America's energy crisis. She reports on matters of national politics with equal skill. As a *Newsday* Washington correspondent. she spent most of the 1976 primary season covering one subject: the financing of the year's presidential campaigns. Time and again Heller was out in front in reporting on where the candidates were getting their funds from and in spotting money problems that eventually proved fatal to several of the candidates' campaigns. Her work was an important part of the reporting of this book.

David Laventhol, editor of *Newsday*, was instrumental in shaping the series on the campaign that originally appeared in *Newsday*. The long hours he spent reading and editing the series that became the basis for this book, and the advice he offered, were very much appreciated. Donald Forst, managing editor of *Newsday*, was responsible for seeing to it that the newspaper series could indeed be expanded into a book. His efforts and counsel were very welcome. I am also indebted to them both for the freedom they gave me to pursue this work.

Pat Golbitz was my editor on this project, and I am especially grateful for the many suggestions she made.

Jim Toedtman, Patrick J. Sloyan, and Jim Klurfeld of *Newsday*'s Washington Bureau helped me plug some last-minute holes.

I also want to thank Sharon Donnelly, who saw to it that *Newsday*'s Washington Bureau continued to function while I was immersed in this undertaking; Susan Drake and Catherine Wood, who helped research campaign facts; and Viola Banks, who typed the finished manuscript.

—Martin Schram

Contents

BOOK ONE

June 9/Plains

Jimmy Carter was wading through the people of Plains.

A hug here, a kiss there, a slap on the back, a handshake. It was 2:15 A.M. and the June 9 sky was black; yet several hundred people were acting as if it were midafternoon as they cheered and greeted the fifty-one-year-old hometown boy who had just finished his campaigning in the last of the primaries of 1976 with a big win in Ohio and second-place showings in New Jersey and California.

Suddenly someone pressed a piece of paper into Carter's palm. He glanced at the paper, mumbled apologies, then pushed through the crowd and headed for the old wooden train depot that had been painted white and converted into a campaign headquarters.

Inside, he glanced again at the paper. It was a telephone message slip.

CALLER: Gov. George Wallace.

MESSAGE: He has something to tell you.

There was a telephone number and a notation that the phone was beside Wallace's bed and that Carter should call regardless of the hour.

For a moment Carter was puzzled. He had already spoken to Wallace earlier in the day as part of a round of courtesy calls he had made to the other candidates. Inside the depot office, Carter went toward a telephone which, according to the note taped to it, was for his personal use. But a reporter was using the phone. Quietly Carter walked past the reporter and up a few steps to a row of telephones separated by shoulder-high wood partitions covered with gunnysacks. He entered the first makeshift booth on the left. His mother, seventy-seven-year-old Lillian Carter "Don't call me Mrs. Carter . . . everyone calls me Miss Lillian"), followed him.

Carter dialed the number and the phone rang at Wallace's bedside. "He said he had been watching on televi-

2

sion that night when I said I was proud to be a southerner," Carter recalled. "And then he said if I had no objection, he would endorse me the following day."

This was the moment when Carter knew at last—without a doubt—that the first ballot was his. He could not be stopped. He had talked so confidently for so long about how he knew he was going to win, but now it was not faith but fact. There would be no last hurrah in Madison Square Garden for George Wallace; he would be releasing his 171 convention delegates and pushing them to Carter instead.

Understandably, Carter told Wallace he had no objection.

The two men talked for a while longer. "He said that the only thing he wanted of me was that I do the best that I could to be a great President," Carter said. "He asked me if I would find the time to come to Alabama to see him. I said I certainly can. He said, 'Can you come tomorrow?' I said 'No, I can't come tomorrow; I have a press conference, got some responsibilities here, where I have to be.'

"So he said, 'Could you come sometime this week?' and I said, 'Yes, I would like to do that because I am going on vacation—Tuesday, if possible'—and I said that I would be there before Sunday night and I'd let my staff work it out at his convenience.

"And he said, 'I am very proud of what you have done and I look forward to seeing you.' "

(Later Carter reflected on George Wallace's closing line—that Wallace was *very proud* of what Jimmy Carter had done. After all, Wallace had been privately bitter, antagonistic, and even derisive toward the self-styled New South governor from Georgia who had beaten him in Florida and trounced him in North Carolina, thus ending forever his campaign dream. It was a dream not of winning the presidential nomination, but of being accepted and respected; a dream of being known North and South as something more than the man who had stood in the schoolhouse door. Carter had shattered this, yet now Wallace was saying he was *very proud* of Carter.

("I think he meant the success of my campaign," Carter later said, his normally soft conversation voice dropping to just a whisper. "The acceptance of a southerner in such a wide geographical area and the over-

whelming victory in Ohio, the sure dominance in the
number of delegates as compared to the other candidates.
It was a very gracious statement he made . . . Animosity
had never been expressed by him or me personally whenever I had been with him. He and I had been very cordial
in our greetings to one another, as I had been with the
other candidates. There had never been any estrange-
ment, animosity.")

Carter and his mother stepped out of the gunnysack en-
closure. Carter, quietly ecstatic, sought out Rex Granum,
the highest-ranking aide who had bothered to make the
trip to Plains from Atlanta, where an official Carter victory party was being held. He told Granum to telephone
the good news to Carter's three top advisers—Hamilton
Jordan, Jody Powell, and Charles Kirbo—who had remained in Atlanta. But above all, Carter cautioned, do
not tell the press. It was important that Wallace not be
scooped on his own announcement.

While Carter was talking to Granum, his mother had
moved on and was telling a few reporters that her son had
just spoken with Wallace.

3:30 A.M. Granum telephones Jody Powell's room at
the Hyatt Regency in Atlanta. Powell gropes for the
phone from the disadvantage of a sound sleep; he fumbles
to make a few notes, sees the futility of it all, figures he
will take care of it in the morning, says he is happy, and
hangs up the phone. Then he makes the call he hates to
make; he phones the hotel operator and has his wake-up
call moved earlier, to 7:00 A.M. He will have to confer
early with Hamilton Jordan. Things have moved far faster
than he or anyone else in the Carter campaign had anticipated.

The morning after—really later that same Wednesday
morning—Carter awoke early and made a couple of quick
decisions. First, he decided he ought to let the world know
that he had the Democratic presidential nomination
locked up. And second, he decided that it ought not to be
George Wallace alone who had put him over the top. So

Carter moved to round up other blocs of delegate support. It took only two phone calls to do it.

The first, in midmorning, was to Chicago's mayor, Richard J. Daley, who controlled 86 Illinois delegates. The call was not unprecedented; Carter had kept in careful touch with Daley throughout the year, calling him regularly every ten days or so. Like courting the banker's chubby daughter, the wooing of Mayor Daley made sense even if it was not strictly an affair of the heart.

"I would say that I called him about every ten days or two weeks," Carter recalled. "You know, quite often we would call his office, at his suggestion and my commitment, and he would not be in and we would just leave word with the staff members that I had called. Sometimes later he would call me back. But I had done this with him and with Senator [Adlai] Stevenson [Daley's favorite son candidate] . . . just as a matter of courtesy, to let them know directly from me how the campaign was going and that I was not a high-pressure person. I never did ask them to do anything specific for me. I just let them know that I needed their support, friendship, and later on I hoped that I would have their endorsements."

Carter had thought for weeks that the Daley-controlled delegates would eventually be his. "Well, I have always thought—through my own analysis, not through any statement of his—that after I did so well in Illinois [winning the preference primary and delegates as well] he would be looking for someone, if there weren't obstacles in his effort, who could do well as the head of the ticket [Daley's Illinois Democratic ticket]. I had shown in my campaign my ability to get votes in his state. So that gave me a kind of a feeling of confidence—not of surety, but of confidence, although that is not something he had expressed to me. I kind of analyzed that myself."

As he dialed that call from Plains to Chicago on the morning of Wednesday, June 9, however, Carter had more reason to be confident than just his own analysis. The night before, Daley had told Chicago reporters that Carter deserved to win the nomination if he won Ohio big (which Carter had then proceeded to do). Now, on that Wednesday morning, the ex-Georgia governor gave the current Chicago mayor a kind of soft-touch hard sell.

"He had never made any definite commitments to me and he had told me earlier that he was not going to make any public commitment until much later," Carter said. "And when I called him Wednesday morning, I told him that I didn't want to put any pressure on him, that I didn't want him to think I would feel aggressive about it, but that I *particularly* would like to have his public statement of support that day."

He got it.

There remained one more call for Carter to make—to the Washington office of Senator Henry (Scoop) Jackson, a man whose presidential hopes Carter had dashed in the Pennsylvania primary, a man who had once attacked Carter bitterly early in the primary season but who had since warmed to Carter. A man who had 248 delegates pledged to him.

Carter had spoken to Jackson several times since the veteran Washington senator had dropped out of the campaign. Jackson, he knew, was leaning toward Carter but wanted to talk to his delegates first; he did not want to be embarrassed by having his own delegates spurn his choice. Carter asked for an endorsement.

"He said that he didn't want me to announce his endorsement," Carter recalled. "That he was going to wait until the following week to make that kind of statement."

But Carter pressed—politely—for something stronger. Jackson finally agreed. "He told me that I could tell the news media that I had had a favorable conversation with him and that I was sure that I would have his support and the support of his delegates—if I didn't quote him on that. So I was very careful to honor that."

Wallace plus Daley plus Jackson. They would officially put Carter over the top, and now all he had to do was to make their commitments public. A group of national political reporters was waiting down by the depot, a few blocks from Carter's sprawling home nestled in the trees at 1 Woodland Drive. He wanted to tell them personally about the phone calls, but first he had to attend to one detail: the selection of his press conference attire. Carter chose denim—freshly pressed blue jeans and a matching jacket. A careful choice aimed at showing that he was no standard establishment candidate.

"The people kind of have an inclination to knock down the frontrunner," Carter said later. "Whenever we'd project ourselves as the underdog fighting the establishment . . . fighting a valiant battle, we did all right. . . . I figured after Wallace, Daley, and Jackson endorsed me, I'd better . . . so I took off my clothes and put my blue jeans on. I generally wear those around Plains, but that was one reason I did it."

January 19/Iowa

"The first time we went to Des Moines, we had a reception at a hotel," Carter recalled. "There were Jody and myself and the man and woman who arranged the reception—and I think that there were three other people. We had enough food there to feed, I guess, 200 folks. So everybody was embarrassed, and somebody finally suggested that 'Governor, why don't you walk down the street . . . and at least you can shake hands with the folks in the courthouse.' "

Jimmy Carter, who became the most sought-after man in the Democratic Party, began to smile as he noted that at least there had been no danger back in February 1975 of the dismal turnout's coming to the attention of the public. "Well," he said, "there weren't any newspeople there to cover the event.

"In a way, it taught us a lesson. I don't like to be a dormant candidate. I don't like to sit in a hotel and have people come to me. I like to go out and meet them.

"The biggest problem I had was not campaign technique, or that I was from the South, or that I had not been in Washington, or that I didn't have any money, that I didn't have a good campaign organization—the problem I had was substantiality of campaign efforts in the minds of the people. Nobody thought I should be taken seriously. And we couldn't take any shortcuts to resolving it except to do better than we were expected to do in two or three of the states.

"We decided early on New Hampshire and Florida; later, we saw that Iowa was a good chance. There are only about 35,000 Democrats there who participated in the 1972 caucuses. We just saw a good chance to build that up with a major media event."

The Iowa caucuses became a major media event. Viewed in terms of the number of participants, the cau-

8

cuses were insignificant—small clusters of people meeting in Legion halls, living rooms, and basement rec rooms. People raising their hands for the candidates they favored in precinct caucuses that would be followed by conventions that eventually selected only 47 of the 3,008 delegates that would vote at Madison Square Garden in July.

But the Iowa caucuses, held on January 19, were Number 1—the first political happening of the election year. So they would be watched carefully and covered heavily by the news media. A good showing could create an initial image that might project a presidential candidate into the lead.

As it turned out, the Iowa caucuses provided a study in miniature of what was in store for the 1976 campaign for the Democratic presidential nomination. The essential factors that would loom so large elsewhere in the following months were present in the wintry campaign in Iowa.

There was Carter's success at personal, grass-roots campaigning; the skill of his advisers at molding an organization; the ability of the Carter people to pick the right moments to make the right moves. There was the example of how Carter formulated his answers to win widespread acceptance within the party, and even the example of the occasional verbal slip—Carter's comment that he favored a "national statute" to limit abortion.

And there also was the hesitation by some of the other candidates and the lack of foresight and breakdown of the organizations of others. All of these factors would become apparent time and time again during the primary elections throughout the spring; and all were apparent in the Iowa campaign.

Once, while driving between Ames and Marshalltown, Carter stopped to do a bit of person-to-person campaigning at Fred McClain's farm. McClain wasn't home. So Carter wrote a note, telling McClain that he was sorry he had missed him and that he had a "beautiful farm." He signed the note "Jimmy" and stuck it on McClain's front door.

Charles Hammer is a theoretical physicist at Iowa State University. He lives with his wife, Hazel, off-campus at Ames. He also is the Fifth Congressional District chairman and a liberal who worked hard for Eugene McCarthy and George McGovern. He briefly had met Carter and his wife, Rosalynn, and after watching Carter answer tough questions in a town called Atlantic, Hammer told a Carter staff member that the former Georgia governor had made a good impression. He also cautioned that Carter should drop his trademark line, "I will not tell a lie." Said Hammer, "That stuff sets him up."

A few days later, Hammer got a phone call. "This is Jimmy Carter," said the caller. "I'd like you to be on the state campaign committee." Hammer was frank. He said he wanted to examine Carter's positions in greater detail first. Carter suggested that Hammer call him back in two weeks and gave him a phone number, a date, and a time —4:00 P.M.

When Hammer called to announce he was joining the Carter campaign, he was surprised to discover that he was phoning the Carter home in Plains, Georgia, and was surprised that Mrs. Carter answered the phone herself.

"Hi, Charlie. How's Hazel?" Mrs. Carter asked.

Hammer, more surprised, told her he was going to be on Carter's state committee. They got to talking, and Rosalynn mentioned that at a reception back in Iowa Hazel Hammer had said that her brother had the same birthday as Rosalynn. Now, Rosalynn asked for the brother's name (Harry Mills) and his address (in Michigan). Even though there was no immediate need to win a friend in Michigan, Rosalynn wrote a note to Mills— only to discover she had lost his address. So Rosalynn telephoned Hazel, got the address again, and mailed the letter.

Tim Kraft arrived in Des Moines in 1975 with a list of politically active Iowa Democrats in his hand. His assignment: to put together a Carter organization in the first caucus state. He had met Carter in 1974, when the Georgia governor had swung through New Mexico and Kraft was working on the successful gubernatorial campaign of Jerry Apodacca. Early in 1975, Kraft volunteered to work for Carter, and he was hired by Hamilton Jordan, Carter's campaign director.

At the time, polls showed that Carter had a national recognition factor that hovered around 2 percent. A standard organizing tactic in political campaigns is to get a big name to head the statewide campaign. But Carter was so unknown, Kraft and Jordan reasoned, that it could be dangerous to have the Iowa campaign headed by a local political figure. Carter would be perceived as a liberal if his chairman were a popular liberal, or a conservative if his chairman were conservative.

So Kraft set out to put together a twenty-person Iowa Carter for President Steering Committee that scattered across the state geographically and ideologically. Because this was a working committee, it in effect gave Carter a quick twenty field offices.

That was the core of the Carter organization: twenty people throughout the state, each recruiting volunteers to work for Carter. Probably the most influential member of the steering committee was Soapy Owens, a former state president of the United Auto Workers who carried the Carter campaign into union halls and meeting rooms at a time when Carter was not perceived as being a union man. Owens had been the subject of some of that special Carter wooing. Carter had called him. Rosalynn had called him. By the time Kraft stopped by Owens' house in Newton (a spur-of-the-moment decision; Kraft was just driving through the area), Owens was about ready to sign on. He told Kraft he was just heading out on a fishing trip, but would "get involved"—he didn't say how—when he got back. Kraft told Carter to give Owens one more call. Carter did, and two weeks later, on October 4, Owens gave a ringing twenty-minute endorsement of Carter before the UAW Community Action Program meeting of 200 union activists in Marshalltown.

When Carter aides began looking for a suitable event to launch Carter's entry into Iowa, they cast throughout the state in search of speaking invitations and came up with just one: a February 26, 1975, banquet in Le Mars (population 8,895), twenty-five miles north of Sioux City, honoring Marie Jahn, whose thirty-eight years as Plymouth County recorder was the longest term that any woman had served in public office in that state. Nearly blind, she was retiring. Carter's appearance at her banquet—eleven months before the January 19, 1976, caucuses—came on the first of twenty-one days that he was to spend campaigning in Iowa.

🏴 🏴 🏴

There was a time, Carter's press secretary and confidant Jody Powell recalls, that various Iowa politicians—"people like Tom Whitney" the young state Democratic chairman—were offering Carter people some early advice: "Stay out. It's not Jimmy's kind of state."

One of the first things Carter did when he came into Iowa in February 1975 was to set up a breakfast meeting with state party chairman Whitney. The breakfast was set for the Savery Hotel in Des Moines, one of the older hostelries of that city. Whitney, not knowing Carter's penchant for punctuality and his impatience with those who do not share same, arrived for breakfast a half hour late.

They talked about what it would take to become President. Said Whitney: "He [Carter] said there was a real need in America for a candidate who would respond to the kind of doubts people have not only about government but about themselves and where they were going. The quality that was most important [according to Carter] was believability—not in terms of a single issue but in terms of human life."

Even then Carter seemed confident that he would win. "I did not believe he was self-deluding," Whitney said. Carter told Whitney to watch him on a local television program. Whitney did. "He was probably the best TV figure, excluding Ted Kennedy, since John Kennedy," Whitney said. "I realized that, in fact, he was an ideal TV candidate. A cool medium, a cool candidate. I wrote him a note and said I was very impressed."

Carter and Whitney met four more times after that. Whitney finally told Carter that although he would remain officially neutral, he would be helpful. But it was not until Whitney sat next to Carter at the head table of a lengthy Iowa fundraiser that he became deeply impressed.

"We spent two hours talking about Christ," Whitney said. "For a moment we shared a concept and a thought process that we both believed is a fundamental need in our society. Which was the concept of love—love thy neighbor. We explored the 'I Am Third' process in which God is first, family and friends second, and I am third. This nation needs a totally loving President."

Whitney says that after Carter learned that a woman active in the Iowa Democratic Party had a son who was an alcoholic and who had been hospitalized as a result, he "made a telephone call to him in the hospital, relating in a very personal way his own witness to personal difficulties in his own life."

"That quality within him ought not to be viewed cynically," Whitney said. "He's got a lot of quality and style—a lot of style. Most people feel perhaps on occasion he tells them less than the whole truth. But they want to believe."

He also remembers another of Carter's personal touches. "He always sent handwritten notes. Initially, at least, he wrote them all himself. Who knows how many he's written? The most important thing is handwritten notes. He wrote them to anyone. He'd get all the names at the meetings he'd go to [Jody Powell usually followed his boss around, noting names and addresses of people Carter met at gatherings]. And he'd write them. They might all have been the same note, but you don't get that from your congressman or senators. It was just class."

The Carter campaign in Iowa was not without its problems. There was, for example, the trip Carter made into blizzard-swept Iowa on January 1, 1976, with his new personal aide, Greg Schneiders, who eventually grew in the job from being a sort of traveling administrative aide to being an adviser of influence as well. Schneiders started out by losing his trenchcoat in the Atlanta airport; the candidate started out by boarding the plane with a 103-degree fever. They stepped off the plane in Iowa and into a minus 45-degree wind-chill factor—"Me with no coat, him with some kind of bad intestinal bug," Schneiders recalled. "What a way to break into a job!"

And there was the more serious problem of Carter's statement on abortion.

He had been interviewed on the telephone by a priest who wrote for Catholic publications. Carter had stated that he personally opposed abortion, but that he also opposed the proposed antiabortion amendment to the U.S. Constitution. The resulting article quoted him on this. But the interviewer had pressed him, and Carter was also quoted as saying that he would support some sort of "national statute" that might, in some unspecified way, restrict abortion.

Carter's opponents charged that he intentionally was clouding his position on the controversial issue, that he was trying to find a position that would seem more popular with the right-to-life people than the other candidates'—all of whom opposed unequivocably an antiabortion amendment.

Carter's abortion problems were further fueled by Rowland Evans and Robert Novak, syndicated columnists who were throughout the campaign among the Georgian's harshest critics. The column talked about "a recent whispered conversation in the basement of the Holy Spirit Church" in Creston, Iowa. Carter had said in a question-and-answer session that he considered abortion "morally wrong" but would not support a constitutional antiabortion amendment. But Evans and Novak said that Carter later told a woman in a conversation—speaking "even more softly than usual," the columnists said—that "under circumstances I would" support a constitutional amendment along the lines of the abortion ban that had been passed in Georgia and was struck down by the U.S. Supreme Court.

Carter finally issued a statement to clarify his position, which, among other things, said: "The confusion in Iowa did not originate because of any change of position of my own. I've had a very consistent position on abortion for several years. I think that abortion is wrong. I don't think the government should do anything to encourage abortion. I believe that positive action should be taken in better education, better family-planning programs, the availability of contraceptive devices for those who believe in their use, better adoption procedures to minimize abortions.

"I do not favor the constitutional amendment that would prohibit all abortions. I do not favor the constitutional amendment that would give the states local option."

With that, Carter attempted to put to rest the controversy on the abortion issue. But a larger, more ominous problem had been born. Comedian Pat Paulsen would describe it by telling audiences how officials had wanted to put Jimmy Carter on Mount Rushmore, "but they didn't have room for two faces."

The image would remain throughout the campaign.

     🏳️   🏳️   🏳️

They were lonely days, those early Iowa days. Carter had no press corps to watch him and at times no staff members to aid him. There were days when he would get up with the sun and hurry out to a small rural airstrip in the stillness of early morning to get a lift in a tiny private plane to another town for another day of handshakes and speech-making, another day of having to make the rounds, introducing himself to unfamiliar Iowans and telling them what he was doing there and what he was all about. "Hello. I'm Jimmy Carter. I'm running for President. I'd appreciate your support."

On occasion, he had the luxury of two staff members to assist him; and there were times when he was torn between his desire for staff companionship and his penchant for punctuality. One morning Carter and his two aides, Jody Powell and Greg Schneiders, arrived at the airstrip for an early departure. Carter and Schneiders boarded the plane, a small Beechcraft; the engines revved and the plane had begun to taxi down the runway when Schneiders reminded the governor that Powell was not on board. Schneiders had the pilot radio the terminal and learned that Powell was inside using a telephone. Seconds later Powell came racing out of the terminal; he ran down the runway, caught up with the idling plane, and climbed on board. Carter, who had been willing to take off without his press secretary, said: "Jody, you've got one friend on this airplane—and it ain't me."

Meanwhile, the other Democratic candidates also were trying to capture the Iowa caucuses. Morris Udall came in early. Birch Bayh came in late. Fred Harris, Sargent Shriver, and Henry Jackson had cranked up in between. But none was able to put together an organization as effective as Carter's. The Georgian's twenty-person steering committee was working well and providing a statewide network of field offices.

Take the case of Morris Udall. He was the first candidate to announce for the Presidency. He had gotten into Iowa early, invested heavily in the state in both campaign time and money, and—like Carter—had sought to build the sort of organization nationally and in Iowa that would give him a head start on the field and would carry him to the White House.

But the Udall campaign proved to be a classic example of how not to begin.

Memorandum

To: Mo, Stewart [Morris and Stewart Udall]
From: Jack Quinn [Udall's national campaign manager]
December 9, 1975
Re: Areas of Immediate Concern

   . . . We've got a reputation, frankly, as the sloppiest campaign in memory. No one knows who is in charge, who can make a quick decision that will stick.

   . . . Moreover, we're genuinely in danger of splitting this campaign into warring factions—anyone who disagrees should give Mankiewicz a call and ask him what happened in 1972 to a campaign which was hopelessly split among headquarters and congressional staff. . . .

   . . . I've had my role defined by Mo several times. Unfortunately, it needs to be done again. Ditto for Terry Bracy. Those roles *must* be clear and concrete. They cannot overlap. . . .

Budget

   Of chief concern to me in this regard is the *process*. . . . I think that on a day to day basis we're a disaster. Stewart calls [Stanley] Kurz. I call Kurz. Coyle calls Kurz. Terry calls Kurz. Jo Baer takes a staff member off the payroll and Stan decides on his own to pay her. This is insanity. . . .

In June 1975 one of Udall's Iowa co-chairpersons, Cliff Larsen, received a master list from the Democratic state committee of people who had attended Democratic caucuses. It was not a "clean" list; there was repetition of names due to people who attended caucuses at various levels (precinct, county, congressional districts). Larsen broke up the list and sent portions of it around the state to various politicians so it could be cleaned up, scrubbed of repetition.

Then on December 23, Ken Levine was dispatched to Iowa by the national Udall staff and he reported back that things were not well in Iowa. He discovered that 80 percent of that master list had disappeared. No one knew where it was. Twenty-four thousand Democratic households were at stake. They resurrected one of the old, "dirty" master lists, and set about trying to use it—repetition and all. "The list we got in June was in the same shape by Christmas," one Udall worker complained.

In Polk County, which includes Des Moines and which has 10.6 percent of the state Democratic vote, the Udall coordinator was a young man making his first venture into politics. When Ken Levine arrived from Washington on December 23, he found the young Udall coordinator hard at work trying to call by himself every name on a list of every registered voter in the county—Democrat or Republican—to tell them to go to the caucuses and vote for Udall.

In one corner of the room, unused and gathering dust, was the Polk County list of active Democrats who had previously attended caucuses—the list of people who had shown they were active and interested and would most likely attend the caucuses this year.

Levine went back to Washington and told Udall to forget Iowa. Rick Stearns, who achieved political fame as the young mastermind of the McGovern delegate hunt in 1972, also scouted Iowa for Udall and told the candidate much the same. But others came back with higher hopes. Ken Bode, a Udall man, conferred with Iowa State Democratic Chairman Tom Whitney (who was a closet Carter supporter trying to remain publicly neutral). Whitney told Bode that Udall might be able to take the state with a big media blitz. And Bode recommended to Udall that he make the effort.

The effort was made, but the problems continued. There were those on the Udall staff who had devised the television spots and who liked them; but there were others who thought the spots were terrible. They consisted of a headshot of the candidate against a stark background, the candidate talking to the people at home—talking too fast, some thought.

Staff bickering continued. Norma Matthews, the other Udall co-chairperson in Iowa, set up an event for Sunday at 8:00 P.M. and no television stations showed up to cover; she set up a press conference at 7:30 A.M. Monday and the TV people again did not show. This made Ken Levine mad. Some felt Levine had taken to poor-mouthing Iowans. He eventually left the campaign—some said he was dismissed—after he shouted across a street at Norma Matthews, "You son-of-a-bitch!" Asked about this, Levine said: "I yelled at everybody in Iowa. They let that mailing list lie for six months. No one showed up for that 7:30 A.M. press conference." He said he left the campaign by mutual consent.

While Udall and Carter had announced their candidacies and gotten an early jump in Iowa, Birch Bayh—an early favorite among a number of pols—was in Washington, thinking about whether he would really run. "He kept thinking and thinking about it," said Bill Wise, Bayh's press secretary. "I recall writing him a memo saying you've got to stop talking about it, thinking about it. Either do it or don't.

"He was out of town, I sent the memo to his home. He had made up his mind to do it just before he got the memo. Did he perceive Carter as a threat? Not really, not seriously. We saw Carter as perhaps knocking over Jackson, as a candidate of the right."

On October 22, Birch Bayh formally entered the race.

"We were aware of the early time he [Carter] was putting in," Wise said. "Our first target was Udall. We felt we had to blunt Udall. He was the more formidable of the candidates on the left. The quicker we could knock Udall out, the quicker we'd get Udall people in [Bayh's corner.] We thought our weakest area was the liberal activists. . . .

"We thought the early primaries would be a holding action. We misjudged what we had to do to get into Iowa. We felt that Udall was strong in New Hampshire. . . . But when we got into Iowa, everyone was saying it was a Carter-Bayh race (not a Udall-Bayh race). Bayh himself started to say that. We began to get sucked in."

While Udall was suffering from organizational unraveling, and while Bayh was having trouble getting it together in the first place (he never did), the Carter machine pulled off what all camps now concede was the major strategic move in the Iowa fight.

"That silly poll in Iowa" is the way Morris Udall referred to the move much later. He was sitting in his Capitol Hill office, reflecting on what might have been, and what actually was.

"People say it was a conservative year, an anti-Washington year," Udall said in an interview after the campaign. "But with just a few breaks I could have been sitting in [Carter's place] and the people would have said this was a liberal year. There were mechanical things, accidental things, failures of strategy. Carter had a brilliant strategy [running everywhere]." And yet, Udall said, it might not have worked without that "incredible flow of press starting with that silly poll in Iowa."

Udall was talking about a straw poll at a Jefferson-Jackson Day fundraising dinner held in Ames on October 25, 1975, and attended by 4,000 people.

The poll was taken by the *Des Moines Register*, which conducts straw polls at many statewide political events, according to city editor Lawrence Paul. People attending Republican Lincoln Day dinners and Democratic Jefferson-Jackson Day dinners had been polled in the past on a variety of topical questions. Logically, the question in the Ames poll would be about who people favored as President. The Carter camp had anticipated that logic.

"We figured that somebody'd take a straw poll or something like that," recalled Carter's press secretary, Jody Powell. "So it gave us a chance to do a little influencing —and also to test our organization. See if it worked. That sort of thing." It was, Powell said, Tim Kraft's idea.

"We turned on the usual paraphernalia of politics as theater," one Carter aide said. Kraft telephoned all twenty members of the Carter steering committee and they in turn worked in their districts to get people to the dinner. In the parking lot that night at Ames, a Carter brigade was hard at work. At the dinner, the steering committee's twenty members acted as floor whips, moving about the hall, persuading fellow diners to support Carter. The other candidates, meanwhile, were concentrating on winning over the audience with the rhetoric of their after-dinner speeches.

Carter won the straw poll with 23 percent of the total. No one else was close. Hubert Humphrey, who was not even on the ballot, came second with 12; Bayh was third with 10; Shriver, Udall, and Harris were further back.

Many national political correspondents were in Ames for the big Democratic dinner—a good place to get an idea of how the first caucus state would go, they figured. They picked up the results from the Des Moines paper. Jody Powell called a couple of reporters to tip them—"on a background basis"—that the *Register* had a poll that was worth looking at.

The event produced a number of stories in the nation's major newspapers. The *New York Times* used the poll results as the basis for a story headlined: "Carter Appears to Hold a Solid Lead in Iowa as the Campaign's First Test Approaches." The straw poll was viewed as the first significant, solid evidence that Jimmy Carter had emerged from the group of semiluminaries running for the Democratic nomination.

And, in fact, the Jefferson-Jackson Day dinner poll was not just a set-up. Iowa was a caucus state—not a primary state—and caucuses are won by the candidate who is able to convince the greatest number of people to devote an evening to a political meeting where they will support him. The poll at the dinner showed that Carter had the organization that could indeed bring out large numbers of supporters.

While the Jefferson-Jackson dinner poll put the spotlight on Carter, it put the pressure on him as well. "That early straw vote had a downside," Hamilton Jordan recalled. "After that poll . . . we *had* to win Iowa."

That, in fact, is just the way the Udall people were trying to picture it. The business of presidential politics, like the business of seduction, is conducted as much with illusion as it is with reality. To be a winner, a candidate must not only perform as well as he can, but he must perform as people expect him to, as well. It is, of course, best to win. But falling short of that, the next best thing is for the loser to make it appear that the winner somehow fell short of his goal.

🏳 🏳 🏳

Confidential

To: Mo [Udall]
From: Jack Quinn
November 19, 1975
Re: Campaign Progress and Strategy (#1)

The Setting—The Competition, Press Perceptions
 . . . Carter is, in my judgment, the only viable contender that you and Bayh have at this point in time. Add Jackson and Humphrey and you have the entire field. . . .
 Carter looks good in Iowa. The J-J dinner poll did two things for him: (1) it lent credibility to his efforts nationwide, and (2) it raised expectation of him in Iowa. Similarly, the Florida convention poll raises the expectation of him in that state and he foolishly predicted a Florida victory, in the traditional sense, over Wallace. I have been hyping his New Hampshire prospects as well and he is thought to be in reasonably good shape there.
 The Carter effort has these goals: (1) an Iowa victory or, at least, second place; (2) strength in New Hampshire (first place or a second to Udall or Bayh); (3) a "startling" victory over Wallace in Florida. . . . After Florida, he takes off and begins a slow drift to the right where he becomes an attractive alternative to Jackson for "God and Guns Democrats."

🏳 🏳 🏳

On January 19, caucus night in Iowa, Jimmy Carter was in New York. He was there by design. He wanted to be handy to the three television network news show interviewers in the morning. Since he was there that night he also attended a fundraising affair put on by Alice Mason, a numerologist who made sure everybody contributed in multiples of "7." Then Carter returned to the Manhattan apartment of Howard Samuels, a veteran of Democratic candidacies in New York, to spend the night.

Carter was asleep by 10:30 P.M. At 3:00 A.M., his aide, Greg Schneiders, entered the bedroom and woke him, saying: "Jody's on the phone with the results from Iowa." Carter went downstairs clad only in jockey shorts (he never wears pajamas) and was told that the news was good. He thanked Jody and he thanked Tim Kraft, the New Mexico transplant who had organized the winter effort in Iowa. "Now I guess we won't have to send you to Alaska," Carter joked to Kraft.

Carter went right back to bed.

THE RESULTS: *Uncommitted, about 37 percent of the vote; Carter, 27 percent; Bayh, 13; Harris, 10; Udall, 5; Shriver, 3; Jackson, 1; others about 3 percent. Just 50,000 Iowans had gone to the caucuses. Fewer than 14,000 of them voted for Carter. In Oyster Bay, Long Island, that would not be enough votes to elect him to the Town Council. But in Iowa, it was more than any other candidate got. In the morning, he appeared on NBC's "Today" show, the CBS "Morning News," and ABC's "AM America." Jimmy Carter had popped out of the pack.*

February 24/New Hampshire

When Birch Bayh looks back at New Hampshire, he recalls the Sunday before election day, when he went to the Wayfarer Hotel outside Manchester to meet with his staff. He had gotten into the race late, but he was looking for a big finish, and so he asked his aides for a review of the plan for getting out the vote.

There was no plan.

"He couldn't believe it," recalled one man who was there. No Bayh delegates were scheduled to be at polling precincts. A frantic effort ensued. Aides went for the telephones; even Bayh began making calls. Some delegates eventually got to the polls, but not enough. Bayh finished third, well off the pace set by Jimmy Carter.

When Mo Udall looks back at New Hampshire, he sees it in terms of days lost.

"I should have taken those eight days in Iowa and gone into New Hampshire," Udall said. He figured that he was picking up 1,000 votes a day near the end for every day he campaigned in New Hampshire. By that measure, Udall fell a little more than four days short in the state primary.

"It was all so close," he said. "If I had gone into New Hampshire [by ignoring Iowa] I would have won New Hampshire. Tiny little things."

When Jimmy Carter looks back at New Hampshire, he sees it as a solid winter of work by family and staff. No major strategy moves, just hard work. "I would say we had far superior organizational structure to Udall and the rest in New Hampshire," he says.

"We kind of played it down—we never bragged about it—but it was there. We contacted 95 percent of the Democratic homes in New Hampshire. And it was a tedious person-to-person relationship. I went into just about all the shoe factories in New Hampshire and a lot of the Beano games. I guess if you went to the stores and restaurants and jewelry shops, coffee shops and barbershops and beauty parlors in New Hampshire and the media centers, at least it would be hard for you to find one of those places where one of my family hasn't been. Chip or Caron or Jack or Julie or Jeffrey or Annette or Sissy or Ruth or any of them."

Carter and Udall and Bayh have explanations for why New Hampshire turned out to be Jimmy Carter's state. But perhaps the biggest factor was a man who didn't run. Senator Henry Jackson's decision not to enter the race assured that the first primary contest of 1975 would be among a collection of liberals, all vying for the votes of the left, and Jimmy Carter, alone to court the center and right of this state's essentially conservative, working-class Democratic Party.

The decision was not reached with unanimity in the Jackson camp. At least one adviser made a strong case very early that this would amount to giving Carter a free pass—a victory that would very likely boost him into the frontrunner's spot early. But back in mid-1975, Jimmy Carter did not exactly look like a force to be feared, and this advice was rejected. Of greater consideration to the Jackson men that time was that their candidate carried a loser image from his disastrous primary showings in 1972, and that he could not afford to start 1976 with a defeat.

Jackson might well not have been able to win in New Hampshire. But it is likely that he could have taken enough of the center and right votes to have permitted Udall to win. "I don't like to think about it," said Hamilton Jordan. "It's just one of those things. But Jackson and Jimmy sure do draw from the same well, and that just might have been the difference."

▨ ▨ ▨

One of Birch Bayh's biggest problems was his campaign image. In a year of anti-Washington slogans, in a year where Jimmy Carter was telling people "I'm a farmer . . . a father . . . a Christian . . ." Birch Bayh was saying—

on television, on radio, on the stump—"I'm a politician."
It didn't work.

🇺🇸 🇺🇸 🇺🇸

The television screen is dominated by the face of Birch
Bayh, handsome, polished, staring straight at the camera
and speaking against a stark, bare backdrop.

"To listen to the other candidates, none of them are
politicians. Even the ones who've held public office say
they're not politicians. Well, I'm Birch Bayh—and I'm a
politician. It took a good politician to stop Nixon's plan
to pack the Supreme Court. And it's going to take a
good politician to break up the big oil companies, to get
jobs for unemployed workers and hold food prices in
line. The question isn't whether you're a politician, but
what kind of politician you are. Because it takes a good
politician to make a good President."

🇺🇸 🇺🇸 🇺🇸

With this appeal Birch Bayh sought to lure the liberal
and moderate vote away from Morris Udall. Udall's
television spots, meanwhile, focused on one of the non-
politicians—former Watergate Special Prosecutor Archibald Cox—who helped bring down the crowd of politicians who created the very crisis in leadership that had
become a theme of every candidate's campaign.

Cox said in endorsing Udall: "Trust in government is
not to be had for the asking. It begins with the trust
that those who govern repose in people. Only a man of
openness and courage can bring us together." ("Bring
Us Together," ironically, was an old Nixon campaign
slogan.)

Back as early as 1972, Carter and Hamilton Jordan
had looked to New Hampshire as the place where Carter
would make his move. Later, Iowa emerged as an op-
portunity for an even earlier test. But all along, in the
Carter master plan, it was New Hampshire first, then
Florida. New Hampshire to make a national reputation,
Florida to show that Carter could wrest the South from
George Wallace.

For the Carter people, in their first venture into
the world of presidential primaries, New Hampshire

seemed in many ways ideal. It was, as Jordan wrote Carter in 1972, "a small state . . . independent and given to the kind of personal campaigning that you and your family are capable of waging."

🏴 🏴 🏴

At 11:00 A.M. on the first Sunday in 1976, a chartered airliner taxied to a stop at the Manchester airport, and out into the bitter chill of a New Hampshire winter day stepped an incongruous assortment of visitors. Ninety Georgians wearing wing tips and double-knits and wide white belts, there to spread the word about Jimmy Carter through the land of the original Yankees. They were mostly middle-aged and well-heeled; each had paid his own way to come up north and politick.

The Georgians, headed by Carter campaign political coordinator Landon Butler, were taken to lunch at a Manchester restaurant and were divided into nine teams of ten each. Each Georgian was assigned to a street route in Manchester and Nashua and each was given a "walk packet"—hand cards assembled in street-address order bearing the name and address of every registered Democrat in the area.

By 4:00 P.M., the Georgians were on the streets, knocking on doors, handing out literature, telling people about how they personally knew Jimmy Carter and could vouch for his record and capability. Ninety Georgians working the streets on one of the coldest days of the year. If a registered Democrat was not home, the Georgians would write a personal note and stick it in the door or the mailbox. The Georgians went at it throughout the next week. Each night they would meet back at the Sheraton Wayfarer, in a special "boiler room" that had been set up to chart the progress of the various teams, engaging in a competition of sorts. By Thursday, the Georgians figured they had talked to 10,000 of the 20,000 registered Democrats on their lists and had left notes for the rest. They returned to the warmth of their Georgia homes and then sent handwritten, hand-addressed, hand-stamped letters to each New Hampshire voter they had met who seemed at all favorable to Carter's candidacy. Six thousand letters were sent in all—personal messages including phrases such as "I liked your cute dog" or "I hope your boy is feeling better."

The Georgians-to-New Hampshire operation was the idea of Hamilton Jordan and the Carter campaign director figures it was the single most effective campaign effort of the year's first primary. "Those Georgians gave Jimmy a lead in New Hampshire that was never lost and was never jeopardized," he said.

Carter and Jordan looked to New Hampshire as a place where, as Jordan wrote in a 1972 memo to Carter, "sure winners have stumbled and dark horses like Eugene McCarthy and George McGovern have established themselves as serious contenders."

Established themselves as serious contenders. McCarthy and McGovern established themselves not by winning; just by doing better than expected. McCarthy finished with 47 percent in 1968 but many people still remember it as a win because he had taken on a President, Lyndon Johnson, and had done well. McGovern scored with 37 percent, second to Edmund Muskie's 47.8 percent, but the Muskie people had been talking about how much bigger they expected their win to be and so Muskie was perceived as having fallen below his own expectations.

So it was that all Carter wanted to do in New Hampshire was *to establish himself as a serious contender,* not necessarily win. Winning came because of the combination of Carter's good fortune (at having Jackson shun New Hampshire and Bayh fumble it) and Carter's good organization, planning, and effort. And things like the plasticized notebook folder with a cover done in a Formica-like imitation of wood and a title page that read: "Jimmy Carter Presidential Campaign—New Hampshire Campaign Manual." Inside there was a section devoted to "Grassroots Projects." A how-to-do-it guide to voter checklists, door-to-door canvassing, telephone canvassing, yard signs and posters, absentee ballots, the crucial get-out-the-vote strategy, and an interesting innovation called "The Postcard Plan."

The Postcard Plan called for volunteers and supporters to go to their local Carter headquarters on Saturday,

February 14, and "simultaneously write messages to every New Hampshire eligible primary voter they can think of." The postcards were supplied by the Carter campaign: green background with a black-and-white photo of Carter in his workshirt, leaning on a fence, apparently down home on the farm. The messages too were supplied by the Carter campaign on a sheet in the campaign manual:

SAMPLE POSTCARD MESSAGES

1. John, I met Jimmy Carter the other day at Yoken's. Jimmy makes sense. I hope all of us in the Portsmouth area will support him February 24.

2. Tim and Judy, Jimmy Carter did a great job straightening out government in Georgia. I think he could do the same thing in Washington. I hope you'll support him February 24.

3. Dear Bill, Jimmy Carter is really an honest guy who would be a great President. I hope you'll vote for him. Kathy and I will.

4. Mona, I'm going to vote for Jimmy Carter. He's a hard worker and does what he thinks is right. That's what we need in Washington.

5. Jim, Jimmy Carter is a businessman like us and has commonsense ideas about making Federal government efficient. We need someone down there who has run a government. Hope you'll vote for him.

6. Joe, I just met a guy who's running for President. Jimmy Carter. He's really different. He's one of us. Vote for him.

7. Georgia, Jimmy Carter had a great record on environment as Governor. He stood up to the Corps of Engineers as Governor. He'll do the same thing as President. I hope you'll vote for him February 24.

The night of Jimmy Carter's first primary election was a quiet, home-style family affair. Carter chose to spend the evening at the home of his Concord campaign chairman, rather than partake in the noise and commotion of the Carter headquarters setup at the frayed Carpenter Hotel. There was Carter; his wife; his sons, Chip, Jack, and Jeffrey; their wives; and three close staff members, Jody Powell, Greg Schneiders, and pollster Patrick Caddell. They passed sandwiches, watched TV, small-talked, and waited for the results.

THE RESULTS: *Carter, 29.4 percent; Udall, 23.9 (4,301 votes behind); Bayh, 16.2; Harris, 11.4; Shriver, 8.7. While en route to a victory celebration on the night of February 24, Carter saw one of his supporters, leaned toward the car window, and flashed a single "V" sign. When he sat back, his wife, Rosalynn, concerned about the Nixonian imagery of it all, said in a quiet voice: "Jimmy, please don't make that sign—and especially, please don't use both hands!"*

Election night in New Hampshire was a many-ringed circus. All of the major candidates were there except the Republican incumbent, President Gerald Ford, and their campaigns had set aside large ballrooms and meeting rooms in hotels and restaurants as places for supporters to gather and party and await the outcome. Political reporters worked the circuit, moving from ballroom to ballroom, interviewing candidates and their advisers. To Stewart Udall, brother of and campaign manager for candidate Mo, the scene stood in vivid contrast to another New Hampshire primary election night sixteen years earlier.

"You know where John Kennedy was on New Hampshire night in 1960?" asked Stewart Udall (who eventually became President Kennedy's Secretary of the Interior). "He was home in Washington—at his house in Georgetown having a quiet dinner with Jackie, my wife and me, and the Ben Bradlees. No TV cameramen, nothing. Then at about 10:30 someone called and gave him the percentages and he had won and that was it."

Interlude: The Kennedy Look

There was something familiar about the man on the
screen. The hair was full, thick—John Kennedy had
hair like that. The dress was casual, sporty, with a blue
shirt open at the neck—Kennedy's dress was sporty, often
open-necked blues, in those scenes at the beach or sailing
off Hyannis.

And there was the full easy smile—"He still has
that Kennedy smile," Carter's long-time media adviser,
Gerald Rafshoon, had written back in 1972, in a memo
about how the Georgian could mold a national image.

Jimmy Carter, on the screen, has the image of "cool"
and the "blurred, shaggy texture" that Marshall McLuhan
said was the best thing John F. Kennedy had going for
him. It was Rafshoon who gave Carter his cool, his blur,
and his shag.

Jerry Rafshoon had recognized Carter's resemblance
to Kennedy when he started handling Carter's political
media campaign in 1966. But he carefully avoided it
—for a time. "I never wanted to capitalize on it,"
Rafshoon said. "I didn't think that it would exactly be a
big selling point in Georgia. . . . I didn't go out of my
way to try to do any Camelot camera angles. And no
shots on the beach and no touch football. . . . I tried
to avoid smiling pictures."

Actually, Jimmy Carter is in many ways more reminiscent of Bobby Kennedy than John. He is of small
stature like Bobby. He is soft-spoken—at times even
mumbling in private conversation—and shy like Bobby.
Rafshoon saw that resemblance, too, but didn't attempt
to project it. "After all, Bobby Kennedy was not too
popular down here."

Jimmy Carter was struggling way back in the field
in 1966 in his first gubernatorial try when Rafshoon
came across his broadcast advertising and figured he
needed some help. The spot was a country-western jingle
that kept prattling: ". . . And Jimmy Carter is his name
. . . Jimmy Carter is his name."

Rafshoon's assistance was accepted. He took all the
money Carter had left, about $70,000, and used it to show
short television spots of Carter—not smiling, but, as

Rafshoon recalled, "playing up his basic appeal of the quiet, sincere, competent, reasonable person."

Carter finished third, narrowly missing a runoff against former Governor Ellis Arnall and the eventual winner, Lester Maddox.

Jerry Rafshoon has been marketing Carter ever since. The head of a successful Atlanta advertising agency, Rafshoon seemed younger than his forty-two years as he moved about his office planning ad strategies in 1976, wearing an open shirt and blue jeans, at times sitting cross-legged atop a desk or table as he conducted a conference.

In 1976, in New Hampshire, Rafshoon's commercials got two-state exposure; the state's residents largely watch Boston television, and the Massachusetts primary was just a week after New Hampshire's. Carter spent $130,000 on TV advertising that served the two state primaries, and another $30,000 on ads over virtually every radio station in New Hampshire. (In later primaries, Rafshoon would purchase radio ads on black stations, country-western stations, and "easy listening" stations.)

The Carter spots concentrated on the candidate as a farmer and working man, talking about his life and family and asking voters to trust him. Many of the spots showed the smile that stirred memories of John Kennedy. They also included the lines: "I'll never tell a lie, I'll never avoid a controversial issue. . . . Watch television, listen to the radio. If I ever do any of those things, don't support me."

The lines played like someone had taped a "kick me" sign to the seat of Carter's pants. Carter's critics seized gleefully on the challenge and sought to unearth anti-Carter evidence. Eventually, documented reports showed that Carter, like most politicians, had at times at least misled and evaded. Later, he dropped the "I'll never tell a lie" portion of his standard stump and advertising litany.

March 2/Massachusetts

"We were the leader. Compared to big shots like Wallace and Jackson, Bentsen, Udall and Bayh, Sanford, I was ahead . . . the dam was broken . . . I was kind of a giant-killer."

Jimmy Carter was up, up, up. Once he and his men had talked about a long and bloody war—thirty primaries and every one a battle. But the sudden victories in Iowa and New Hampshire had changed all that. Now they were talking about a quick kill. Their strategy was so right, their judgment so fine. They could do no wrong. The nomination just might be won in a couple of weeks. A "high-risk strategy," Hamilton Jordan called it.

The Carter master plan had always been to concentrate first on New Hampshire's February 24 primary to establish a national reputation and then on Florida's March 9 primary to take the South away from George Wallace. The Tuesday in between, Massachusetts' March 2 primary, had never been big in their plans. A couple of months before the Massachusetts election, in fact, the Carter staff—fortified by a private poll—had become downright negative about the Bay State primary. The survey by Patrick Caddell in December 1975 showed Sargent Shriver with 18 percent, Wallace with 13 to 14, Jackson with 10, Carter barely surfacing with 3, and 40 percent undecided.

But the post-New Hampshire euphoria led to a radical shift in sentiment among Carter men. On New Hampshire's primary night, they gathered in the Carpenter Hotel in Manchester and decided to extend the media spots that had been showing in Boston during the final week of that primary.

The next day, Caddell's staff reinforced the optimism with a report on what he calls a quick "panelback," returning to interview people who had been polled in December. The sample was small, but Carter's progress

32

seemed substantial. Their candidate was in the high twenties; Jackson and Udall were in the low teens.

Another poll, by a network, showed Carter with a 5- to 6-point lead. By now, as virtually every member of the Carter inner circle—including Carter—recalls, there was strong support for a major push in that final week in Massachusetts.

If Carter was going to be officially running in Massachusetts, his aides began to reason, then he should run all-out. Try for the quick kill in Massachusetts; then a Florida victory over Wallace would be just a mop-up. Carter would have scored a farm belt win (Iowa), a true Yankee win (New Hampshire), a northern industrial state win (Massachusetts), and a southern win (Florida).

"We had a real tough argument about Massachusetts— about whether to leave Florida and go into Massachusetts," Carter said. "There was a good argument for that. If we had won Massachusetts the week after New Hampshire—we weren't supposed to do anything, you hip?—it would have made Florida unnecessary. Of lesser importance.

"I must say that the mistake, if there was one made in Massachusetts, was my own. Because—I think this is accurate . . . Hamilton Jordan, the campaign manager, warned me to put more time in Massachusetts, and I was reluctant to do it in order to maintain a high commitment to Florida." But Caddell said in an interview: "I guess I'm the most guilty party for Massachusetts. I wanted Jimmy to go for the kill."

(Note: Unlike Carter and a number of other top Carter aides, Jordan said he does not remember that he was advocating that Carter spend more time in Massachusetts than Carter wound up spending. "If a mistake was made," Jordan said, "we all made it.")

The Carter camp decided to make a big investment in money—especially television ad money—but not in the candidate's time. Carter did not appear in Massachusetts in the last five days of the campaign.

Greg Schneiders looks, at first glance, much like the strain of bright young men that seem to be pulled to candidates' sides to function as aides de camp. He is twenty-nine, clean-cut, dresses conservatively and still wears dark-rimmed glasses; he has the job that in the Nixon circumstances was Dwight Chapin's and in the Ford White House was filled by Terry O'Donnell. He seems at first glance to be out of the same mold; capable and efficient, upwardly mobile, but verging on humorless. Right and wrong. Schneiders is a newcomer to politics —he ran a couple of ultra-in restaurants in Washington, D.C. (Whitby's and The Georgetowne Beef Company), and he is a capable and conscientious man. But he is also partial to mixing business with wit.

At the time of the Carter inner circle's great debate over Massachusetts, Schneiders gave Carter a memo of his own. "I realize that you are constitutionally unable to contemplate a planned defeat. . . ." the memo began. Carter read the first sentence, paused, looked at Schneiders and said: "That's right."

The memo went on to make the case that if Carter effectively decimated his opposition so early, an effective Stop Carter movement might then be organized —with plenty of time in which to operate. Thus, it said, Carter might have a more serious problem in the long run if he did win Massachusetts.

It was a prophetic memo, for it did reflect the tentative plans of some of those liberal politicians from Washington who mistrusted Carter. In the nighttimes of debate and drinking at the two bars of Boston's Parker House Hotel during the Massachusetts campaign, liberal operatives confided to a reporter that they had just such an idea. If Carter won in Massachusetts, they said, there would immediately be a major effort to urge organized labor to abandon Jackson and join with McGovern liberals in a new alliance behind Hubert Humphrey. If Carter lost Massachusetts, the liberals said, the movement would be made more difficult because it would then lack urgency.

Eventually, when Carter eliminated his opposition in Pennsylvania, a Stop Carter movement did form. Frank Church and Jerry Brown came in and landed some sharp blows in the later rounds. Had Carter won in Massachusetts and gone on to take Wallace in Florida, it might have spurred still earlier Stop Carter efforts—

and Carter might have had trouble holding on to win the fight.

≋ ≋ ≋

One of the central factors of the Morris Udall campaign in Massachusetts was the endorsement of Archibald Cox, a professor who is widely known and respected in the liberal circles of New England for the way he stood up to Richard Nixon and forced the President to touch off his Saturday Night Massacre in order to continue his Watergate cover-up.

It was Stewart Udall, Mo's brother, who was responsible for wooing and finally winning the Cox endorsement, according to Terry Bracy, aide to candidate Udall.

Cox had served in the Kennedy administration too, Bracy recalled. "Stu Udall started talking to Ken Galbraith and Archie Cox in late 1974. Archibald Cox's first major speaking engagement after he was fired was a testimonial dinner for Mo in Arizona. Cox always had a special feeling about the Udalls. . . We were wooing him over a matter of months. . . . Ken Galbraith told Stu to go right at Cox but to be careful, that Archie was sensitive." Finally, Cox agreed to endorse and campaign for Mo Udall, "after a number of long talks on an intellectual basis," Bracy said.

≋ ≋ ≋

On Monday, February 23, the League of Women Voters held one of its forums for candidates. It was televised over the Public Broadcasting System network.

That evening somebody asked a question about tax reform (Carter had said that the present tax system is a disgrace). Specifically: Would his tax reforms include eliminating the income tax deduction for home mortgages?

Carter said that "would be among those I would like to do away with" as part of his sweeping tax-reform proposal. It was an uncharacteristic answer—uncharacteristic in that it was not carefully thought out and structured.

Carter left immediately after the show. As his car was pulling out, his aides Greg Schneiders and Jody Powell ran into the street and flagged down the driver. Powell told Carter through the window that he was getting some questions from reporters seeking details of the mortgage plan. Carter told him to say that it would be part of his overall, comprehensive tax-reform program and that it would be based on studies and cut the tax rate for the average taxpayer by 40 to 50 percent. The car pulled away.

"He was operating on about three cylinders on that answer," Powell said months later.

The Carter people were slow to assess the impact, but it was just the opening that Udall, Bayh, and Jackson had been seeking. Jackson hit the hardest. He charged that Carter's "proposal" would mean "American home-owners will have to pay $6 billion more in taxes." Jackson also said: "He'd better do some homework before he comes up with fuzzy ideas." Carter would wear that "fuzzy" label the rest of the campaign.

Newspapers began taking note of how all three Democratic candidates had suddenly ganged up to run against —and attack—Carter. "We were in trouble," Bayh's press secretary Bill Wise said months later. "We were looking for some way to break out of the pack of candidates who were all saying the same things . . . we had to take the risk. We had nothing to lose. Apparently the Jackson people came to the same conclusion. Udall also at the same time. People thought there was an organized cabal against Carter. There was nothing further from the truth. We all decided independently."

The Carter men were unable to decide whether it would be better to slash back at the combined attackers or take the high road and deal with it in a statesmanlike manner. Carter basically did neither.

Carter made one attempt to deal with the attacks during an appearance at Faneuil Hall, Boston's historic meeting place, and wound up sounding like Richard Nixon. There Carter was asked about the criticisms; he replied that he himself could bear them without damage but that the attacks "may hurt the country."

After that he went to campaign in Florida, doing his business as usual and basically ignoring the charges of his opponents.

In those days, the controversy didn't seem very important to the candidate and his advisers. They were still savoring New Hampshire. Carter predicted, "I'll finish ahead of Jackson and Wallace. . . . I won't be embarrassed." Jody Powell kept telling reporters that Carter would do "very well."

The Carter people remained convinced that their candidate would be able to sail through on the strength of his momentum, his media spots, and his cover stories in *Time* and *Newsweek*. What they got, instead, was their first lesson on what it means to have "soft" support. People had been saying all along that Jimmy Carter's vote was "soft," but few in the Carter camp had a good idea of just how bad that can be for the candidate. They just weren't very concerned with details such as that.

"Soft vote," Jody Powell said by way of formulating a definition, "is the voters who don't care enough to come vote for you in the rain."

THE RESULTS: *It did not rain in Massachusetts on election day. It snowed. A near blizzard. "That abominable snowstorm," Carter later called it. Fifty-five percent of the eligible Democrats went to the polls, about the same percentage that voted in 1972. But not many of them were Carter's. For the first time he discovered how soft support can melt.*

Carter, the favored "frontrunner," finished fourth, with a bare 14.2 percent. Jackson won with 22.7 percent; Udall finished second with 18; and Wallace was third with 17.1.

Scoop Jackson had relied heavily in Massachusetts on the get-out-the-vote abilities of a young political neophyte, Bob (Skinner) Donahue. And Donahue did not let the veteran senator down. His organization worked smoothly, getting Jackson voters to the polls despite the heavy snow and wind. The twenty-six-year-old Donahue said at one point that he had some 500 cars in the field on election day.

Donahue had also picked some key precincts for the Jackson people to watch on election night. The Jackson advisers gathered in the senator's hotel suite in Boston to watch the returns. The early key precincts were all Boston precincts. Wallace won them all, but Jackson came in a strong second, and the rest of the pack was far behind.

Jackson and his advisers knew then that they had it won.
They would win the election in the suburbs and outlying
areas. But the impact of Wallace winning in Boston precincts stunned one in the Jackson crowd—Daniel Patrick
Moynihan, a tall gray-haired man of Harvard with a Hell's
Kitchen background and a Brahmin air, an individualist
who served both Kennedy and Nixon, and who has long
been a puzzle to people who like to put ideological labels
on all those who dabble in politics.

Moynihan couldn't get over it. "Look at what American
liberalism has done!" he exclaimed at one point, according to a friend who was in the room. "It's pushed Boston
so far that it's voting for George Wallace! John Kennedy's
city! Bobby Kennedy's city!"

Soon the results were official and the Jackson suite was,
in the words of one adviser, "a slightly delirious place."
The man who in 1972 was the symbol of the political
loser was now a winner—victorious in his first test of 1976.
There were backslaps and handshakes and hugs and cheers
and, in the midst of it all, Jackson, Moynihan, and writer/
adviser Ben Wattenberg were trying to take a serious
look at just what the election meant. They moved through
the bustle of ecstatic well-wishers, found no corner
satisfactory, and wound up talking politics in the senator's
bathroom. There, with their voices amplified by the acous-
tical mix of plumbing and tile, they agreed on a basic
point: the Jackson victory had, as they saw it, changed
the landscape of American politics—actually it ratified a
change that had already taken place. The electorate had
recognized that the Vietnam War was over. Jackson was
a hardliner, a hawk in this state that was the nesting
place of doves. Yet his support of the Vietnam War effort
had not been a damaging campaign issue. Neither were
his get-tough positions on negotiations with the Soviets on
arms, on Jewish emigration, or on détente in general.

Jackson and advisers had been well aware that the
senator was probably the most unpopular with Soviet officials of the entire field of candidates. In fact, at one
point during the bathroom conference that night, Wattenberg exclaimed: "How'd you like to be a fly on the wall in
the Kremlin tomorrow?"

It was a heady time for Scoop Jackson and his men, and
in that night of euphoria they concluded that the Massachusetts election marked the end of the New Politics era

of the Democratic Party, the end of the era of liberal control that had spawned the candidacy of George McGovern. The party was moving his way, Jackson felt that night, and if it continued on that course, he believed he would be the Democratic nominee.

The coming months would show that Jackson was right on the first point but wrong on the second.

🏴 🏴 🏴

On Massachusetts primary night, Jimmy Carter was in Florida. He awaited the returns in a room on the top floor of his hotel, a room that carpenters were transforming into a restaurant, a room that was still bleak, with bare boards in place where plush, padded dining room booths would someday be. First the results came by phone and later by television.

Carter sat stunned.

Late in the night, he went to a telephone and called his public opinion analyst, Pat Caddell, who had remained at the Boston headquarters. As Caddell remembers it, the candidate's voice was pure ice. Carter simply asked, in slow, measured tones of controlled rage: *"What happened?"*

Caddell explained about the snowstorm and the soft vote and how people who favored Carter apparently had not felt so passionately about him that they wanted to go out in bad weather just to vote for him. Caddell also noted that at least Carter had done well among the black voters of Roxbury. Carter listened silently.

Later that night Greg Schneiders tried to cheer his boss by looking for some saving grace. "Well," Schneiders said, "if we didn't do well in Boston, we must have done well in some other section that we can emphasize to the press." Carter replied emptily: "With fourteen percent, we didn't carry much of anything." End of conversation.

🏴 🏴 🏴

Looking back sometime later, Jody Powell candidly discussed his own mistakes: "Our expectations jumped considerably [after New Hampshire] and we conveyed these expectations to the press—repeatedly—which was a stupid thing to do. . . . I'd gotten myself in a mental set. I'd been

shooting off my mouth when I should have been quiet. . . .
Later, as a result, we became overly cautious."

Hamilton Jordan put it this way: "It's a lesson—every
time we get cocky, we get knocked on our ass."

The Early Days

Archery, Georgia, is a state of mind—an undefined and unorganized community, Jimmy Carter calls it—on a road that stretches across the low flatlands between Savannah and Columbus, just outside Plains (population 683). There is no signpost saying where Archery begins or ends. People just know.

It was a place on a dirt road, during the Depression, where trains would stop if someone put a red leather flag in the switch. A place where two white families and about twenty-five black families lived. One of the white families was that of the section foreman of the Seaboard Railroad. The other was that of James Earl Carter. His oldest son was born on October 1, 1924. He was named James Earl Carter, Jr., but everyone has always called him Jimmy.

The Carter farm was a pleasant, basic place. The wooden clapboard house was heated by fireplaces and a wood-burning stove. Water was drawn by a hand pump. An outdoor privy stood in the back yard. Dogs, chickens, guinea fowl, ducks, and geese came and went as they pleased.

Jimmy Carter tells of the farm and his family and his early life in *Why Not the Best?*, his autobiography, which was published to coincide with his run for the Presidency. The publisher, Broadman Press, specializes in religious works. On the jacket it has included an advertisement for two of its other books: *Modern Stories of Inspiration*, described as "true stories of people who have heard God through the clouds and in the middle of the storm," and *Politics and Religion Can Mix!*

In his book, Carter portrayed his boyhood in Archery and Plains in romantic Faulknerian passages laced with humble beginnings and Poor South adversities. Among the most interesting portions of the book are the sections in which Carter talks about his father's feelings toward blacks. Carter recalls that when he was a child during the Depression, Archery society was built around a black leader, Bishop William Johnson, who represented five or six states in the African Methodist Episcopal church. One of Johnson's sons, Alvan, was educated and lived in Boston. "He was the only black who habitually came to our front door," Carter writes.

Whenever we heard that Alvan was back home for a visit, there was a slight nervousness around our house. We would wait in some combination of anticipation and trepidation until we finally heard the knock on our front door. My daddy would leave and pretend it wasn't happening while my mother received Alvan in the front living room to discuss his educational progress and his experiences in New England for this was one of the accepted proprieties of the segregated South which Alvan violated. Even when Bishop Johnson came to see my father, he would park in front of the store and send one of his drivers to the back door to inform my daddy that he would like to see him, and Daddy would go out to meet the Bishop in the yard.

Earl Carter was a community leader: one of the early directors of the Rural Electrification Administration's local program in the Plains area, a member of the Sumter County School Board, and—one year before he died of cancer in 1953—he was elected to the state legislature. He ran a diversified farm and had a small store next to his house where he sold overalls, work shoes, sugar, salt, flour, meal, Octagon soap, tobacco, snuff, rat traps, and products off the Carter farm: syrup, side meat, lard, cured hams, loops of stuffed sausage, and wool blankets. He was a respected man in his community, respected by both blacks and whites. In his book, Carter tells about how one of the prize possessions of Archery was the Carter family's battery-operated radio. He writes:

All our black neighbors came to see Daddy when the second Joe Louis-Max Schmeling fight was to take place. There was intense interest, and they asked if they could listen to the fight. We propped the radio in the open window of our house, and we and our visitors sat and stood under a large mulberry tree nearby.

There were heavy racial overtones encompassing the fight, with Joe Louis given a good chance to become the new black heavyweight champion of the world. He had lost in his first boxing encounter with Schmeling, but in this return match Louis almost killed his opponent in the first round.

My father was deeply disappointed in the outcome.

There was no sound from anyone in the yard, except a polite, "Thank you, Mister Earl" offered to my father.

Then, our several dozen visitors filed across the dirt road, across the railroad track, and quietly entered a house about a hundred yards away out in the field. At that point, pandemonium broke loose inside that house, as our black neighbors shouted and yelled in celebration of the Louis victory. But all the curious, accepted proprieties of a racially segregated society had been carefully observed.

Earl Carter was a deeply conservative man, a product of his place and his time. He was a rural, Deep South man who never finished high school and never questioned the propriety of racial segregation. Jimmy Carter protrayed well his father's racial insensitivities in his book, and he later had times when he seemed uneasy about the picture he had painted of the man who he maintained was both his father and his "best friend." In June, for example, after he had the nomination locked up, Carter got into a rambling chat with reporters on board his airplane, beginning by trying to explain George Wallace and winding up talking about his father instead.

Jimmy Carter had been asked if he viewed Wallace as "evil" or "ugly." Carter shook his head.

"No, you have to remember that the Congress of the United States, the Supreme Court, the governors of I guess every state in the country all accepted racial segregation. The Supreme Court ruling was separate but equal. Congress didn't pass the Voting Rights Act. There was no one-man, one-vote rule until just a short while ago. So Wallace is the last remaining public official on the scene who was part of that nationwide attitude.

"I don't know what would have happened had I been governor back in 1960, or 1955, whenever it was, I don't know. But I was lucky enough to come along after the crisis took place in the South. When I was trying to exemplify as a church member, and so forth, equality of the races, in a fairly timid way compared to what I could have done, that was just the embryonic stage of my political life. It was an accepted thing. Very fine governors like Ernest Vandiver of Georgia accepted the inequities that were in existence.

"So Wallace is anachronistic in that he's come over into this modern age. But it's not quite fair to say that he was malevolent or that he was ugly. And I think he capitalized on the racial issue by standing in the schoolhouse door. I don't know if he had any visions of what might proceed from that. My guess is that he did it at that time for Alabama consumption. I would guess that subsequent to that he thought about running for President. As you know, when he first ran for President, it was in a very tentative way. He only entered three primaries. I think he was surprised at the acceptance he got there [in Maryland, Wisconsin, and Indiana]. . . . He didn't have to mention race anymore. There's no doubt that he used the race issue."

A reporter interrupted to say that Carter is viewed as a better man than Wallace. But Carter, already victorious, was in a mood to be charitable.

"That's a mistake. It's easy for people to look back on the war in Vietnam and say, 'That's a terrible war, we never should have been there.' It's easy for people to look back on the South and the rest of the nation and say, 'We should never have had racial discrimination and blacks should always have been able to vote.'

"Somebody came out the other day and talked to my mother and asked her, 'How does it feel to have been married to a racist?' Well, you know, if my daddy was still living, he would be part of the modern, enlightened consciousness between black and white people. He died in 1953. Even the black people who lived at home never thought about, you know, equality and riding in the front of the bus and going to the same school as whites.

"It's not right to stigmatize people into generic groups or as individuals because of the times they lived in and when they got their reputation and shaped their political image."

Jimmy was the oldest of the Carter children. Gloria was born about two years later. Ruth was born when Jimmy was five and his only brother, Billy, when Jimmy was thirteen.

"Ruth was always his [Earl Carter's] favorite child," Jimmy told reporters during that same lengthy, free-flowing airplane conversation. "Gloria was much more rebellious against Daddy than Ruth was. Ruth was just her father's little girl. . . . I don't know, I can't explain it psychologically . . . Gloria always had a mind of her own; I'll say that. . . . [But] I think Ruth was Daddy's favorite, and it was kind of an accepted thing. I didn't feel any jealousy over it. Gloria and I were almost of equal age and we were competitors with each other."

Carter's mother, Lillian, recalled that, in fact, it was Gloria who was the leader of the Carter children as they were growing up on the farm outside Plains. "Gloria tended to be more aggressive," she said. "She was bigger then he [Jimmy] was—he was of small stature and she was larger from the time she was five. She was more or less the leader of my children. . . . He teased them and pulled their hair, but they usually got along just fine. Once she hit him with a monkey wrench and he shot her in the behind with a BB gun."

Jimmy had been a very sick baby. "Until he was two years old, he had colitis, and he almost died," his mother recalled. "It was so prevalent. He had diarrhea and would be constantly passing blood. He was in and out of the hospital, and we tried to do everything we could for him, changing one diaper after another, and there was always so much blood. A country doctor from Montesula—he told me what to do. He told me to make a saturated solution of corn starch for Jimmy, and that worked. But it was a terrible time."

His mother likes to tell how Jimmy worked diligently at his farm chores. "Jimmy never complained about doing his chores," she said. "I remember when he was older, his friends used to drive up to the house and ask him to go with them. But he used to just smile and wave and do his work. We never let him stay out in the field in the middle of the day—he's so fair, he blistered easily."

In his early boyhood, until he was about fourteen or

fifteen, virtually all of Carter's playmates were black. "That's all I played with," he said. "We used to wrestle, fight, fish, swim, and have footraces and play baseball. There was never any deference shown me at all because I was white." In his book, Carter writes of his black boyhood friends:

> We hunted, fished, explored, worked and slept together. We ground sugar cane, plowed mules, pruned watermelons, dug and bedded sweet potatoes, mopped cotton, stacked peanuts, cut stovewood, pumped water, fixed fences, fed chickens, picked velvet beans, and hauled cotton to the gin together.
>
> In addition to the many chores, we also found time to spend the night on the banks of the Choctawhatchee and Kinchafoonee creeks, catching and cooking catfish and eels when the water was rising from heavy rains.
>
> We ran, swam, rode horses, drove wagons and floated on rafts together. We misbehaved together and shared the same punishments. We built and lived in the same tree houses and played cards and ate at the same table.
>
> But we never went to the same church or school. Our social life and our church life were strictly separate. We did not sit together on the two-car diesel train that could be flagged down in Archery. There was a scrupulous compliance with these unwritten and unspoken rules. I never heard them questioned. Not then.

As a youth in Plains and as a young adult as well, Carter felt uncomfortable about the racial segregation that was a fact of life in the South. But he kept his disquietude largely low key. "Jimmy was never really critical [about segregation]," Rosalynn said once. "He just quietly let people know what he thought. He never had any hot arguments or debates on it."

Eventually, as an adult, Carter did take a stand against the racist elements in his hometown, and later, as governor of Georgia, he won the support of blacks for such emotional, symbolic acts as ordering that a portrait of Martin Luther King, Jr., be placed in the state capitol. His stand on the race issue has angered a good many of his fellow Georgians; indeed, not even all the members of his family shared his view. One who did, though, was his mother.

"Yes, he got that from me," Lillian Carter, Jimmy's mother, once told Helen Dewar of the *Washington Post.* "I've always been like that. My father was never a racist, and I grew up trying to be compassionate and kind to everyone. . . . I've stood alone in Plains, Jimmy and I have stood alone."

As Earl Carter was a traditional southern conservative, a segregationist as a matter of course and principle, Lillian Carter was a liberal, uncommon and even a maverick in the rural Deep South way of life. She was the daughter of a rural postmaster in south Georgia, one of eight children. She graduated from high school, received a nursing degree at Grady Hospital in Atlanta, and then promptly married Earl Carter and settled into a life alongside the Seaboard railway tracks outside Archery.

Rosalynn Carter, who was a friend of Ruth's long before she married Ruth's brother Jimmy, always considered Lillian Carter to be outspoken on matters of racial segregation, even when she was without allies among the white population of Plains. "I remember that Jimmy's mother was always a baseball fan," she said. "And when Jackie Robinson joined the Dodgers she went around telling everyone 'I'm for the Dodgers—because they're the team with Jackie Robinson,' and everyone would be shocked. You can imagine how that went over in Plains. Even now she likes the Atlanta Braves, but the Dodgers are still her team."

Lillian Carter says she didn't really become outspoken about race relations until the civil rights movement took hold in the South in the late 1950s and early 1960s. "When my husband was alive and the children were growing up," she said, "there was no such thing as segregation and integration. There were things for the blacks and things for the whites. That's all. My husband never joined anything against blacks, and you should know that everything I did as a nurse (caring for blacks) was done with my husband's consent. . . . My liberalism came much later, during the civil rights movement. I was for the blacks, who have been so mistreated. And that's when word got out that I was so liberal—and I was. It wasn't a frightening time—I was never afraid of anything in my life, except snakes, and that was a different period."

When she began to speak out in favor of equal treatment of blacks in the South, Lillian Carter says that it was made very clear to her that her views were resented by others in the community. "People would throw oranges and banana peels at my car," she said. "There were many things I wanted to say publicly. But I did not."

There was always in Lillian Carter a strong strain of independence. When Earl died in 1953, she set out to remake her life. She was a housemother to a fraternity on the Auburn University campus. She started up a small nursing home in Blakely, Georgia. And then in 1966, she was watching television one night when an ad for the Peace Corps came on the screen. "Age is no barrier." So at age sixty-eight, she sent away for information, and soon after she announced to her sons that she was volunteering for service in the Peace Corps. She would request assignment in either Africa or India.

Lillian Carter went to the University of Chicago to study the Marathi dialect as preparation for teaching nutrition to the people of India. Then the Peace Corps got word that family-planning aid was needed in India. So Mrs. Carter went back to school to learn Hindi so she could be of service in that program.

Vikhroli is a small town near Bombay. Lillian Carter did family-planning work there and eventually was transferred to a clinic there to make use of her nursing skills.

Years later, as she looked back on it, Lillian Carter spoke of the personal frustrations, doubts, and suffering she endured as she tried to go about her Peace Corps work in India. In her interview with Dewar of the *Washington Post,* she said, "India was killing me. I just couldn't bear it. I couldn't touch the dirt, the blood, the lice, the leprosy. I hadn't the strength to bear the horrible cruelty and indifference." So Mrs. Carter said she went up on a hillside and prayed. "And Christ let something come into me, and I knew I could do anything. I could wipe up blood . . . and blood had always appalled me, and I could touch leprosy without running to scrub my hands raw. I could stay in India."

Lillian Carter was more than seventy years old when she returned to Georgia from her service in the Peace Corps. She had worked herself into a weakened state, losing thirty pounds while in India. She was so debilitated that her children insisted on using a wheelchair to transport her from the plane to a waiting car. Within a short time, though, she regained enough strength to set out on the lecture circuit, telling organizations about the Peace Corps and its work.

During Carter's campaign for the Presidency, his mother, then seventy-seven, assumed two diverse roles: she looked after Carter's youngest daughter, eight-year-old Amy, while her parents were off politicking; and she moved energetically about the business of being an available and quotable Carter figure for reporters who had suddenly become fascinated with the fact of a Deep South country boy who was taking on the whole of the Democratic Party and winning. She developed a good number of favorite lines.

"Don't call me Mrs. Carter—that's Jimmy's wife," she would admonish good-naturedly. "Everyone calls me Miss Lillian."

Also: "Everybody in Plains either loves me or owes me."

Also: "Jimmy says he'll never tell a lie. Well, I lie all the time. I have to—to balance the family ticket."

And: "Sure I'm for helping the elderly. I'm going to be old myself someday."

She is a small but solid-looking woman with striking white hair, a face etched with the lines of her years, and blue eyes that sparkle with life every time she gets off one of her favorite lines and sees that it is well received. Once, when dining with several reporters, she accepted a drink of their wine, but allowed as how she was just a little disappointed that they did not have anything more substantial to offer. "You probably shouldn't put this in the paper," she said. "Some of my friends don't know I take a toddy now and then."

Carter's uncle, Tom Gordy, his mother's youngest brother, was an enlisted man in the navy and he was fond of sending Jimmy postcards from each of his port stops. From the time he was in grammar school, Carter looked forward to attending the U.S. Naval Academy at Annapolis. As a youth, he wrote the academy and, without telling them his true age, requested a listing of their entrance requirements. He said later that he virtually memorized the catalogue word for word.

"I had ridiculous and secret fears that I would not meet the requirements," Carter later wrote in his book. "Some of the physical requirements listed in the catalogue gave me deep concern."

Childhood fears. They are so real at the time and yet so often they are quite the opposite of what is to become adult reality. So it was with Carter, who thought his problem was his teeth. " 'Malocclusion of teeth' was my biggest theoretical problem," wrote the man whose teeth and grin were to become more of a political trademark than his views on any of the issues of his day. "When I ate fruit, the knowledge that my teeth did not perfectly meet interfered with my enjoying the flavor.

"There was another requirement which caused me to worry, one called 'retention of urine.' I was always ashamed to ask whether that last clinging drop would block my entire naval career!"

As he has frequently announced in his campaign speeches, Jimmy Carter became the first member of his father's family to graduate from high school. In a revealing passage in his autobiography, Carter says that his father had supported Congressman Stephan Pace in each of his campaigns in the hopes of securing an Annapolis appointment for Jimmy. Had the Carters been New Yorkers, this would have come off like standard Sammy Glick; it is, in fact, the sort of long-term cunning and determined calculation that was passed from father to son in the Carters of Georgia and which became very much part of Jimmy Carter's way of operating. In 1942, Jimmy Carter got his Annapolis nomination.

Soon after his arrival at the naval academy, Carter—stubborn and proud of being a Georgian—set out to make it clear to his upperclassmen that there is one song that is most unsuitable for dinner music: "Marching Through Georgia." He succeeded in proving to his classmates mostly that he was well reared. The incident occurred during the standard, ritual mealtime hazing at the academy.

"We were plebes," recalled Robert Lee Scott, who was Carter's roommate for two years. "And at the dinner table one day Jimmy was ordered by an upperclassman to sing 'Marching Through Georgia.' Well, Jimmy absolutely refused—he flat refused to do it. And so Jimmy got belted pretty good on the rear end with a bread platter—I mean knocked quite a ways. But he held true. He didn't sing it."

Scott, who then lived in Arizona but now coincidentally lives just outside Atlanta, recalls Carter as a "private kind of guy. . . . He didn't need to be very studious because he was intelligent enough." Midshipman Carter did not date much, Scott said. One of their most memorable times, he said, was when Carter of Georgia and Scott of Arizona decided to see the big city. "We took a weekend in New York City," Scott said. "It's not that anything special happened. We just took in the sights. But for us it was really something."

Carter writes in his autobiography of how interested he was in classical music and how he and his roommate would spend their money on records and listen to them for hours. He drops names like Tristan and Isolde, and Liebestod. According to Scott, Carter's interest in the classics was acquired. "He was only slightly interested in music [at first]," Scott said. "I had been interested in classical music and got him interested in it. We chipped in on a record player and records, and he really got taken by it. When we were ready to graduate, we finally had to decide who would get the records and it turned out that he finally bought my half."

Carter graduated 59th out of 820 in his class of 1947—a class which was graduated in 1946, incidentally, after being rushed through the academy in three years in hopes of catching up with World War II. Carter set out to build a career in the navy. Eventually, he was picked to participate in the nuclear submarine program headed by Admiral Hyman Rickover, whom he frequently mentions as a person he admires.

He tells the story in his book of the time that he and a friend ran into his sister Ruth and a friend; they wound up double-dating at the movies—Jimmy's friend and Ruth, Jimmy and the other girl, Rosalynn Smith. At home that night, Carter says he told his mother about the date with the Smith girl. Mrs. Carter asked her son if he liked Rosalynn. "She's the girl I want to marry," Carter says he replied. He is unabashed in reporting this Andy Hardy dialogue to the world in his autobiography.

Jimmy liked Rosalynn and Rosalynn liked Jimmy and it was not long before they were married. But it took years for Rosalynn to realize that her husband had gradually come to give her a shorthand name: "Rosie." In fact, she says, she had gone through more than two decades of marriage before somebody asked her whether she liked it when Jimmy called her by the nickname. "I said he never does call me that," Rosalynn Carter recalls. "And I really believed that. I'd just never noticed it. And then one day just a short time later, we were at home and Jimmy called to me, 'Rosie, get the telephone.' . . . So he does call me Rosie sometimes after all. I don't particularly like it."

After they were married, Rosalynn accompanied her husband on tours to Hawaii; San Diego, California; New London, Connecticut; and Schenectady, New York. Then, after the death of his father, Carter reports that he and Rosalynn had their first real fight. He wanted to quit the navy and live in Plains; she preferred a life of wider horizons, free from the family influences back home. Carter won, and back in Plains he set about building a family seed peanut business.

🇺🇸   🇺🇸   🇺🇸

While Jimmy Carter was busy building a peanut farming business, his cousin Hugh was busy making a killing on worms.

BIG MONEY IN FISHWORMS

Dear Sir:

Billions of fishworms needed yearly and not ½ enough people are raising them to supply this huge demand! . . . **You can make profit fast.** . . . Our simple, detailed instructions show you how to raise and sell worms. . . . **Hurry, this is your big opportunity to make money fast.**

Yours Sincerely,
Hugh A. Carter
Plains, Georgia

PRICE LIST

Carter's Pure Bred Hybrid Red Wigglers

(Perfected After 20 Years of Breeding Experience)
1,000—$8.95 . . . 5,000—$42.50 . . . 100,000—$800.00

FISHBAIT LITERATURE
By
Hugh A. Carter, world's largest worm grower

"18 Secrets of Successful Worm Raising." "What to
Feed and How to Feed the Hybrid Red Wiggler."
"Over 300 Questions and Answers on Worm Raising."

Eventually Hugh Carter began to diversify. He went
into crickets as well. "Raising the Gray Cricket and How
to Raise and Sell the Hybrid Redworm." But worms were
bigger than ever, and Carter had to subcontract his
cricket business. Actually, it wasn't just the worms that
took up so much of Hugh Carter's time. It was the worms
and the politicians. For Hugh Carter took his cousin's
seat in the Georgia State Senate when Jimmy made his
first run for governor in 1966. And he then ran Jimmy's
second—successful—race for governor in 1970. "I finally
had to job my crickets," he said. "I just didn't have time
for them anymore."

In Plains, Carter served as a member of the Sumter
County school board. "It seems hard to believe now," he
writes in his book, "but I was actually a member of the
county school board for several months before it dawned
on me that white children rode buses to their schools and
black students still walked to theirs! I don't believe any
black parent or teacher ever pointed out this quite obvious difference."

At about this time, the White Citizen's Council movement was springing up throughout the South as a way of
trying to fight off integration. Carter refused to join the
local Council—he refused when several influential Plains
men told him that he was the only white man in the area

who had not joined, and he refused when they later returned with some of Carter's customers warning that his business would suffer if he did not join. The ensuing boycott was small and short-lived.

Carter was a deacon at his Baptist church in Plains, a small and segregated institution. He failed to attend one meeting at which the eleven other deacons and the pastor voted unanimously to propose to the entire congregation that blacks be physically barred from the building if they attempted to attend worship services. When the matter was brought before the full congregation later, Carter urged that blacks be permitted to enter the church if they wished. Of the 200 people at the meeting, about 50 voted. Of these, Carter writes, only six voted to open the services to all who wished to worship: Carter, his mother, his wife, his two sons, and one other member of the congregation.

Jimmy Carter paid his politicking dues. He began his public service with quasi-political jobs: state president of the Certified Seed Organization, Lions' Club district governor, local planning commission chairman, Georgia Planning Association president, and member of the county library board, hospital authority, and school board.

In 1962 Carter ran for the Georgia State Senate. On primary election day at one polling place, in Georgetown, which was on the Chattahoochee River, Carter came upon some irregularities—for example, his opponent's literature being on the voting table and the election supervisor suggesting that this was the man to vote for and then watching the ballots being marked and occasionally reaching into the box to see how the votes went on ballots he couldn't see. Eventually, about 300 people had voted, Carter says, and there were 433 names in the ballot box and 126 of them had voted alphabetically and at times ballots had been folded together in clusters of four or eight when they were dropped into the ballot box.

If Carter's version is accurate, it was not only ballot-box stuffing but a clumsy job of it. Carter lost the election and after a lengthy and flip-flopping series of rulings, he was eventually elected. His successful challenge was due in large measure to the work of an Atlanta attorney,

Charles Kirbo, who had been hired to handle the Carter case, and an assisting attorney, Warren Fortsom.

Kirbo and Carter grew to be quite close, and a sort of father-son relationship developed between the attorney and his young politician/client. Eventually Kirbo became well known as Carter's closest adviser and confidant. Fortsom too achieved fame of sorts; he was from Americus, which is the nearest big town to Plains, and was a prominent citizen, being county attorney and a member of the school board and the Rotary Club and a church director and an ex-marine; but after recommending in the mid-1960s that a biracial committee be set up to ease tension in the town, he and his family were harassed by crank phone calls and ostracized by their townsfolk, and he was superseded as county attorney by a specially appointed "assistant attorney." Eventually Fortsom and his family were effectively forced out of town and they moved to Atlanta. All because he dared to be moderate enough to call for a biracial committee.

In 1966, Carter ran for governor. He passed up what he felt was a sure shot at a congressional vacancy to go for the state's top job. And he fell short. He came in third, behind former Governor Ellis Arnall and fried chicken segregationist Lester Maddox, just missing the runoff. Maddox had become famous mostly because he had run a segregated fried chicken restaurant in Atlanta and he had made the ax handle his symbol—an instrument for driving blacks out of his restaurant. Maddox represented a colossal insult not just to blacks but to all of mankind. Maddox won the runoff and became Georgia's next governor, and the people of that state were saddled with a Cro-Magnon image of their own making.

One notable thing about Jimmy Carter is that he is stubborn. Also, determined and hard-driving. Having been defeated once for governor he made up his mind that he would not rest until he became governor. He began his 1970 gubernatorial campaign almost as soon as the 1966 balloting ended. It was as if his 1966 campaign had never stopped. He went right on stumping the state and shaking hands. Maddox was barred by law from running again. This time, Carter's opponent was of a different stripe—former Governor Carl Sanders, a lawyer and a moderate who had been a generally popular political figure in Georgia and had a good following among the blacks. Sanders was the overwhelming early favorite; people paid little attention to the chronic campaigner from Plains.

With Sanders well ensconced with the moderate left, Carter moved after the right. He painted Sanders as a figure of the Atlanta country club set and labeled him "Cufflinks Carl." He portrayed his opponent as a big-spender liberal, and here he had some good fortune. It seems that a button manufacturer, in an effort to cut costs, had recycled some old Hubert Humphrey buttons by putting a new finish on top of the old and turning them into Sanders buttons. But some nervous scratcher in the Carter camp absently peeled off the Sanders surface one day and gleefully discovered Humphrey. "Scratch a Sanders and get a Humphrey" became a quickie campaign jingle that did Sanders no good in Georgia. Carter also encouraged the segregationist elements by saying that he hoped to have the Wallace vote on election day (which was true, he would later explain, because he hoped to have votes of *all* people, liberals and conservatives, blacks and whites).

It was not a gentlemanly campaign. Pro-Carter forces distributed in redneck areas an Atlanta newspaper photo showing Sanders getting doused with champagne by two black Atlanta Hawks basketball players in a victory celebration. Carter denied personal involvement in the circulation of the photo.

Carter won.

On January 12, 1971, Carter, who was a product of a segregated society and who had been elected in part by successfully courting the Wallace vote, stood in the state capitol building and declared in an eight-minute inaugural address: "I say to you quite frankly that the time for racial discrimination is over. No poor, rural, weak, or black person should ever have to bear the additional burden of being deprived of the opportunity of an education, a job, or simple justice. . . ."

Carter's speech attracted national publicity and later, when *Time* did its cover story on the new breed of politicians who are governors of the New South, Carter was on the magazine's cover.

Running for President

The drive that made Jimmy Carter the choice of the 1976 Democratic National Convention began during the 1972 Democratic National Convention in Miami Beach. Advisers Hamilton Jordan and Gerald Rafshoon sought to have Carter considered for Vice President and found that they had trouble in just getting to see George McGovern's advisers.

"Boy, were we ever naive!" Jordan recalls.

The two men hoped to convince McGovern's advisers that the South Dakota liberal would fare better with a southerner—Carter—on the ticket. So they went to the Doral Beach Hotel and asked to see Patrick Caddell, then McGovern's pollster (now Carter's), because they had a poll supporting their position.

"A bullshit poll," Rafshoon later admitted. It was a poll that had been taken for a U.S. Senate race in Georgia. A question had been asked about how McGovern would do against Nixon and another asked how McGovern would do if Carter were his running mate. Obviously McGovern did much better in Georgia with the governor of Georgia on the ticket.

Jordan and Rafshoon were kept waiting one floor below the Doral floor that served as the McGovern convention headquarters for staff members, including Caddell. Almost an hour had passed when another McGovern aide, Alan Baron, saw the two Carter men waiting and asked: "What are you guys doing?"

"Waiting to see Pat Caddell," Rafshoon replied. Baron offered to help out. He led the two Carter emissaries up a back stairwell to Caddell's floor and guided them past the guards and into the right room. (It is one of the delicious ironies of politics that Baron later played a role in the Carter story of 1976, as well—only this time he became one of the key figures in a last-gasp Stop Carter movement.)

Once in the room, Jordan and Rafshoon laid out their case and Caddell listened politely. "He said things like, 'uh huh. . . . oh, wow,' and said, 'I'm going to think about recommending a southerner.' And he thanked us for stopping by," Jordan says.

Eight minutes after they had been ushered in to see Caddell, the Carter men were on their way out, chagrined. They had seen Carter as one of the major figures of the party, *the* leading southern moderate. The McGovern people obviously had not.

"I thought people were going to fall all over Jimmy at the convention," Jordan said later. "But he was just one of thirty or forty guys there."

That night, Jordan and Rafshoon talked a bit about how Carter's national image needed improving. The conversation progressed in succeeding days to how Carter was just as qualified as any of the presidential aspirants. "We got to thinking, 'Hell, if we work at it for four years, we just might be able to take any of these guys,'" said Rafshoon.

Other Carter advisers talked about it, too. They included Peter Bourne, a psychiatrist who had set up a drug rehabilitation program for Carter in Georgia. On July 25, 1972, Bourne wrote a memo to Carter, suggesting for the first time that he run for President.

Meetings followed, usually in the Atlanta apartment of Hamilton Jordan. After one such session, Jordan, Rafshoon, and Atlanta businessman Landon Butler went to the governor's mansion. Carter greeted them, wearing blue jeans and a T-shirt, the clothes he often favored during his off-duty hours. Jordan spoke for the group and outlined their view that a southern alternative to George Wallace could make it in 1976. They figured then that Florida Governor Reubin Askew was better known outside the south than Carter—"if Jimmy was one percent toward his goal, then Askew was fifteen," said Jordan. But the men urged Carter to run.

"Yeah, I've thought about it," Carter replied, after hearing his advisers' arguments. He, too, had been figuring that he was as capable as any of the better-known politicians he had met—many of them men who had come to Atlanta seeking his help in their own presidential efforts. "During 1971 and 1972, I met Richard Nixon, Spiro Agnew, George McGovern, Henry Jackson, Hubert

Humphrey, Ed Muskie, George Wallace, Ronald Reagan, Nelson Rockefeller, and other presidential hopefuls, and I lost my feeling of awe about Presidents," he writes in his book.

As the meeting at the mansion drew to a close, Jordan recalls that Carter gave them some simple instructions: "It's an enormous undertaking. We're got to work at it. Think about it. And we've got to keep our mouths shut."

     🏳️   🏳️   🏳️

The meeting with Carter led to the preparation of a couple of documents. One was a memo from Rafshoon to Jordan on how Carter should go about getting himself a national image. The memo showed that Rafshoon had spotted the Carter attribute that four years later was to become the Carter trademark—the smile. Specifically, Rafshoon noted, it was a "Kennedy smile," an image Rafshoon had shunned in past campaigns in Georgia but now planned to exploit nationally.

     🏳️   🏳️   🏳️

The Rafshoon Memo

1972.

As for a national image . . . I believe that despite the accusations of back-sliding by the liberal press, that Jimmy's image in national circles and in the media has not changed much since inauguration. He is still the man who said the time for racial discrimination is over. . . . He still has a Kennedy smile. . . . *What he does not have is much depth to his image. He is not as well known as many other big-name politicians in the U.S. and is not known for the heavyweight ideas and programs that he is capable of articulating.*

Getting this across should be the No. 1 priority now. The first phase of any Carter campaign should be to formulate a heavyweight program and project a heavy-weight image, all at the same time, trying to infect other southern states and other regions with the Jimmy Carter "good guy" brand of populism. It will take more than the hand-shaking and the projection of "I under-

stand the problems of the average man" image to put
Carter over. *This is still his greatest asset and it must
be projected but he will also have to convince the
press, public and politicians that he knows how to run
a government (he has a record to prove this).* . . . He
knows about the problems of the cities . . . the races
. . . the economy . . . and the problems of the world,
national defense, foreign affairs.

Timing

1973 will be a very quiet year on the political front
but there are a lot of preparatory things that can be
done. This is the phase when Jimmy's accomplishments
in Georgia—such as reorganization, control, ecology,
and the upgrading of positions for blacks—can be
heralded nationally. I see 1973 as the year in which
Carter is projected as the heaviest of the governors in
accomplishments and the year in which the rest of the
country gets a good look at him as a governor. It's
really his last chance for this because in 1974 we will
have mid-term elections and he needs to shift gears
then for another phase of his publicity.

In general, I see the publicity phases as follows:

Phase I 1973: Projection of the Carter record and
knowledge.

Phase II 1974: Carter as a leader in the Democratic
Party and someone involved in bringing it back.

Phase III 1975: Carter as a heavyweight thinker,
leader in the party (denote in Phases One and Two)
who has some ideas for running the country and is
going around the country talking about them and who
may have presidential ambitions.

Phase IV 1976: Carter—a presidential candidate.

Each of these phases runs into the succeeding phase
and is an integral part of the overall buildup. They all
cannot be accomplished at the same time but they all
must be accomplished at the time allotted in order to
evolve into the next phase. Phase I must be accomplished early enough to make the others work.

The second important document was written by Hamilton Jordan (he pronounces it "Jurd'n"), who had been a Carter man ever since he heard Carter speak back in 1966—when Carter was running for governor the first time and Jordan was a twenty-one-year-old youth working at a summer job spraying mosquitoes. Jordan had been impressed enough to sign on with Carter, trying to line up the youth vote. Eventually, Jordan would wind up as Carter's 1976 presidential campaign manager, a stocky and athletic type who had learned to be tough and exacting on some occasions and beguiling and charming on others.

In 1972, at the age of twenty-seven, Hamilton Jordan drafted the master plan that would ultimately carry Jimmy Carter to the Democratic presidential nomination. Jordan dated his memo to Carter November 4, 1972—just a day before Richard Nixon's landslide victory over George McGovern. The Jordan memo turned out, all in all, to be a remarkably accurate assessment of a political situation that would exist four years later.

It talked about how "the New Hampshire and Florida primaries provided a unique opportunity for you to demonstrate your ability at an early stage of the campaign" —Carter eventually won both and was on his way.

It talked of Carter's need to select a large industrial traditionally Democratic state where he would have to ultimately confront his opponents and suggested Pennsylvania and Ohio—Carter eventually scored his biggest victory in Pennsylvania, and he scored a victory in Ohio that was so smashing it touched off a wave of endorsements that guaranteed him the nomination.

The memo also talked of how Carter must develop expertise in foreign affairs and suggested he make trade mission trips to South America, Europe, the Mideast, and Japan—and Carter did.

It urged him to write a book—he did.

It talked of how he would have to work to woo and win the leaders of the media world, the "eastern liberal news establishment"—he tried.

It talked about how "compatible and comfortable" he appeared to be with Senator Henry (Scoop) Jackson, but warned him not to continue to praise Jackson in his speeches because Jackson could turn out to be one of his 1976 opponents. Jordan assumed, though, that Senator

Edward Kennedy would run and that he would be the early favorite to win the nomination.

For all its accuracy, the Jordan memo began, surprisingly, with an error. Jordan said that a serious effort by George Wallace in 1976 *would* preempt Carter's candidacy. (The copy of the memo now in Jordan's file shows "would" crossed out and "could" inked in its place, along with a penned notation: "I have changed my mind about this. 9-10-74 H.J.") Throughout the memo, Jordan seemed to view Carter as a basically conservative southerner who could be an alternative to Wallace. Jordan also was critical of Edmund Muskie's 1972 efforts to enter all the primaries, and he praised George McGovern's strategy of carefully picking his primary battlefields; later, of course, Carter and Jordan would agree that Carter indeed ought to enter all of the primaries.

≋   ≋   ≋

The Jordan Memo

November 4, 1972.

. . . The New Hampshire and Florida primaries provide a unique opportunity for you to demonstrate your abilities and strengths as a candidate at an early stage in the campaign. As you know, New Hampshire's primary traditionally has been a place where sure winners have stumbled and the dark horses like Eugene McCarthy and George McGovern have established themselves as serious contenders. New Hampshire is a small state which is rural and independent and given to the kind of personal campaign that you and your family are capable of waging. It only voted about 84,644 people in the primary this year, and I believe that your farmer-businessman-military-religious-conservative background would be well received there. It is not too early to begin to make some contacts with people there, learn something about the state, and be looking for an appropriate opportunity to make a major speech or address there.

Florida, as it follows the New Hampshire primary, affords an excellent opportunity to build on a good showing. It is not too early to begin thinking of people who should be contacted in Florida. . . .

. . . I could go on and on, but the point that I would like here is that we need to begin thinking *now* about party rules vis-a-vis primary states and your own effort. It is here where the nomination will be won or lost.

Establishing a National Image

. . . I believe that Rafshoon's comments and overviews are excellent. In keeping with his strategy and sense of timing, it is necessary that we begin immediately to generate favorable stories and comments in the national press. Stories in the *New York Times* and *Washington Post* do not just happen, but have to be carefully planned and planted.

I would hope that we could relate the accomplishments of your administration to the theme that revitalized state government is the key to solving many of the problems in this country today as has been demonstrated in Georgia by Gov. Jimmy Carter. The thrust of your national press effort should be that state government is working in Georgia and is solving the problems in meeting the needs of ordinary citizens. By emphasizing this theme and making your own political plans a secondary consideration, I believe you would have the forum and excuse you need to appear on television talk shows, write articles for national publications and serve as an obvious example that revitalized state government is where the action and the interest are.

. . . A particular problem facing the Democratic Party is that its preoccupation with senators has resulted in many of its members having already been unsuccessful candidates for national office—Humphrey, Jackson, Hughes, Harris, Bayh, Muskie, Eagleton and McGovern being the most obvious.

For all these reasons, we have reached the time when a governor who can demonstrate an understanding and ability in foreign affairs and domestic issues can be seriously considered for the presidency. . . .

. . . A lot of the research and leg work that needs to be done in the next year or so could be attributed to a possible race for the U.S. Senate. We could involve more people with less risk using this as an excuse for briefings and position papers on foreign affairs and domestic issues.

The Years in Between

. . . I believe that you should attempt to develop the image of a highly successful and concerned former governor of Georgia and peanut farmer living in a small rural town, speaking out on the pertinent issues of the day. Once your name begins to be mentioned in the national press, you will not lack for invitations and opportunities to speak in major groups and conventions. . . .

If you are in general agreement with Rafshoon's thinking, we should begin immediately to (1) generate favorable stories in the national press on the accomplishments of your administration, (2) develop and/or maintain a close personal relationship with the principal national columnists and reporters, and (3) take full advantage of every legitimate opportunity for national exposure as long as it is couched in terms of what you have accomplished in Georgia.

We should compile a listing of regional and national political editors and columnists who you know or need to know. You can find ample excuse for contacting them—writing them a note, complimenting them on an article or column and asking that they come to see you when convenient. Some people like Tom Wicker or Mrs. Katherine Graham are significant enough to spend an evening or a leisurely weekend with. . . .

Like it or not, there exists in fact an eastern liberal news establishment which has tremendous influence. The views of this small group of opinion-makers in the papers they represent are noted and imitated by other columnists and newspapers throughout the country and the world. Their recognition and acceptance of your candidacy as a viable force with some chance of success could establish you as a serious contender worthy of financial support of major party contributors. They could have an equally adverse effect, dismissing your effort as being regional or an attempt to secure the second spot on the ticket.

Fortunately, a disproportionate number of these opinion-makers are southerners by birth and tradition and . . . subconsciously desire to see the South move beyond the George Wallace area and assert itself as a region. . . . It is my contention that they would be fascinated by the prospect of your candidacy and would treat it seriously through the first several primaries.

In keeping with these recommendations, we should begin to: (1) Foster relationships with political columnists that you know. Establish relationships with those you don't know.

(2) Utilize Don Carter's [a cousin, and publisher of the Lexington, Kentucky, *Herald*] contacts to create situations where you can get to know key people. For example, let Don Carter invite Tom Wicker and Max [Frankel] to spend a weekend visiting with both of you on Cumberland Island.

(3) Generate stories in national . . . trade magazines on particular accomplishments. . . .

(4) Hire a professional, first-class speechwriter, researcher. When you go out of state you need to have something of substance to say. The same applies when you address national conventions in Atlanta. This is and should be a full-time position.

(5) Review and read portions of the *New York Times, Washington Post, Wall Street [Journal]* and other national selections every day. Despite its liberal orientation and bias, the *New York Times* is the best paper in the country and possibly the world. One cannot keep track of national politics or international affairs by simply reading the *Atlanta Constitution, Time* and *Newsweek.*

(6) Learn to speak from your prepared text. I have heard Jody and Rafshoon both say that this is your only shortcoming as a candidate and that this skill can be easily developed through practice.

(7) Schedule appearances on network talk shows, the focus being "Making State Government Work" or some tangible accomplishment of your administration.

(8) Write a book or column on some pertinent issue or topic with the focus on how a problem was confronted by your administration. . . .

Staff needs

Schedule of Tasks For the Next Six Months

Description of Task	Target Date
1. Read *N.Y. Times and Washington Post* daily.	Immediately and continuing
2. Hire professional speechwriter who can devote full time to research in preparation of speeches on pertinent issues of the day.	Jan. 1, 1973
3. Log up on your schedule beyond March 1, sufficient time for briefings, meetings and out-of-state speeches and trips.	Immediately
4. Devise plans to insure better follow-up on speeches to national groups and conventions, to include letters to key persons and acquisition of lists of convention participants.	Immediately
5. Begin to develop national files for special emphasis on primary states.	Immediately
6. Visit Sen. Kennedy and get to know him. He may tell you unequivocally that he is going to run. Such a meeting will give you some idea as to how you should proceed.	Jan. 1, 1973
7. Meet with Sen. [Henry] Jackson to determine if he has plans of his own. If not, seek his support and advice.	Jan. 1, 1973

Target Date

8. Make courtesy call on Gov. Jan. 1, 1973
   Wallace. If this is impossible,
   call him and sek his advice on
   national Democratic chairman.

9. Meet with Dean Rusk. Ask him Jan. 1, 1973
   to assume responsibility for
   educating you on foreign affairs and to develop a continuing program which would include regular briefings, a reading list and the establishment
   of a formal task force. Ask
   that he submit program outline to you in six weeks.

10. Meet with Don Carter. Ask Jan. 1, 1973
    him to develop a list of nation-
    al editors and columnists you
    should know. Ask him to as-
    sume responsibility for liaison
    work with national press and
    be responsible for developing
    a realistic program that will
    permit you to spend some
    time with each of these. Ask
    that he submit listing and pro-
    gram in four weeks.

11. Ask Philip Alston to prepare Dec. 1, 1973
    listing of potential financial
    contributors who can be in-
    volved in an early stage and
    can be trusted. Schedule time
    with each of these.

12. Meet with Morris Dees. Try to Jan. 1, 1973
    involve him in your effort. His
    national fundraising expertise
    as well as his ability to make
    a sizeable contribution is
    needed.

Target Date

13. Hire full-time persons to co-ordinate various aspects of early campaign.   Jan. 1, 1973

14. Begin to look for person with good reputation and contacts in Washington who can plan major role and campaign. Try to identify this person by target date.   June 1, 1973

15. Schedule weekend meeting for Advisory Committee. Outline to them their role in your effort.   March 1, 1973

16. Identify persons who can assume responsibility for developing a continuing program on education on pertinent domestic issues of the day to parallel Dean Rusk's activities in foreign affairs. Stu Eizenstat is a possibility.   March 1, 1973

17. Decide if you're interested in pursuing the chairmanship of the National Governor's Conference. If so, you will need to talk with Mandel about this soon.   Before Dec. 3, 1972

18. Select someone to devise complete budget for next two years. Mr. Kirbo should be involved.   Jan. 1, 1973

19. Assign someone responsible for accumulating data on national campaign cost with projection on media expense,   March 1, 1973

polling and primary state campaign. Jerry Rafshoon would
be a possibility.

☆   ☆   ☆

When Democratic National Chairman Robert Strauss
came to Atlanta to give a speech on March 5, 1973, he
dropped by the governor's mansion to talk with Jimmy
Carter. Charles Kirbo was there, too—he was an old
friend of Strauss. As they sat on the porch having a drink,
it was not surprising that the talk was of politics.

As they recall it now, Strauss thinks it was Carter
who brought up the idea and Carter and Kirbo think it
was Strauss. At any rate, by the time dinner was ready,
the plan was that Jimmy Carter, who would be going
out of office in 1974, would serve that year as the chairman of the Democratic 1974 congressional campaign committee, a generally routine and thankless job.

Strauss may have been mildly pleased with the arrangement; the Carter people were tickled to death. The Rafshoon plan was on schedule: *"Phase II 1974: Carter as
a leader in the Democratic Party and someone involved
in bringing it back."*

Carter traveled around the country on the assignment,
making friends. In Rochester, New York, he helped Democrat Midge Costanza in her unsuccessful effort to unseat
Republican Congressman Barber Conable. Two years later
she was Carter's earliest New York supporter and served
as co-chairperson of his state campaign.

In Palo Alto, California, while helping a congressional
candidate, Carter dropped in on an environmental meeting aimed at saving the Stanislaus River. There he got
up and said a few words, and by the time he sat down
he had himself some key supporters for his still unlaunched
Carter for President effort. Rodney Kennedy-Minott, a
history professor and veteran political organizer in the
area, had been impressed by Carter, his environmentalist
outlook, and his willingness to attack the Army Corps of
Engineers and the federal bureaucracy. Kennedy-Minott
wrote Carter and volunteered to help him if he ever ran
for President. Kennedy-Minott later served as his California co-chairperson.

In Washington, Carter worked with Bill Dodds, political director of the United Auto Workers, and Mike Miller, political director of the Communications Workers. It was the Georgian's first chance to get a good feel for the union leaders who are so important to any Democrat who wants to win in the northern industrial states. And it was their first chance to get to know him. Two years later, Carter received the endorsement of UAW President Leonard Woodcock.

Where Carter went, Jody Powell went too, keeping a notebook with the name, address, and phone number of every person that Carter met. On several occasions, Powell, Hamilton Jordan, and another Carter aide, Frank Moore, traveled apart from Carter to conduct campaign workshops around the country—and each time they broadened their list of national political contacts.

Carter and his aides did not receive a salary from the party. But their travel expenses—$6,000 to $10,000, Jordan estimates—were paid by the Democratic National Committee. Whenever possible, Carter and his aides stayed as house guests of the Democrats they were meeting—not really to save money, but because, as one Carter man observed, "It helped to build the close personal relationships—the family-type relationships—that are so important when you are later asking people to give of themselves and bust their humps for you."

Robert Keefe, executive director of the Democratic National Committee—and later the director of Scoop Jackson's campaign—approved the hiring of Jordan as executive director of the campaign committee. Keefe soon knew that Carter actually was running for President while he was heading the Democratic campaign committee. "Early on, some people left some things around that they should not have left," Keefe said. "I found them on my table." Keefe passed the intelligence information to Strauss. But neither Strauss nor Keefe did anything about it. "Carter was paying his own freight," Keefe said. "He was working like a bastard for the committee. It was not like he was milking it. . . . He did it in very good taste. . . ."

After the November 1974 congressional election, Carter visited Capitol Hill and walked into the impressive office of the House Majority Leader to meet briefly with its occupant, Representative Thomas (Tip) O'Neill (D—Mass.) "I'm going to be the next President," Carter said to O'Neill, according to the recollection of the large, white-haired, classic old pol who has long believed that no presidential year is complete if there is not a Kennedy in the race. "I know you're supporting Teddy Kennedy, but he's not going to run. [Kennedy had officially taken himself out of the race in September, citing personal reasons.] Hubert Humphrey will make a lot of noise, but in the end he won't run either. Jackson won't get off the ground. The man I've been running against—Mondale—just announced he's withdrawing."

Tip O'Neill, who looks like he was appointed to the role of House Majority Leader by Central Casting, had seen enough bright-eyed politicians come and go that he was not impressed by the softly drawled hard sell of this guy from Georgia, whom he really did not know. "Tip just did not take him seriously," reports one close associate of O'Neill's.

Walter F. (Fritz) Mondale, a senator from Minnesota, had spent a year sampling his chances to win the Democratic presidential nomination; he had traveled widely and tried to spark some political enthusiasm. He found none. On November 21, 1974, Mondale announced that he was withdrawing from the contest. "Basically, I found I did not have the overwhelming desire to be President which is essential for the kind of campaign that is required," Mondale said then. (Later, when he was being chosen by Carter to be his vice-presidential running mate, Mondale would say that it was not that he did not have the stomach for the tough campaign; rather, he said, he just had campaigned hard and had found he was not making progress. Mondale had hovered around 3 and 4 percent in the polls in 1974. But it is worth noting that this is higher than Jimmy Carter was—in fact, Carter was not even ranked at the time, he was so unknown.) The *Washington Post* devoted considerable space to the Mondale withdrawal, playing the story on page one. The next-to-last paragraph of the Mondale story said that Robert Keefe was resigning as executive director of the Democratic National Committee to head the Jackson campaign. And the last paragraph of the story said that Governor Jimmy Carter of Georgia planned to announce officially on December 12 that he would be running for President.

December 12, 1974, Atlanta. Jimmy Carter stood before more than 2,000 well-wishers, including Apollo 11 astronaut Edwin (Buzz) Aldrin. Live television carried Carter's words to his fellow Georgians:

"As of this time here, in the state that I love, surrounded by friends of mine from all over the nation—in fact even from the moon—I want to announce that I am a candidate for the Presidency of the United States."

For all his memos, for all his planning, for all his maneuvering, Jimmy Carter still had two basic problems when he set out in 1975 on his presidential campaign. Not many people knew who he was. And not many cared.

In Philadelphia, Carter scheduled a press conference in a downtown hotel and nobody showed up except the candidate and his press secretary, Jody Powell. "We soon learned that things had to be pre-existing events for him to get any coverage in many cities," Powell recalled. "Either that, or else we had to finagle." Later Powell got Carter onto a television talk show in Des Moines by agreeing to talk about subjects other than politics. He told viewers about Plains, Georgia, and a recipe for cooking fish.

JIMMY CARTER'S CATFISH RECIPE. Ingredients: catfish (or bass); Heinz 57 Sauce; Bisquick or pancake mix; corn oil.

Method: Cut fish into strips like French fries. Marinate fish in Heinz 57 Sauce for several hours. Coat fish with dry Bisquick or pancake mix. Fry in oil. May be served hot or cold.

So it went on the campaign trail in 1975 for the galloping gourmet who in 1976 would become the Democratic Party's presidential nominee. In each state, Carter and his aides set about trying to establish some sort of organization, building as often as possible on contacts Carter had made in the past—including some from his work as the party's 1974 campaign chairman. Carter stuck to a schedule that eventually took him to forty-six states and the District of Columbia in 1975. But that is not to say things steadily improved for the Georgian as he set about the business of getting nationally known.

"By midsummer," Carter's press secretary and traveling aide Jody Powell recalls, "in every state we'd go into, some of Jimmy's supporters would pull me aside and say 'When are you going to get him on "Meet the Press" or "Face the Nation"'?"

"They knew they were working hard in their area, but they had no idea—and saw no evidence—that we had anything going on anywhere else. They each thought they were the only ones working for Jimmy in the whole country, and you could tell clearly from the way they said things to me that their concern was that if Carter only had a press secretary who was worth a damn, he'd have been on 'Meet the Press' and 'Face the Nation' and 'Issues and Answers' already. Well, that just might have been true. But in those times, I was doing a better job of going around and lowering people's expectations than Jerry Brown ever thought of doing."

In those days, Powell was Carter's constant traveling companion, his personal aide, driver, spokesman, and issues expert combined. In 1968, as a political science graduate student at Emory University, Powell had written a paper disputing the theory that a Wallace-type third party would inherit the southern vote. In 1969, he wrote to Carter and told him about the paper and volunteered to help in the coming gubernatorial campaign. Powell had earlier been dismissed from the Air Force Academy for cheating, a fact he frankly admits. He told Carter about that black moment in his past; Carter told him to forget it. As Powell frequently drove Carter throughout the state, the two had many lengthy discussions of strategy and issues. Powell, who was thirty-two during the 1976 run for the Presidency, had emerged as a man of mature judgment and candid, self-effacing style who functioned as press secretary and whose counsel on strategy, issues, and public relations had the attention and respect of Carter.

Back in 1975, there wasn't much Powell could do about getting Carter frequent prestigious bookings like "Face the Nation" or "Meet the Press," but he did come up with a way of letting Carter workers around the country know that at least they were not alone. The Carter campaign began sending out a nationwide newsletter, carrying clips from newspapers in every area Carter visited. Thus the

Carter workers could see that at least their man was getting good local press coverage.

In 1975 Carter was doing more than just worrying about local press coverage. One glaring weakness in the presidential candidacy of the ex-Georgia governor was that he had no experience in foreign affairs—certainly nothing that could be compared favorably with the many men of Washington who had their eye on the White House. That was one reason why he seized on an opportunity in May to go to Japan as a member of a trilateral commission composed of North American, European, and Japanese representatives of government and the academic communities, as Jordan's 1972 memo had advised.

The commission effort was funded by the Rockefeller Foundation and its broad purpose was to bring together persons from the three geographic areas to discuss a variety of global matters. "We knew this was no opportunity for us—or anyone else—to get much media attention," said Jody Powell. "But we figured it was of good long-term benefit."

(As governor, Carter had traveled to Central and South America in 1971 to talk up business and investment opportunities in Georgia—including the sale of Lockheed aircraft. In 1973 he traveled to Europe on another state industry and trade mission; and he made a side trip over to the Middle East, where he arranged to meet with officials including Golda Meir, a meeting that he was not at all reticent to mention during his presidential campaigning before Jewish audiences three years later.)

While in Japan, Carter met with the then-current Prime Minister Tanaka, the future prime minister (Miki), and the past prime minister (Sato). And with his eye on future relationships, he also contacted various American reporters based in Tokyo at the time and arranged to meet with them for drinks and conversation. Some of the reporters wondered at the time what the sense was of spending time talking with a former governor of Georgia, but to Carter it was just part of the "long-term benefits" he has always looked for. (A couple of the reporters have since made their way back to prestigious jobs with major newspapers back home.)

"We didn't expect any story out of that get-together and I don't think anyone filed a line of copy on it," Jody Powell said. "But the thinking was that if you do

things like that wherever you go, eventually you get so
you're not a stranger to everyone."

      📧   📧   📧

In mid-1975, Morris Udall's legislative assistant, Terry
Bracy, received a telephone call from a man who said he
was, as Bracy recalls, "the just-dismissed desk coordinator
for the Northeast for Jimmy Carter." The man said he
worked out of Atlanta. And he told Bracy that he had
taken some files with him when he left—including media
files and "basic Carter strategy, Carter contacts."

The man offered the Udall official a dirty tricks proposition of sorts.

"I asked him what he had," Bracy said. The caller gave
him a rundown. "I was really disturbed," Bracy said.
"This really bothered me." Bracy thought for a brief moment about the political career of Donald Segretti. Then
he told the caller to "go fuck yourself" and hung up.

Bracy promptly called Hamilton Jordan, Carter's campaign manager, who was based in Atlanta. As Bracy remembers it, "I said to him, 'We have got a problem. One
of your former guys has your stuff on the bidding block.' "

Jordan suggested that Bracy "go public" about the telephone call and the offer. "I said, 'Ham, I'm not dying to
go public.' " Instead, Bracy gave Jordan the name of the
ex-Carter man who had called him.

Jordan appreciated the way Bracy dealt with the matter.
"Those Udall people were very decent and honorable in
the way they handled it," Jordan said. "They acted truly
first class."

Jordan called the young man in Arizona, where he
lived. "I called the kid and told him I knew he'd left here
mad. I told him I'd heard some rumors that he'd been
saying some things about files—I just said rumors; I
wanted to protect Bracy. I told him I'd looked over my
files and there were some things missing and that I'd
hoped it wasn't true what I'd heard but that if anything
surfaced, we'd have to take quick legal action.

"I was just bluffing him out of it. . . . I really didn't
know what was missing or anything. But we never heard
anything about it after that."

It was about a month and a half before Bracy mentioned the incident to Udall. There was no need to tell

him in advance of rejecting the offer of stolen files, Bracy said. "That's what he would have expected," Bracy said. "Yes, we got tough and nasty in Michigan and in Ohio, but we stuck to the rules. I don't know of any dirty tricks. . . ."

There were tricks played in the campaign, but they were within the accepted rules of politics. On one presidential forum night in Louisville, Sylvia Chaplin, a Udall advance woman, discovered before the session that the podium to which the microphone was attached was far too short for her 6-foot, 5-inch boss.

Ms. Chaplin bought four reams of paper, each six inches thick, and placed a ream under each corner of the lectern. Then she did her work by decorating the new bottom with red, white, and blue bunting. That night, Udall stood tall as he spoke, looking straight at the audience. The other candidates had to stare at the ceiling to make themselves heard.

While Jimmy Carter was spending 1975 trying to get national recognition, six of his rivals, all philosophical allies, were trying to eliminate each other. Morris Udall, Birch Bayh, Sargent Shriver, Fred Harris, Milton Shapp, and Terry Sanford were six liberals in a race where they felt there was room for only one.

In September the liberals converged on Minneapolis to contest for the support of 1,500 liberal activists of the Midwest. Each addressed the meeting. The contender who drew the greatest applause was Harris, who could stir any crowd with his angry shouts against the way Washington ran things within the United States and overseas. Diplomacy was being conducted in secret, Harris thundered, and at home "the issue is privilege."

It was a long day of rhetoric and Bayh was the last speaker. He was the best known of the hopefuls and on that day the least impressive. In his opening remarks he did not talk of issues; instead, he spoke of his record in the Senate. To those familiar with his work on Capitol Hill, he responded to questions with less ability than he had shown in Washington.

This was just one of a string of unimpressive campaign performances by Bayh. His inability to attract a large following early in the primary year surprised many Democratic politicians, including a number of his opponents for the nomination. Among these were Jimmy Carter and his advisers, who believed all along that Bayh would be stronger than he proved to be.

Although it was Harris who received the applause, it was Udall who apparently won the support. The *Washington Post* conducted a straw poll at the Minneapolis meeting, found that Udall was a strong favorite, and said so in a big front-page story. He was the first choice of over half the audience at the meeting.

One of the most expensive investments of time and money by the liberal candidates was their effort to win the backing of the New York group known as the New Democratic Coalition. The endorsement of the NDC would "isolate the others from liberal support," Birch Bayh declared. And liberal support was viewed as the key to winning the New York primary.

"Our first target was Udall," Bayh's press secretary, Bill Wise, recalled. "We felt we had to blunt Udall. He was the more formidable of the candidates on the left. The quicker we could knock Udall out, the quicker we'd get Udall people in [Bayh's camp]. We thought our weakest area was the liberal activists. That's why we spent so much time and effort with the New Democratic Coalition. The NDC was significant. It makes it so much easier to get on the ballot in New York. We put in a helluva lot of early time, money, and effort to make that point."

One of Udall's top advisers also recalled the NDC campaign. "The time, concern, and energy we spent on the New Democratic Coalition was, I think, an outrage. An outrage because I was led to believe that was where it was at. We had to prevent Birch Bayh from getting that NDC nomination."

Udall adviser Ken Bode worked out a system in which he had the Udall delegates and the Harris delegates in constant communication at the NDC convention December 6, united in a common goal: Stop Bayh.

Sixty percent of the delegates were needed in order to

win the support of the NDC. Bayh was stopped just short.

"Two months from now," New York Assemblyman William Hoyt of Buffalo had said in making an endorsement appeal for Bayh, "the only name you're going to hear upstate is Birch Bayh." By the time of the New York primary, however, Bayh's name was not heard anywhere. He had already been knocked out of the race.

In October 1975 Broadman Press, publishers of religious books, came out with the first printing of Carter's combination autobiography and campaign book. Its title, *Why Not the Best?*, seemed to work two ways: it seemed to reflect the Georgian's self-assured nature as he went about trying to convince people that he was going to win the presidential nomination even if they did not think so (his book might just as well have been titled, "I'm the Best, You're O.K."); but as Carter saw it, the title was not immodest; it merely reflected the message he carried away from his job interview with Admiral Hyman Rickover when he was applying for the nuclear submarine program. (Rickover had asked Carter if he had always done his best at the naval academy and Carter had said no, not always, and Rickover had paused and finally responded: "Why not?")

Carter's book reflected a theme that became a central trait of his campaign. It offered something for everyone. It begins by quoting Reinhold Neibuhr and Bob Dylan and Dylan Thomas. It talks of his days fishing and fighting and getting whipped by his father for misbehaving and goes right into quotes of Sören Kierkegaard and Paul Tillich; it tells of his passion for Tristan and Isolde and talks of the music of the Liebestod and the next sentence is, "I became an expert on the recognition of the world's ships and planes during that time [at the U.S. Naval Academy]."

Something for everyone.

🏴 🏴 🏴

A symbolic moment in the California State Democratic Convention, held early in 1975 in Sacramento: Mo Udall, after repeated attempts to meet privately with Governor Edmund G. (Jerry) Brown, finally was told to come by at night. "We lope over from the hotel at about

11:15 P.M.," Udall aide Terry Bracy recalls. "We were thinking, 'There's no apparent purpose to this. What fool would stay up to do this?' Just as we were walking into the governor's office, we meet Jimmy Carter walking out. Always one step ahead."

In early December 1975 a Carter supporter in New York called the Carter headquarters in Atlanta to report a bit of Manhattan cocktail-circuit gossip. There had been a cocktail party at the Automation House and someone who is in the magazine business said that *Harper's* Magazine had signed Steven Brill to write a piece about Carter—"and he's going to do a number on us."

In early January 1976 a person supporting Birch Bayh in New York contacted a person running as a Carter delegate in New York to pass on a warning. There is going to be a piece coming out in *Harper's* that will be just devastating to Carter—"so you better stay away from him."

At a reception a few weeks later in Washington given by the Energy Action Committee, Alan Baron told some people about a *Harper's* piece by Brill that did so much damage to Carter. He said he had an advance copy of it and people could take a look at it if they wanted.

Jody Powell called *Harper's* editor Lewis Lapham to see a copy. They were receiving queries about the article, and there were apparently advance copies of the article around. Could the Carter people have a copy too? Lapham eventually agreed and Carter got his first look at what *Harper's* would be printing in its March edition.

It was titled "Jimmy Carter's Pathetic Lies." By Steven Brill.

There were many hard swipes at Carter in the lengthy *Harper's* piece. But there was nothing in the piece that was as devastating a shot as the title itself. Had the article been called simply "The Jimmy Carter Story" it could have pulled off its anti-Carter attack with a touch of class. As it turned out, the title alone created an aura of a cheap shot. In fact, the Brill piece contained some elements that were well reported and some that were not. The article dealt in large measure with Carter's political career in Georgia—controversies about his earlier campaigns and his stewardship of the state in his years as governor.

Because he received an early copy of the *Harper's* piece, Powell was able to prepare a lengthy point-by-point rebuttal to the article by Brill. Some of Powell's points were in fact refutations; others were just responses. The Powell document proved indeed effective as a political tool; it took the edge off the Brill attack. The *Boston Globe,* for example, wound up running excerpts from the Brill piece and excerpts from the Powell responses on the same day.

Postscript: One of Jody Powell's rebuttals concerned a letter quoted in the article. Brill said it had been sent by Carter to a woman, Mrs. Lena Mae Dempsey, who had written him complaining about his endorsement of Jackson instead of Wallace at the 1972 Democratic convention.

Dear Mrs. Dempsey:

I have never had anything but the highest praise for Governor Wallace. My support for Senator Jackson was based upon a personal request from our late Senator Richard Russell shortly before his death. I think you will find that Senator Jackson, Governor Wallace and I are in close agreement in most issues.

Let me ask you to consider one other factor before I close. There are times when two men working toward the same end can accomplish more if they are completely tied together. I think you will find that Governor Wallace understands this.

Please let me know when I can be of service to you or your children in Atlanta. I hope I have been able to give you a slightly better impression of me.

Sincerely,
Jimmy Carter

Brill was right. The letter did exist and it was sent. But Powell responded:

The letter to Mrs. Dempsey was written by a staffer, never seen by Gov. Carter, and did not accurately express his views. Several hundred letters each day often were answered from the Governor's office by staffers; inevitably a few of these staff responses were not exactly what the Governor would have written. Had the writer of the article asked, he would have been told of the three-letter-initial code used to identify staff letters.

The unfortunate choice of words by one staffer in one letter is hardly a test of the national leadership ability or the personal integrity of the Governor. . . .

Powell too was right. It was "the unfortunate choice of words by one staffer." What his response did not go on to say, however—but which Powell acknowledged without hesitation when asked—was that the "staffer" who wrote the letter had been Powell himself.

The Carter master plan for winning the nomination would have been useless without money to make it work. On December 12, 1974—the day he announced his candidacy—Carter began his fundraising with letters asking some 30,000 Georgia friends and associates to contribute to his campaign. Another letter was sent to about 500,000 other people culled from lists of Democratic National Committee telethon contributors and McGovern campaign contributors. That was the first large-scale Carter fundraising drive.

Up to that time, the Carter money effort had been made strictly in Georgia. In August 1974 twenty-seven people were invited to a pool party at the home of Bill Schwartz, an Atlanta real estate man and friend of Carter's. "We were really grubbing," recalled Frank Moore, a Carter finance coordinator. "About half of them were Jimmy's friends and the other half could afford to give." The affair raised $40,000. By the end of 1975, Carter had raised $850,000.

In 1975 Morris Dees, who had been successful in massmailing fundraising efforts for McGovern and who had helped set up similar systems for several of the 1976 Democratic candidates, officially signed on with Carter.

In December 1975 Dees proposed a "double-up" effort, in which all people who had given Carter $100 or more —some 1,800 people—would be asked to match their previous contributions. "The idea got a lot of horse laughs around here because the campaign had twisted people's arms to get them to pay $100 in the first place," Dees said.

The double-up letter, sent out over Carter's signature, was pitched to the Florida primary and his hopes of defeating Wallace.

Mr. John Doe
100 Main Street
Atlanta, Georgia 30303

Dear Mr. Doe:

We have done what seemed impossible.

I have emerged early as the Democratic candidate who has broken from the pack. . . .

The hour of decision is at hand.

Whether we can maintain our winning momentum until the early primaries and defeat Wallace in Florida on March 9th depends on you.

A bumper crop of peanuts, I learned years ago, is not made at harvest time but in early spring when you prepare a good seed bed. When I beat Wallace in Florida, the nomination with be within reach. To do this, I need $500,000 by December 26 to tie up prime TV time, buy billboards, and reach Florida voters.

We have wisely spent all the funds raised this year. Many of my key staff members are now going without pay to release new funds raised to be used for media advances.

To be very frank, our campaign's success may well depend on raising the Florida media funds prior to December 26th.

It is not easy to ask your help once more when I know how generous you have already been.

But history has always been made not by the multitudes but by the determined and courageous few. The $xxxxx you have already given is helping write a new chapter for America.

I believe so strongly that our government can be decent, truthful, fair, compassionate and efficient and I need your help so urgently that I am going to ask you and each donor to make a personal sacrifice.

Please send me another $xxxxx in the enclosed

stamped envelope. I'm asking each donor to "double-up" at this critically important time. I know the financial strain this may create with the holiday season at hand. But I pray you will answer our urgent need even if you have to borrow the funds.

Just think how shocked my opponents will be to learn we doubled our total contributions in just two weeks. Not only will this show unprecedented loyalty and faith from my friends but it will make political history.

Will you reach out your hand to me, once again? Rosalynn and I will do our best to never disappoint you.

Sincerely,
Jimmy Carter

P.S.—On December 26th I hope to announce to the press the success of our "Double-up for Carter" drive. Please rush your check.

The plea brought in $225,000. And after that Carter wrote to his donors every month, asking them to give again. He raised more than $1 million using this technique.

Beat Wallace in Florida. That was the message of Carter's double-up letter and that, in fact, was the foundation of the original Carter master plan. Carter had to win in Florida to show that he could take the South from George Wallace; he had to show that he alone could restore the solid South to the Democratic Party in November. Only then could Carter prove that he could be a winner nationwide.

Carter had started out sticking to his original plan—doing better than he expected, in fact. He won in Iowa and he won in New Hampshire. The plan called for him to ride this bandwagon momentum straight to a victory in Florida over Wallace. But on the way, Carter had let himself get sidetracked; he had tried for a win in Massachusetts on March 2, and he had built up expectations for his showing there. And he had been crushed. He had been buried by opponents, including the two men he now had to face in Florida, Jackson and Wallace. His momentum was gone. He had shifted his sights and he was paying a price. He had sabotaged his own bandwagon. Perhaps, he feared, irreparably.

March 9/Florida

A minor difference of opinion exists among the members of the Carter staff. Some say that when Jimmy Carter is angry the veins in his temples throb. Others insist that when he is angry it is his jaw muscles that throb.

Carter's temples and jaw muscles throbbed through much of the week that separated the Massachusetts and Florida primaries. They throbbed on airport tarmacs when Carter stood in the hot sun with microphones being shoved in his face as soon as he stepped off his plane. They throbbed in crowded motel meeting rooms as he held his question-and-answer sessions. They throbbed at a fish fry that turned into a press conference in Green Cove Springs.

"I'll be glad to repeat myself again—or else you can play your tape back to yourself," Carter snapped at a reporter who sought to question him.

On another occasion: "Do you want to stop talking so I can give you my answer or do you want to go ahead and ask a second question as well?"

When he wasn't snapping at the press, Carter was launching harshly worded attacks against Scoop Jackson. And even against George Wallace.

"He was off balance after Massachusetts," Hamilton Jordan said much later.

"The campaign was less sure of itself at that point than at any other time," recalled Greg Schneiders. "Massachusetts was the first sign that we were fallible."

"He was kind of at loose ends then," said Jody Powell.

"It was a case of not having cleaned it up and talked out in advance where we were headed."

Of the attacks on Wallace, Powell said: "We'd realized all along that doing it didn't cut with the voters. Frankly, even he knew that it wasn't the thing to do."

Jerry Rafshoon was in a phone booth in the Washington National Airport on the day after the Massachusetts election, working his way through five dollars in dimes while waiting for his plane, when his secretary at the office told him that Jimmy Carter had been calling. Carter was at Cape Canaveral being briefed on missiles; he couldn't come to the phone right then. Rafshoon left the number of the telephone booth he was using and waited for Carter to call back. A woman entered the booth.

"Can you use another phone?" Rafshoon asked.

"Why?" asked the woman.

"Jimmy Carter is trying to call me," Rafshoon replied.

"So what?" said the woman, depositing her dime.

Carter finally got through to Rafshoon. He wanted to make a new rush TV spot for the Florida campaign—a spot countering Jackson's efforts to play up the Carter home mortgage snafu. Carter wanted to tape the spot that night.

Gerald Rafshoon Advertising, Inc., went to work and finally located a small, private studio on the outskirts of Jacksonville that could be used that evening. Rafshoon made his way to Jacksonville and he and Carter went to the studio. Rafshoon's script for the TV spot opened with something like: "One of the candidates has been talking against my position on tax reform." Carter wanted to blast Jackson by name. But he eventually agreed that there was no need to give Jackson the free publicity. The rushed spot was put on the air in Florida the following day.

In press conferences and interviews that week, Carter's attack on Jackson centered around Jackson's ad in the *Boston Globe* which proclaimed in large letters: "I AM AGAINST BUSING." Said Carter: "Senator Jackson ran a campaign centered around the busing issue . . . an emotional issue . . . one that has racial or racist connotations. To build a campaign on an issue . . . that has already created disharmony, and sometimes even bloodshed, is to me the wrong approach to politics. I wouldn't do it. But Senator Jackson did. It's legal. I don't think he is a racist. I think he recognized an emotional issue and capitalized on it."

Carter's attack on Wallace was broad-based: "Governor Wallace's position on the race issue is well known. And part of his support probably comes from the race issue—I don't think there's much doubt about that. . . . But Wallace's support also comes from a wide range of voters and beliefs—partly because they think he's going to clean up the federal bureaucracy. It's obvious he can't do it. He hasn't done it in Alabama. Part of it is because they think he's going to give the poor people a better break from taxation. Obviously he can't do it. He hasn't done it in Alabama—that's the most regressive tax structure in the nation, in Alabama. Part of his support is because he wants the federal courts to be out of the administration of government. Obviously Alabama is a horrible example, because for all practical purposes, the federal courts are running many important elements in the Alabama government. . . ."

＊＊＊

Massachusetts. The specter of that snowstorm election verdict hung heavily over the Carter caravan as it crisscrossed sweltering Florida early in that final week.

Massachusetts. It was now very much a part of Florida, the Carter men feared. In Tallahassee at a businessmen's lunch, Carter received telephoned word that his campaign phone survey had shown his positive rating slipping and his negative rating climbing. There seemed to be a correlation between those statistics and the fact that Carter headquarters in Florida were receiving more and more phone calls from people wanting to know just what Carter was going to do with their tax deduction on home mortgage interest. Massachusetts. That damn Massachusetts.

But tucked into the bitter lessons of Massachusetts was the first indication of what proved to be a pleasant discovery to many of the Carter men. "It was the great surprise of '76 for us." Carter's pollster, Patrick Caddell, said later. "We got the black vote in Massachusetts. We never dreamed we would, but we got it. Roxbury went for Jimmy. That was the one good thing about Massachusetts."

This pointed up what was to become the truly phenomenal thing about the Carter campaign: the candidate was able to attract large numbers of people from a wide range of disparate backgrounds, interests, and beliefs. Rednecks and blacks, McGovern liberals and hardline hawks, labor leaders and corporation executives, people who wear denim because it's good to work in and people who wear denim because it's good to party in.

Massachusetts, it turned out, gave the Carter people a good healthy scare. But it proved to be not as significant in Florida as several other factors. Chiefly, the liberals seeking the nomination had challenged Carter in the other states, but to a man they had bypassed Florida. They feared that Florida would be Wallace country once again, just as it had been in 1968 and 1972. As they were to do throughout the 1976 campaign, the liberals fought this year's battles on the basis of the past years' wars. Many Democrats feared in the beginning that Wallace would be a large and unpleasant problem for all the party in 1976, that he would do well outside the South in this year when people were so turned off by politics as usual. So they were content to let Carter have a clean shot at Wallace in Florida. After all, if the unknown Georgian should pull an upset win, they reasoned, he would be easy to pick off later.

🇺🇸 🇺🇸 🇺🇸

SCENE: Vero Beach, at the high school gym. The stage is bedecked in red, white, and blue, but in the crowd some people waiting for the candidate are pointing up at the eerie piece of furniture that sits on the stage front and center. "Look, he's got to set behind that little bulletproof thing now," a man in a straw Wallace boater says to his wife. "Poor fella. Look what it's like for him now." Wallace is wheeled in and is placed behind the lectern that is strangely small, with short wooden (lead-reinforced) walls and bulletproof glass that separate the candidate from the crowd.

Empty seats predominate, but Wallace pretends not to notice. The people applaud his lines enthusiastically but the hoots, shouts, and rebel yells of old are largely missing.

🇺🇸 🇺🇸 🇺🇸

George Wallace 1976 was not George Wallace 1972 . . . or 1968 . . . or 1964. His people talked about Franklin D. Roosevelt, who was crippled yet a leader and unifier. But George Wallace had never been a national leader

—certainly not a national unifier. His South had moved on from those early days of racial confrontation; blacks now starred on Alabama football teams and rednecks cheered them. His anti-Washington theme—lambasting the pointy-heads and the bureaucrats with briefcases full of peanut butter sandwiches—was no longer just his. Anti-Washington had become the gospel of Campaign '76, sung frequently with more sophisticated lyrics by a full choir of candidates—liberal, moderate, and conservative. (On the Republican side, even the President of the United States, Gerald Ford, would try his hand at running against the federal government.) It just might be that this could not have been the year of even a healthy George Wallace. But the fact that he was crippled could not be overlooked. FDR campaigned and won before the days of the ubiquitous video eye; newspapers then did not dwell on pictures of Roosevelt being lifted, doll-like, from his auto to his wheelchair; and certainly there were never reports of a time when his handlers dropped the dignified Roosevelt. Roosevelt grew to be the national leader and unifier; Wallace grew to be a national curiosity. People came to his rallies and their attention was riveted not on the man and his message, but on things like the midget-sized bulletproof lectern—just high enough to protect a candidate in a wheelchair from being wasted once and for all, eerie with its bulletproof glass rising from a base at less than waist high. It is cruel but true: you can't win votes sitting in the schoolhouse door. George Wallace would not be a major factor in the campaign of 1976; but the liberals, always fighting the last war, would not realize that until they read it in the newspapers.

SCENE: Temple Emanu-El is a symbol of Hebraic strength in Miami Beach and on March 7 its chapel looks like Shea Stadium on cap day. A capacity crowd fills the huge downstairs seating area and there is standing room only in the semicircular upper deck. It is a pep rally populated by people of years, wrinkled and bent yet tanned and alert. They are cheering and hollering for the hometown hero, Scoop Jackson, and he is turning them on with his pledges of support for Israel and tough talk against the Soviets. Interestingly, the Temple

Emanu-El crowd cheers just as lustily for a towering, florid-faced Irishman who was recently signed by the Jackson team after playing for both the Boston Kennedys and the Washington Nixons. Daniel Patrick Moynihan, the world's tallest leprechaun, had won himself a new constituency months earlier by sounding a hard line as America's ambassador to the United Nations, and now as designated hitter for the Jackson team Moynihan is being greeted as though he were Moshe Dayan. He loves it.

Jackson was running statewide, but he was focusing really on locking up the heavily Jewish areas of Miami Beach and North Miami Beach, looking to carry the South Florida Gold Coast districts and at least come out of Florida with a sizable number of delegates. The Jackson people did not really expect to carry the state. But they did expect to carry Miami Beach. To this end, they had set up a squad of condominium commandos trained to mobilize, at the drop of a leaflet, the thousands of retired people who live in the tall New Yorkish apartment buildings that have overrun the once beautiful beachfront like ugly barnacles that have gotten the best of a once sleek ship. Susan Weiner, a twenty-six-year-old Jackson volunteer, has put together a most effective condominium organization, complete with condo captains, and lists of condominium people needing rides to the polls; eventually they ensure Jackson a good South Florida vote.

Carter strategists, meanwhile, did not want to concede even Miami Beach to Jackson. The Carter effort was headed by a Lutheran minister, Roger Volker, who hoped to be able to convince the Jewish voters that only Carter had a chance of beating George Wallace, who was the man who they really did not like. He hoped to convince them not to throw away a vote on Jackson, but to vote for Carter instead. And after all, if the Miami Beach Jews went wild over Daniel Patrick Moynihan, perhaps Carter had a chance with them too.

SCENE: On the same weekend that Jackson and Moynihan are working Temple Emanu-El Jimmy Carter goes to Yeshiva. He dons a yarmulke at the Jewish

center school in the south end of Miami Beach, but it
does not help. He only looks like "Jimmy," chief of the
Mouseketeers. His audience has some elderly people,
some middle-aged people, and a lot of children who are
fidgety and noisy and bored; later most of the adults say
they came not because they are Carter supporters but
just because they were curious. Jimmy Carter, still in
yarmulke, tells them all about his trip to Israel and how
he talked with Golda Meir and how he toured the country
in a car that he emphasizes was made available to him
by Mrs. Meir. His words about Israel are about as strong
as those of Scoop Jackson, but somehow, with this constituency, Jimmy Carter does not make it. He comes off
like grits at a seder.

It was traveling Georgians, not transplanted Yankees,
who provided the big boost for Carter's Florida campaign. First there was family: Rosalynn campaigned for
weeks throughout the state; others in the Carter clan did
too. And then there were busloads of Georgians, traveling across the border to carry the Carter campaign to
even the smallest areas of northern Florida.
"I could depend on 1,000 Georgians in Florida,"
Carter recalled months later. "And they were almost like
my family. And if they went to a barbershop and said,
'I know Jimmy Carter—he was our governor and he reorganized the government and he reformed our prison
system, so forth, would you vote for him?' Very often
that barber would say, 'Yeah, I'll vote for him' and say,
'I met Chip, you know, six months ago. I remember
Chip.' He's easy to remember." That personal investment
of time—Carter's time, his family's time, his friends'
time—was too large to be wiped out by something that
happened in faraway Massachusetts.

SCENE: In the shade of trees heavy with gray moss,
on the steps of a farmland courthouse at Brooksville, the
local bank president is saying a few words about "the
next President of the United States." Up to the microphones comes Jimmy Carter, smiling shyly. "My folks

have all been farmers," be begins, and he tells them all about Plains and raising peanuts. "I'm the first member of my daddy's family to finish high school. . . . Something's gone wrong with the government in Washington— we feel like outsiders. . . . Now I don't want any of you to vote for me this year unless you want the federal government reorganized. . . . I'm campaigning hard and I don't intend to lose; I believe you're looking at the next President of the country. . . . What this country needs most of all is a government that is as good and honest and decent and truthful and fair and compassionate—and *filled with love*—as the American people are."

There is a knot of about 200 people clustered under the trees listening to the campaigner who is talking their language. They are applauding at all the right places and then some. They are Wallaceites and moderates, town folk and farmers who have come in for supplies and even just to hear the speech; those in the cluster are all whites; but a small number of blacks are hanging around the fringes of the crowd. "I'd like to see him elected," Cecil Bishop, a retired citrus grower, is saying. "Liked Wallace, but he can't win. This one can win. And we need a man from the South." By now Jimmy Carter is making his way across the lawn toward the street. A heavy-set white woman pushes forward and then when she is within reach of the candidate she gets shy about being there. Carter reaches out and pulls her toward him and gives her a hug and a kiss. "Oh, Lord bless you, Jimmy," she gushes. "I'll be praying for you." Carter walks over and does a round of handshaking in the Snacks 'n' Stuff Restaurant. A black woman who is eating there reaches out to receive a handshake and suddenly recoils in embarrassment; she wipes the grease of fried chicken off and she is thrilled, beaming and saying incredulously, "How *about* that?" As Carter is crossing the street to his motorcade car, a Cadillac with ego plates reading "FDC" drives by and slows. "Hello, Jimmy! Good luck!" the man behind the wheel says, and he drives off.

Wallaceites, blacks, people who drive pickups and people who drive Cadillacs. Jimmy Carter is scoring well with them all in Florida. He is pictured by many as the liberal in the three-man race (Milton Shapp is in the race too, but he is making no headway at all); yet Carter is also drawing support among conservatives. A good part

of his ability to attract voters of varied philosophies was
due to the careful, deliberate way Carter constructed his
position statements on many controversial issues. It was
apparent that Carter had concluded that strident positions
on issues are unlikely to win much support for a candidate, but they sure can make him some vociferous enemies
among those who feel strongly—and oppositely—from
him on any given issue. The Carter appeal was to faith
and trust. So he decided to trim a bit, tacking first to the
left and then to the right, a wily navy veteran trying
most of all to sail through the sea of emotion-triggering
issues without striking any perilous mines.

"Sure, Jimmy has worked out answers on controversial
issues so as not to anger people," Jody Powell said later.
"Why not try to find a solution—a way of getting it done
—so as not to piss off a lot of people and create more
problems than we started with?" Powell is asked about
Carter's way of handling questions on amnesty for Vietnam draft dodgers. "His answer on amnesty," Powell replied, "is a classic example of how to say something and
not piss off people."

Carter on amnesty. It is not an answer; it is an art
form—carefully constructed so as to diffuse the emotions
of the subject and come up with something for everyone.
The shorthand of it is that he starts out by saying he is
against amnesty, but he winds up saying he is for pardon.
And he tells interviewers, when asked, that he thinks
there is a difference, even though Webster defines
"amnesty" as a "general pardon."

This shorthand explanation does not do Carter justice.
His answer actually works like this:

"I'm not in favor of amnesty . . . In my county, where
I'm from, we don't have a dentist or a doctor or a phar-
macist. There's a lot of ignorance there. But when boys
were drafted, they didn't know where Sweden was. They
went and fought and died. Others came back. . . ." He
goes on to talk about how when he came home from
the navy he was a hero to his townspeople, just for having gone; but when his son came back from Vietnam he
was not treated as a hero at all; people were not proud

of where he had been and what he had done. The divisions of Vietnam still run deep.

"So when I become President," he goes on, "although I do not want a blanket amnesty, I will issue a blanket pardon to those people [who dodged the draft]. . . . Amnesty is saying what you did was right. . . . A pardon says it was wrong but you are forgiven. . . . It is time to get the Vietnam War over in our country."

So, too, Carter staked out a position on the air force's controversial new B-1 bomber that was somewhere in between those of the B-1 backers and the B-1 opponents. "I oppose production of the B-1 bomber at this time. I believe that research and development should continue. The decision on the production of this weapon system should be made by our next administration." (Which, Carter says, would be *his* administration; so Carter thus left unclear just what he as President would do about the B-1.)

And on welfare reform, Carter would sometimes stress that he would cut off payments to all those who were able to work but would not; and other times (frequently before black crowds), he would emphasize that "Ninety percent of the people on welfare cannot work and ought to be treated with love and compassion by the government."

While Carter was amassing broad-based support from many diverse groups, he seemed to have genuine problems winning any sizable expression of support from one special group: his fellow governors. The people who had presided over their states at the time Carter presided over his, who met with him and talked with him as equals during the various governor's conferences, were not fond of him.

Some of the other governors said privately they resented the way Carter wound up getting the major share of the publicity at their regional and even national governors' conferences—how, as they saw it, he always seemed to get out of the meetings in order to get into places to be able to get in front of the television cameras first. "They got mad because he was just better at doing the political thing than they were," is how one of

Carter's aides once expressed it. Perhaps. At any rate, he was not the most popular man inside the meeting rooms of the governors' conferences.

Calvin Rampton, Utah governor for years, was once quoted as saying: "Of the forty some Democratic governors that I've known personally, I'd rank Carter about thirty-ninth." ·

Governor Patrick Lucey of Wisconsin said: "A number of the governors are upset about Carter's statements on revenue sharing. He thinks states should be excluded from the program. We are surprised to hear that from a former governor. . . ."

Wendell Ford, a former chairman of the Democratic Governors' Conference, was quoted as saying: "I don't know of any governors or former governors that he has contacted for support. That might indicate how much support he has among his former colleagues."

Among the governors not fond of Carter was Florida's Reubin Askew. Askew reportedly felt he had been led to believe at a meeting that Carter would back him for the chairmanship of the Southern Governors' Conference. But Carter wound up backing Dolph Briscoe of Texas, who had been endorsed as well by Wallace.

In the Florida primary, Askew was under considerable pressure to back Carter as an alternative to Wallace. Instead, Askew, still bitter, took no position. (After the Florida primary, he came out for Jackson.)

Carter could have used Askew's help in Florida. But he found help from other sources. Among them was the United Auto Workers. Jackson was the man with the union ties in the Florida primary, and so the Georgian and his advisers were pleased at being able to wind up with some union help of their own—from Florida UAW people. And even the UAW's powerful president, Leonard Woodcock, showed up at a dinner party Carter attended in St. Petersburg. Woodcock emphasized to reporters that he was not making any endorsement at the time. Not yet. But he also spoke very warmly, very openly, about Carter.

THE RESULTS: *Election night in Florida was the first of the big election-night gatherings of the Carter clan.*

Twenty-five or thirty relatives and friends gathered in the Carter suite at the Carleton House Hotel outside Orlando.

They wound up celebrating a victory. Years ago, Carter and his men had figured that Florida would be the place where they could knock off Wallace and show Carter to be a viable southern alternative. And Florida was the place where they did just that. Carter finished with 34.3 percent, Wallace had 30.6, Jackson, 23.9. Jimmy Carter was a born-again frontrunner.

Some of the Carter people celebrated through the night, but the candidate had a busy schedule ahead. He was getting ready for bed at 12:30 A.M. when there was a knock at his door. Someone passed the word that several of his Florida UAW people were outside. Carter put his pants back on and went out to chat with them. Barefoot.

Interlude: The Morning After

The morning after his dismal fourth-place finish in Massachusetts, Jimmy Carter had been testy. The morning after his stunning first-place finish in Florida, Jimmy Carter was . . . testy.

"He was in a testy mood," recalled Greg Schneiders. "He discovered that he had been booked on 'Issues and Answers' and that an interview had been promised to Hunter Thompson [the sage of *Rolling Stone*], on the flight to Chicago. He complained to Betty [Rainwater, an assistant press secretary] that he was being overscheduled. He'd planned to sleep on the flight." Carter gave Thompson forty-five minutes and slept the rest of the time. Thompson turned out to be much enamored of Carter, and wrote an article highly favorable to the Carter campaign.

It is one of the things about Carter that he can fall asleep anywhere, anytime. A deep, good sleep. He can sleep right up until he reaches his stop, then wake up, straighten his hair, and go out and shake a few hands and make his speech.

March 16/Illinois

To say that Richard J. Daley was a mayor and be done with it is like saying that MacArthur was a soldier. Richard Daley was a master of the uses of power—power at the local level where it affects people directly, where people see what you are doing for them and see what they can do for you in return—the sort of power that makes a person something more than just a mayor; the power that makes a boss.

Richard J. Daley was a boss, but he was not without his problems, some of which have been visible at Democratic National Conventions. In 1968, when the convention was held in his city, the police turned disturbances into major riots with head-smashing billy clubs and brutal tactics. "A police riot" was the official verdict of an investigating commission. Television at the convention caught Daley making a singularly dramatic and obscene gesture at Senator Abraham Ribicoff, who had the temerity to call the storm-trooper police brutality that was occurring in the streets what it truly was.

Then in 1972, a year of McGovern and reform, Daley lost control of—and was tossed out of—his own Illinois delegation. An unceremonious thing to happen to a man of his clout. Daley reacted in the only style fitting a political boss. He came back. Came back strong. He won reelection in 1975 to a sixth four-year term as mayor, renewing his political power.

Jimmy Carter has a fine appreciation for the uses of political power. And so it is that he long ago developed a fine rapport with Daley.

Shortly before the Democratic Convention of 1976, Carter was asked to reflect on just how important the seventy-four-year-old mayor of Chicago was in American politics.

"He's important," Carter said. "You know, the county

chairperson of a south Georgia rural area and the county chairperson of a metropolitan county in Pennsylvania or New York, they look on Mayor Daley as a sort of surrogate for them. He represents [a Democratic Party] establishment figure . . . who supported McGovern after McGovern had kicked him out of the [1972] convention. He was a professional and his word was his bond, and they look to him as an exemplification of what they are. And his support therefore is significant in the eyes of the media, in the eyes of the delegates whom he can influence, and in his posture as a loyal local Democratic official. . . .

"So in many ways, Daley is important. I like Daley personally, I have known him for five or six years. As a matter of fact, at the Kansas City convention [the mini-convention the Democrats held in 1974], when we took a crucial vote on the . . . rules, I was sitting with Daley, talking to him about politics and government. When I went to the Illinois delegation to meet with them before the actual deliberations at the Kansas City convention . . . , Mayor Daley welcomed me and he introduced me.

"I made about a five-minute speech, and there was a tremendous response from the Illinois delegation. He insisted I bring my wife up to the stage and introduce her to them. And when I finally walked out of the room, they were still applauding. And that would not have been possible without Daley's friendship."

This was two weeks before December 12, 1974, the day on which Carter officially announced his candidacy for the Presidency.

James Wall, editor of the *Christian Century,* led the fight for George McGovern in the suburbs of Chicago in 1972. In 1976, the primary scene in Illinois was being dominated by Daley, who was running a favorite-son effort in the name of Senator Adlai Stevenson. James Wall, meanwhile, was looking for a candidate to back.

First he thought he would go with Fritz Mondale. But Mondale decided not to run. Next he thought he would go with Sargent Shriver. He was introduced to him, but did not hear from Shriver again.

He also took Mo Udall on a tour of his suburban area. But he did not hear from Udall.

On May 1, he had met Jimmy Carter. The Carter people kept in touch, and as Wall explained: "I'm from Georgia originally. I went home and talked to his staff." Then on October 20, Wall said, "Jimmy came to my home and asked me to become his state chairman. That's exactly the way he functions. I told him the mayor thing has been my big trouble. Jimmy said, 'I will take care of that. The mayor and I have a good relationship.' "

According to Wall, Carter told the mayor that, even though he was going to put up a slate of delegates in the suburbs of Chicago, its members would vote for Daley to head the delegation. There would be no repetition of 1972. Daley, said Wall, was not dissatisfied.

🏳 🏳 🏳

Dear Friends,

You may already know that my brother, Jimmy Carter, is running for the office of President of the United States.

My reason for writing you is to acquaint you with a most important facet of Jimmy, one that couldn't possibly be pursued with any depth by the press or television, and that is his quality of deep personal commitment to Jesus Christ and his will to serve Him in whatever capacity he finds himself.

A growing number of national commentators have stated that they are deeply impressed with Jimmy's grasp of national and international affairs and his proven capacity of governing with fiscal responsibility and compassion for human needs. What usually is ignored in such analyses is that our nation's greatest need is for a President who will render spiritual leadership. This, in my opinion, is one of Jimmy's greatest qualifications.

As one who knows the importance of Christ in your personal life and who I'm sure wants our nation to be under His blessings and guidance—please pray for Jimmy. And if you share my feeling that he is the best candidate, I urge you to actively support him.

On Tuesday, March 16, the Illinois Primary will be held. Please call your friends and neighbors to go

with you and cast your vote for Jimmy in the Pref-
erential Primary and for his delegates in your particular Congressional District.

Sincerely in Christ,
Ruth Carter Stapleton

Ruth Carter Stapleton is Jimmy's youngest sister, and
she is a gospeler who specializes in a ministry of "inner
healing." She does not specialize in politics but she does
believe that politics and religion can—and should—mix.
So it is that she wrote her letter, which was sent to a mailing list of a couple of hundred names; the above copy
was marked to be sent to a Lithuanian Center.

A very attractive woman, blond and blue-eyed and
always fashionable in wardrobe and makeup, Ruth Carter
Stapleton campaigned hard for her brother, bringing an unusual religious element into the realm of politics. While
others tried to sell Carter on the basis of his grasp of
governmental issues, she sold Carter on the basis of his
belief in Christ. America should be "under *His* blessings
and guidance," was her message, so "please pray for
Jimmy."

She came to the campaign trail as a corporate executive
of sorts: she and her husband, Fayetteville, North Carolina, veterinarian Bob Stapleton, formed "Behold, Inc.,"
as a nonprofit organization which is the umbrella for her
practice of the ministry.

She had come to her present practice of the ministry
as a mother of four, after experiencing a period of profound personal unrest. She had gone from being a daughter
pampered and favored by her father to being a coquet-
tish southern belle and then to being a superreligious
Baptist who eschewed frilly clothes and all makeup. "I
hated myself and subconsciously wanted to die," she told
the *Washington Post*'s Myra MacPherson. "People lit
candles, prayed for me. A psychiatrist said, 'You're suffering too much—there's no way to help you. You need
medication.' After I exhausted every resource, I had to
come to grips with the fact that the problem was inside
me."

Stapleton also told MacPherson that she has since had
a couple of religious "experiences," and she told her in
the spring of 1976 of the most recent one, which occurred

two years earlier. "I woke up in my sleep and there was this light, this glow in my room. Something inside me said I was moving into a place of 'unconditional love.' My total healing took place when I fully realized God was a God of love, not one who punished."

As she travels the country, giving speeches and practicing "inner healing," she professes a ministry that is an unusual mixture of psychology and religion. She takes her patients back to their childhood and then conducts them on a trip of faith and imagination, traveling through their troubled childhood, but this time traveling with Jesus. She talked about her work during a small press conference she gave at the Democratic convention. Syndicated columnist Garry Wills was among those who gave wide circulation to her story of a person she called "Zeb," which she offered when asked to describe her greatest healing experience.

"Suddenly the idea came to have Zeb visualize Jesus walking through each room of his childhood home, filling it with his love and light. When Zeb refused to go into the upstairs bathroom, I knew we had the key to one of the locked doors of his past. After much encouragement and with the assurance that Jesus would walk with him, together they opened the door to that bathroom. Through sobs and mild hysteria, Zeb told me his uncle had walked in on him many years ago as he stood there masturbating for the first time. Memories of his uncle's roars and cursing rebukes flooded his mind in that moment. I repeated the words continually, 'Jesus, Jesus, Jesus,' throughout his story. As Zeb began to regain his composure, he visualized Jesus there in the room blessing him, blessing the room, blessing his life, and most important, blessing the part of his body that Zeb had so hated and had rejected."

Late in January 1976 Ken Levine went into Illinois as the first Udall operative to enter the state. He was thinking about trying to set up something for Udall in Liberal Representative Abner Mikva's Chicago area district and in the liberal University of Illinois communities of Champaign and Urbana. Mikva told him to forget it, that the people of his district didn't know Udall. It went the same way in the university town. The ex-McGovern people were either for Carter or did not want to get involved. Levine then tried the 13th Congressional District.

"I made a presentation in the thirteenth—Libertyville," Levine told a friend later. "I said, 'Hey, Mo Udall is a liberal guy.' They said, 'Hey, we're going to go uncommitted. We don't know Mo.'"

Udall passed on Illinois. So did Scoop Jackson.

George Wallace did not. Wallace campaigned hard in the weeks following his loss in Florida, trying to get his campaign together again. Illinois was March 16 and North Carolina was March 23 and his opponent in both places was Jimmy Carter.

Wallace fought gamely in Illinois, trying to convince people that he was physically capable to be President. He told a press conference the day before the election, "Some people are paralyzed in the head, but I'm only paralyzed in the legs. I wouldn't be involved in the primaries if I couldn't do this. My health is fine. Doctors have assured me I'm all right. But if you want an acrobat for President, then I'm not your man."

THE RESULTS: *Wallace was not the people's man in Illinois. Carter scored a substantial victory in the presidential preference vote, defeating Wallace 48 percent to 28 percent. Shriver polled just 16 percent and was finished as a candidate. Harris received 8 percent and was never a factor after that.*

But Carter's most politically impressive showing was not his victory in the preference vote, but his second-place finish in the delegate voting.

Carter had not even fielded delegate slates in seven of the state's twenty-four districts in and around Chicago. He and his advisers had been saying how they would be happy if they won a total of 20 delegates in Illinois.

Instead, Carter won 55 delegates—second to the 85 pledged to favorite-son Stevenson; Wallace only three. Carter delegates defeated Stevenson's in many downstate races, including areas where Stevenson delegates were popular local officials. Daley, who more than anything else admired people who can win, was impressed. And Daley said so in his own way: "His was a campaign that some respect must be paid to."

Interlude: Reorganization

> All of these changes combined to permit the
> slashing of the administrative costs of government
> more than [in] half. . . .
>> —Jimmy Carter, on his reorganization of Geor-
>>   gia's bureaucracy, in his book *Why Not the
>>   Best?*

Rick Cobb is a Jimmy Carter man. He is deputy director. of the Georgia Office of Planning and Budgeting.
He is a true Carter believer who originally came to the
state for a few months to help Carter implement his famous government reorganization and who became converted and stayed on. He is a man who says: "I'd work
for Jimmy Carter anywhere—anytime."

About the only thing Rick Cobb won't do for Jimmy
Carter is vouch for all of the campaign claims Carter
made about the success of his reorganization effort. Cobb
definitely believes that the reorganization was a great
success. But he concedes that it probably was not as great
as Carter likes to say it was.

Example: Carter's claim in his book, his campaign
speeches, and brochures that he cut state administrative
costs by 50 percent. "I wouldn't be surprised if Jimmy
really thinks that's true," Cobb said. "Was fifty percent of
the state government's administrative costs actually cut?
No, it wasn't. But more cuts were made in administrative
costs than in any other area. . . . It's just that we have no
idea how much was cut and it would take a special audit
to find out."

Later, a Carter campaign spokesman, Rex Granum,
said that the former governor has no statistics to back up
his 50 percent figure. "It's just an estimate," Granum said.
And Carter, when told of the comments by planning
official Rick Cobb, conceded that perhaps the savings
claims had been exaggerated. Eventually Carter stopped
making the 50 percent savings claim in his campaign
speeches.

Carter did stick to one other controversial set of reorganization statistics however. He has always referred to
how he eliminated 278 of 300 state agencies, leaving
Georgia with just twenty-two. Actually, there were only

sixty-five budgeted state agencies, commissions, boards, and so on when he took office. The remainder were not receiving any funds and in many cases they existed on paper only. Also, according to Rick Cobb, the total of existing state agencies and commissions and such was reduced by Carter to thirty, not twenty-two." "Even when he was governor," Cobb said, "Jimmy would say in speeches how we'd cut it down to twenty-two. And then we'd meet with him and say, 'No, Governor, it's really twenty-nine or thirty or whatever.' But he just stuck with twenty-two, and it's a small point, really."

Carter's media adviser, Jerry Rafshoon, commented much later on the numbers controversy that Carter's reorganization claims touched off. "I guess it was a mistake to get into a numbers game on reorganization," Rafshoon said. "The point is that reorganization was good."

March 23 /North Carolina

"I spent more time on my knees the four years I was governor in the seclusion of a little private room off the governor's office than I did in all the rest of my life put together because I felt so heavily on my shoulders that the decisions I made might very well affect many, many people."

Jimmy Carter was standing on a riser on a patio of a sprawling, modern, luxurious home in Winston-Salem, North Carolina. More than seventy-five wealthy contributors had come to this fundraiser. The night was chilly, but the party had moved out to the patio because it was the best way to accommodate such a large crowd.

They had come expecting to hear a political talk. Instead they were treated to the rare spectacle of a presidential candidate discussing publicly the intimacies of his religion and the relationship he feels he has with God.

He told them about "a deeply profound religious experience that changed my life dramatically" in 1967.

"I recognized for the first time that I had lacked something very precious—a complete commitment to Christ, a presence of the Holy Spirit in my life in a more profound and personal way. And since then I've had an inner peace and inner conviction and assurance that transformed my life for the better. . . . I don't think I'm ordained by God to be President. . . . [The] only prayer that I've ever had concerning the election is that I do the right thing. And if I win or lose, my religious faith won't be shaken."

Carter elaborated on his comments the following day at a press conference. "In 1967, I realized that my own relationship with God, with Christ, was very superficial. And because of some experience I had that I won't describe . . . I came to realize that my Christian life, which I had always professed to be preeminent, had really been a secondary interest in my life.

104

"And I formed a very close, intimate personal relationship with God, through Christ, that has given me a great deal of peace. . . .

"It was not a profound stroke of miracle. It wasn't a voice of God from heaven. It was not anything of that kind. It wasn't mysterious. It might have been the same kind of experience as millions of people have who do become Christians in a deeply personal way. . . . I don't think God is going to make me President by any means. But whatever I have as a responsibility for the rest of my life, it will be with that intimate personal continuing relationship. . . ."

On that chilly North Carolina evening, and in the day that followed, Jimmy Carter talked about the very intimate, very personal nature of his religious beliefs to a degree that perhaps no presidential candidate has before. It had been a question from one of the campaign contributors standing on the patio that night that had gotten him talking about his beliefs. But Carter had been questioned about his Southern Baptist convictions before and had limited himself in the past to short, simple replies about how religion is separate from politics. Why had he responded in such intimate detail this time?

"The questioner wanted to know if I was going to disavow my religion or my religious beliefs in order to get votes around the country," Carter recalled. "This question had come up several times before in audiences and I would try to give a brief answer like yes or no or that's the way I feel. I had talked to my wife a lot and that question was coming up with increasing frequency, so I thought for once and for all with all the reporters present I would answer the question a little more completely and have it over with. And there was no surge of questioning of me by the news media until after Richard Reeves wrote an article about me in *New York* Magazine, ascribing my political success to a spiritual desire on the part of the American people that I was meeting. I have never known how to assess the impact of one reporter's writings upon another reporter's, but apparently that article had a great deal of effect on the interest of other reporters in that subject.

Question: "Does Carter regret having discussed his private religious beliefs so publicly, and in such detail?"

Carter: "In retrospect I would have done the same

thing. I don't see any legitimate alternative to it. The people have a right to understand the religious beliefs of their future President. And this was a legitimate inquiry when Al Smith ran and when John Kennedy ran, and when we have our first Jewish nominee that's going to become an issue and I think that is expectable and certainly proper. At the beginning it created very serious political problems for me among some of the Jewish voters and some of the Catholic leaders because of the past prejudice that had been exhibited in the Deep South against Jews, against Catholics, against blacks, and others, and there had to be a learning process on their part, a teaching process to some reticent degree on my part just not to bury the issue once it was raised. And I think that as people began to realize that the Baptists believe in strict separation of church and state and that Truman was a Baptist and that I have served in public life for about fourteen years and have never tried to mix our religious beliefs and public service in an improper fashion, I think that the problem has attenuated substantially."

So it was that Carter came to talk about his Southern Baptist beliefs during his campaign through North Carolina. It was a move that may well have helped him win that Bible Belt region. And while Carter maintains he does not think his comments turned out to be a political plus in that primary, he also conceded that he probably would not have gone into the matter of his religious beliefs in detail had the question come that day in a northern primary.

Question: "Would you have answered the question as fully at a fundraiser in Boston?"

Carter: "No, I doubt it. The people in North Carolina knew what I was talking about and I didn't have to define terms or explain to them the basic tenets of a Southern Baptist or of the Methodist faith. So I was talking to a group of people among whom knowledge of my faith was very widespread already. I didn't have to define terms. I didn't have to tell them that the Baptists believe in separation of church and state and we have no hierarchical arrangement that might tend to dominate me from the church structure. They know that just as a normal part of their lives."

Carter's "deeply profound religious experience" came,

he says, late in 1966, following his gubernatorial defeat, and in the early part of 1967. As a result, he now considers himself a "born again" Christian—the term means that he has had a spiritual rebirth, that he has thus begun a new life, committed to Jesus, with a new love for his fellow man.

Ruth Carter Stapleton has been widely quoted as recalling the day when her brother, Jimmy, underwent this "deeply profound religious experience." After Carter's 1966 defeat, she has been quoted as saying, he sat outdoors and "put his face in his hands and cried like a baby." As Mrs. Stapleton told it to Myra MacPherson of the *Washington Post,* Carter went for a walk with her through the pine woods and there Carter said to his sister, "You and I are both Baptists, but what is [it] that you have that I haven't got?"

"I said, 'Jimmy, through my hurt and pain I finally got so bad off I had to forget everything I was. What it amounts to in religious terms is total commitment. I belong to Jesus. Everything I am.'

"He said, 'Ruth, that's what I want.' So we went through everything he would be willing to give up. Money was no problem, nor friends, nor family. Then, I asked, 'What about all political ambitions?' He said, 'Ruth! You know I want to be governor. I would use it for the people!' I said, 'No, Jimmy.' But he really meant it and became connected with part-time religious work. So he went to Pennsylvania and New York on a Baptist missionary tour for less than a year. Jimmy's a Baptist and to commit to life Baptists think you have to go off and be a missionary somewhere."

Carter is not happy with the way his sister, Ruth, recounts the story of his religious experience. Quietly, and apparently a little uncomfortably, he takes issue with her on the question of his weeping and the profundity of that one walk in the woods. Carter said: "There was never any crisis in my life that took place in one single day, one single walk in the pine woods. There was never any one time when I sat in my sister's presence weeping. That's been exaggerated grossly. I did walk in the woods and talk to my sister Ruth about that. The problem in my life that had been created by that 1966 loss was the fact that my life seemed to be without purpose and that I was overly concerned about the defeats, that I had lost an interest in other people, individually, to a great extent, that I didn't get any sense of accomplishment when I achieved success and I felt like my religious beliefs were shallow and just a matter of self-pride. And Ruth and I had a long talk and it was a very important conversation for me, but there was no flash of revelations, no weeping. But there was a series of circumstances during that period of about a year or two that was in the last part of '66, first part of '67, and it gave me a renewed insight and a much clearer understanding of what my religious teachings, throughout my life almost, had meant. But that one particular episode was exaggerated a little bit because of my sister's subjective involvement in it."

Carter also took note of that period in his life in a televised interview with Bill Moyers, former press secretary to President Johnson and now a journalist and commentator. "I was going through a stage in my life there that was a very difficult one," Carter said. "I had run for governor and lost. Everything I did was not gratifying. When I succeeded in something, I got no pleasure out of it. When I failed at something, it was a horrible experience for me."

Moyers, himself a graduate of the Southwest Baptist Theological Seminary, channeled the hour-long interview into a revealing conversation in which Carter talked at length about his view of God and religion.

Q: "What drives you?"

A: "I don't know exactly how to express it. As I said, it's not an unpleasant sense of being driven. I feel like I have one life to live—I feel God wants me to do the best I can with it. And that's quite often my major prayer—let me live my life so that it will be meaningful. And I enjoy tackling difficult problems, and solving them, and the meticulous organization of a complicated effort. It's a challenge. Possibly, it's like a game. I don't know. I don't want to lower it by saying it's just a game—but it's an enjoyable thing for me."

Q: "How do you know—this is a question I hear from a lot of people—how do you know God's will?"

A: "Well, I pray frequently—not continually, but many times a day. When I have a sense of peace, and self-assurance—I don't know where it comes from—what I'm doing is a right thing. I assume, maybe in an unwarranted way, that that's doing God's will."

Q: "What do you think we're on earth for?"

A: "I don't know. You know, I could quote the biblical references, through creation, that God created us in his own image hoping that we'd be perfect. But we turned out to be not perfect, but very sinful. And then when Christ was asked what were the great commandments from God, which should direct our lives, he said to love God with all your heart and soul and mind, and love your neighbor as yourself. So, I try to take that condensation of the Christian theology and let it be something through which I search for a meaningful existence. I don't worry about it too much anymore. I used to when I was a college sophomore, and we used to debate for hours and hours about why we are here, who made us, where should we go, what's our purpose.

"But I don't feel frustrated about it. I'm not afraid to see my life ended. I feel like every day is meaningful. I don't have any fear at all of death. I feel like I'm doing the best I can, and if I get elected President, I'll have a chance to magnify my own influence maybe in a beneficial way. If I don't get elected President, I'll go back to Plains. So I feel I have a sense of equanimity about it, but why we're here on earth I don't know. I'd like to hear your views on that subject."

Q: ". . . Do you have any doubts? About yourself, about God, about life?"

A: "I can't think of any. I, obviously, don't know all the answers to philosophical questions and theological questions—the kind of questions that are contrived. But the things that I haven't been able to answer in a theory or supposition, I just accept them, and go on—things that I can't influence or change.

"I do have, obviously, many doubts about the best way to answer a question. Or to alleviate a concern. Or how to meet a need, or how to create in my own life a more meaningful purpose, and to let my life be expanded, in my heart and mind. So doubts about the best avenue to take among many options is a kind of doubt that is a constant presence with me.

"But doubt about my faith? No. Doubt about my purpose of life? I don't have any doubts about that. . . ."

Q: "What's the most significant discovery Jimmy Carter has made?"

A: "Well, I think I described it superficially a while

ago. I think it affected my life more than anything else. This is embarrassing a little bit for me to talk about because it's personal, but in my relationship with Christ and with God, I became able in the process to look at it in practical terms—to accept defeat, to get pleasure out of success, to be at peace with the world. For instance, one of the things I derived from it, again in a kind of embarrassing way, when I stood out on a factory shift line like I did this morning [in Erie, Pennsylvania—the General Electric plant]. Everybody that comes through there, when I shake hands with them, for that instance, for that instant, I really care about [them] in a genuine way. And I believe they know it a lot of times. Quite often I will shake hands with women who work in a plant and I just touch their hands, and quite frequently they'll put their arms around my neck and say—God bless you, son, or good luck. I'll help you and good luck.

"But it's a kind of relationship with people around me, but I don't want to insinuate that I'm better than other people. I've still got a long way to go."

In every state, in almost every speech, Carter talked about a special relationship that he believed he had developed with the people. He said frequently that he felt he would be a good President not because of any special talents or managerial skills that he had, but "because of the close, personal, intimate relationship I have established with each and every one of you." He would say this in living rooms, where he was addressing a coffee klatch of two dozen people; and he would say it in large halls, where he was addressing hundreds—and where his words "close . . . personal . . . intimate relationship" would echo through the building as the people in his audience nodded affirmatively.

Wednesday, the morning after the Illinois primary. George Wallace is having breakfast in his room at the Raleigh, North Carolina, Hilton, and he is a very disappointed man. He had been hoping for 25 to 30 delegates out of Illinois and he got only three. Now he knows that it is the end of his era. He was beaten by Jimmy Carter in Florida and he was beaten by Jimmy Carter in Illinois. Now he is in North Carolina and he is not going to win there either.

During breakfast, Wallace summons his press secretary, Billy Joe Camp. He tells Camp that he is considering pulling out of the race and he thinks he probably should. He cites the futility of the effort and the difficulty in just getting around. He asks Camp for his view.

"I said I couldn't disagree with him," Camp recalled. "But I said that I felt he ought to first talk to others in his staff and his family—his son, his brothers."

Wallace consulted with the others by phone. Some argued that he could probably get a good number of delegates out of North Carolina. "They felt maybe lightning would strike," Camp said. Wallace relented and stayed in the race.

North Carolina was the first time, according to his aides, that Wallace was really depressed about his political prospects for 1976. "It just didn't hit until North Carolina," said Billy Joe Camp. "More than anything else, it was the fault of our organization. We just didn't have a polling firm. And that was a huge mistake. A huge mistake. We only could go by the polls we read in the papers—and we sincerely felt they were wrong. We just really felt we were going to win in Florida, and we felt we were going to do better in Illinois."

Wallace was also buoyed by phone calls he received during the Illinois and North Carolina campaigns from Hubert Humphrey, Scoop Jackson, and Bob Strauss (chairman of the Democratic National Committee). None of them wanted to see Carter walk away with the nomination, and Wallace had the impression that they all wanted him to stay in the race; they told him things about his effort being courageous and that he had gotten a good vote, all in all, and not to give up.

So Wallace kept on fighting. He had been running for years by attacking Washington's bureaucrats and politicians, making himself at least part of the legend of his time. Now he attacked, for the first time, the Deep South politician who had finally done him in.

"He talks one way today and one way tomorrow," Wallace said. ". . . Jimmy Carter is a warmed-over McGovern. . . . He's seen fit to talk about me in Illinois and in Florida, so I say turnabout's fair play, and I'll talk about him in North Carolina."

Wallace had long been bitter over the fact that Carter would not nominate him for President at the 1972 convention (Carter spoke for Scoop Jackson instead). Now, in North Carolina, Wallace's bitterness against Carter boiled to the surface. In a remarkable interview with Elizabeth Drew of *The New Yorker* Magazine, Wallace repeatedly mocked Carter's stump promise that "I will never lie to you; I will never misleeeeeeed you." (It is something to hear George Wallace do an imitation of a southern accent.)

"He was my friend when I was popular," Wallace said in that interview. "He said he was for me when he thought I'd die. . . . He talks about spending all that time on his kneeeeeees. Well, I'm going to church tomorrow, but I don't go around talking about my religion."

THE RESULTS: *Carter won 53.6 percent of the vote; Wallace, 34.7. George Wallace never again would be a factor in the primaries.*

🇺🇸   🇺🇸   🇺🇸

Memorandum

To: Governor, Hamilton, Jody, Bob, Charles, Jerry, Rick
From: Pat Caddell
24 March 1976
Subject: General Memo

. . . The single greatest danger in presidential politics is "hubris." The arrogance of early success can doom almost any campaign. In the flush of early victories there is too often the belief in the inevitability of a candidacy. . . . In those heady days we [the McGovern campaign of 1972] believed that in coming so far in the end we could not be denied. In doing so, we sowed the seeds for the campaign's destruction. . . .

[When a] campaign changes from a state primary campaign to a national campaign . . . the ability to control and dominate the media coverage—the extent to which these tools are utilized to send signals and broad messages to the electorate—becomes critical. . . .

I don't think there is any question that we must win Wisconsin, avoid embarrassment in New York, and beat Jackson in Pennsylvania, and then in Indiana, to effect a quick kill in the primaries. . . . My position is, unless we can put together a first-ballot victory or damn close to it, this party will deny us the nomination. Popular with the elites, we are not. . . .

Of immediate concern are the next few primaries and a summary of each from what we know follows:

Wisconsin—While we are ahead in Wisconsin, the situation is precarious. Udall has moved up in the last few weeks, and among the most likely voters in a 40 percent turnout, we lead 27 percent to 20 percent. If the turnout were 25 percent or less, we trail Udall 28 percent to 22 percent with 18 percent for Jackson. . . . The voters who presently express "no preference" or "none of the above" seem to be Udall-inclined liberals. . . .

New York—Downstate city data indicates that we are only trailing Jackson by a small margin in the city. Indeed, among likely voters we were running even, 20 percent to 20 percent. . . . I fear that in a low-vote primary, though, where organization is crucial, we would do worse, due to our lack of voter ID and get-out-the-vote effort. . . .

Pennsylvania—This state is [likely] to be the "OK" corral of the campaign between Jackson and us. With three weeks of campaigning, except for days needed in the states that follow, we should be able to defeat Jackson. We trail by a few points in the data we have, which was completed before Illinois and North Carolina. In this state, we must effectively find a way to cut Jackson's blue-collar employment issue. . . . This is the first major northern state where the black vote should reach 15 percent or more. This is our greatest edge, and Ben Brown must work particularly hard on a massive get-out-the-vote campaign. . . .

Indiana—This should be the next state Jackson will contest us in, but I suspect with farmers, blacks, and

Midwest labor folks, he may have picked the wrong place. . . .

Speech, Issue Themes—This area of the campaign is the one in need of the most attention. We have passed the point when we can simply avoid at least the semblance of substance. This does not mean the need to outline minute, exact details. We all agree that such a course could be disastrous. However the appearance of substance does not require this. It requires a few broad, specific examples that support a point and it requires a better definition of these priorities and approach. . . . We need to have set formal addresses—no matter how distasteful—maybe every 10 days, for the purpose of articulating thematic program approaches and priorities, and to satisfy the press, elites, and eventually the public that we are "presidential" and competent. Also, we need to utilize this approach to send "signals" to interested groups and particularly to the suspicious but open liberals. . . .

Of all Carter's advisers, none had the candidate's confidence and respect that Charles Kirbo did.

Charles Kirbo is a down-home country gentleman from the farmlands of Georgia. He is Deep South. Up until just a few months before, he had been a familiar sight driving his 1967 green weathered Chevy pickup truck into downtown Atlanta and parking it in the garage of an ultra modern new building, then taking the elevator up to one of the South's most prestigious law firms, where he worked in wood-paneled, expensively furnished elegance. He switched to a sedan: "They kidded me so much about that old truck that I don't use it anymore."

Kirbo is easily the slowest-talking man in the Carter campaign. He seems to weigh each word carefully before he says it, and gives it one more good look as it's coming out of his mouth. Kirbo used to drop by for consultation regularly when Carter was governor. "I never did have a parking space," he recalled. "So I'd just park my truck next to Jimmy's car. And sometimes there'd be a new young policeman on the beat, and he wouldn't know and he'd make me move. It just got me in trouble."

It was Kirbo who first tutored the young aspiring politician when they took some of his votes away years ago when he was running for the state legislature. Kirbo represented Carter in a voting-fraud case and won, and he's been tutoring Carter ever since.

Kirbo has no staff title, no official responsibility. "I just kind of float in and out and help a bit if someone asks me to," he said. He is most commonly described by the members of the Carter staff as a father figure to the candidate. The Carter men and women call each other Jody and Hamilton and Betty and Jerry. They call Carter Jimmy. They call Kirbo "Mr. Kirbo." He is gray-haired, tall, always courtly; he walks with a gait slowed by age; his nose is red and weathered. Yet he is just fifty-nine—just eight years older than his "son figure," the candidate. . . . He was the oldest member of Carter's inner circle and also the most conservative. His politics came from the old South, from his days as an attorney in Bainbridge.

Two days after Caddell wrote his "hubris" memo to Carter, Kirbo offered some observations and suggestions of his own. He concerned himself with how to handle the Wallace supporters and the Jackson supporters.

"Hamilton is doing a good job developing labor support," Kirbo wrote Carter, "but I wish we could get elected without some of the leaders of labor who are now supporting Jackson. I know we must continue to try and put them all together and I know that they are important, but I do not believe it would be fatal if they all went to Jackson. . . . If we should by fortune do well in Wisconsin and New York, I think we ought to consider letting the labor leaders come to us instead of chasing after them."

Kirbo also suggested that some special apparatus ought to be set up to establish relationships with various delegates controlled by Jackson and, especially, Wallace.

"The Wallace make-up of delegates are likely to be people who can be reached through some of our friends, particularly after it has been demonstrated that he cannot win," Kirbo wrote. ". . . I think Hamilton should select another group that we will call Group X. We can keep them informed as to the number of delegates controlled by Wallace and others and the background of these delegates. Then Group X can develop methods and people to make contact outside of the activities of the Tracking Operation. I have in mind people like Griffin Bell."*

---

* The Carter campaign ultimately contacted a number of Wallace delegates and their friends through Kirbo and Frank Moore. But Griffin Bell was not a part of that effort, according to Kirbo. "He had a phasing out problem with the courts," Kirbo said, referring to the fact that Bell was retiring then as U.S. Court of Appeals judge. ". . . when he got where he could operate, it [the effort] was just about over. . . . Also, it turned out that Griffin Bell's type of friends turned out not to be the type of people we needed. . . . They weren't party-worker type people."

Bell said in the Senate confirmation hearings on his nomination to be Carter's Attorney General that he helped the Carter campaign by (1) raising money during the Pennsylvania primary, (2) preparing a speech, (3) giving some legal advice on the difference between a pardon and amnesty, and (4) preparing the questionnaire that was given to Carter's propective vice-presidential nominees.

At one point, Senator Donald Riegle of Michigan asked whether there was some connection between Bell's decision to leave the Court of Appeals and his involvement in the Carter campaign.

Bell: "If I had done that, I would not have enough judgment to be Attorney General because at the time I left and while I was in the process of leaving, Governor Carter had not even won a primary . . . People were saying that they did not know him."

Senator Bayh: "Excuse me, Judge. Would you not look at me when you make that comment?"

April 6/New York
and Wisconsin

Patrick Caddell, at age twenty-six, has been around. He was twenty-two when he entered the ranks of the political geniuses, running the public opinion polls that helped George McGovern come from obscurity and win the 1972 Democratic presidential nomination. And he was twenty-two when he entered the ranks of the political losers, as McGovern was buried by a Nixon landslide.

Now he was the only experienced national campaigner in Carter's inner circle. His March 24 forecast of the upcoming campaign pointed up important problems. Later he summed up the Carter strategy for the simultaneous New York and Wisconsin primaries like this: "Our strategy for April 6 was to somehow avoid disaster."

April 6. A two primary day. New York—to the Carter people working in their plastic modern offices down on Peachtree Drive in Atlanta, New York looked like foreign territory; hostile foreign territory. Wisconsin—for months it looked like the party would not even permit this primary to be binding on delegate voting because the state was allowing Republican-Democratic crossover voting.

"New York was frightening," Carter aide Greg Schneiders conceded months later. "We were intimidated. We started out not knowing what the hell was going on there. We didn't have any presence there." What was worse, the names of the individual candidates originally were not going to be on the ballot in New York. Just the names of the delegates—and Jackson had a big jump on Carter in lining up the prominent Democrats as delegates.

Jimmy Carter was uncomfortable about New York, too.

As early as December 1975 he campaigned upstate, but shied from politicking in New York City. "I'd have to walk down the street naked to attract any attention here," Carter said.

And as late as mid-June, after he had the nomination won, Carter was uneasy when he appeared at the Waldorf Astoria before a meeting of the New York delegation. He mumbled some lines in his speech, blew others, and received only mild applause. (Moments after Carter left the room, California Governor Jerry Brown entered and was greeted with a standing ovation, cheers, and shouts.)

As Carter's plane flew south from New York that June day, a reporter noted that the candidate had not looked as much "at home" before the New Yorkers as he had before other groups. Carter replied, "I didn't."

Question: "Did you get the feeling that you're still trying to prove things to them, that they're still examining you?"

Answer: "I did. . . . There are some groups with whom I feel perfectly at home. And some I don't. But, in general, I'm able to accommodate different kinds of groups fairly well. But I'm not always successful."

New York

Early in the campaign, in 1975, back before Jimmy Carter was traveling with a large entourage and staff, Carter was forced to endure a wait of more than three hours in LaGuardia Airport because his plane had not arrived. Carter had this thing about punctuality—he insists on it, and so the delay put him in a sour mood.

Carter went into a small waiting room to pass the time. A sofa and some chairs were there and Carter, fatigued, saw an opportunity to at least make up for nights of lost sleep. He dozed off almost immediately. The one aide traveling with him, Jody Powell, sat watching. Soon it dawned on Powell he had a problem. There were some phone calls he just had to make and there was no phone in the room. If he left Carter sleeping alone and went to make the calls, the governor might awake and find nobody there. What would he think? But the calls had to be made.

So Powell hit on a compromise. He opened the door

—it made an annoying thunk—and went out to make his first call. The door closed with another thunk. After the first call, Powell raced back and opened the door—thunk—just to check on his boss, saw he was still sleeping, so closed the door—thunk—and ran back to the phone booth. After the second call he ran back to peek in again. Thunk. Carter was asleep and all was well. Thunk. So he went back to the phones. Then back to his boss. Thunk. Thunk. Finally, Carter raised his head and squinted in the direction of his aide.

"If you want to come back and check on me every ten minutes, leave the door open," Carter said.

"Well, I just . . ." Powell said, launching into an explanation of just what he'd been trying to do.

Carter listened to his aide's concern for his well-being and offered a low-key reply: "Well, you've told me and I'm awake." And he rolled over to try to pick up where he had left off, as Powell returned to the phones. Thunk.

In December, Carter's campaign manager, Hamilton Jordan, met with Theodore Sorenson, the former speech-writer for President Kennedy, and William vanden Heuvel, an attorney who long had been identified with the Kennedy crowd. Sorenson is said to have pushed hard for vanden Heuvel to head the Carter campaign in New York.

But Carter already had Midge Costanza on his team. He had met her in Rochester in 1974, when he was serving as the Democratic campaign chairman and she was trying to unseat Representative Barber Conable, a Republican who still holds the seat in Congress. The Carter people had Costanza run the upstate effort, vanden Heuvel the downstate campaign. Some people on the Carter national staff did not think much of vanden Heuvel's efforts, but Carter believes that vanden Heuvel was instrumental in eventually securing the endorsement of New York City Mayor Abraham Beame (after the New York campaign, but when he needed Jewish support).

The Carter strategy for New York was to pick up as many of the state's 274 delegates as possible and to discredit the New York election so that it would not be considered a major primary.

Carter charged frequently that the New York primary system, which called for the use of ballots carrying the names of all the delegates but not the candidates' names, was a disgrace and represented an attempt by the party bosses to thwart the people's will. The system was changed three weeks before the vote.

🇺🇸 🇺🇸 🇺🇸

The Jackson strategy was quite different. It was to get out in front early and win. Win big. Carter's strategy was to run in every state. Jackson's was to win in the big industrial states, where he would have plenty of backing from big labor and party regulars. New York was the core of his big-state strategy.

For years, Scoop Jackson had been a leader in the Senate on the making of policies foreign and domestic. He was particularly familiar as a hardliner in matters of military defense and—important for many New Yorkers —he was known as a supporter of Israel and of Jewish emigration from the Soviet Union.

Scoop Jackson did not have to feel uneasy about New York, and he did not have to tell New Yorkers who he was.

As early as November 1974, a year and a half before the New York primary, he was raising money in New York through a fundraiser in the large Fifth Avenue apartment of insurance executive Leonard Davis. It had been attended by a number of prominent New Yorkers: Governor Hugh Carey, Morris Abrams, William Zeckendorf, philanthropist Jack Goldfarb, union leader Gus Tyler, city Environmental Commissioner Robert Lowe, and Representative Ogden Reid. That night, $60,000 was collected, and Jackson had similar success throughout the New York campaign. He raised big money and he spent big money.

🇺🇸 🇺🇸 🇺🇸

New York is a city of fine restaurants. When Scoop Jackson sought to do some political courting before the campaign got started, he chose the restaurant at La-Guardia Airport. Jackson sat unrecognized and talked with Queens Democratic Chairman Donald Manes. All of the candidates had been wooing Manes, but at this meeting he opted for Jackson, a decision which probably had more to do with Manes's interest in clout than cuisine. "I liked many of the things he was saying—and I thought he could win," Manes recalled.

Manes proved a key to Jackson's effort. With the New York ballot being kept deliberately confusing by the prominent state and county party leaders, who did not want the candidates' names on the ballots, it was imperative that a slate of big-name, easily identifiable people be corralled to serve as delegates for a candidate who hoped to win. Manes proved quite adept at putting together a list of prominent people.

The Carter people thought Midge Costanza did a good job in upstate New York, considering the limited amount of time and, mainly, money Carter spent in the state. "But," said one national Carter campaign official, "Midge made a couple of tactical errors." He cited her challenges, in Carter's name, of Jackson delegates in three upstate districts in a campaign where Carter was trying to discredit the process and trying to appear to be a victimized underdog. Carter was not aware of the challenges upstate and he held a press conference decrying the fact that Jackson was challenging his delegates and saying that this was dirty politics; when reporters asked him why he was doing the same thing, he looked surprised by their questions and said he was not. "This, then, undermined our strategy of trying to discredit the election process in the state," the Carter official said.

Greg Schneiders had known about the challenges made by the Carter people upstate but had not gotten around to telling Carter of them yet. "I probably should have told him about them earlier but I didn't think he was going to say anything about them in that press conference," Schneiders said. He went to Carter immediately afterward and said: "We have a problem here. We are challenging in three districts." Carter said that was not right, that vanden Heuvel had told him they were not challenging. Schneiders replied that was technically correct: vanden Heuvel was not challenging—downstate; but Costanza was—upstate.

Three weeks before election day, the legislature voted to change the election rules so that candidates' names would appear on the ballot. Looking back, some Carter advisers say this led them to pull back from their strategy of just trying to hold down their embarrassment on April 6 and go for a win instead. "We ran a public opinion poll in New York the week of the election and we were even with Jackson," Carter recalled later. "But the people didn't vote and the organization didn't turn out people. . . . The turnout is very important. Very important. I have always done better when the turnout is large. Because the ones who are casually interested in politics like me. . . ."

The change in the election ballot, putting the candidates' names on after all, turned out to be significant to the Jackson people as well. "It changed the game completely," said Ben Wattenberg, a Jackson adviser. "From then on we had to scrap our 'Palm Card' strategy and step up our media strategy."

The Jackson people had hoped to make use of a complex, computerized system for mailing postcards to every registered Democrat in the state, back when it appeared that the candidates' names would not be on the New York ballots. The plan was for these cards to serve as "palm cards," to be carried into the voting booth to serve as delegate voting guides. The cards were going to say: "If you're planning to vote for Senator Jackson, these are the delegates in your district and this is where you vote. . . ." The Jackson campaign spent $50,000 on the computer effort. "But we scrubbed the whole project and waved good-bye to all that money when the law was changed. . . ." said Dick Kline, Jackson's finance coordinator. "We went into a hurry-up media campaign, especially heavy upstate. So we not only lost the $50,000 on the mailing, but we had all the added, unexpected expense of the last-minute media things."

All through his New York campaign, Jackson—buoyed by his Massachusetts victory—had been predicting that he was going to win "by a landslide" in New York. He said it everywhere he went. At times, early on, he mentioned a two-to-one margin; later he scaled it back to saying his "landslide" could be achieved by just capturing a majority of the 274 delegates. Every time he spoke the word "landslide," his aides cringed. They urged him —even argued with him—not to say it; time and again in primaries past, candidates have fared poorly because they set their public goals so high that even a good victory that fell just short of the mark was treated as a defeat.

Jackson's words were the yardstick by which his campaign was judged, and in the end he did not measure up.

THE RESULTS: *Jackson finished on top, but won just 38 percent of the delegates (103 of the 274). Udall finished a surprisingly strong second with 25.2. Carter was buried deep in fourth place with just 12.8 percent —beaten even by uncommitted slates, which took 23.7 percent.*

But there was another set of New York statistics that proved to be even more decisive: the spending statistics. The Jackson campaign went unaccountably wild, spending big bucks at three times the rate of any of the other candidates—and while it won him New York, it eventually cost him later in Pennsylvania, when he simply went broke. Jackson spent $891,698 in New York. Carter spent $293,377 and Udall just $139,770. (Add in Wisconsin spending and Jackson spent for the combined April 6 primaries $942,002 compared to Udall's $600,002 and Carter's $462,103.)

Wisconsin

"The decision to go into Wisconsin was announced to Carter by Hamilton." Announced. Greg Schneiders had chosen the word carefully; it described precisely the way Carter's campaign operation worked.

Throughout most of the campaign, the major decisions about where Carter would go and how long he would spend there—even about which states he would concentrate on and which he would slough off—were made by Hamilton Jordan and Jody Powell, or, occasionally, another top aide. Financial decisions were left to Robert Lipshutz. Media decisions were made by Jerry Rafshoon—

in fact, it was not until April, when Carter happened to be attending a meeting in Rafshoon's office, that the candidate even saw the television ads that had been running throughout the country and helping him win for months.

Many campaigns of past years were doomed in part because the candidate tried to do too much himself. Some insisted on at least reviewing all major decisions and all media efforts. Carter did not. He delegated authority.

"We did that sort of thing really in 1966 when I first began political campaigns and I found that it worked well," Carter said in an interview after the primaries were over. "I used the same procedure, the same attitude, while I was governor, in the management of the state's affairs, and it worked well. As you can well see, the details of campaign scheduling and emphasis on issues in the advertisements were worked out long ago there with my staff in the formative months of the campaign planning. So that we were fairly well agreed, compatibly, on what should be done. I trust them completely to do a good job. When a deviation from the basic concept was at issue, I was always consulted on it. But I did not want to be responsible for scheduling, or the wording of television advertisements, or emphasis on issues. I trusted my polling group and news secretary and campaign manager and advertising agency to do that thoroughly. And I never doubted their ability to do it."

Originally Wisconsin national committeeman Don Peterson was the state vice chairman of the Udall campaign. But he had a falling-out with Stewart Udall and became independent. Then a friend of his told a story about another friend from Georgia who had worked in Carl Sanders' campaign against Carter in 1970. Carter, once elected, asked the man to take a state government position; the man pointed out that he had, in fact, supported and worked for Carter's opponent. According to the story, Carter replied: "I don't care. Just integrate the parks, but do it without disrupting anything."

The story hit Peterson just right. "It impressed me tremendously," he said. Later, when a Young Democrats convention was held in his hometown of Eau Claire. Peterson agreed to host a reception for Carter. He was impressed again. And he was impressed once more when he later got a personal note of thanks that began "Dear Don" and was signed by "Jimmy." Peterson wound up a Carter man and even journeyed to Pennsylvania to help the Carter cause there.

After the Florida primary, Hamilton Jordan had written a memo to Carter saying that the campaign was about to start a new phase. While still intending to run everywhere, it would now be possible to pick and choose among the states where campaign effort would be emphasized—targets of opportunity, where Carter had a chance to eliminate an opponent. The memo said the Carter campaign ought to look to eliminate Udall in Wisconsin April 6 and Jackson in Pennsylvania on April 27. At that time, most of the top Carter advisers had the staying power of the two men reversed. They figured Udall could soon be eliminated, but that Jackson, who had so stubbornly fought on in 1972 despite a clearly hopeless cause, would stay to the convention at Madison Square Garden.

Morris Udall did not have much to do after Massachusetts, back on March 2, except to think about and plan and campaign for the primaries on April 6. He had bypassed Florida and Illinois and North Carolina and was hoping to finally win in Wisconsin.

Udall desperately needed Wisconsin. There was a deep belief in his camp that the Carter vote was fragile; they remembered how soft Carter's support had been in Massachusetts. Udall stumped hard through the state that is a mix of Midwest progressive thought, farm vote, and ethnic blue-collar big-city vote.

Three weeks before the election, Udall returned to Washington feeling optimistic after three straight days of campaigning in Wisconsin and met with some of his top advisers—his brother, Stewart, his media adviser, John Marttila, and his pollster, Peter Hart. They were meeting in Udall's congressional office to go over a new poll Hart had done. The news was bad. Carter, 34 percent. Jackson, 24. Udall, 17. Wallace, 15. Undecided, 10. No matter how they tried to analyze and rationalize, it did not seem to help. Even if Udall captured every one of the undecided, it would only give him 27—still well behind Carter.

Mo Udall sat on the sofa, staring silently. "It was almost cruel," Stu Udall recalled. "To hit him with something like that after he'd just been campaigning there so hard. I wish they'd told me first so I could have lied to him a little, just to soften the blow."

The Udall brothers left the office and drove out to Mo's home together. In the car, the candidate offered a crisp analysis. "Well, it's all over, isn't it?" he said, making it more of a statement than a question. Stu nodded. "Yes, I guess so."

Stu Udall recalled, "We both agreed that, well, he's going to lose—but at least let's go down with class. Don't whine. We were just so sure that we were going to lose, and lose badly, in Wisconsin. You just can't come back from a 2-to-1 deficit in three weeks."

Udall, dispirited, returned to see the campaign through in Wisconsin.

At times, Udall found himself in the same city as Carter; and in these times, the Secret Service found the situation rather confusing. The Secret Service gives each candidate a code name to be used on its walkie-talkie bands, and, in fact, in all radio communication. And the Secret Service, in its collective wisdom, had given Udall the code name "dashboard" and Carter the code name "dasher." There were times when Udall agents would move into action thinking they had received a radio alert that their man was coming, only to discover that it was a smaller, sandy-haired man from Georgia who was headed their way instead.

Ten days before the election, Peter Hart gave the Udall camp a more encouraging report. Udall was coming on strong. He had passed Jackson and was closing in on Carter. The figures: Carter, 34; Udall, 30; Jackson, 15.

The Udall advisers were pleasantly stunned. It was a chance for John Marttila to do his thing again.

Marttila heads the Boston firm that has handled media for John Lindsay and Boston Mayor Kevin White. His big television campaign for Udall in the Massachusetts primary had pulled the tall, lanky Arizonan to a surprising second-place finish—a showing that had forced Birch Bayh to abandon his presidential bid.

Now, Marttila's ads apparently were working again. Another big media push could put Udall over the top in Wisconsin.

Udall had planned to raise and spend $350,000 for Wisconsin. His fundraiser, David Thorne, had said it could be done. But ten days before the primary, only $100,000 had been raised. Udall's brother, Stewart, doubted Thorne's assurances that the remainder would be on hand by primary day. Stewart Udall argued that the television ads, which would cost $25,000, should be taken off the air in Wisconsin.

Stewart Udall met in New York with Thorne, Marttila, and Tom Kiley, a Marttila associate, on Monday, a week before the primary. He told them to turn off the Wisconsin television and radio advertising. Marttila argued against pulling the ads, but Stewart Udall was firm. Marttila was distressed. He had not expected to lose the argument. He telephoned Morris Udall, then campaigning in Wisconsin, to appeal.

Udall decided he had to review the figures. He flew to New York for a meeting the next day, Tuesday. The meeting, set for the morning, did not start until the afternoon. Mo Udall overruled Stewart. It was only $25,000 more, he reasoned, so let the ads roll. Marttila went for the telephone. But his call to the television stations was too late—just about forty-five minutes too late. The last of the television air time already had been committed to others.

For two and a half days, the Udall ads were off the air in Wisconsin while Carter's commercials were filling the airways. The delay in arranging Udall's funding turned out to have been the most significant thing in the Wisconsin primary.

Meanwhile, the slow trickle of funds had also forced a decision to cancel a Udall mailing to 100,000 rural households—Udall's only mailing of the Wisconsin campaign. The cost was budgeted at $20,000. Representative David Obey, a key Udall adviser, was upset; at least the mailing had to get to his district in the northeast corner of the state. A revised mailing plan was set covering 23,000 households at a cost of just $6,500. But it was decided that the money was not there. This too was scrapped.

The Wisconsin primary that Udall had once thought could not be won had turned out to be very winnable. But the Udall campaign was stalled by bad planning and bad budgeting—by bad staffwork and bad guesswork. In retrospect, it is easy to see that Udall money was misspent. Marttila remained upset that Stu Udall had refused to spend that comparatively small amount of media money in the last days of Wisconsin. Stu Udall, meanwhile, was upset that the Udall campaign had spent precious money in New York—$139,770—even though he had made the decision early on that the Udall effort would concentrate in Wisconsin in an effort to secure that vital, first primary win, and that spending in New York was to be done only after it was assured that Wisconsin needs had been met.

And, perhaps most puzzling of all, the Udall people eventually managed to spend $180,345 on the next primary down the line—April 27 in Pennsylvania, where Udall was never a major factor and was in fact destined to finish well off the pace. "We scraped up and borrowed to have $70,000 for media in Pennsylvania," Stu Udall concedes. Why had they not put the Pennsylvania money into Wisconsin? "We weren't thinking that way," he replied.

On election night, the early returns were heavily Udall. So were television network projections of ABC and NBC. The two networks predicted a Udall victory.

As the television projections rolled in, the Marc Plaza Hotel's ballroom in Milwaukee was filled with the sounds of Udall joy. Beer and liquor and victory elated the crowd as it set about celebrating the first Mo Udall victory party of 1976.

Joining the shouting, and saluting all with upraised glass, was a man whose face was flushed and very familiar. Almost, but not quite the face of the enemy; it was Jimmy Carter's look-alike brother, Billy. Billy shook hands, laughed, and joked with Ella Udall.

"I'm good friends with the Udalls," Billy Carter said. "They're misinformed, but they're nice. I came down to say hello." Udall aides said that in Green Bay, Billy Carter cheerfully had helped them put up some Udall posters.

Billy Carter, the candidate's beer-bellied cherub of a brother, was, at age thirty-eight, more at ease sitting in the gas station he runs in Plains sipping a can of Pabst Blue Ribbon than he was foraging on the campaign trail. Jimmy has always said that his brother was more like their father than he. And Billy agrees. "People say I'm more like my father than Jimmy. That's because we look alike. And I'm more outgoing than Jimmy. I enjoy a party, too."

People often ask Billy Carter about his childhood of growing up with Jimmy. "That was nonexistent," he says. "I was four when Jimmy left for college." But Jimmy did manage to leave a lasting impression on his younger brother. "He was a very good student, and every year I used to hear about it from the teachers. Put it this way. He finished at the top of his class. In a class of twenty-seven, I was number twenty-four or twenty-five."

Billy Carter was sixteen when Earl Carter died. "I was closer to my father than the rest of them [family]. They were all gone as I was growing up, and I was almost like an only child," he said.

"Right after Jimmy came back [following the death of their father], I joined the marines. It was right in between everything—after Korea and before Vietnam. I traveled to the Philippines, to Japan, and to Thailand. I didn't intend to come back to Plains. I gave a lot of thought to it, and planned to make a career out of the marines.

"But I was married with two kids then. When you reenlisted, it was for four years—at least that's how it used to be in the marines—you had to spend one tour of duty overseas and I didn't want to leave them and do that. I went to college [Emory University in Atlanta] and flunked out. Then I worked for a construction company that did work all over the Southeast. I can't even remember the name of the company. Then I came back to Plains."

He ran the family warehouse business while Jimmy was governor and prides himself on its growth while he was in charge. They expanded the capacity of the warehouses and bought a new peanut sheller. In 1976, the business was valued between $2 million and $3 million, and their agreement in July with the National Bank of Georgia, mortgaging the buildings to establish a $1-million line of credit, is a reflection of the size of the business. "I have a tremendous cash flow," said Billy Carter. "One day I might go buy a farmer's crop and I might need $500,000. I might get it back the next day, or I might still need more on hand."

Father's Day is big doings in the Billy Carter household. For Father's Day 1976, his five children, ranging in age from eight to twenty, gave him a green football jersey bearing the number "6" and his nickname "Cast Iron," a reference to his protruding stomach and its ability to withstand all sorts of abuse—notably his fondness for beer.

Where there's Billy, there's beer. His Amoco gas station became a landmark in Plains because it was the only place to buy beer in town; some said he pumped more beer than gas. It was a place for Billy and his friends to gather daily, sitting on worn-out chairs and wooden boxes, drinking.

The other gas station in Plains, a Fina station owned by Frank and Albert Williams, dealt strictly in automotive needs. "That pretty much decides their business," said Plains Mayor A. L. Blanton. "Billy gets the drinkers and the Williams boys get the Baptists."

Jimmy and Billy have the same trademark Carter smile; but that aside, they are not likely to be confused. "I'm not a political person. I'm blunt and sometimes folks don't like it, I don't go to church because I wasn't pushed into church. I catch hell for my beer drinking from some folks . . . but I don't mind it."

As the 1976 campaign progressed and as the national media began to discover that the Carter family and hometown were good copy, Jimmy Carter's relatives and friends developed favorite stories and quotable *bon mots* that they became fond of laying on each reporter who passed through Plains. One of Billy's favorite lines: "I got a mamma who joined the Peace Corps and went to India when she was sixty-eight. I got one sister [Ruth] who's a holy roller preacher. I got another sister [Gloria] who wears a helmet and rides a motorcycle. And I got a brother who thinks he's going to be President. So that makes me the only sane person in the family."

Two defeats in one night—an upset in Wisconsin and a humiliating drubbing in New York—could have been disastrous to Carter's campaign.

Late in the night, Carter went to the NBC affiliate station in Milwaukee to do a taping for the morning news show. Carter was thinking about doing two tapes: one as if he had won, the other as if he had lost, so they could use the one that proved accurate. NBC insisted on just one tape.

Back at the Carter headquarters at the Pfister Hotel, Pat Caddell began analyzing the returns that were still out. They included paper ballots and a lot of rural votes. Caddell screamed at the Secret Service agents to contact Carter, contact Jody Powell. Stop Carter from conceding. Meanwhile, Greg Schneiders was at the television studio, telling Carter that he ought to give NBC a statement that would be acceptable, win or lose. The Georgian agreed. Carter fuzzed the issue in his taped interview.

Once back at the hotel, Carter had an idea. He asked if there was a newspaper that had done the same thing the networks had done—predict a Udall victory. Carter was thinking of the great moment when Harry Truman held aloft a newspaper—the *Chicago Tribune*—with the premature headline saying that Dewey had won the Presidency in 1948.

Carter's aides came back with the *Milwaukee Sentinel*. The headline said "Carter Upset by Udall." But the late returns gave Wisconsin to Carter. It was 2:00 A.M., and Carter's supporters were still waiting. Carter greeted them, and held the newspaper high above his head, Truman-style. That picture—of Carter's winning in Wisconsin —became the focus of April 6. "It obliterated that disaster in New York," Caddell later said.

The Udall staff members—and Billy Carter—were still in the Marc Plaza's Bombay Bicycle Club eating pizza and drinking as the Udall lead slipped away with the night. Shortly before 2:30 A.M., they were greeted by a group of cheering Carter supporters bearing the news that it was Carter who had won. Billy Carter joined his brother's backers and let loose a triumphant rebel yell.

THE RESULTS: *Carter won 37 percent of the vote; Udall, 36. Carter won by less than 5,000 votes out of the more than 670,000 cast.*

Two liberals stayed on the ballot in Wisconsin and received what could have been crucial Udall votes. Harris got 8,265 (about 1 percent) and Shriver got 5,139 (also about 1 percent). Had either man come out in advance for fellow-liberal Udall and had his backers followed his wishes and voted for Udall, either the Harris votes or the Shriver votes would have been enough to put Udall over the top.

Months later, Udall sat in his House office and reflected on how things might have been changed had he only spent the money right away for the media and the mailing.

"If I'd only known then what I know today," Udall said, sitting on a government-issue sofa, his face somber as he thought once more about this fact that will haunt him always. "I'd already gone into debt. . . . My wife was concerned. I'd seen candidates going on the lecture circuit [to bail themselves out of heavy debt]. . . . Maybe putting up my home for mortgage. . . . [But] I promised my wife I wouldn't. Ella, she loves her home. . . . We had hit all our friends. We were over our heads. All of the scrounging, the borrowing hadn't done it. . . . [But] one more turn of the wheel would have done it."

There is no doubt in the minds of most of the Udall people that the campaign was lost by the delay that shut Udall off the television stations in that final crucial weekend plus the mailing of 100,000 letters that were never sent.

And there is no doubt either in the minds of the Carter men. "That had to be the difference," Hamilton Jordan conceded in an interview a couple of weeks later. "A weekend of television has to be good for 5,000 or more votes easily. It had to make the difference. That's how they lost it. That's how we won."

April 27/Pennsylvania

Memorandum

To: Campaign
From: Pat Caddell
8 April 1976
Re: Implications of Wisconsin

Analysis of Wisconsin

. . . Our survey was completed on Thursday evening, when the weighted results stood Carter 38%, Udall 27%, Jackson 8%, Wallace 7%, 5% no preference, and 9% undecided. Another survey by an outside source, completed on Saturday, showed the results to be 38% to 28%. As I explained at the time, we expected the 5% no preference vote to go to Udall as they were far more liberal than the electorate in general and more favorable to him or not to vote at all. However, the analysis I have done also shows that the undecided votes went overwhelmingly to Udall and some to Wallace. Indeed, Wallace almost doubled his vote on Tuesday both from our survey and the other survey. . . . Why the wholesale defection of the undecideds?

In our survey on Thursday, we noted only two disturbing notes. First, the leading Carter negative on open-ended responses was the category "not specific, wishy-washy, changes stands," which went from 3% in our first poll to 11% in the last survey. Also, the agreement to the projective statement "Jimmy Carter always seems to be changing his positions on the issues" rose from 23% in survey 1 to 33% in survey 2. . . . More important, the CBS poll [taken as people

133

left the voting booths] indicates that 43% of the voters agree to a question similar to ours that Carter was not specific enough and vacillated on the issues. This would suggest that the 33% figure we saw rose and may well have cut us.

. . . This problem must be overcome. We must defuse the "no specifics and changes positions arguments." They seem to be rising. And inevitably unchecked lead to perceptions of Carter as "untrustworthy" and "dishonest." We can see some of that already in Pennsylvania. Also, Carter must no longer stay on the defensive—every time that happens, whether in Massachusetts, Wisconsin, or New York, we are hurt badly. . . . We must assume a national campaign posture and stay on the offensive on change of issues. Otherwise a vacuum emerges and our opponents and the press will rush to fill it with adverse attacks and issues.

🏴   🏴   🏴

One-third of the people were thinking Carter was fuzzy on issues, and Carter had not been able to win any of the "Undecided" voters on election day. The Carter advisers moved to combat the problem. Jerry Rafshoon, who in this campaign has earned himself a reputation as one of the most savvy in the business of political media, came up with a cut-rate plan to counter the image that Carter is a man who does not discuss issues. He took Carter's existing television spots and had an announcer read a new introduction: "Jimmy Carter on the issue of health care," he said for one; "Jimmy Carter on the issue of unemployment," he said for another; and so on.

Rafshoon also had the announcer read a new voiceover closing to the existing taped commercials: "If you see this *critical issue* the way Jimmy Carter does, then vote for him."

The specifics of Carter's now issue-oriented television commercial message had not been sharpened. But his image had. The spots were aired throughout the Pennsylvania primary campaign.

🏴   🏴   🏴

On April 2 Carter was interviewed by Sam Roberts, the chief political correspondent of the *New York Daily News*. An article based on the interview ran two days later. The sixteenth paragraph, on page 134, said: "And, asked about low-income scatter-site housing in the suburbs, he replied: 'I see nothing wrong with ethnic purity being maintained. I would not force a racial integration of a neighborbood by government action. But I would not permit discrimination against a family moving into the neighborhood.'"

Ethnic purity. Jimmy Carter had said it, and the *Daily News* had attached no special importance to it, and the New York and Wisconsin primaries came and went without the matter's being raised.

But a CBS official saw the phrase and suggested that correspondent Ed Rabel, who was traveling with the Carter organization, question him about it. Rabel did, at a press conference in Indianapolis on the day of the New York and Wisconsin primaries.

Question: "What did you mean by ethnic purity?"

Answer: "I have nothing against a community that's made up of people who are Polish, Czechslovakians, French-Canadians, or blacks who are trying to maintain the ethnic purity of their neighborhood. This is a natural inclination on the part of people. . . . I've never, though, condoned any sort of discrimination against, say, a black family or other family from moving into that neighborhood. But I don't think government ought to deliberately break down an ethnically oriented community deliberately by injecting into it a member of another race. To me, this is contrary to the best interests of the community."

The questioning continued at South Bend, Indiana, and at Pittsburgh. Carter kept talking about the value of "ethnic purity" of neighborhoods. And he elaborated—warning of "black intrusion" into white neighborhoods and of "injecting into [a community] a member of another race" or "a diametrically opposite kind of family" or a "different kind of person."

Only two staff members, Greg Schneiders and Betty Rainwater, were with Carter. Rainwater was one of Jody Powell's assistant press secretaries. They were alarmed. Carter was not.

As soon as the questioning began, Schneiders wrote Carter a memo. It said that there was nothing unacceptable about Carter's basic points, but that, as in the abortion controversy in Iowa, the specific language should be clarified. The problem, he said, was the use of "ethnic purity" and the other phrases that are emotional and generate controversy. Don't use them, Schneiders said.

Schneiders gave the memo to Carter in South Bend. He and Rainwater got in the car with Carter. Carter said he did not think the words were offensive. He didn't intend them to be; he didn't think they would be taken that way. There is no telling whether the issue will prove to be good or bad for his campaign effort, Carter said.

Schneiders reasoned with Carter to no avail. Rainwater did the same. Later Schneiders and Rainwater separately called Jody Powell, who had stayed in Milwaukee after the Wisconsin vote. "Betty called first," Powell recalled. "She said, 'I think we've got a real problem developing here.' Greg called. It was a situation that was hard for me to make a persuasive argument [with Carter]. It was relying on their perceptions, which were clearly different from his—and I was arguing through them to him."

Hamilton Jordan was among those not overly concerned. "I thought it would pass," he said. "I felt it was a serious mistake, but that it wouldn't last. I was surprised when Betty Rainwater called from South Bend and told me how Jimmy's explanation [at the press conference] went over."

And then there was the view of Kirbo.

When Kirbo heard about the ethnic purity situation, he decided to go out to the Carter headquarters—a place he then rarely visited—to be available for consultation. "I knew a flap was going on, so I came out," he said. "I just happened to walk in on a meeting. Well, they asked my views, and I said it was my feeling that if we keep on going with the issue—you know, issue an explanation and all that—it would just keep going on. I've just seen it happen time and time again—you make a mistake, and then you keep fanning it, and it just keeps hurting you. So then they said that some of Jimmy's black supporters were embarrassed because they'd stuck their necks out for Jimmy, and all that.

"Well, I thought about that, and then I said that is different. If Andy Young wants him to apologize, then he ought to."

Andy Young is Andrew Young, a black Democrat, then

a congressman from Atlanta and a former top aide to Martin Luther King, Jr. According to his staff members, Young was distraught after learning of Carter's initial comment, and was upset even more by the candidate's subsequent explanation. Young had been Carter's first and only prominent black backer, and his credibility, as well as Carter's, was at stake.

"This doesn't mean to me he's a racist," Young said publicly. "It means he made a terrible blunder that he's got to recover from. I just think it's an awful phrase. I don't think he understood how loaded it is with Hitlerian connotations."

The next night Carter was in the Bond Court Hotel in Cleveland. He washed out his socks and underwear in the bathroom sink; he called his wife; and he called Young. By the next day, he was convinced that he had to admit he had made a mistake. He had to apologize.

"I think most of the problem has been caused by my ill-chosen agreement to use the word ethnic purity," Carter said in a statement upon arriving in Philadelphia. "I think that was a very serious mistake on my part. I think it should have been the word 'ethnic character' or 'ethnic heritage.' . . . I do want to apologize to all those who have been concerned about the unfortunate use of the 'ethnic purity.' I don't think there are any ethnically pure neighborhoods, but in response to a question and without adequate thought on my part, I used a phrase that was unfortunate. . . . I was careless in the words I used. . . . I have apologized for it. It was an improper choice of words."

It took Carter days to switch from his original view about his remarks, but he finally apologized. His backers had been saying that it was just a case of his saying something while overtired. His critics had been saying it was a veiled appeal for the Wallace vote in the suburbs. No one knows Carter's motive for sticking so long with his original phrasing—except Carter. "The reason for the delayed reaction," said one of Carter's close advisers, "was in part because he is stubborn when under attack." Looking back, Jody Powell later said: "The situation made Greg [Schneiders] more forceful in the future and willing to go to the mat with Jimmy."

Hamilton Jordan had seen that the Pennsylvania primary could provide Carter's best chance to make a big impression in a northern industrial state. "After the Massachusetts primary," he added in an interview, "it became clear that Pennsylvania would be more than that. It would be our chance to take on Jackson man to man." So immediately after the Massachusetts primary, Tim Kraft—who had engineered Carter's Iowa victory—was sent to Pennsylvania. He had almost two months to organize support for his candidate there.

One of Kraft's easier tasks was winning endorsement for Carter from Pittsburgh Mayor Peter Flaherty. Kraft asked him if he intended to be an observer or get involved. Flaherty said that he would strongly support Carter. "You should meet Jimmy Carter," Kraft said. Flaherty flew to upstate New York to meet him. And then he made his endorsement.

In Massachusetts, Kraft's efforts had been surpassed by the Jackson staff's, especially by the get-out-the-vote work of twenty-six-year-old Bob (Skinner) Donahue. But the Jackson people then rejected Donahue's request that he be put on Jackson's national campaign staff, and Donahue was unhappy. Kraft heard about it and contacted Donahue. The ex-Jackson man wound up running the Carter get-out-the-vote campaign in Pennsylvania.

Kraft hired a professional telephone service and set up a 100-phone bank in Pittsburgh and another 100-phone bank in Philadelphia. The two banks were used in making 250,000 to 300,000 calls.

But on paper, at least, no one had an organization to match Scoop Jackson's. Philadelphia's Mayor Frank Rizzo had come out for Jackson. So had I. W. Abel, the head of the steelworkers' union, most of the state's prominent labor leaders, and most of the state's Democratic organization.

But it did not come together for Jackson. One reason was that the Jackson people just did not see the situation as clearly as Carter's. "I don't think Pennsylvania [was considered] a crossroads state until it was upon us," said Bob Keefe, Jackson's campaign manager. "Until mid-March it was not clear that Wallace would not be a factor. . . . We should have invested more heavily in building an organization in Pennsylvania."

Abel and his steelworkers and the other unions never

really came up with the hard-working day-to-day campaign work necessary to make a man a winner. Keefe said he was surprised at the failure of Abel and the other labor leaders to deliver. "We believed Abe was going to help to a greater degree than he helped," he said. "Hubert had suggested to him that he help. Labor leaders suggested that he help. He suggested back that he was doing all he could. But we started working in a crazy season. He had his own [union] election coming up. Abe's handpicked successor bombed out and another handpicked successor had a couple of opponents. The steelworkers have a real election with ballot boxes. . . . So he was worried about his election. That's the nature of our business. . . ."

In Reading, two days before the election, another Jackson official recalled asking the business agent for an 11,000-member steelworkers local what it was doing for Jackson. "Nobody ever contacted me," was the reply.

"Fred Lebder, the Fayette County commissioner, was our key guy in Pennsylvania," Keefe said. "Fred Lebder is a typical local leader. He runs Fayette and he was supposed to worry about everything outside of Philadelphia. He filed for Congress . . . and he was running for a month before we knew about it. A lot of his reports, shall we say, lacked substance." (As it turned out, Lebder's attempt to divide his efforts between Jackson's campaign and his own proved unsuccessful. He lost the congressional primary.)

During the Pennsylvania primary, Keefe said, he kept talking to Hubert Humphrey's administrative aide, Dave Gartner. "It was their opinion that helping us was the best thing they could do," Keefe said. Later, however, Jackson men would be bitter over the Humphrey connection—stung most of all by the Pennsylvania labor men who admitted to Joseph R. Daughen of the *Philadelphia Bulletin* that their first choice was Humphrey, and that they were working for Jackson mostly because it was the best way to help Humphrey.

Udall, who had not spent the extra $30,000 on media and mailing in Wisconsin, was spending money again in Pennsylvania. He was campaigning hard despite a survey by Peter Hart two and a half weeks before the election which showed Carter with 34; Jackson, 25; and Udall, 15. "We kept telling ourselves, 'If we can just get the liberals,'" Udall recalled. "We thought the liberals might coalesce in Pennsylvania—that the liberals were going to rally there."

Udall recalled how he was working a street in Philadelphia when a couple came out of a doctor's office with a two-year-old son who was wearing an eye patch. He had had an eye removed due to cancer. Udall stopped, talked to them, told them he too had lost an eye and asked them to keep in touch if they needed help. He said it not only made him feel good, but it got him great publicity.

If it was Philadelphia publicity he wanted, why, he was asked, did he spurn a rare invitation to address the city council at its regular meeting? Charley Bowser, a black lawyer, had arranged the opportunity for him. No other candidate had access to the council. It could have meant big television coverage in Philadelphia and even statewide. Instead Udall had gone to a fundraising breakfast in Washington. Udall looked genuinely amazed. "I didn't know about that [the city council invitation] until this minute," he said, almost two months after the Pennsylvania election.

Perhaps the most significant development in the Pennsylvania primary happened three months before the election, well outside the state boundaries, when the U.S. Supreme Court issued a ruling that prevented the Federal Elections Commission from disbursing matching funds to the presidential candidates until Congress reconstituted the commission on a constitutionally acceptable basis. The last checks were sent out on March 22. A month later, the candidates were in a cash squeeze.

Jimmy Carter managed—thanks to some prudent planning and good fortune. Scoop Jackson did not.

The Planning: Bob Lipshutz, Carter campaign treasurer, had insistetd during the Wisconsin primary on saving some money for Pennsylvania. "That was the decisive break," Pat Caddell said later. "We had a big jump on the media. We were the only ones with the money for it. We were on for about ten days unchallenged."

The Good Fortune: When the Carter campaign committee needed money for Pennsylvania, it was able to quickly borrow $100,000 from the Fulton National Bank of Atlanta on the strength of Jimmy Carter's personal financial statement.

The Carter campaign also borrowed another $175,000 from Citizens Southern National Bank on the basis of its accounts receivable—money due it from the Secret Service and the press for airplane charter trips. And they borrowed another $500,000 from the Fulton National Bank against matching fund submissions awaited from the Federal Elections Commission.

Still, Carter needed more.

"In Pennsylvania, we had to have about $350,000 in a hurry," Morris Dees, Carter's national finance chairman, recalled. "So I called a national finance committee meeting in Georgia and invited 650 people to come. We sent out Mailgrams and asked each person to raise $1,000 and bring it with them. We had about 400 people show up and they brought $150,000 with them. Had at least that much more in pledges which came in very quickly. So the week of the Pennsylvania primary (two weeks before, actually) we were able to put over $300,000 in the bank."

For Jackson, the situation was much different. "Pennsylvania was not prepared to go," Bob Keefe recalled. "We had not put the energy and resources there. We had applied them to New York, Massachusetts, and Florida. We spent way too much money in Florida."

The Jackson for President Committee spending records on file at the Federal Elections Commission tell the story of the faulty planning of the Jackson campaign.

In Massachusetts Jackson spent $657,393.

In Florida he spent $558,437 (in an election he was not really trying to win).

In New York he spent $891,698.

In Pennsylvania, his showdown with Carter state, he spent just $163,305.

"If we spent the same money in Pennsylvania as we did in Florida, we'd have won it. We didn't have any money to spend in Pennsylvania in the last three weeks."

Jackson would have been helped by smart planning and budgeting in a number of other states as well. Jackson officials spent $36,267 in California and $23,740 in Ohio —but Jackson had been blown out of the race long before those June 8 primaries came. He spent $13,866 in Iowa, in a half-hearted effort; $50,304 in a third place effort in Wisconsin when he was really concentrating on New York that same day; $44,728 in New Hampshire in a belated effort to win some delegates while staying out of the popularity vote (all he got out of this was a little media exposure in Massachusetts).

Jackson had a reputation for being a dull candidate and dull public speaker. But in the end he blew the election not on the stump but on the drawing board.

"By the time we got to Pennsylvania, it was a pity," said Hershey Gold, Jackson's national finance chairman. "But had we built the grass-roots organization, we could have made a good showing despite a dry bank account."

"Money isn't the ultimate weapon," he said. "How do you make $13 million do the work of $20 million? You do it by adding people—volunteers. Carter had the volunteers. He had the ability to do a literature drop of 50,000 pieces in a couple of hours," Gold said. "We used to struggle and flail around trying to get a little literature drop made—trying to find people to do it."

From their vantage point in Atlanta, the Carter people had always figured that Jackson had a bottomless source of wealth in that foreign place, New York. And Keefe, who had given Hamilton Jordan his start at the Democratic National Committee a couple of years earlier, was certainly a pro. So in Pennsylvania, the Carter people were amazed to find themselves facing what seemed to be a phantom opponent in Jackson. They had expected to find Keefe's presence everywhere, but they saw little evidence of his work. It was only then that they came to believe stories that had been circulating about how Jackson, that veteran of Washington back rooms, was hurting for money—how Jackson was left to depend on the unions to keep their word and deliver for him. But the unions did not deliver and Kraft's Carter organization did.

THE RESULTS: *Carter's "ethnic purity" controversy turned out to be no handicap. Carter won 37.2 percent of the vote; Jackson, 24.7 percent; Udall, 18.8. "In Pennsylvania it was a genuine pleasure," said Tim Kraft later. "It was like being in the cockpit of a powerful jet."*

Jackson took the train from Philadelphia to Washington on Wednesday morning with his press secretary Brian Corcoran. From Washington's Union Station, they walked several blocks to Jackson's office.

There, on the red chairs in Jackson's large inner office, they sat and contemplated what was left of the future. With them were Bob Keefe; Sterling Munro, the campaign administrator; Ben Wattenberg, an adviser; Dick Kline; and Walter Skallerup, the controller and legal adviser.

Wattenberg was the only man who wanted to continue the campaign. The group estimated that it would take another $1 million; the Federal Elections Commission had $400,000 for Jackson, but where would the additional $600,000 come from? The financial men offered no encouragement.

Labor leaders wandered in and out. They said they would do whatever Jackson wanted.

Ahead lay Indiana. Tough by any odds. Carter would win the southern part of the state. Jackson recalled how in 1960 he had been stumping the state for Kennedy and how people kept asking him: "Are you another one of those Catholics for Kennedy?"

No decision was reached Wednesday. Keefe said that he and Hubert Humphrey had talked, and that Humphrey asked him what was happening and that Keefe said honestly he did not know. Keefe called Humphrey at 8:10 A.M. the next day and said that Jackson was likely to drop out. Humphrey asked if Keefe had read the *Washington Post's* editorial page. No? Humphrey read him the last paragraph of an editorial that said Humphrey could only bring discredit upon his career by entering the race now.

On Thursday afternoon, Jackson, Keefe, and some Jackson supporters watched live television coverage of Humphrey's press conference. Humphrey was teary-eyed as he said he had decided not to get into the campaign.

The Jackson people thought it all out again. Indiana, Keefe recalled, "would be bum. There was no money spent there. Texas was going to be bum. It would be another two weeks before we could see anything. Connecticut looked promising. Nebraska, Maryland, Michigan might be good." But, he added: "Scoop felt there was little likelihood that he would be the nominee." It wasn't worth going deep into debt. He decided to drop out. His active campaign was over.

▰ ▰ ▰

Interlude: HHH

In 1948 a young, idealistic mayor of Minneapolis electrified the Democratic National Convention. "To those who say that this civil rights program is an infringement of states' rights . . . the time has arrived in America for the Democratic Party to get out of the shadows of states' rights and walk forthrightly into the bright sunshine of human rights," Hubert Horatio Humphrey declared in firm, ringing tones. Strom Thurmond and his fellow-archright southerners walked forthrightly out of the Democratic Party and founded the Dixiecrats as a strong civil rights plank was passed. At age thirty-seven, Hubert H. Humphrey had catapulted to national prominence as a leader among liberals.

In 1960 a now-established senator mounted an energetic campaign for the Democratic presidential nomination. Hubert H. Humphrey criss-crossed the country lining up support, but was defeated first in Wisconsin and then in West Virginia by a well-oiled, well-financed John F. Kennedy machine. "I am no longer a candidate for the Democratic presidential nomination," a crushed Hubert Humphrey declared. "I shall run for reelection to the United States Senate."

In 1964 a fiery veteran of sixteen years in the Senate stumped hard after being chosen as the Democratic vice-presidential candidate. Hubert Humphrey rode into office on the tail of Johnson's landslide victory over Barry Goldwater.

In 1968 a Vice President shackled to a hated war policy that ripped the country apart won the Democratic presidential nomination. But Hubert Humphrey could not bring himself to cut his ties to the Johnson war policy until it was too late. He was edged by Richard Nixon and he left Washington a crushed and crying man.

In 1972 a sixty-one-year-old freshman senator fought again to win the Democratic presidential nomination. But Hubert Humphrey was now Old Politics. He was thrashed soundly by a young, liberal crowd that rallied behind Senator George McGovern.

In 1976 the juices were flowing once more. The quadrennial glands that had secreted in sync with the presidential campaigns for so many years were pumping once more in that venerable and politic body that was once home to the young Turk of 1948. Powerful people in labor and within the Democratic Party had been urging the sixty-five-year-old Happy Warrior to make still one more run at the White House. "I get tempted. I get tempted because people call me. But I've gone around many times already asking for help. Asking people to please help me. And I'm tired of it. I don't want to have to go around and ask people to help me. I don't want to go to people anymore," Humphrey said back in March.

He preferred then to let others make the run, hoping for a deadlocked convention. But then Jackson collapsed in Pennsylvania, and Jimmy Carter appeared to have a clear field, and the pressures from labor people and party people mounted again. And so on Wednesday, April 28, Humphrey called nine advisers to his office to figure out what he should do.

In his office, Humphrey took off his suit jacket and outlined the possibilities. There were three options open: an all-out campaign which included entering the New Jersey primary; the authorization of an "exploratory committee" that would gather funds, assemble supporters, and lobby uncommitted delegates for votes; and, finally, nothing.

Humphrey asked each person to give his views. Most argued for an all-out fight, starting with the New Jersey primary with its filing deadline of 4:00 P.M. the next day.

A few argued against this. It would be hard to build an organization, to raise the money needed so desperately to mount an effective campaign that would win the voters in time for the June 8 New Jersey vote.

Then, if he announced he was going to wage an all-out fight, there would be intense pressure for him to enter the Nebraska primary, where the vote would be held May 11. His name was on the ballot there but he had absolutely no organization in the state. Senator Frank Church (D—Idaho) already was campaigning hard to win Nebraska. It would be tough, very tough.

Max Kampelman, the lawyer who had been Humphrey's legislative aide some years ago, showed the senator a draft of a speech he had prepared announcing his candidacy. Humphrey scanned it and thanked him. He already had received memorandums from at least two congressmen, and a senator had outlined what he could say in giving his reasons for campaigning in New Jersey.

One of his secretaries entered the meeting and handed him a note. Humphrey smiled and read it out loud. It was from his wife, Muriel, and it said: "Whatever you decide to do is all right with me. And wherever you decide to have dinner is all right with me."

Muriel Humphrey had been reluctant to have her husband try again. Humphrey remembered his wife's attitude as he read the note. The secretary, he thought, "must have gotten the message wrong."

Despite the obstacles, Kampelman wanted him to fight it out in New Jersey. So did Walter Mondale, the other senator from Minnesota, who had voluntarily withdrawn his own presidential bid months before. So did Minnesota millionaire Robert Short, former owner of Washington's baseball Senators, who took the national pastime out of the nation's capital and moved it to Texas (a capital flight by a rich baseball man who wanted to get richer).

Erie County Democratic Chairman Joseph Crangle of New York also urged Humphrey to enter the race actively. He didn't really know the senator but he long had been a supporter of his. "Certainly," Crangle said afterwards, "he could win New Jersey."

But would New Jersey be enough, particularly if Carter sailed through the other primaries? Crangle counseled that Humphrey could be the issues candidate—a dramatic figure who could effectively counter Carter's anti-Washington, anti-big government themes.

After each of the nine spoke individually, there was a general discussion. Humphrey asked a lot of questions but did not reveal his inclinations.

The answers were somewhat different then. The nine were divided about evenly on the subject. Those against, according to one person present, basically said: "You've already served your country and the party. It'll be a terrible grind and strain on you to do it again."

Another person at the meeting said: "There was a recognition underlying the whole thing that this was an intensely personal decision. I could not tell at the end of the meeting which way he was leaning. He said, 'I will go home, talk to Muriel, and sleep on it.' "

On Thursday morning, Humphrey and his wife sat down in their library. They discussed the strain on their personal lives that such a campaign would bring. "I told her that as far as I could see, I should not enter the primaries," Humphrey said.

Still, he left the question open and left for the office, arriving at 10:40 A.M. His physician and confidant, Dr. Edgar Berman, had talked to him the evening before and was convinced he would run. Berman was so certain that he telephoned John Y. Brown of Louisville, the former owner of Kentucky Fried Chicken, to come up to Washington and run the Humphrey for President campaign.

Brown promptly boarded a plane and flew there. Meanwhile, Humphrey telephoned Henry Jackson and Morris Udall, two of the Democratic presidential contenders. He encouraged both to stay in the race. He did not call Carter because the former Georgia governor's campaign manager, Hamilton Jordan, had called him—making Humphrey think that Carter would be telephoning later. He did not.

Humphrey telephoned New York Mayor Abraham Beame, who told him to run in New Jersey. He called AFL-CIO president George Meany.

At 11:45 A.M. he called his wife and, during a ten-minute conversation, decided that he would not, after all, campaign. He called his daughter, Mrs. Nancy Solomonson, and told her of the decision. At 12:20 P.M., he dictated a statement announcing his intentions to his secretary, Marsha Greenwood, and went off to a labor committee luncheon.

"There was no overriding factor," said his administrative assistant, David Gartner.

"It was a personal decision," John Y. Brown said. "He didn't want to expose himself."

"Hubert is a gentleman," Dr. Edgar Berman said. "To be cut up by the press again would have been pure anguish. He thought it [the primaries] would be a very iffy affair among three candidates. It just didn't happen."

But Berman added that he thought that despite all of that, with two or three more days to think about it, Humphrey might have entered anyway. Deciding to stay out, Berman said, "I think was a mistake."

On Thursday afternoon, Hubert stood next to Walter Mondale in the Senate Caucus Room and read the statement his secretary had typed. So momentous was his announcement that network television had cut into its soap operas to carry Humphrey live. The senator pulled a white handkerchief from his pocket and wiped tears from his eyes. "Really, I'm not crying," he volunteered. "Those [television lights] are really bright on my sensitive eyes. I've cried before but that's when I lost. This time, I prevented that." •

Hubert Humphrey would not run for the Presidency, he would not pursue once more the goal which had forever eluded him. "One thing I don't need at this stage of my life is to be ridiculous," he said. "I haven't thought about a deadlocked convention since eleven A.M."

He actually had not come to a decision until 11:45. On Tuesday, two days earlier, one month before his sixty-fifth birthday, the voters of Pennsylvania—considered his most loyal followers outside his home state—had turned overwhelmingly to Jimmy Carter in the presidential primary.

But he did say there was always the chance of a miracle —a chance that the convention would deadlock and that the nomination might somehow still be his. "I shall not seek it," Humphrey said. "I shall not search for it. I shall not scramble for it." Then he paused. "But I'm around."

Another Interlude: Fiasco

From Pat Caddell's memo of March 24, 1976: ". . . This campaign needs now at least one excellent, brilliant writer, who can pull together ideas and statements for the governor and who has good political sense. Someone who knows how to capitalize on opportunities and also how to avoid disaster. This person needs to work with Jody, and may need to travel. I think under the right circumstances Shrum may be available."

Back in 1972, Robert Shrum was known as a very heavy, very talented, very liberal political speechwriter. He was a 290-pound, twenty-nine-year-old man who had written for New York City Mayor John V. Lindsay and for the unsuccessful presidential campaign of Edmund

Muskie. He had eventually joined the George McGovern staff. In April, 1976, Shrum had lost 140 pounds (through the discipline of lots of exercise and little food) but none of his talent and none of his liberalism. On the advice of Pat Caddell, he was brought into the Carter inner circle.

Shrum was recruited during the Pennsylvania primary campaign in an effort to defuse the charge that Carter was fuzzy on issues. He quit just nine days later and eventually made his dissatisfaction public, charging that not only was Carter fuzzy on issues, he was *deliberately* fuzzy on issues.

It was, in all, a rather short political metamorphosis. On Monday, April 19, Shrum sat in on his first staff meeting devoted to issues. And by Thursday, April 22, he recalls, he was a discouraged and disillusioned man; he sat on the steps of a Holiday Inn that night talking with Caddell until three A.M., unburdening himself of his doubts. On Monday, April 26, Shrum wrote a victory statement for Carter to use after the votes were counted the next day; but he didn't wait around to join in the celebration. Instead, he took the 5:41 Metroliner from Philadelphia to Washington, where he sought the advice of friends.

"After I wrote that victory statement, it all came back to me again—all the doubts and uncertainty," Shrum recalls. "It wasn't any blinding revelation that let me know what I was going to do—I don't believe in stuff like that. But the more I thought about it, the more I became certain about what I had to do. I believed at that point that Carter was going to be the nominee and then be elected the next President. But by then, the only thing I kept trying to calculate for myself was 'Has this been long enough for me to make the decision to quit?' My initial thought was that I would quit but that I just would never say anything publicly about why I was quitting."

Caddell, who remained a friend of Shrum's even after the whole embittering experience, called at one point. In Shrum's words: "Pat told me if I was going to resign, to please shut up, at least." But in the end, Shrum says, he was most persuaded by a Washington friend who offered this counsel: "If you talk about it publicly and you turn out to have been wrong, how will you feel? You'll feel a bit foolish. But if you *don't* talk about it and you turn out to have been *right* [about Carter], how will you feel?" As

Shrum saw it, he had a duty to let people know how things were as he saw them.

And so, less than a week after the Pennsylvania primary, Shrum went public by giving reporters copies of the letter of resignation he had written to Carter, charging the candidate with "an attempt to conceal your true positions." He talked in interviews of manipulation and deception, and later elaborated on his feelings in an article he wrote for *The New Times Magazine*.

Shrum gave a lengthy list of examples of cases in which he felt Carter had deliberately fuzzed issues. He said that although Carter had publicly pledged to cut the defense budget by 5 to 7 percent, he had been told privately that Carter "might favor a substantial increase."

He said that Carter had decided not to support a plan to give automatic eligibility for black-lung disease benefits to miners who had worked thirty years because "the plan is too radical." He said Carter told him: "It would offend the operators. And why should I do this for Arnold Miller [the United Mine Workers president] if he won't come and endorse me? . . . I don't think the benefits should be automatic. They chose to be miners."

When trucking executives had wanted to know where Carter stood on changes in trucking regulations, Shrum quoted Carter as saying: "I want to give them enough reassurances to satisfy them, but give them as little as I have to." He also wrote that Carter wanted to tell the trucking industry people that "I oppose the diversion of the highway trust fund to mass transit"—but that an aide reminded Carter that "you're already on record as favoring it."

Shrum said that while preparing what the Carter campaign labeled a "comprehensive" economic policy statement that was released during the Pennsylvania primary, Carter cautioned that he wanted his advisers to make sure that the statement did not "commit me too much."

And he said that Carter had rejected a suggestion that he make another statement on the Mideast situation. He quoted Carter as saying: "We have to be cautious. We don't want to offend anybody. . . . I don't want any more statements on the Middle East or Lebanon. Jackson has all the Jews anyway. It doesn't matter how far I go. I don't get over four percent of the Jewish vote anyway, so forget it. We get the Christians."

In his letter that was written to Carter—and released to reporters—Shrum also said: "You say you wish to keep your options open. Within reason that is understandable. But an election is the only option the people have. After carefully reflecting on what I have seen and heard here, I do not know what you would do as President.

"I share the perception that simple measures will not answer our problems; but it seems to me that your issue strategy is not a response to that complexity, but an attempt to conceal your true positions. I am not sure what you truly believe in other than yourself.

"I have examined my reactions closely. I have attempted to justify a different conclusion. But I cannot rationalize one. Therefore I must resign."

The Carter people were clearly stung by Shrum's decision to go public with his damaging accusations and comments. Jody Powell maintained to reporters that Shrum was not being paid the $23,000 he said he was earning, and said that in fact Shrum had not even been on the payroll. "I think what he is doing now is childish and hurtful," Powell said. "I don't question his sincerity. . . . He, like anyone else, has said things about people and things that would be embarrassing if quoted back to him."

Carter appeared upset when reporters questioned him about the Shrum affair during a stopover in Terre Haute, Indiana. "Shrum has never been on my payroll," Carter said. "I don't feel inclined to comment on this young man's statement. . . . [Shrum] obviously wrote the letter for the news media. . . . I'm not a liar and I don't make any statements in private contrary to those I make in public."

May/Ups and Downs

Jimmy Carter had defeated them all. Birch Bayh and Fred Harris. Henry Jackson and Milton Shapp. Lloyd Bentsen, Terry Sanford, George Wallace, and Mo Udall. With the exception of Udall, who would press to the end, propelled by a number of second-place finishes, they all had stopped running by the end of April.

But the primaries went on. Two fresh challengers, Frank Church and Jerry Brown, arrived. And a movement known as "ABC" (Anybody But Carter), which actually was an effort to win the nomination for Hubert Humphrey, was formed.

As it turned out, Carter's new opponents were simply too late. Jimmy Carter had won the nomination when he defeated Jackson in Pennsylvania. The new challengers would slow him, but they would not stop him. He would lose in ten primaries in May and June. But he would win in ten, and his delegate total would keep climbing. The new opponents did their jobs pretty well, and Carter at times did not do his very well, but in the end, he had too much momentum for it to make a difference.

⊜   ⊜   ⊜

On May 1, Texas held the year's only Saturday-night primary. Senator Lloyd Bentsen, who had dropped his national presidential effort before New Hampshire, was still running as a favorite son. The Texas primary was the most difficult to qualify for, according to Carter campaign director Hamilton Jordan. He told of a conversation he had about Texas with Charles Kirbo, Carter's closest adviser/confidant. "I told Kirbo early on that I couldn't see spending the extra $6,000 or $7,000 it would take to get on in all thirty-one districts in the state," Jordan recalled. "We were on in twenty-five, and I figured that was good enough, Bentsen being a favorite son and all. But Kirbo put things in proper perspective for me. He said, 'Never put yourself in the position where you can't realize your own potential. Spend the money.' We did."

Carter wanted Texas badly and he worked the state well, while Bentsen appeared unsure of whether he really wanted to allow the primary to be a test vote on his statewide popularity. Carter was proving a formidable opponent.

At a rally in Dallas sponsored by the Southern Methodist University Law School, a rally attended by a largely middle-class college and white-collar worker crowd, one person got up to apparently give the needle to the Georgia governor. The questioner noted that Texas had a large Spanish-speaking population and asked if Carter had anyone on his staff who spoke Spanish. The Georgian handled the question the way Ted Williams used to handle a lazy, hanging curve. He clouted it out of the park. Carter answered the question in Spanish: "Yes, I do. I speak Spanish myself. And my staff will be happy to send you a detailed position paper on any issue you wish."

The audience erupted in applause.

Carter's national staff members became fond of quoting their Texas coordinator, Bob Armstrong, who gave them comfort and confidence by saying: "We're riding a fast horse. All we have to do is hang on and wave our hats."

Carter swept Texas, picking up 122 delegates compared to Bentsen's mere 8. Three days later, Carter had another big day. He carried his home state of Georgia with 83.9 percent of the vote, smashing Wallace. He carried Indiana with 68 percent compared to Wallace's 15. He carried the District of Columbia 39.7 to Udall's 26.1. And he came in a respectable second to Wallace in Wallace's Alabama, 50.8 to 27.4.

May 1 plus May 4 meant a whooping 258 delegates for Carter in a single week. "We were in another euphoria as we headed for Nebraska," Caddell recalled. "Euphoria Number Three."

Challenge: Church in Nebraska

The only campaigning competition Carter had for Nebraska's May 11 primary was Frank Church, a newcomer. As the Carter people saw it, Church posed little threat.

Frank Church had picked his spot and his strategy carefully, planning months ahead. At fifty-one, after spending twenty years in the Senate, Church had looked at the large early field and figured that many of the candidates would knock each other off. Then, he hoped, he would come on with a rush in the West, cap his crusade in California, and take a large bloc of delegates to Madison Square Garden in July.

"To those who say it's too late, I reply that's it's never too late—nor are the odds ever too great—to try." Church declared in his Idaho City announcement speech, his voice searching for emotion and emphasis in the Boys State oratory style that he has never lost. "In that spirit, the West was won, and, in that spirit, I announce my candidacy for the Presidency of the United States."

That was his plan. But the collapse of Scoop Jackson was a damaging blow to the Church strategy, and then the emergence of Jerry Brown knocked it haywire.

Church had counted on Jackson being strong throughout the primary season. "He figured Jackson would beat Carter in New York [he did] and beat Carter in Pennsylvania [he did not]," said one of Church's closest advisers. "Then he would be out front and then there would be an initial surge for Humphrey, and then people would begin to wonder whether they really wanted to be saddled with all that old baggage Humphrey brings with him, and then here would come Frank Church, a fresh face with years of experience, who had just done an impressive job with the Senate Intelligence Committee [investigating the CIA]. Church thought he would inherit the antiwar people of McGovern and the old-line Democrats. But the one thing none of us foresaw—the one astonishing thing of the campaign—was the Jackson catastrophe."

"The plan was to finish big in California," said Bill Hall, former press secretary to Church. But Brown's decision to run wiped out Church's California hopes. After the popular young California governor announced his plans to run, Church remarked dolefully, according to Hall, "I made a mistake in not patenting that late, late strategy."

In November and December of 1975, Church had considered making an early bid for the Presidency by jumping into the Massachusetts primary. He had earlier given his word to Senate Majority Leader Mike Mansfield, upon being named chairman of the Senate Intelligence Committee, that he would not use the committee as a launching pad for a presidential campaign. But he could have reasoned that the *public* hearings of the committee had ended before the Massachusetts primary, thus freeing him to enter. A couple of his advisers, Geoffrey Shields and Jerome I. Levinson, were said to have urged him to get into the race early. But Church opted to wait.

On March 10, six days before he announced his candidacy, Church seriously contemplated not making the run for the Presidency at all. This was well before the Jackson collapse in Pennsylvania; it was, in fact, just after Carter had defeated Wallace in Florida. Church saw Carter as being already stronger than he had expected the Georgian to be. He talked with his advisers about forgetting the whole thing and with his family as well. Church's son, Forrest, who is getting a doctorate from the Harvard Divinity School, urged him to make the race.

Church made the race. He came into Nebraska well before the election and worked the state hard. He campaigned there just as he had campaigned in his nearby Idaho. Jimmy Carter, in contrast, spent one day in Nebraska. He was, after all, in the middle of what Caddell called "Euphoria Number Three": he was fresh off a week that had given him 258 delegates; and he had a new Caddell poll, taken just a week before the Nebraska election, that showed him well ahead, with Church mired deep in the pack. So it was that the Carter men decided to spend the candidate's politicking time elsewhere, where he was needed. They were supremely confident about Nebraska.

The Nebraska ballot contained the names of all persons who had been mentioned anywhere, anytime in connection with a run for the Presidency. Caddell's poll a week before the election showed Carter in the low 30's with noncampaigners Hubert Humphrey and Edward M. Kennedy bunched behind with a total of 25 percent. Church had just 16 to 18.

Good enough grounds for euphoria. And so the Carter camp stopped polling. None of the Carter men bothered to ask if the people who were saying they were for the non-candidates, Humphrey and Kennedy, would really wind up voting for a man they knew was not running. Not even Caddell paused to ask. "That was my major mistake," he said later. "Not concentrating on the second choices. Not asking if the Kennedy and Humphrey votes would stay there or would they go elsewhere. Well, they all went elsewhere—and they all went to Church."

The Church people were never confident. Their candidate spent at least twelve days in the state. "We were wondering right up to election night whether we'd just wind up packing it all in after Nebraska," said one Church aide. "After all, California had already been shot out from under us. So if we couldn't win in Nebraska, forget it."

It was not until just before election day that Caddell got the inkling that something was wrong. And that was not exactly due to his scientific skill and method. Rather, it was because Gene Pokorny called his mom and dad. Pokorny, Caddell's Cambridge Research, Inc., partner, just happened to call home to Nebraska and in the course of things asked his parents who they were voting for. Church, the parents said. Pokorny was stunned. Why? he asked; didn't they know he was polling for Carter? Yes, they knew. But, they said, it was just that Church had been out there campaigning and Carter didn't even care enough to come.

THE RESULTS: *Church wound up beating Carter by 1 percentage point (38.8 to 37.8)—a margin of less than 2,000 votes. Carter was in Washington on election night, politicking at a congressional fundraising dinner for Democrats. Peter Bourne, who was with Carter that night, told another Carter aide that the candidate had been really upset with that one. Carter said that if they had only spent one more day in Nebraska, it could have made the difference. His staff men, kicking themselves, agreed.*

"A clear case of misreading—a clear case of stupidity," Jody Powell said candidly. "It wasn't like New York, where we might not have known the political system. In Nebraska, we damn well should have understood. If we can win in Georgia, we damn well ought to be able to win in Nebraska. . . . Nebraskans got the impression that we don't care about Nebraska and screw you. I guess I don't blame them. In Georgia, we'd feel the same way if someone campaigned in Georgia the way we campaigned in Nebraska.

"All this crap about us having a well-planned, flawless campaign that moved from obscurity to stardom is—is ridiculous. But Jimmy delegates authority in areas like strategy, and the good thing about him is he can live with the mistakes his people make."

Said Carter: "None of us realized what was happening in Nebraska until it was over."

The same day, May 11, was the only primary in which Carter did not actively campaign. West Virginia favorite son Senator Robert Byrd ran virtually unchallenged in his home state and wound up beating George Wallace 88.5 percent to 11.5. Carter did not campaign against Byrd because he figured, correctly, that he would have Byrd's delegates in the end. It is the sham of the American political process that when Byrd announced his candidacy early in the campaign year, he swore that he was not just a one-state candidate, that he would be running a truly national campaign. It is proof of the strength of the American political process that no one believed him.

Challenge: Brown in Maryland

It is the legend of Jerry Brown that he is the antipolitician.

He shuns the new $1.3-million California governor's mansion and lives in a nearby apartment, sells the governor's limousine and rides in a Plymouth, cuts his top aides' salaries, and lobbies successfully against his own pay raise. He returns free passes, free memberships, and other gifts sent by special interests; he halts the giving of free briefcases to state bureaucrats because he hates paperwork. He gives state janitors the same $68-a-week pay increase he gives state judges, cuts spending requests for liberal favorites such as education, does not give autographs, does not go on out-of-state trips—not even to national governors' conferences—and shuns traditional party fundraising functions and party patronage pleas.

Yet one year after his election, the respected California poll found that only 7 percent of respondents thought Jerry Brown was doing a "poor" job as governor.

Only 7 percent. Most politicians are born with a higher negative rating. At age thirty-seven, Edmund G. Brown, Jr. (don't-call-him-Pat's-son), is setting records for voter popularity.

Jerry Brown is—by the only measure that really counts —the ultrapolitician.

Sacramento politicians find it hard to peg Jerry Brown. He is the Jerry Brown of the Jesuit past (and, some say, Zen present) who stunned a senior state legislator during budget deliberations by sending a young aide to ask him, in effect, if he was guilty of knee-jerk thinking. "The governor wants to know if your belief that the poor are hungry is just a middle-class assumption."

When he campaigned for the governorship, a lot of people assumed that he represented a return to liberal causes after eight years of Ronald Reagan. "He was Pat Brown's son, and everyone figured that Jerry Brown's election meant that the faucets would start flowing again," said one of the state's most prominent Democrats. "Well, everybody was wrong."

Brown is not big on public speeches: his first state of the state address lasted just seven minutes; his second, eleven. Antipol.

But he is adept at winning over liberals and conservatives with a style that is effective, but unaffected, and with rhetoric that sounds like recycled Reagan. "At the state level, I think we ought to be doing more of what the federal government is doing now. And in the state, I think more ought to be done at the county level instead of pyramiding a lot of these new agencies that are unresponsive, unelected, and rather obscure." Ultrapol.

When Brown ran for governor in 1974, a number of education and labor people grumbled privately that they kicked sizable amounts into Brown's campaign fund because they assumed he was a liberal who would favor their spending requests. But Brown says, "I never promised them I'd be a big spender. When I kicked off my campaign, . . . I said I will not raise general taxes. So all of these people know that once you say you're not going to raise taxes, it obviously imposes a certain limit. Now some people said, 'Well, this is the son of Pat Brown,' so people thought they'd get more programs and more money." But Brown admits he did not tell his education and labor contributors that he was going to clamp down on their programs either. Antipol/ultrapol.

Does he consider himself a liberal? "John Stuart Mill was a liberal," he says. "By the standard indices, I guess people would think I am. . . . But I am not restrained by the metaphors and mythologies associated with the term. . . ."

Sacramento politicians make no pretense of having adjusted to Brown's modus operandi. A bachelor with a lifestyle on the modified bohemian plan, Brown says he works best at night. He handled the prolonged farm labor crisis by calling management, labor, and state officials into his conference room at about 8:00 P.M., keeping them there until 3:00 A.M.—with a break for a meal of Japanese food. Meetings on two succeeding nights lasted even later, and when an agreement was finally reached, he stunned those present by having them sign copies of the written accord—so that no faction later could deny having agreed to any section that might have proven unpopular with the people they represented. Antipol/ultrapol.

In February of 1976, back when Brown was proclaiming "I'm not locked in and I'm not locked out" about running for President, a visiting Eastern reporter asked the young governor if he thought he would make a good President.

The governor exhaled and sagged back into the sofa like a collapsed balloon. "Gee . . . let me think . . . I have to give that one some thought. . . . I mean, I just don't know."

There was no ringing formal declaration when Jerry Brown got into the presidential race. He just sort of let the statement slip out—parenthetically—in a chat with a few reporters after an art exhibit that, by the way, he intended to run for President, at least as a favorite son. Later he confided that he would begin a national campaign by going into Maryland.

Maryland was to be a testing place for Brown. It was too late for him to field a slate of delegates, but he could still have his name placed on the ballot for the presidential preference vote. It would be a way of finding out whether people outside California were interested in the politics of lowered expectations that Brown had been applying to the California electorate in his appealing, Zen-conservative way. He was the most popular figure in California political history, if the polls are an accurate measure; but no one —not even Brown—was sure how his politics would play east of the Rockies.

While Jimmy Carter was making it on a pitch that said he was a peanut farmer/engineer/navy officer/husband/ father/Christian, Jerry Brown was making it on a pitch that he wasn't even a traditional governor. No mansion, no limo, no five-point programs, no promises that things would get better.

On April 28, Brown made his first trip outside California since he had been elected governor eighteen months earlier. From the time he hit Maryland, his campaign was something different from anything that had transpired in Campaign '76. He did not have crowds, he had mobs. They were not warm, they were bobby-soxer enthusiastic. They were not like the crowds around Carter or Udall or Jackson or anyone else in this campaign. They were more like the jumpers and squealers that used to surround Bobby Kennedy.

The rise of Jerry Brown was phenomenal. Just two weeks after he had announced his candidacy, before he had made a single campaign speech or taken a single trip outside of his state, Jerry Brown had a higher nationwide rating than three of his rivals—Jackson, Udall, and Church.

Brown arrived in Maryland May 28 and was welcomed at the Baltimore International Airport by Governor Marvin Mandel, a number of top Democratic and labor leaders, and what the *Washington Post* noted was the largest group of newspeople to gather in the state since the resignation of Spiro T. Agnew. Brown went to a nighttime rally in the ballroom of the Baltimore Hilton that drew 2,000 people, many of whom had been urged to attend by party and labor officials.

"I'm not a Santa Claus with a bag of tricks," Brown told his audience. "I'm just an ordinary guy who works hard and comes home late."

The Maryland politicians fell into line. "A West Coast

Jack Kennedy," Lieutenant Governor Blair Lee III bubbled. "I like him. And it looks like a lot of other people do too."

"He definitely made points here—there's no question about it," Baltimore City Council President Walter Orlinsky, who had been wearing a "Holding for Hubert" button for weeks, told the *Washington Post*. "We're getting a media star here. Everyone wants to see him. The question is: will he wear?"

Brown wore. His headlines read like a political Horatio Alger. "Brown Gets Big Welcome in Maryland" . . . "Motorcade by Brown Is a Blitz." He was different; when a television interviewer stuck Brown with a long, boring question, Brown replied with a long, boring answer—and then added: "I don't know if that answers your question, but at least it fills up some air time."

Sally Quinn of the *Washington Post* caught a number of the Brown irreverencies in a lengthy piece in the paper that serves Washington's populous Maryland suburbs.

The article was widely read and its anecdotes widely quoted, and people saw a politician who offered them a refreshing change of pace.

Like the time Brown led a group of reporters on an inspection of a garbage dump and said: "What is the inner meaning of this? Why are we here? What are we doing?"

Like the time in a Westinghouse plant when he was shaking hands, saying absently, "I hope you'll vote for me." And one woman replied, "I will," and Brown did a classic double-take. "You will?" he blurted. "But you don't know anything about me."

Like the time he was asked which political philosopher he looked to for inspiration and he replied somberly, "Thomas Hooker." Reporters wrote down the name and finally someone asked just who Thomas Hooker was. "I'm just being facetious," replied Brown. "He's the only obscure name I could remember from political science class."

Brown had the Maryland Democratic political machine, headed by Governor Marvin Mandel. The party regulars were backing Brown in part because Mandel does not like Jimmy Carter and in part because the labor-backed party officials do like Hubert Humphrey. He was, then, Jerry Brown, the machine antipol. It was Stop Carter politics well played. The only person who did not play the game well was Carter. The Georgian had never succeeded in checking the "soft-on-issues" label and it was starting to catch on, and this was reflected in the polls.

There were two primaries going on May 18th—the other was in Michigan, where Carter felt he was doing very well against Udall, what with having such diverse endorsements as those of United Auto Workers President Leonard Woodcock and auto industry giant Henry Ford, and Detroit's black mayor, Coleman Young. They represented constituencies that at times would barely speak to one another. Carter and his strategists felt good about Michigan; they chose to tackle Brown head on in Maryland.

Caddell's Maryland polling showed Carter behind Brown by 4 points. Nationally, Carter negative ratings were starting to climb, from the low 20's up to 30 to 33 and up to the mid-30's in the West. Nebraska had shown that Carter was indeed still vulnerable. "Now we were getting pounded all over the place," Caddell said.

Carter moved to stop the slide by stepping up his efforts in Maryland and stepping up his rhetoric as well.

Carter stumped the state attacking Brown head on, attacking him for being against government reorganization. Carter said that reorganization is essential, that it must be done and that he intended to see that it was—that 1,900 federal agencies be chopped down to just 200. He gave no examples. But he pressed this argument, even in the suburban areas outside Washington, which are heavily populated by people who work in the bureaucracy Carter was promising to whittle down to size.

The last Carter polling, done the Thursday before election day, showed Carter 7 to 8 points behind. "We were getting killed by the Catholics, by the women, and mainly by Brown," Caddell said.

       🏴   🏴   🏴

"I made a mistake—that was a serious tactical mistake I made in Maryland," Carter said. "Going in and running against Brown and running against the establishment . . . if ever there was a state in the nation that has the political establishment that's still dominant, it's Maryland. It worked well in Pennsylvania and we didn't understand Maryland well enough to analyze it. So that was a mistake. . . . I should have run a positive, statesmanlike campaign in Maryland. I ran just the opposite. . . . As I said, it was a mistake. We finished with Pennsylvania and did the polls in Maryland. We were behind and we could either write off Maryland or run against the political machine. That was a mistake."

Jimmy Carter had at least one fan among the government workers living in Maryland. William Richard Salter, who was active in the American Federation of Government Employees and who worked at the Department of Corrections, Washington, D.C., was a Carter man. He figured it would be nice to have a President he could talk to.

"Jimmy and I used to debate every Friday afternoon," said Salter, who called himself "Richard" when he grew up with Carter in Plains but who now is called "Bill" by his friends. "We were the captains of our teams [each year from eighth to eleventh grades]. There were usually three on a side. I don't remember the things we debated, except that Jimmy was always a stickler for the facts."

Salter recalled that Carter—"an excellent student . . . tops in his class . . . a natural leader"—once played hookey from school. "One day in the spring of 1941, about fifteen of us, went to a movie—some kind of a clown movie—over in Americus about eight miles away. We had to submit to a good whipping from the principal before we could get back to school. [A wooden paddle.] Then we got a whipping from our parents as well. Our parents made us abide by the rules."

In fact, young Carter was frequently out on a limb. "Part of our life was spent climbing trees," Salter said. "One of the things we used to do was two of us would climb about thirty to forty feet up a young pine tree and bend it to the ground. Then one would jump off and the other would fly off to another tree. Four or five of us would get together and do that."

Challenge: Udall in Michigan

Three weeks before the Michigan primary, Peter Hart did a statewide poll for the Udall people. The results were not bad; they were disastrous. Hart showed Udall trailing Carter by a whopping 52 percent to 19. "We just assumed we were going to lose and lose badly. . . . But we also thought we just might be able to hang on to the end—because if we did, and if the convention was truly an open convention, we thought Mo just might be able to end up as Vice President."

Once he got to Michigan, Mo Udall played hardball. "Udall's Quick Carter Quiz" was one of his biggest ploys, a checklist his campaign circulated asking questions about where Carter stood on welfare reform, right-to-work, and the reduction of specific federal agencies. Then there was the Udall cartoon—a thirty-second TV spot narrated by actor Cliff Robertson (John Kennedy in *PT-109*), showing two cartoon faces of Jimmy Carter, smiling and frowning at each other as conflicting Carter statements on issues were read.

The cartoon was negative advertising at its best—biting and effective. It also infuriated the Carter forces. And they responded with their version of hardball politics, low and inside. On May 14, addressing a group of black Baptist ministers on behalf of Carter, Detroit Mayor Coleman Young, who is black, said: "I am asking you to make a choice between a man from Georgia who fights to let you in his church, and a man from Arizona whose church won't even let you in the back door."

It was a blatantly unfair, bigoted attack aimed at discrediting the man because of his religion (in fact, Udall had long been unhappy with his church's views on the role of blacks and he had said he left the Mormon church —Church of the Latter-day Saints—as a youth because of its policy of excluding blacks from the church hierarchy; but all of that is really beside the point now). Carter was asked repeatedly to repudiate Coleman Young's comments, but he would not. The Carter people felt that Udall's cartoon advertising was unfair. "Let Udall stew— he deserves it," one Carter aide said. Carter let Coleman Young's comments stand.

On Tuesday, election day, Hamilton Jordan flew from Washington to Detroit so he could be with his candidate when the returns came in. It was one of the few election nights that he bothered to make the trip. Usually he let others stay at the governor's side, but this time there would be some meetings and decisions to make. And besides, this was looking like a very uncertain night.

Jordan was wearing blue jeans and a windbreaker and he drummed his fingers nervously as he contemplated the night ahead. "I don't like it," he kept saying. "I just don't like it. I'm starting to feel good about Maryland. Jimmy spent a lot of time there and I think he may pull it out. But this Michigan thing is something else. It's slipping away. It's that damn crossover."

Caddell had picked it up in Sunday night's polling. Democrats were deciding to cross over and vote Republican in this primary. To vote in the Ford-Reagan contest. And most of those Democratic crossovers were coming away from Carter.

Back in early May, Caddell had found Carter beating Udall decisively—45 to 20. He surveyed daily. Crossovers were running steady at 7 to 8 percent. But another 15 percent were saying they would consider crossing over, and they were prospective Carter voters by a 3 to 1 margin.

"Sunday night it all came apart," Caddell recalled. "We'd lost eight percent in crossovers. I really hit the panic button. Soon ten points of our twenty-point lead was gone in a matter of twelve hours."

Caddell projected the trend. If it continued at its present rate for the next twenty-four hours, Carter and Udall would be breaking even. Or worse. "The Udall people weren't polling," Caddell said. "They didn't even know what was going on until I finally told some of them over a drink."

On the plane, Jordan was figuring that as in the past the crossover would be conservative Wallace Democrats who wanted to vote for Reagan. A reporter flying with him bet that they would be more liberal Democrats, interested in helping out home stater Gerald Ford and seeing to it that Michigan did not boost Reagan toward the White House. Jordan was wrong on that, and he was wrong on Maryland.

He had been basing his hopes on a poll from an outside source.

🏳 🏳 🏳

On Monday, the day before the election, the *Baltimore Sun* published the results of a poll that brought encouragement—false encouragement, it turned out—to the Carter forces. The *Sun* poll said that the contest remained tight and that Carter was gaining strength more rapidly than Brown; a 3-point climb for Carter compared to just a 1-point rise for Brown. ". . . However, the separation between the two candidates appears to be of less significance than the slowing down of the impressive growth of voter support for Mr. Brown over the past month," the *Sun* reported.

🏳 🏳 🏳

THE RESULTS: *Carter forces felt they had narrowed the gap in Maryland. But on election night, it turned out that the gap was moving the other way—it had become a grand canyon, as Brown smashed Carter by 48.3 percent to 36.9.*

🏳 🏳 🏳

Detroit, election night. Carter campaign television adviser Barry Jagoda is making arrangements for the use of the Sheraton Cadillac Hotel's ballroom for a Carter election-night victory gathering. The hotel manager says he will need payment. Jagoda tells him to send the bill to the Carter headquarters in Atlanta, Box 1976. No deal, the manager says. It must be cash. Jagoda tells him not to worry. The manager does not reply, but instead takes the Carter man over to a file cabinet and extracts a folder marked "uncollected." Inside is a bill, still unpaid, made out to the John F. Kennedy Campaign, dated 1960.

Jagoda rounds up the cash.

🏳 🏳 🏳

In Detroit, the Carter people were undergoing what Caddell later called "the worst night of the campaign." This was not supposed to be a close race; yet here was

Carter, close to blowing it, close to suffering a disastrous double defeat at a time when he was supposed to be pulling away with the nomination won.

CBS—perhaps because they had been right in delaying the Wisconsin prediction when the other networks trumpeted Udall—was holding off in declaring Carter the winner. In the hotel bar, Jordan was saying how he was happy to have the 2-point victory they seemed to have shortly after midnight. Jordan by then was calm. Caddell was a nervous wreck; he did not get to bed until 5:00 A.M. (which proved awkward since he wound up having to rush back to New York to give a speech Wednesday morning). Carter says he fared better that night than his wife. "Well, I have to admit, I don't suffer when I think I'm going to lose," he said. "My wife does more than I do. In Wisconsin when we thought we had lost, I felt good. I had done the best I could. . . . I never thought I was going to lose in Michigan all through the night. . . . I went to bed fairly early when I was ahead, and when I woke I knew I'd won."

THE RESULTS: *Michigan went to Carter by less than 1 percent—43.5 to 43.2 And by a margin of just over 1,000 votes out of 659,000 cast. Democrats—mostly Carter Democrats—had crossed over into the GOP primary in large numbers to help home stater Gerald Ford defeat Ronald Reagan.*

On election night, Carter sat in his suite watching the returns. He sat slumped in a chair, staring at the television, his face mirroring concern, frustration, and disappointment. But when he went downstairs to greet his supporters in the hotel ballroom and to be interviewed by reporters he was smiling, apparently happy and confident and very much turned on.

He told reporters about how his delegate totals had climbed significantly that night and about how he had now received such a large number of votes throughout the long primary season. He smiled, he waved, he shook hands, and then he rode the elevator upstairs and went to bed, an unhappy winner.

For Udall, it was the fifth time in six primary contests that he had finished second—and the third time he had missed beating Carter by a few thousand votes or less.

Udall said later that he had never realized how close he was to defeating Carter in Michigan. Had he known, he said, he would have done one thing different: "I should have pushed my colleagues [from Michigan] in Congress."

ABC: HHH

In the year of the American Centennial, 1876, the country was treated to the spectacle of at least nine prominent politicians vying to be the next President. On Friday, May 19, 1876, *The Daily Graphic,* an illustrated evening newspaper in New York, ran a front-page cartoon entitled: "Merry-Go-Round for the White House Bound." The cartoon featured each candidate on a hobbyhorse, trying to spear with his lance the brass ring labeled "Presidency" as the merry-go-round spun. Accompanying that cartoon was a poetic caption that summed up the campaign of each contender:

> What time the newsman turns the crank,
>   The riders, in a whirl,
> From BAYARD, with his Bourbon bounce,
>   To CONKLING, with his curl,
> On hobbies mettlesomely high,
>   Career before the public eye.
> See TILDEN, saccharinely sly,
>   Come beaming to the tilt,
> With trophy called canal reform,
>   To deck his lance's hilt.
> While thoughtful THURMAN, just behind,
>   To ALLEN'S anger rides resigned.
> And BRISTOW brave, to battle borne,
>   Another prize parades—
> A badly broken Whiskey Ring;
>   But, HAYES, by recent raids,
> Has made a yet more gorgeous gain
> From fierce Inflation, faced and slain.
>
> Then mighty MORTON, martially,
>   Whom Ku-Klux-Klans would kill,
> Rides hot upon the track of BLAINE,
>   Who, staunchly seated still,

At all unknightly knaves can scoff,
And parries Slander's serpent off.

Upon his lithe and legal lance
  Each wears a riven king;
Yet hangs there one on high each
  Would fain as victor bring:
The Presidency goes with this,
And what a joke if all should miss!

—O.C.K.

The punch line of that political cartoon-poem of 1876 was the strategy of Hubert Horatio Humphrey in 1976. He would sit on the sidelines while the crowded field of Democrats rode the circuit, sticking their necks out, trying to spear the presidential ring with their lances and—he hoped—sticking each other in the process. It was a strategy that would work only if the primary elections proved truly divided, with no one emerging as a front-runner. When Carter beat Jackson in Pennsylvania, Humphrey was under great pressure from labor people and other long-time supporters to get into the race. But he decided he would not.

On April 29 at a press conference in which he announced this decision, Hubert Horatio Humphrey had declared: "The one thing I don't need at this stage in my life is to be ridiculous." But a few weeks later, Humphrey was reconsidering. It was just a month ago that he had ruled out an active candidacy. But now, his spokesmen were saying, Humphrey was going to take one more look at the political picture.

Urging Humphrey to make a final effort was the "ABC" movement. On May 18—as the Carter people were awaiting their election-day fate in Maryland and Michigan—a group gathered in a suite at the Hay Adams Hotel in Washington bent on sealing Carter's fate for him.

There, over breakfast Danish and coffee, they held the first meeting of what became known as the ABC movement. It stood for "Anybody But Carter," but this was a misnomer, since it really meant Humphrey instead of Carter.

The meeting was in the suite, just across Lafayette Square from the White House, belonging to Joseph Crangle, the Buffalo Democratic chairman who was trying

to put together a movement that would carry the nomination to Humphrey. Jackson's man Bob Keefe was there;
so were Udall's men Jack Quinn and Mark Shields; and
McGovern's aide Alan Baron, who ironically had been the
man who helped Carter's two aides get in to see the then
McGovern pollster Pat Caddell back in 1972, when they
were trying to convince McGovern to pick Carter for Vice
President. (This time, Baron was not seeking to aid Carter
but to bury him.)

"It was a meeting to take inventory," according to one
of the participants. "To see where things stand, where
there were holes for Carter." A second meeting took place
one week later in Baron's apartment. All but Shields attended, plus several newcomers: Representative Paul
Simon (who was working with Crangle on the Humphrey
project); Arnie Miller, formerly an aide to Representative
Allard Lowenstein and later a McGovern aide; and Steve
Ross, a political adviser who was with Humphrey in 1972
and Jackson in 1976.

They gave advice to Crangle on how he could set up a
boiler room operation for Humphrey and where to go
looking for uncommitted delegates and Humphrey support. (A boiler room operation of about thirty people was
eventually set up.)

They suggested people for Crangle to hire, and talked
about how some Humphrey contributors ought to back
Udall in Ohio. The machinists' union did.

The ABC people had a few moments of satisfaction in
Rhode Island: an uncommitted slate beat Carter's dele-
gates—largely through the campaign of Jerry Brown. A
two-headed slate favoring Humphrey would result in New
Jersey voters electing more uncommitted delegates than
Carter delegates.

But by then it would be too late.

On St. Patrick's Day, novelist Patrick Anderson was
celebrating, perhaps in part out of his affinity for the Irish,
but probably more because the paperback rights to his
latest book had just been auctioned off for a healthy $250,-
000. His book was *The President's Mistress* and it was
written, according to Anderson, "to entertain the reader
and enrich the author."

Patrick Anderson, a talented writer, was becoming a man of books. He had written *The President's Men,* a well-respected study of the White House staff of Lyndon Johnson; two highly acclaimed novels—*The Approach to Kings* and *Actions and Passions*—and he had ghost-written the Watergate tell-all of ex-Nixonite Jeb Magruder.

Anderson was also known to the Jimmy Carter crowd. At a Washington, D.C., party months ago, Anderson had met two Carter advisers, Peter Bourne and his wife, Mary King. Anderson had worked in Virginia for George McGovern while Bourne had worked with the Veterans Against the War in Vietnam and King had worked actively in civil rights causes, so they had things to talk about. Bourne and King began to tell Anderson how impressive they thought Jimmy Carter was (Bourne earlier had been brought to Georgia by then Governor Carter to set up state drug rehabilitation programs). They told him about how Carter liked to read Dylan Thomas and listen to Bob Dylan. At about that time, *The New York Times Magazine* had been talking to Anderson about doing a piece on a prominent political person—maybe Rockefeller, they said. Anderson countered, how about Carter? The *Times Magazine* agreed and soon Anderson was off to Plains, where he was courted in true Carter style. "I spent the night at Jimmy's home in Plains," Anderson recalled. "I was very favorably impressed."

Anderson's cover story article on Carter appeared in the magazine on December 14, 1975, titled, "Peanut Farmer for President." It reflected the author's admiration of the candidate. "It was certainly a very favorable article," Anderson said. "People much later would come up and tell me that it was that article that turned them on to Carter."

Now, on St. Patrick's Day, with the paperback rights to his latest book safely auctioned, Anderson decided that he could take a rest from his personal writing to devote himself to the politics of 1976. He called Peter Bourne and Mary King and told them to pass the word that he would be willing to do some political writing for Carter if the candidate wished.

It turned out that the Carter people had just made their move on another speechwriter, Robert Shrum, and so nothing was done. But on May 11, almost two months later, after the Shrum fiasco—and after the storm cloud it produced had settled—Jody Powell called Anderson and asked if he was still interested in writing for Carter. Anderson was. He and Powell conferred, and then Anderson drove into Washington, D.C., from his home more than an hour away in the rolling Virginia farmland community of Waterford, to get things settled and meet briefly with Carter. The candidate was in Washington for a Democratic congressional fundraising dinner at the Washington Hilton, and his conversation with Anderson was brief. It occurred in an elevator.

Anderson: "Governor, I hope I can help you."

Carter: "Well, we'll have some fun."

Anderson caught up with the Carter campaign on election night in Michigan and rode the candidate's plane out to Oregon to politick the West Coast. One of his first tasks was to help Carter with a speech he was giving in the heart of Jerry Brown country—an address to the California State Legislature in Sacramento. Carter entered the capitol by walking through the old wing, through the door where the sign is posted warning that the building is not structurally sound and that people enter at their own risk. His speech contained this central message: "If I had to sum up in one word what this campaign is all about, that word would be faith."

Another early task of Anderson's was to write a speech on conservation and the environment for Carter in Oregon, a truly independent and environment-minded state. Anderson soon discovered that traveling with the candidate was not the best place to write an issue-oriented speech. The campaign suffered from a lack of research at hand; there was Anderson, sitting just a few seats away from the candidate (who was busy reviewing memos and giving interviews), and he was unable to find out just what the candidate had been saying on the environment and just what new positions had been recommended. Someone in Atlanta had that information but it was difficult if not impossible to pass the detailed issue material rapidly to a speechwriter traveling with Carter. Anderson wound up going home to work on the speech. Anderson was well into the writing when the Carter strategists changed their minds. Carter already had the environmentalist vote in Oregon, they figured; but he needed to go after the business people. "No need to antagonize the business community with more conservation stuff," said one Carter official. Anderson was told to forget about the speech. "I was getting a little depressed," Anderson recalled. "I felt I wasn't doing much to help the campaign."

At noon on Wednesday, May 26—the day after the primaries in Oregon and five other states—Jody Powell telephoned Patrick Anderson's home in rustic Waterford, Virginia. "You've got to come back," Powell, who was in New York, said. "We've lost our theme. The thing is adrift. You've got to come back and write a new speech."

Powell and Patrick Caddell felt that the soft-on-issues stuff was crippling Jimmy Carter. Back in Atlanta, Hamilton Jordan was less concerned. But he was content to leave the issue decision-making up to others, and so it was that Powell put out his call for Anderson.

Within a couple of hours, Patrick Anderson was driving in his well-worn, well-rusted old Buick convertible along the highway that goes through Leesburg and to Washington's National Airport. Ideas came to him as he drove and he began scribbling notes on a pad at his side as he sped toward the airport.

"I see an America that . . ." Anderson wrote on his pad and continued it with a visionary ideal of the future. "I see an America . . ." he wrote again and he added another visionary goal.

The speech was good. Impressive.

William Safire would later write that the "I see an America" construction was nothing new—that it had been written by him for Richard Nixon and before him it had been used by Franklin D. Roosevelt in 1940, and before him by James Blaine, who was running for President 100 years before Carter, in 1876.

"I don't think I was consciously aware of it having been used before," Anderson said later, laughing. "I thought, as I was driving down that highway, that I had hit on a brilliant new idea."

Anderson caught an Eastern Airlines shuttle to New York and went directly to meet with Powell at the Madison Avenue office of Barry Jagoda, Carter's television adviser. There he turned his scribbled notes into a speech.

Meanwhile, Carter was engaging in a form of rare but essential politicking that night. He had driven from Newark to the Waldorf Towers in New York City, to a meeting he had requested with former Israeli Prime Minister Golda Meir. Carter had met Mrs. Meir when he was in Israel before becoming a candidate for President (Hamilton Jordan's 1972 memo had suggested a visit to the Middle East). Now, at a time when the Carter strategists were very concerned about Carter's ability to win and hold the Jewish vote, the audience with Mrs. Meir was looked on in the Carter camp as a much-needed coup. The former prime minister was sensitive to the fact that she might be used for political purposes. She did not want any photographs taken of her meeting with Carter and would make no statement about it. "It's purely private," her secretary said. But the next day's newspapers still carried photos of Carter leaving the Waldorf Towers after his meeting with Mrs. Meir. And they quoted Carter describing her as "an old friend."

After the meeting, Powell, Anderson, and Jagoda rode in Carter's limousine back to Carter's hotel in Newark. Powell remembered that he had left his briefcase in Jagoda's office, which is in a five-story brownstone. Carter said it would be all right to go there to pick it up. The limousine drove up to the curb and Jagoda, who is in his calmer moments a whirling dervish of activity, burst out the door and raced into the building—just as a neighbor who lives there was walking down the stairs carrying a basket full of laundry with a box of Cheer balanced delicately on top.

"What's the matter, Barry? Running for President?" the neighbor asked.

"No, I'm not," Jagoda replied, and jerking a thumb toward the limousine at the curb he added: "But that guy is." The neighbor peered at the long black car and Jimmy Carter leaned toward the window and waved.

In the limousine, on the way back to Carter's hotel, Anderson handed Carter a copy of the speech he had written and had shown to Jody. Typed across the top was a note:

JODY: HERE ARE SOME IDEAS AND PHRASES THAT GOVERNOR CARTER MIGHT PLAY WITH. I THINK THE IMPORTANT THING IS THAT HE MOVE FROM ANY ATTACK ON THE STOP CARTER MOVEMENT TO A POSI-

TIVE AND PASSIONATE STATEMENT OF HIS VISION OF
THE AMERICAN FUTURE. THIS SHOULD BE INSPIRA-
TIONAL, KENNEDYESQUE IF YOU WILL, BUT I THINK IT
IS WHAT A LOT OF PEOPLE ARE HOPING FOR. PAT.

The speech was the one that became known as Carter's
"vision of America" speech. Carter liked it and used it in
the future on a number of occasions—including as part of
his acceptance speech. This was the core of the message:

I have a vision of an America that is, in Bob Dylan's
phrase, busy being born.

I see an America that is poised not only at the brink
of a new century, but at the dawn of a new era of responsive, responsible government.

I see an America that has turned her back on
scandals and corruption and official cynicism and has
finally demanded a government that deserves the
trust and respect of her people.

I see an America with a tax system that does not
cheat the average wage earner and with a government that is responsive to its people and with a system of justice that is evenhanded to all.

I see a government that does not spy on its citizens
but respects their dignity and their privacy and their
right to be let alone.

I see an America in which law and order are not a
slogan but a way of life, because its people have
chosen to bind up their wounds and live in harmony.

I see an America in which your child and my child
and every child, regardless of its background, receives an education that will enable him to develop
to his or her fullest capacities.

I see an America that has a job for every man and
woman who wants to work.

I see an America that will reconcile its need for new
energy sources with its need for clean air, clean water, and an environment we can pass on with pride
to our children and their children.

I see an American foreign policy that is consistent
and generous and openly arrived at, and that can
once again be a beacon for the hopes of the entire
world.

I see an America on the move again, united, its

wounds healed, its head high, an America with pride in its past and faith in its future, moving into its third century with confidence and competence and compassion, an America that lives up to the nobility of its Constitution and the decency of its people.

I see an America with a President who does not govern by vetoes and negativism, but with vigor and vision and positive, affirmative, aggressive leadership.

This is my vision of America. It is one that reflects the deepest feelings of millions of people who have supported me this year. It is from them that I take my strength and my hope and my courage as I carry forth my campaign toward its ultimate success.

This was the "inspirational" and "Kennedyesque" and "positive" and "passionate" statement Anderson had wanted Carter to make. But the writer had set up this message with an introduction that attacked Carter's opponents.

My critics . . . want to stop the people of this country from regaining control of their government. They want to preserve the status quo, to preserve politics as usual, to maintain at all costs their own entrenched, unresponsive, bankrupt, irresponsible political power.

At a labor meeting in Cincinnati, Carter read the speech virtually as Anderson wrote it. But as Carter and Anderson should have expected, reporters covering the event naturally focused their attention on Carter's harsh, name-calling attack on his opponents, rather than the uplift rhetoric Carter and Anderson had wanted.

"We blew it," Anderson said later. "So we did the next best thing, and went with the new vision again." Carter read the vision of America speech again at a gathering in Akron. But after the speech, a reporter asked Carter something about Udall's television ads, and Carter lashed out against the Udall ads, and the vision speech was bumped out of the news for a second day. "The new vision had bombed again," Anderson observed. Eventually Carter got his vision speech into the news. And when the Carter advisers decided to buy five minutes of nighttime television on all three networks for Sunday, June 6, the "I see an America . . ." theme was a strong part of the message. It was delivered by Carter in a setting unlike his previous television ads; it was not Carter talking while on his farm or politicking with voters; it was just Carter sitting in front of a bare backdrop, staring at the television camera, giving a speech. It was costly, and it was not one of Carter's most impressive campaign tools despite the quality of the words Carter was saying.

Much later, when Carter, Powell, and Anderson were lunching at the Carter house in Plains, the former governor turned to his press secretary and said: "The thing Shrum didn't like about me—one of the things Schrum didn't like about me—is that I always wanted to change and rewrite his speeches. Pat's the only writer I've ever used who didn't get his feelings hurt when I changed things."

May 25/Oregon Plus Five

The Western Forestry Center is a magnificent, modern wood-and-glass structure that sits in the midst of the great stands of Douglas firs outside Portland. Jimmy Carter's motorcade pulls up to the door at lunchtime and the candidate, beaming as always, emerges and handshakes his way inside. This is a Carter fundraising luncheon and the candidate himself is the drawing card. "It would be suicidal if I was to say one thing in one state and another thing in another," Carter says during his luncheon address. "If anyone would play a tape showing I'd made different statements in different states, I'd be proven a liar. I'd have to pull out of the race"—he pauses—"almost."

Carter is pleased to note that the large and airy room is virtually filled with about 200 people. But, in fact, it is a paper crowd. There just had not been enough tickets sold for the event and so many of the audience were recruited at the last minute to attend the Jimmy Carter campaign luncheon free of charge.

Oregon was just one of six primaries being held on May 25. But it was the only one that was being vigorously contested. The two prime candidates on the ballot were Jimmy Carter, who was from faraway Georgia but who had a national reputation as the Democratic frontrunner, and Frank Church, who was from neighboring Idaho—so close a neighbor, in fact, that there are parts of eastern Oregon which are fed by Boise television stations and have come to know Church as well as they know their own senators and congressional representatives.

Church had a national reputation that was well known in Oregon. He was a dove in a state that had produced some of the great antiwar leaders of the United States—the late Senator Wayne Morse was one of only two senaators who opposed the Gulf of Tonkin Resolution, which became the justification for Lyndon Johnson's buildup of the U.S. war effort in Vietnam; its senior senator, Mark Hatfield, was a Republican moderate and staunch opponent of the Vietnam War effort.

Other primaries being held on May 25 offered little contest. In the West, there was Idaho, where Church would win overwhelmingly. And there was Nevada, which has so many economic, geographical, and personal ties to California that Brown would win easily.

Las Vegas. Pir Marini of the Thunderbird Lounge is looking splendid in his white-on-white suit, and, as the candidate walks into the auditorium rally, he strikes the piano keyboard with what he considers an appropriate theme: "What the World Needs Now Is Love Sweet Love." Later he says, "It was my own idea. Did you like it?"

The music was appropriate. For "love" is a dominant theme of the standard Carter campaign speech. The former Georgia governor tells voters at every stop that he expects to be a good President because of the "intimate personal relationship" that he has established "with each and every one of you" during his campaign swings throughout the country. And he has carefully chosen as the closing line of his speech the message that what the United States needs is "a government that is as good, honest, decent, truthful, capable . . . and filled with love . . . as the American people are."

In the Southeast, on May 25, there were Tennessee, Kentucky, and Arkansas, where Carter would win by huge proportions.

Only Oregon offered a true contest.

Mickey Kantor, campaign manager of Brown for President, was at home and in bed at midnight when the telephone rang. It was his boss, the candidate, calling. Jerry Brown was in the East, where it was 3:00 A.M., and he was up and awake and thinking politics—Oregon primary politics. Brown needed some answers. "What is the situation and the law for write-ins in Oregon?" Brown asked.

Kantor recalls that he gave Brown some general, factual answers. "No, that's not good enough," Brown replied with the clear hint of annoyance in his voice, according to Kantor. "We've got to be specific. We've got to know all the details. We've got to know if we need computer mailings and how to go about them. We've got to know just how we can tell every Oregonian precisely how he can vote for Jerry Brown."

Brown was upset and Kantor says he had a right to be. The Brown forces were about to mount a difficult write-in effort in Oregon, where Brown had gotten into the race too late to get on the ballot. "We had been at it up there only thirty-six hours and we didn't have the detailed information for Jerry," Kantor recalled. "But he was right. We couldn't afford a single delay or a single error. We only had nine days to do everything."

Kantor hung up the phone after finishing his talk with Brown and immediately called the campaign's computer specialist, Frank Tobe, at his hotel in Oregon. Tobe was not in his room, but he had left word of his whereabouts. It was after midnight and he was still in the offices of an Oregon computer company, checking out procedures. Different counties had rules for just what they would accept as a valid write-in vote—"Brown" or "Jerry Brown" or "Brown for President," etc. The Brown campaign needed a computerized mailing to tell each voter just how to write in Brown in his precinct.

The Jerry Brown write-in effort in Oregon was for real. It was a skilled, computer-age effort that was attempting to capitalize on Brown's extensive West Coast press notices and appeal, realizing that the drive was bound to suffer from the last-minute nature of it all and the fact that many people just did not perceive Brown as a genuine presidential contender—although his Maryland victory did much to compensate for the latter.

🇺🇸   🇺🇸   🇺🇸

Betty Roberts, a leading liberal Democrat in the state senate, was one of the Carter co-chairpersons in Oregon; Fred Heard, a leading conservative Democrat (a converted Republican) in the state senate, was the other.

Together they gave Carter the political contacts and philosophic diversity that were definitely helpful in that beautiful, green, independent-minded state. But what they did not bring the Carter campaign was a smooth-running operation; it was the sort of thing the Carter brass had found in most of the states where they opted for using established state politicians to head their effort rather than importing someone of unknown political reputation but known organizing skills, such as Tim Kraft in Iowa and Pennsylvania, Chris Brown in New Hampshire, and Phil Wise in Florida.

Two weeks before the Oregon election, a Carter official came into the state and was shocked by what he later termed "a real lack of organization—people who should have been contacted, including name Democrats, just had not been called; there just were no good lists."

At one point Hamilton Jordan called a leading Carter official in California, Rodney Kennedy-Minott, and asked him to get some California volunteers up to Oregon to help campaign. Kennedy-Minott did, and he showed up himself to help with some of the last-minute fundraising. "I asked for the names of the potential donors—they handed me a shoebox," he said. "It was full of cards, but there were no notations as to who had been called already and who had not. So I just took the cards and began calling."

Several weeks earlier, the Carter strategists had looked confidently ahead to Oregon. Early in May, the *Portland Oregonian* had published a poll showing Carter cruising ahead of the pack with 32 percent. Trailing were noncandidates Humphrey (15 percent), Kennedy (10), Church (8), Udall (7), and Jackson (5).

But that was before Church and Brown had scored their upset victories in Nebraska and Maryland. It was before Carter's scare in Michigan. And it was before Brown had begun his write-in effort in Oregon.

Carter had planned to fly home from the West Coast to rest in Plains on the weekend before the Oregon primary. But on Thursday, Carter's strategists told the governor to change his plans, and then they announced to reporters traveling with Carter that the candidate would remain in the West throughout the weekend to campaign, primarily in Oregon. Jody Powell, and later Carter himself, unabashedly told the reporters that the reason Carter had changed his plans was that things were looking even more promising for Carter than they had anticipated, and they wanted to capitalize on this good fortune. They said they had learned of this new prosperity from a poll by Patrick Caddell. They flatly refused to release the figures of the Caddell poll, though they were willing to talk about it. "Our political strength is much greater than we had anticipated," Carter said, strolling the aisle of his chartered jet and explaining the schedule change to reporters. "We discovered a much more likely prospect of picking up delegates . . . than we had anticipated. . . . The poll shows I'm in a good position in Oregon."

It was much the same language that Jody Powell had used the night before in talks with reporters. And it simply was not true.

In fact, Caddell's secret poll had shown that Carter's lead had slipped dangerously—and that there was now a real possibility that Carter might suffer the political humiliation of finishing third to a write-in effort, the last-minute effort of Jerry Brown. The figures of the Caddell poll were subsequently back East in *Newsday* that Saturday, and they were subsequently confirmed by Caddell after the Oregon primary had taken place.

The Caddell poll showed that Carter's lead over Frank Church had plunged to just two points, 24 to 22, among the candidates whose names were listed on the Oregon ballot. And when the poll-takers had added the name of Brown to the list, the results had been even more startling: Brown finished first with about 24 percent, with Carter a couple of percentage points behind and Church trailing Carter by several more points. The Carter officials realized that there was no foolproof way of measuring anticipated votes for a write-in effort, because the mere action of putting Brown's name before the people being surveyed gave Brown more of an advantage than he would have in the voting booth, where his name would not be listed, and where the voter would have to go through a rather involved write-in procedure to cast a ballot for Brown. Still, the Carter strategists were clearly concerned about what the results showed. None of this justifies the unprofessional efforts of Carter and Powell and others to mislead reporters about the nature of their poll.

The episode of Oregon and the poll was one of the few times Carter and his advisors yielded to temptation and compromised integrity in the swirl of campaign pressure. Just why they acted as they did can be understood, but not justified, by recalling what they were going through at that time. After Pennsylvania, it had seemed that they had the nomination won; they had defeated every Democrat in the race. But then came the new faces of 1976— Church and Brown—the crumbling of what had once seemed so safe in Michigan, and now the erosion of their base in Oregon.

"We were all kinds of off balance in that couple of weeks beginning with Maryland and Michigan," Hamilton Jordan said later. "The Maryland thing—I thought we'd do better. And I was really uptight about Michigan. I mean, we'd just come so far and now all this—it seemed like a bad dream. I kept saying to myself, 'This can't be happening. We're not really going down the tube. Not after all this.' But then, every time I got to feeling uneasy during that time and after, I'd always go back to the figures. I'd look at the delegate count and the delegate projections. And then I'd feel better. I got back on my feet mentally. I knew the numbers were there. I knew we'd be all right."

What Jordan did on those days when he was feeling depressed about what was happening to his campaign was go over to his locked files and pull out a memo dated March 18, 1976, which was from him to Carter.

The memo contained a section on "Carter Delegate Projections." Jordan and Carter's brilliant young delegate coordinator, Rick Hutcheson, had put together a set of projections that Jordan said in the memo were "realistic and, if anything, conservative." Jordan's memo listed low and high estimates for each state. The figures gave Carter a total low projection of 969 delegates by the end of the last round of primaries on June 8 and a high of 1,509— four more than were needed to win the nomination.

The March 18 memo was based on an erroneous assumption: that Jackson would probably stay in the race until the end (in 1972 he had, after all, stayed in so stubbornly and for so long in his winless effort) and that Udall and Wallace would stay in for a while but would eventually fold. It turned out that Udall stayed but Jackson pulled out early, as did Wallace.

The Jordan memo had some projections which proved too low, some which proved too high, and many which were right on target. "It was those figures that gave me faith in May," Jordan recalled. "Every time I got worried, I went back to the numbers."

THE RESULTS: *The numbers in Oregon did not bring Carter a victory, but at least they saved him from disgrace. Church won with 34.6 percent of the vote. But Carter beat back the Brown write-in by 27.4 percent to 23.3. Idaho went to Church, as he beat Carter by 80.3 percent to 12.1. Nevada went to Brown, 52.8 percent to Carter's 23.3 and Church's 9.0.*

But Carter more than offset these defeats with decisive victories in three delegate-rich border states. He beat Wallace in Tennessee, 78.0 percent to 11.0; he beat Wallace in Kentucky, 59.3 to 16.9; and he beat Wallace and Udall in Arkansas, 62.8 to 16.8 to 7.5, respectively. Carter won 90 delegates in these three states, plus 20 in his defeats in the West, giving him a total of 110 for the day, compared to Church's 30 delegates won that day and Brown's 13. As Jordan said, it was the delegate numbers in that month of May and on. May 25th in particular that cushioned the crushing fact that Carter had fared poorly in the only real contest of the day, in Oregon.

Jimmy Carter was weak out West. He learned that in Oregon, where he had campaigned hard, passing up a weekend at home to politick, but was lucky to escape the humiliation of showing third behind a Jerry Brown write-in. In fact, he would go the entire primary season without ever winning in the West. He took Texas away from Lloyd Bentsen in a strong showing in that southwestern state. But he went on to suffer defeats in Oregon, Idaho, Nevada, Montana, and California. It was a matter that would worry his campaign advisers throughout the primary season and into the fall presidential campaign as well.

Jimmy Carter was in New York City on May 25, the night of the elections in Oregon and five other states. It was careful planning that brought him there. Carter was in the East because, among other reasons, Oregon is in the West; he wanted to make sure that the television stations that night and the news stories in the morning would reflect as heavily as possible on Carter's victories in the border states, softening the blow of the defeats that were to come in Oregon, Idaho, and Nevada.

As it turned out, the emphasis on the television networks and in the newspapers the next morning reflected the fact that Carter had won three out of six rather than the fact that Carter had been beaten in the only real contest of the night. Had Carter stayed in Oregon to wring his hands and fret, the balance of the stories just might have shifted.

"We got by a lot lighter on the Oregon primary night than I was expecting," Hamilton Jordan conceded later. "I was afraid we would get hit over the head about that Oregon defeat. But the way it was played, it came out okay."

In his suite at the New York Sheraton, Carter was watching the returns on television and talking with his aides. One reporter, David Nordan, political editor of the *Atlanta Journal,* was permitted by Carter to sit in the suite and watch the governor watching the returns. An aide told Carter that Ted Kennedy had said earlier in the day that Carter was "intentionally . . . indefinite and imprecise" on issues.

"A hint of anger" flashed in Carter's eyes, according to Nordan, as the former governor replied: "I'm glad I don't have to depend on Kennedy or Hubert Humphrey or anyone like that to put me in office."—pause—"I don't have to kiss his ass."

Indeed, he did not. Carter had just summed up in a single phrase a strategy that had once taken his campaign manager seventy pages to explain in a 1972 memo, and which had taken pundits many column inches to analyze. Jimmy Carter was done with the May primaries. He was in the home stretch of a race that he had been running everywhere. He was winning some and losing some, but winning delegates all the while. He figured that if he finished the primaries on June 8 with 1,200 delegates, the delegates he needed to finally reach the 1,505 required for the nomination would eventually drift his way; he would be so far ahead of the rest of the candidates that they would have nowhere else to go. They would come to him. He did not have to kiss anyone's ass.

June 1/The Little Three

Late in May, Jimmy Carter conferred by telephone on a couple of occasions with one of his prime political advisers. The conversations led Carter to make two key changes in his campaign schedule.

"Everybody here in Rhode Island is going to vote for you," Rosalynn Carter told her husband in one of the telephone conversations. "But they're going to vote for you in November. I think you ought to come up here and create some enthusiasm . . . so people will come out and vote in the primary."

"We can carry South Dakota," Rosalynn reported to her husband in the other phone conversation. "We've got great support . . . people are working day and night . . . but they've never even seen you or met you." If he would just touch down in South Dakota once or twice, it could make a tremendous difference, Rosalynn told her husband.

On both occasions, Carter took his wife's advice and had his schedule changed to include quick visits to Rhode Island and South Dakota. The moves proved to be important, and as other members of the campaign staff would say later, they proved to be correct. Carter and his staff had been looking past June 1 and June 8, when the primary season would wind up with three big state elections: California, Ohio, and New Jersey. But the three small state elections on June 1—in Rhode Island, South Dakota, and Montana—had to be dealt with first. The amount of delegates they would pump into the overall nomination process would be few. But the damage that could be done by suffering severe setbacks just a week before the three big elections of June 8 could prove substantial. And this is why, most of all, Carter took his wife's advice and made stops in Providence and Sioux Falls and Rapid City.

"Jimmy would always tell me, 'If you go to something

that's been planned for you, you'll never get a true feeling for what the situation in that area is really like.'" Rosalynn Carter said as she reconstructed the phone conversations she had with her husband back when she was in Rhode Island and South Dakota. "He'd say, 'If you get to the shopping centers and to factory shift lines, that's where you'll learn what people are really thinking.' And that's what I tried to do."

Rosalynn Carter campaigned across the country throughout much of 1975 and 1976 to help her husband win the Democratic presidential nomination. But rarely during the campaign was she at her husband's side. The Carters figured that they could cover more ground if they were in two places at the same time—Jimmy in one, Rosalynn in the other—and that is how they worked it for more than a year.

Over the years, Carter had come to greatly respect his wife's political judgments and instincts—"She has very good judgment of people in politics," he once told a member of his campaign staff. And in the 1976 campaign, Rosalynn Carter was a major asset to her husband's drive for the Presidency—and, in her own way, an aggressive campaigner as well.

It was not always that way.

Rosalynn Carter is a soft-spoken woman, very attractive, with dark hair and dark almond eyes, but also very shy. It is said that when he ran for governor in 1966, Carter had to push his wife to get her to campaign for him, coach her in such basic political arts as how to hand out a brochure on a street corner. One of Carter's deputy press secretaries, Betty Rainwater, recalls that years later Carter gave her similar instruction. "I was just sort of wall-flowering it," she recalled. "You know, standing on a corner and holding out brochures for someone to take if they wanted them. And Jimmy showed me how to do it in a pleasant but more forceful manner. He told me, 'You know, my wife, Rosalynn, used to have the same problem. But don't be afraid. She learned, and you can too.'"

Actually, Rosalynn had been used to getting things done, but in her own subtle way. Three years younger than Carter, she had been the best friend of Carter's sister, Ruth, and so she was in and out of the Carter house outside Plains frequently.

But she and Carter never went out on a date until

Carter came home from Annapolis for a brief stay. In his book, Carter talks as if it were really his doing, how he and a friend had asked Rosalynn and Ruth for a movie date. Rosalynn recalls that it just did not happen that easily. "I had hung around his house for a month getting him to notice me," she said. "And he didn't ask me out until two nights before he was going back to Annapolis. Well, the next night he already had a date with another girl. But we had kind of a late date that second night. . . ."

Carter recalls telling his mother after their first date, "She's the girl I want to marry." Rosalynn recalls that when Carter asked her to marry him, she turned him down. "I was just eighteen and a sophomore in college," she said. "I was so young. I just wasn't thinking like that." That following February, she accepted.

When his father died, Carter wanted to give up his naval career and settle in Plains to run the family warehouse, which was just a very small business operation at the time. This provoked the first serious argument between Carter and his wife, Carter says.

"That's true," Rosalynn Carter says. She just did not want to give up the life that had taken her to Hawaii and New York and Connecticut and move back into the lap of the family in Plains. "I was young," she said. "I had been traveling, I had three babies. I think I liked the independence. It's hard to recall now just how it was then, but I think I thought that if I came home, I'd be more restricted . . . my mother, Jimmy's mother." She hastened to add: "I never did regret it, though."

During their first year back in Plains, Carter ran the entire business himself. "He kept the books, he loaded the goods, everything," says Mrs. Carter. But as the business grew, Rosalynn Carter assumed the bookkeeping duties for the Carter family operation. "Looking back on it," she said, "I can see where our give and take developed. I kept the books in the warehouse and he'd come in and ask my advice. He'd ask me, 'Should we do this or should we do that to make more money? Should we get more peanuts, sell corn?' That sort of thing."

But keeping books in a warehouse and politicking in a campaign were two very different things.

Edna Langford is a close friend and political traveling companion of Rosalynn Carter's. They met back when Carter was running for governor and the Langfords came to work on the campaign. The Carters' son, Jack, and the Langfords' daughter, Judy, met in the campaign and eventually married. Mrs. Langford recalls how difficult campaigning used to be for Rosalynn Carter.

"In the 1970 campaign, we set up a meeting over in the bank building in Calhoun and about fifty or sixty women were there in the audience," she said. "And when Rosalynn came in the back door and when she walked out front, her eyes got big and kind of fearful and she looked at me horrified and said, 'Do I have to make a speech?' She said she'd never made speeches before except to her missionary society and her garden club."

In April 1975 Rosalynn Carter and Edna Langford set out from Atlanta by car to work the Florida panhandle—to politick for a presidential primary that was almost one year away. "Jimmy just told us to go to Florida and make friends," Langford recalled. "Make friends in George Wallace's territory and show them that there was an alternative. So that's what we did."

In Tallahassee, they contacted Rosalynn's former fifth-grade teacher, Eleanor Ketchum, who had just been named Florida's Woman of the Year. "I said, let's have a get-together with thirty or forty of the active women in Tallahassee," Langford said. "Well, she sent out 400 invitations—and 308 of them came."

From there, the two women set out on a lonely trek through the small towns of the Florida panhandle, the most conservative, the most redneck, the most Alabama-like Wallace country in Florida. Quincy. Marianna. Bonifay. Chipley. They would hit the town and walk in unannounced to the local newspaper office and the local radio station and try to get Mrs. Carter interviewed and get her picture taken. "Sometimes nobody would know anything about Jimmy," Langford recalled. "So if we were told by someone in the newspaper to come back later, of course we didn't have time to wait around for that because we had to go to the next place. So I would say, 'Wouldn't you like to get somebody to come out and take her picture—maybe take a picture with Mrs. Carter and you?'" And often they would, and then it would lots of times wind up on the front page. "We'd always have

Rosalynn holding a Jimmy Carter bumper sticker, so people would get to know his name even if they didn't read the story. And at the radio stations, if the boy didn't know what to ask, sometimes we'd write down the questions for him.

"Once, we went into one newspaper office and there was only one person inside. It was about nine-thirty in the morning and so she called her editor—woke him up—and asked him what should she ask Rosalynn. Well, the editor said to ask her how she would restructure Vietnam. Restructure Vietnam! And so she did, and Rosalynn answered: 'I don't know anything about restructuring Vietnam.' "

In Panama City, the two women were eating in a restaurant near the beach when Rosalynn looked over and saw a car with a press sign on it. Then she saw another. "Where are the press people?" she asked. Edna Langford spotted a Rotary Club sign, and the two women got up from their table and left—even though they had just ordered their meal. (They paid the bill.)

"I just went in and went up to the president of the club," said Langford. "And I said to him, 'I'm Edna Langford from Georgia and my daddy was a Rotarian and my husband is a Rotarian and I've got someone here who I think you'd like to meet.' And he was delighted and we both spoke before the group. . . . And there was a woman there from a newspaper with a camera and she put it in the paper."

There were times during the campaign that Rosalynn Carter even advised her husband on the handling of thorny issue questions. For example, in March 1976 she let him know that he had botched the question on home mortgages and tax reform in Massachusetts and that he was continuing to botch the issue every time it was raised.

"I called him from Florida about that home mortgage exemption," she said. "Everywhere I went I was getting questions on what Jimmy had said about [perhaps eliminating] that home mortgage exemption. Jimmy would always answer the questions by going into all the details of how it was going to be part of his comprehensive tax-reform program . . . and it just wasn't getting through. I told him he did not have to do all that. Just be brief. Say, 'I'm not going to raise your taxes' and explain that no tax-reform proposal of his would cost them more money."

There was a time, in Rhode Island, when the Carter people figured they would take the contest without too much difficulty. But then the new faces of 1976, Brown and Church, moved in. Both had scored impressive wins over Carter and together they had seriously shaken Carter's once-comfortable view of Rhode Island.

On the Wednesday before the Rhode Island election, Brown's official schedule showed him spending the next three days in California on "state business." But then on Thursday Brown decided to take another gamble, just as he had in Oregon—only with less time before the election to do his work. He announced that he would fly to Rhode Island and spend three days campaigning for the uncommitted slate, spending some $25,000 on a last-minute radio, television, and newspaper advertising campaign.

Along with his extensive media campaign, Brown put together a hurried, but effective, organization that managed to round up a group of uncommitted delegates he could endorse. Brown and his people worked the small state vigorously, stumping for the uncommitted slate, and had considerable success in getting their message across.

Church, meanwhile, was helped by three of his Capitol Hill colleagues—one of them being Mo Udall. Church and Udall had worked out an understanding: Udall would concentrate on beating Carter in South Dakota and would not campaign in Rhode Island, even though he remained on the ballot there and had a slate of delegates pledged to him; Church, meanwhile, would not run in South Dakota. Dennis J. Robert II, Udall's Rhode Island state chairman, was quoted shortly before the campaign as confirming the existence of this meeting of political minds.

The other two Capitol Hill colleagues helping Church were Senator Claiborne Pell and Representative Edward P. Beard. The two men campaigned with Church through the state, helping him with voting groups such as teachers and the elderly. On Sunday, Church announced the endorsement of the officials from three unions: the vice president of the Rhode Island Federation of Teachers, and officials of the United Steelworkers of America and of the barbers' union.

Carter was still considered the favorite right up to election day in Rhode Island, but his lead was viewed as slim, and his concern was sufficiently larger. He took his wife's advice and scheduled a Memorial Day appearance in Providence, to march in a holiday parade and hold a press conference. He left Rhode Island and made two more stops that day—one of them in Rapid City, South Dakota—before turning in for the night in Sacramento.

A few weeks before the South Dakota primary, Pat Caddell's people took a statewide survey and tabulated the results. Just as they had in Oregon, the Carter strategists decided once again—at all costs—to keep the poll results secret. Only this time the Carter people were not afraid of being embarrassed, as they had been in Oregon. Just the opposite. They just did not want Udall to know how well Carter was doing. Jimmy Carter had scored 45 percent, 12 to 13 points better than Mo Udall.

"It was the best kept secret of the primary," Caddell said later. "For us, South Dakota was really part of the Ohio [June] primary. Udall thought he would do well in South Dakota and have something going by the time he hit Ohio. But our poll showed us that those were our kind of farmers. And Udall didn't know it. The Udall people just kept thinking it was in the bag and we didn't tell the reporters or anyone otherwise."

The Carter people were careful; they kept looking nervous about South Dakota, even as they brought Carter into the state twice, Rapid City and Sioux Falls.

THE RESULTS: *In Rhode Island the turnout was small, as Rosalynn Carter had warned, but it was large enough for Jerry Brown. His uncommitted slate upset Carter by a 798-vote margin, 19,035 (31.4 percent) to 18,237 (29.9). Church came in third with 16,423 (27.6). "We gave a home to a lot of people who were homeless," said Brown Campaign Manager Mickey Kantor. "A lot of our people were Jackson people in Rhode Island."*

In Montana, Church easily defeated Carter, who did not try to make it much of a contest, 59.9 percent to 24.8.

In South Dakota, Carter kept Udall's winless streak alive. He beat Udall 24,573 to 20,055—41.1 percent to 33.5. "It took the wind out of Udall's sails," Caddell said. In fact, it did more than that. It gave Frank Church an argument for going into Ohio along with Udall and Carter, rather than letting Udall have a clean shot at trying to knock off Carter in that large midwestern industrial state.

June 8/The Big Three

June 8. It had always been clear that this would be the most important date on the Democratic primary calendar. June 8. A three-alarm climax fight for the presidential nomination—540 delegates on the block in three populous states, California, Ohio, New Jersey. June 8. The date was so well known throughout the primary season that politicians did not refer to it by month or numeral. Some called it "Big Casino." Others called it "The World Series."

Jimmy Carter and his aides had visited California early and had prepared for months—even years—to make that a major fight. California was, after all, the traditional end-of-the-primaries contest, with the convention's largest delegation as its prize. But when Jerry Brown got into the picture, California pretty much got out. The state would go to Brown, it became clear, and the only question was how many of California's 280 delegates could be won by the also-rans. With the delegates now being divided proportionally—no more winner-take-all—it was still possible to finish second and come away with a whopping 100-plus delegates. Possible, but not probable. For Jerry Brown was still rolling along with a record 85 percent popularity figure within his own state. And buoyed by his showings in the East, Brown could demonstrate to his home staters that people in Maryland and Rhode Island had taken him seriously as a presidential candidate and that they ought to as well. Brown figured to own most of California on June 8.

New Jersey, with its 108 delegates, offered a potentially appealing prize. There was an uncommitted state that had the backing of a number of the state's party bosses, and there were internal divisions and uncertainties and a confusing ballot structure and a separate beauty contest and delegate-selection balloting that clouded the outlook in the state.

And there was Ohio, with its 152 delegates, and its large industrial blue-collar and midwestern middle-class Democratic Party. "It became clear by the beginning of May that Ohio was going to be the big windup of the primaries," Hamilton Jordan said. "And that was fine with us."

Patrick Caddell explained why. "Ohio was always our strongest state," he said. "It had a lot of southerners who had settled there and a lot of rural voters. It was not as liberal as the other two states and it had no crossover voting provision." Caddell's organization polled constantly in Ohio, and the results show that Carter was never in trouble in Ohio. He cruised along in the high 40s in the Caddell polls, a lofty position which left him able to look down with amusement at the Punch and Judy performance that was being waged by his opponents.

Mo Udall and Frank Church came roaring into the state in the beginning of June, each suggesting that the other pull out.

Church: "He [Udall] cannot be a viable candidate after having gone so many times to the voters [without winning] —and he must realize that himself. Those who are looking for an alternative candidate in Ohio will have to look for a winner . . . he's had ample opportunity to win." Did Church want Udall to withdraw? "That is a judgment he himself must make. . . ."

Udall: "He hasn't taken my advice [to stay out of Ohio] during this campaign and I'm not likely to take his, . . . I don't think Frank Church should be pronouncing me dead or out of the race. He has 50 to 60 delegates. I have over 300. I expect to win Ohio and go into the convention as a viable candidate. . . . If Carter slips and falters, I'm in a better position than anyone else to get the nomination. I know it's a long shot. I can recognize a long shot as well as anyone else. I look at one every morning when I shave."

California

"I invented it and put it into a system. Five media markets in one day—a record for media politics. I was, and am, quite proud of it."

Kent Brownridge is an artist who works in the medium of message. He is by profession the marketing director of *Rolling Stone*. He is by choice "a politics junkie—a lot of us at *Rolling Stone* are politics junkies." So it is that in the spring of 1976, Kent Brownridge cooked up on Jimmy Carter. His specialty is the media event, and on June 1, 1976, he put on an art show of sorts up and down the state of California.

California is a sprawling state of more than twenty million diverse people who are linked together by a love of the sun, a fondness for the sea, and little else except a tenuous necklace of affiliated and independent television and radio stations. It is a state that is top-heavy with broadcasters and reporters and photographers and camera-people, full-timers and free-lancers, and even media groupies. Candidates can politick and win in California without even shaking a single hand; but they cannot politick and win without holding a single media event.

A media event is a by-product of the performing arts that is often without cultural, social, or even aesthetic value. It is the sort of thing that does not necessarily look impressive in person—it may, in fact, look perfectly ridiculous and may even *be* perfectly ridiculous. But if it guarantees that the candidates will get on television in one of the local news shows that night, then it is good.

Once Jerry Brown said that he would run in California, that traditionally important end-of-the-campaign primary looked a lot less winnable, and therefore a lot less important, to the Carter people. The trick, then, was for Carter to get whatever was going to be his in California with as little expenditure of money—and mostly of the candidate's highly valuable time—in the state as possible. There were, after all, campaigns to be waged in Ohio and New Jersey. So a five-day visit to California was cut down to just two days, and Kent Brownridge had orders to do the best he could.

Brownridge was not a part of the Carter national staff; he was a volunteer who was experienced in politics, a former Californian, and a Carter fan. He boiled a week's worth of publicity into a day's worth of politicking. Yet he says: "I don't think the governor even knows me. I don't think he knows my name."

Brownridge convened a quick school for advance people and trained Carter volunteers in the art of building crowds, screening the people the candidate would spontaneously meet while the cameras were rolling, and, in short, marketing the candidate. Index cards would be prepared, one for each person Carter would meet; flash cards telling him the name of the person, what they were interested in, and at times what to say.

"The thing was we had to hit all of the major media markets in what was really one day's worth of campaign," Brownridge said. "And what we wanted to do was focus on specific issues—show people that he was not wishy-washy on the issues. So we set up an extremely fat schedule. Go into one media market. Do one specific thing tailored to the one issue we wanted to emphasize. And get out."

This was Jimmy Carter's June 1:

7:15 A.M.—*handshaking at Sacramento Municipal Utilities Truck Yard.*

Carter talked about employment. Dozens of workers crowded around and the cameras caught the scene. "We bought out the coffee wagon. Gave free coffee to everyone, and they just crowded around and the governor talked to them. He was a real pro. We gave them a half hour and that was it. Cut it and on to the next place."

7:45 A.M.—*en route to Sacramento Municipal Airport. 8:20* A.M.—*fly to Oakland. 8:55* A.M.—*arrive Oakland. 9:30* A.M.—*tour Alpha Bates Hospital.*

Carter talked about health care. "First he went upstairs, with the cameras following him, to meet some patients who couldn't pay for their bills. We introduced each patient. There was a card for each. [Sample: Patient John Doe. Pneumonia. Illness is not covered by health insurance. Ask: Do you have insurance to cover this illness?] Then he went downstairs to make a statement before all of the press. It was a regular room in the hospital which we'd packed with people in white coats and stethoscopes —so it looked very healthish. . . . It wasn't hard to get them to come. After all, this was big haps for the hospital. If you had a boring job emptying bed pans, then this to you is big time. . . . The press just went bullshit. They'd never seen anything like it before.

"For the patients, we had to find people who could not pay and then we picked people with tubes running out of their noses and all sorts of medical contraptions strapped on their bodies. . . . I know we're taking advantage of people with hardships with what we're doing in a way, but a guy like the governor can do it in good taste."

Upstairs, Carter was led to the bedsides of five patients.

The last patient Carter was scheduled to visit was an elderly lady with tubes in her nose and an intravenous unit in her arm who apparently was so ill that her breathing came in difficult, raspy gasps. She was seemingly unaware of what was going on around her. Carter's television adviser, Barry Jagoda, who is modest in stature and a giant in energy and intensity, took one look at the woman while Carter was still down the hall and ran nervously for the nearest doctor. "Doc, tell me—is she going to die when he gets there?" Jagoda wanted to know, horrible visions clearly running through his head. The doctors assured him she would be all right. But Jagoda wanted to make one final check to satisfy himself. He raced back to the woman. Jagoda, who has dark hair and a full, dark beard, walked to the side of her bed and leaned over. The woman looked up at the swarthy Jagoda, reached her hand toward him, and asked him in a thin wisp of a voice: "Governor Carter?"

Jagoda got Carter downstairs as quickly as possible. He was out the door less than an hour after he had arrived.

10:15 A.M.—*en route to airport. 11:00* A.M.—*fly to Long Beach. 12:30* P.M.—*reception with senior citizens at Bixby Park.*

Carter talked about senior citizen issues. "We had three thousand senior citizens at that park. Three thousand! It's always hard to build a crowd, and when you have a special requirement—that they be old—it's even harder. Well, we made three thousand phone calls. Put out forty thousand leaflets. And we had this little secret—we had buses bring them in, but the buses were kept very carefully hidden [from the press]. . . . And we also gave away a free lunch to anyone who came. That was also a secret. They'll always come out for a free lunch."

1:15 P.M.—*en route to airport. 1:55* P.M.—*fly to San Diego. 2:35* P.M.—*arrive San Diego. 3:05* P.M.—*brief remarks at Mae L. Feaster School.*

Carter talked about education. "Attending were students, parents, and teachers—we got teachers to come who weren't teachers at that school. So it was a little hokey. . . . It was the least successful of our events." This was in part due to the fact that there had been in-fighting between local and traveling Carter staff people. And it was in part due to the booing. It seems that someone had reminded Carter that they were just a few miles north of the Mexican border, and so Carter, who is so fond of showing that he knows Spanish, tried out a few welcoming lines on the crowd. There was silence, and a few boos. Carter thought they hadn't heard him well enough, so he gave his little all-Spanish welcome again. More boos. The advance people had neglected to tell him that this was a conservative, virtually all-white neighborhood area of people who just did not think highly of Chicanos.

3:45 P.M.—en route to airport. 4:20 P.M.—fly to Los Angeles. 4:55 P.M.—arrive Los Angeles airport. 5:40 P.M. —arrive at Martin Luther King, Jr. Hospital dedication.

As the Carter entourage made its way down the state of California, from media event to media event, Patrick Anderson sat in the bus, writing. He had awakened at 3:00 A.M. in his Sacramento hotel with the idea and now, on the bus, he was putting together and polishing a speech for Carter to give at the last stop—a serious and meaningful stop at the end of a contrived-for-the-media day—a speech at a dedication of a wing at the Martin Luther King, Jr. Hospital in Los Angeles.

The speech was not a health-care speech, but a race-relations speech. It was a little bit of Carter's autobiography and a little bit of New South. It was a white southerner paying tribute to a black southerner. A rural Georgian praising the coming of civil rights. "It was the best thing I've ever written for him," Anderson says. It may, in fact, have been the best speech Carter gave in the entire campaign, in content, in delivery (see Appendix). Anderson showed the speech to Carter and Powell at noon and they liked it.

Carter made only one substantive change. Anderson, a northern-thinking liberal, had written a dig at George Wallace: "When I started to run for President, there were those who said I would fail, because there was another governor who spoke for the South, a man who once stood in a schoolhouse door and cried out, 'segregation forever!' "

Carter, a practical southern politician, took a blue-ink pen and shortened the paragraph so it would simply read: "When I started to run for President, there were those who said I would fail because I am from the South."

Powell had the speech typed and distributed to the traveling press corps. In general, traveling press corps provide the nation with a vital and essential service: humbling those who are at the center of, or trying to get to the center of, power. With the writer, Anderson, clearly in earshot, the reporters read over the speech next and began singing, "We Shall Overcome."

In fact, it was an impressive speech.

In his autobiography, in his speeches, and in his interviews, Jimmy Carter made note of the fact that *War and Peace* was one of his favorite boyhood books. He probably never stopped to think of it, but there was much about his California campaign operation that was reminiscent of Tolstoy's classic. Internally, the organization was often at war and seldom at peace; and its leadership ranks alone had more characters than a Russian novel.

All of this is not merely because of the people involved; it is due in large measure to the state in which they operated. California is a beautifully schizoid political place; it is at least two states in one: northern California, which is a world that looks to San Francisco for leadership, and southern California, which revolves around Los Angeles. Statewide campaigns usually find themselves in a northern California versus southern California split, and the Carter campaign was no exception. They had problems putting together a smoothly functioning unit in 1975 and on June 8, 1976, they were still trying to get things organized.

Carter had met Rodney Kennedy-Minott early in his presidential travels, back in 1974 when he was out in Palo Alto doing his work as chairman of the Democratic congressional campaign committee and getting around the country in the process. Carter had grown to like Kennedy-Minott, and so had Hamilton Jordan and the rest of the Carter men. He continued to be close to the candidate and his crew throughout the campaign.

When the Carter campaign set up operations in California in 1975, Kennedy-Minott headed the effort in the north with the title of California Chairperson, and Terry Utterbach was then working as Southern California Coordinator. Technically, according to the Carter staff in Atlanta, Utterbach was under Kennedy-Minott; as Atlanta saw it, Utterbach wanted a larger share of the control, and then he wanted a salary, and soon he was no longer with the Carter organization.

Ben Goddard, a political adviser out of Colorado, was brought in. As the national Carter staff saw it, Goddard had a Number Two role to Kennedy-Minott, but he had the titles Western States Regional Campaign Coordinator and California State Campaign Coordinator, and their roles at times seemed to overlap. Meanwhile, various California political figures began making themselves available to the Carter organization; each sought a prominent role in the decision-making and each sought to advise the candidate on what he ought to do and when and how he ought to do it. State Senator Omer Rains and Los Angeles County Supervisor Ed Edelman were among the California political establishment figures who became active in the Carter campaign. Rains was titled Western States Co-Chairperson; Edelman was Co-Chairperson of the California Carter campaign.

"California was one state Ham [Hamilton Jordan] was intimidated by," said one of Carter's top national campaign officials. "Hamilton kept letting these people join and he kept giving them titles and each thought he was running things. They all fought most of the time and little grass-roots organization developed. They spent their energies on each other."

All of this left Carter and his national staff members in a difficult position. His administrative assistant, Greg Schneiders, was heard on at least one occasion to observe that he had a hard time knowing which advice to follow when one of the California hierarchy was telling him what Carter *had* to do. "I never knew who to listen to in California." Schneiders was quoted as telling a friend.

Consider the night of May 20. Carter had been the guest of honor at a lavish fundraising dinner at the Beverly Hilton Hotel and at 10:30 P.M. he had gone up to his room and was getting undressed for the night when State Senator Omer Rains appeared. He said that a group of Chicanos was waiting downstairs and Carter had to go talk to them, that Carter had not yet met with the Chicanos and it was imperative that he do so. So Carter put his shoes on and went downstairs to see the group.

The Chicanos had a list of questions they wanted answered; Carter gave them a general talk and told them to give him the list and he would have his staff issues people send them the answers. They presented Carter with the list and went on to complain that Carter California official Ben Goddard was not serving Carter well in California—that only State Senator Rains (who had set up the meeting for them) was doing a good job. Meanwhile, Goddard had by chance walked into the room and heard their comments; he walked in because he had been searching for Greg Schneiders to set up a meeting because he wanted to pass the word on to Carter that State Senator Rains and Ed Edelman were not doing their jobs well. Edelman, meanwhile, had cornered Schneiders three times that night to warn him that the other Carter officials had California screwed up. Edelman pressed that Goddard had been allowed to talk to Carter and was certain Goddard was complaining about Edelman; so Edelman said he wanted a chance to talk to Carter to present his side of it. Schneiders relented and scheduled Edelman to ride out to the airport with Carter the next morning.

Late that night, both Goddard and Kennedy-Minott talked to Carter's administrative assistant and expressed concern over what Edelman would have to say to Carter. But when Schneiders told them the conference would be at 8:00 A.M., on the way to the airport, Goddard and Kennedy-Minott were visibly relieved; Edelman will never make it that early, one of them said to the now thoroughly puzzled Schneiders. At 8:00 A.M. the next day, Edelman was nowhere to be found when Carter stepped into his car and left for the airport. (As Edelman later recalled it, the reason he did not show up that morning was that Schneiders had said he would call him the night before to make sure the arrangements were okay. "Schneiders never called," he said. "I tried to reach him but couldn't. I just didn't want to go down there in the morning and look foolish—you know, to try and push my way in.")

People in the California operation were constantly threatening to quit and go public with their dissatisfaction, according to people on the Carter national staff. The clash of personalities in the California Carter campaign continued right up to the end. Just a day before the primary election, in fact, Carter's national finance director, Morris Dees, dismissed Los Angeles attorney and fundraiser

Herb Hafif, who had been involved in a dispute with several Carter staff members for some time, as co-chairperson of Carter's California fundraising committee.

In the end, the Carter campaign in California had more friction than fire. "Perhaps the basic problem was that none of us could make up our minds," Rodney Kennedy-Minott said candidly. "I couldn't and I don't think some in the headquarters in Atlanta could either. After Brown came in, I contacted Hamilton and I said, 'Now I don't think we should make a big effort out here.' And then later, I started getting excited about the way it was looking and I thought we should make the effort. And then, at the end, I know we were right to concentrate on Ohio instead."

"We became mesmerized by the popular vote total," Kennedy-Minott said. "We booked Jimmy into San Francisco and Los Angeles on his last swing out here. I think that was a mistake. Had we booked him into Orange County and the Central Valley, the Sacramento Valley—rural areas—we probably would have picked up some more delegates per district. But we were mesmerized—we succumbed to the lure of all those votes in the LA area."

Beverly Hills. Hundreds of people have paid $100 a plate to attend the Carter fundraiser. The festivities are opened with an invocation from a rabbi. The rabbi takes note during his remarks of the fact that campaign seasons necessarily produce "the painful banalities, the hectoring . . ." by political candidates.

Just before the fundraising dinner, candidate Carter met in a hotel suite with a group of Los Angeles Jewish leaders. There he made some remarks that are unusual when compared with most candidates' standard cocktail party commentary.

"I'm going to tell you something you don't like," Carter said. "I'm a devoted Southern Baptist. There has been a great deal of concern expressed to me by Jewish leaders about my beliefs. . . . I'm a devoted Baptist. . . . I ask you to learn about my faith before you permit it to cause you any concern. . . . There is no conflict between us [concerning the] separation of church and state. . . . I worship the same God you worship."

Carter and his strategists were concerned about the Jewish vote for much of the campaign, and they were especially concerned about it as they worked toward a big finish in Ohio, New Jersey, and California. They had gone to great lengths to set the meeting in Manhattan with Golda Meir and to secure the endorsement of New York City Mayor Abraham Beame.

"One of the leaders of the Jewish Community," Carter later said, ". . . explained to me that they'd been concerned about my stand on Israel, first of all. Then they were concerned about my Baptist beliefs. [Because so many southern rednecks had proved to be hateful anti-Semites.] But they were also concerned about the degree to which I was committed to the Great Society and New Deal programs. Because if there was social unrest . . . intersocietal conflict, quite often the Jewish people were the ones who suffered. Incipient prejudice there—that was something that was explained to me by a professor. I don't know whether it's true or not."

New Jersey

James P. Dugan was spending a four-day weekend of getting-away-from-it-all by sitting in his Sahara Hotel room in Las Vegas wearing a telephone in his ear. He was the chairman of the Democratic Party in New Jersey, and here he was in Las Vegas watching his grand plan for the June 8 primary come apart in his hands. Hubert Humphrey had just let him down by going on television April 29 announcing that he was not going to campaign for the Presidency. Dugan, an erudite and effective party boss, had carefully constructed a slate of big-name delegates .that would be officially uncommitted, but would in fact be backing Humphrey. Then Humphrey had withdrawn and now Congressman Peter Rodino, the state's most prominent Italian-American office holder, and Newark Mayor Kenneth Gibson, the state's most prominent black office holder, were pulling their names off the slate. And Dugan was not happy about the whole thing, and he was having his problems.

"Rodino and Gibson abandoned ship the weekend I was

in Vegas," Dugan recalled. "So there I was in the god-
damned room all weekend talking on the telephone with
Rodino—who always had been a willow in the wind—
and with Gibson. And I was having real problems getting
people to come aboard a sinking ship."

On the fourth and final day of his vacation, Dugan made
it out to the poolside. If he could not cure his troubles, at
least he would try to tan them. He was sitting there reading the *Las Vegas Sun*—"reading all those stories about
the Howard Hughes wills"—when he saw a box that said
that Jerry Brown would be arriving in town to make an
appearance at a function with Nevada's lone congressman,
James D. Santini. This set Dugan to thinking. "We needed
a campaigner—someone to put some excitement into our
race," Dugan said. He contacted Santini's office and found
out that Brown would be arriving at about the same time
that he would be departing, and so a meeting between the
California governor and the New Jersey chairman was set
up for the Las Vegas airport terminal the next day.

The meeting was brief. Dugan told Brown about how
he had put together an uncommitted slate and how its
delegates had been pro-Humphrey. "I'd like to give you
the opportunity of coming into New Jersey," Dugan recalled telling Brown. "But since you've come in late,
you can only do it if you come in support of my uncommitted slate." Brown was interested and the two men
agreed to meet sometime the next week in New Jersey.

It turned out that they met on May 15 at a party Diane
von Furstenburg, the dress designer, threw for the Manhattan cognoscenti. The two men left the party and went
to Brown's room in the New York Hilton. There Brown
said he wanted to come into New Jersey, but that he wanted
to come in and campaign for a de facto Brown slate.
Dugan balked at this.

"No," Dugan recalled saying. "You're not going to get
anything out of New Jersey unless we get our uncommitted
slate in. If we elect them, then you'll get a fair shot at
getting delegates out of the slate."

As Dugan saw it, he had put together an uncommitted
slate and then had it pledged to Humphrey. He felt that
he could not abandon Humphrey because (1) he had
given Humphrey his personal commitment; and (2) "tacti-
cally, we would have looked foolish, starting out uncom-

mitted and then going for Humphrey and then switching
to Brown."

As Dugan remembers it, Brown agreed then to come in
on Dugan's terms, but then—following Brown's impressive
drubbing of Carter in Maryland—the Californian reinsti-
tuted his original demand that the Dugan slate come out
as a Brown slate before he would agree to come in and
campaign for it.

As the Brown camp remembers it, Brown never agreed
to come in on Dugan's original terms.

"We just couldn't go with terms like that," Mickey Kantor, Brown's campaign manager, recalled. "It made us look
poor—lowly."

"So we talked with them again, and Dugan and the New
Jersey people came up with the two-headed monster."

The New Jersey uncommitted slate, put together by
Dugan and headed by Senator Harrison Williams, would
be for Hubert Humphrey and/or Jerry Brown.

Among those pushing the uncommitted slate, however,
was a knowledgeable carpetbagger, Joseph F. Crangle,
Democratic Leader in New York's Erie County (Buffalo),
and one of those who had been at the ABC (Anybody
But Carter) meetings pushing Humphrey.

Carter had the support of one well-known party boss,
Harry Lerner of Essex County (Newark).

Throughout the candidacy of Jerry Brown, people had
speculated that he was really just Hubert's stalking horse
—he would try to create a deadlocked convention; the
convention would turn to Humphrey; then Humphrey
would name Brown as his Vice President. Brown liked
Humphrey and admired many things about him. But he
and his people had strongly rejected the implication that
he was Humphrey's stalking horse. And now, in New Jersey, he had become Humphrey's stablemate.

The Humphrey/Brown stable was bolstered by the return of a campaign warhorse who had seemingly been put
out to political pasture. Edmund G. Brown, Sr.—Pat
Brown—had volunteered to campaign for his son back
in Maryland, but his offer had been spurned. The senior
Brown, former governor of California and the man who
had sent Richard Nixon down to defeat in the 1962 California gubernatorial contest, had reportedly heard the
thanks-but-no-thanks not from his son, but from his son's
campaign manager, Mickey Kantor. But in New Jersey, a

RUNNING FOR PRESIDENT

Paul Bereswill/*Newsday*

Governor Jimmy Carter of Georgia.

Dick Yarwood/*Newsday*

Jimmy Carter talks with reporters at a press conference during the 1976 Democratic National Convention.

Dick Yarwood/*Newsday*

Democratic staffers Barry Jagoda (left) and Greg Schneiders (right) in the Carter press room.

Dick Yarwood/*Newsday*

Hamilton Jordan, Carter's campaign director, talks on the phone.

Paul Bereswill/*Newsday*

Jimmy Carter arrives in New York for the 1976 Democratic National Convention. Just to his right is New York Mayor Abe Beame.

Jimmy Carter on his way to address the California delegation to the Democratic convention. With him are Governor Jerry Brown (left) and Senator John Tunney of California.

Press Secretary Jody Powell.

Dick Yarwood/*Newsday*

Carter pollster Pat Caddell.

Henry Mills

Gerald Rafshoon, Carter's media adviser.

Dick Yarwood/*Newsday*

Dr. Walter Stapleton, Billy Carter, Sybil Carter, and Jimmy's sister Ruth Stapleton in their hotel suite in New York City. Dr. and Mrs. Stapleton wear their convention ID cards.

Just before he makes his acceptance speech, Jimmy Carter gets a kiss from his wife. Daughter Amy looks on.

Dick Kraus/*Newsday*

Dick Kraus/*Newsday*

The entire Carter clan and assorted Mondales wave to the packed hall at Madison Square Garden as the Democratic convention draws to a close.

Joe Dombroski/*Newsday*

Jimmy Carter and Walter Mondale acknowledge cheers at Madison Square Garden. Their wives and Amy Carter are behind them.

William Senft/*Newsday*
Jimmy Carter and his wife Rosalynn waving to the crowd at
Schuetzen Park, North Bergen City, N. J.

Stan Wolfson/*Newsday*

Jimmy Carter, with coat over his shoulder, shaking hands after his speech at Brooklyn College.

Jimmy Carter speaks to a crowd from a platform alongside his campaign train during a whistle stop at Trenton, N. J.

Dick Kraus/*Newsday*

Dick Yarwood/*Newsday*
Jimmy Carter and his grandson Jason.

Dick Yarwood/*Newsday*

Press Secretary Jody Powell and his aide Betty Rainwater.

Carter's campaign director, Hamilton Jordan.

Dick Yarwood/*Newsday*

Dick Yarwood/*Newsday*

Miss Lillian Carter talks to the press.

Amy Carter with her father, Jimmy, and mother, Rosalynn.

David Pokress/*Newsday*
Gerald Ford takes a last look at Washington D.C., the city
he worked in for 28 years. *Marine One,* the President's
helicopter, passes over the Capitol building.

Dick Kraus/*Newsday*

James Earl Carter, Jr. is sworn in by Chief Justice
Warren Burger.

The Carter family walks along the parade route after the
swearing-in ceremonies. Left to right: Grandson Jason, 15
mos., held on shoulders by his father, Jack; Jimmy Carter;
his son, Chip, and wife, Caron; Amy and Rosalynn Carter.
At right is secret serviceman.

Joe Dombroski/*Newsday*

state big on the boss system and old politics, Pat Brown was more than welcome. He was wanted. And he came back to stump for his son (and Humphrey).

Late in the campaign, Dugan and Jerry Brown were sitting in a car in Trenton.

"How did my father do campaigning here?" the young governor asked.

"Great—a lot of people think he should be the candidate," Dugan joked.

Later, Dugan elaborated on the role of Pat Brown. "The truth is, he went over like gangbusters. He was terrific. He went to Atlantic City and he did a fundraiser and he worked the boardwalk, and he went and spoke before the county pols, he spoke opposite one of Jimmy Carter's relatives, his wife Rosalynn or his sister. And he went over great."

Looking back, Dugan figures that Humphrey was both a plus and a minus in the New Jersey primary. "He helped us, but he also hurt us," Dugan said. "He hurt us because of that April 29th thing of his. He made four or five appearances in the state, and there would be times when Hubert would be standing next to me and he would make a statement to reporters that he was not a candidate. And then the reporters would turn to me and ask me, and I would say that he was going to be the next nominee and the next President.

"But Jerry Brown was all plus. He added that degree of excitement. He was the alternative to all the pols. A very electric candidate. Young, good looking. He takes a different view of politics and he does not make the classic political speech. He was very effective."

Candidates campaign in New Jersey by making sure they get on television in Philadelphia and New York City. These are the stations that serve the south and the north, respectively, in that strange large industrial state-without-television. It is this televisionless fact of life that has made New Jersey politicians all the more dependent on strong party machines. The lack of television may have hurt political independents and challengers, but it has been a boon to bosses.

(A quick digression: There was a time years ago when Channel 13 was serving New Jersey on a commercial basis. In 1957, Democrat Robert Meyner was running in the gubernatorial election against Republican Malcolm Forbes, and he purchased the hour from 10:00 to 11:00 P.M. for a big windup to his campaign. Forbes, concerned that he would need a rebuttal, purchased the block of time immediately following Meyner. But after fifty-five minutes of his commercial, Meyner signed off with a thank you, the Star Spangled Banner was played, and for the last five minutes of his time, Meyner showed just the test pattern. Most viewers figured that the station had gone off the air. They turned off their television sets and went to bed, leaving a furious Forbes to beam his rebuttal to darkened homes.)

Carter was scheduled to leave New York City by train and go to Philadelphia—to make a time-consuming stop for a press conference—before doubling back to Trenton to get on with his genuine New Jersey politicking. But in New Jersey, Phil Wise, a young Plains, Georgia, man who had become in this campaign a savvy state coordinator and political operator, was more than a bit perturbed about the scheduling of that Wednesday. The Carter schedulers had booked the candidate into Trenton at 2:00 P.M.—after the Philadelphia media stop—to talk with government workers at the state capitol. No good, said Wise; it has to be lunchtime so Carter can pull an audience from among state workers who are out strolling the capitol lawn. Wise wanted the Philadelphia stop scratched. The Carter men were assured by politicians wise in the ways of the Philadelphia media that the television stations would gladly come up to Trenton to cover Carter. So the Philadelphia press conference was cancelled and the candidate went directly to Trenton—and only one Philadelphia TV station showed up.

"The boss was pretty mad about that one," a Carter aide later acknowledged. Did Carter bawl out anyone on the staff or raise his voice in anger? "No," the aide said. "When he gets mad he gets very, very, very quiet. And he just glares right through you."

Southern New Jersey, the suburbs of Philadelphia, and the farm areas were Carter country. "But the further north we went, the harder it was for us," Wise said. "These were the areas to the north that were heavily settled with ethnic groups, Catholics, et cetera."

Carter continued to have problems with the Catholic and Jewish voters. Some Catholics were unhappy with his failure to come out for strong antiabortion measures. And both the Catholics and the Jews were still distrustful of this politician who would discuss so openly his personal religious convictions. But it was not until the primary campaign was over that the public had one of its most fascinating glimpses of the religious side of Jimmy Carter.

June 19. Jimmy Carter is preaching.

He is standing on an auditorium stage, before some 2,000 predominantly white Christian laymen, under a huge banner that reads "WHO'S IN CHARGE?" (there is a small cross painted in the center of the question mark). The man who is to be the Democratic nominee for President is preaching.

"The biggest blessing we have is our belief in Christ," Carter is saying. "It gives us an unchanging core around which our lives can function."

It is Saturday, midday, and Jimmy Carter has come to this national gathering of the Disciples of Christ in the Purdue University auditorium in Lafayette, Indiana, to give a speech that is more evangelical than political. The Disciples of Christ is not his church, but it is the church of Charles Kirbo, his closest adviser. He had agreed about a year ago (before he was the Democratic frontrunner) to address this gathering that is the Department of Church Men, Division of Homeland Ministry, "Sessions '76 Program."

The program for the day had begun with music—a modern piano piece and a song led by a very rotund man in a white jacket, black shirt, bold black-and-white striped pants, and white patent leather shoes that glossed almost as much as his slicked dark hair. But the highlight of the day is Jimmy Carter, who is, in the words of one of his aides, *"witnessing*—witnessing his faith in Christ."* An airplaneload of television crews and photographers and reporters and technicians—who travel with Carter because he will soon be the Democratic Party's presidential nominee—is also on hand to witness Carter *witnessing*, and report it all to the outside world.

He talks of Christ and God and government. "I think if you analyze the parables of Christ . . . Christ was concerned more than anything else, about pride. . . . I always thought my political leaders told the truth and that our nation stood for what was right in the eyes of God. Maybe it was too much for the national pride. . . . In the last few years, we've seen—with the Vietnam War, the bombing of Cambodia, the Watergate tragedy, the CIA revelations—that the goodness of our nation is not as sure anymore as it once was."

And he talks to the Christian laymen, perhaps more than anything else, about his own faith in Christ and how it developed and how he had been asked to do missionary Christian work in Pennsylvania but at first didn't want to go. "So I prayed about it and I decided to go." It is designed to show the virtues of both religion and himself. He talks at one point about how hard it is for men to overcome pride and actually show emotions such as crying, and at another point of how he found himself "with tears running down my cheeks" after doing some Christian missionary work. He talks about doing missionary work with Eloy Cruz, whom he describes as a "dark-skinned Cuban" and "the best Christian I ever saw."

He talks about how in Massachusetts, "I was asked to go and witness among Spanish-speaking people" and about how he was able to do this because he speaks Spanish; and then he proves this by speaking a sentence with careful emphasis, phrase by phrase—first Spanish and then English. ("Nuestro Salvador tiene los manos que son muy suaves, y El no puede hacer mucho con un hombre que es dura." "Our Savior has hands which are very gentle, and He cannot do much with a man who is hard.") He speaks this and translates it with pride; it is apparent— and understandably so—that Jimmy Carter of Plains, Georgia, who often says he is the first of his father's family to finish high school, considers it a badge of honor and accomplishment to be able to demonstrate his grasp of a foreign language.

His speech is quiet and low key, and his gestures are the same—he punctuates his soft comments with his favorite soft gesture, done mostly with the wrist, with his hand moving in a semicircle first toward his chest and then toward his audience. Yet he holds and impresses his audience of Christian laymen, and he moves them to scattered shouts of "Amen!" at one point when he says with emphasis: "What power lies in this auditorium! Four or five thousand men knowing a truth that never changes!"

Then his preaching is done and the man who will soon be the Democratic candidate for President adjourns to a nearby church bookstore so he can autograph for various churchmen copies of his book, *Why Not the Best?* It is almost 1:00 P.M. when Carter takes off from Lafayette and flies back to Georgia.

▄▄▄ ▄▄▄ ▄▄▄

Ohio

Jimmy Carter was not going back to California.

His spokesman, Jody Powell, announced this into the airplane's public-address-system microphone as the Carter charter was flying to Toledo. A last-minute swing west had been scrapped in favor of more campaigning in New Jersey and Ohio.

Later Carter was asked why. He told a press conference that it would be the best use of his time and so on. Finally he said: "I've already told you more than I know on the subject." That was probably true. For Carter was not involved in the crucial strategy decision to bypass California. Powell made the decision based on phone calls with Carter people in Atlanta and the states involved. He analyzed the situation and he made the decision and then he told Carter, who accepted it.

"That's the way things are done in this campaign," explained a Carter campaign official. "The single most valuable commodity we have is the candidate and his time. He needs to be at his best in his public appearances. So he trusts his staff to handle a lot of the decisions, strategy and otherwise."

Milton Gwirtzman, a Washington attorney and veteran of Democratic political campaigns, was along on the Carter charter primarily to give advice on issues. Sometimes Gwirtzman sensed the need to diversify. Such an occasion came as Carter was strolling the grounds of the Ohio capitol in Columbus, pausing for interviews and handshakes. Gwirtzman noticed a statue there paying tribute to General

William Sherman, the Ohioan famous for having marched
his Union Army troops through Georgia during the Civil
War. Sensing a media field day and Carter disaster, Gwirtzman rushed ahead and deftly diverted the governor to a
path that prevented photographers from snapping the obvious picture of Carter—who refused to sing "Marching
Through Georgia" as an Annapolis plebe—marching past
the huge bronze Sherman.

≋   ≋   ≋

Carter was advised long ago about the importance of
cultivating cordial relationships with individual reporters
and influential editors and publishers. But he often seemed
uncomfortable around the press. He is not given to the
easy back-and-forth banter and joking that some politicians, such as Morris Udall and Edward Kennedy, find
so easy.

One morning, Carter had scheduled an early press conference at a Holiday Inn, and most of the reporters were
in the conference room waiting for him to arrive. Several
others were in a separate anteroom, downing a last cup of
coffee. Another reporter, who obviously had difficulty wak-
ing up, arrived at the same time as Carter; the reporter
headed for the coffee room instead of the press conference
and Carter followed, sensing an opportunity for a cup of
coffee and fellowship before going in to face the cameras.
The straggling reporter was dressed in a loud, almost gar-
ish, blue-and-white-check summer suit.

"Dressed for the beach?" a colleague asked. The late-
arriving reporter replied, "No, I just got confused. I
thought this was California." A third newsman interrupted: "This year Ohio is California." (The reference is
to the fact that this year the heavily contested big last race
of the campaign is in Ohio, not California.) Through it all
Carter stood with the group, smiling, apparently happy to
be part of the discussion but nevertheless silent and too
shy to inject himself into it.

Finally, a reporter asked Carter if he was aware that
one columnist had suggested that there ought to be still
one more primary vote—this one to be conducted not
in a state but at the upcoming National Governors' Conference. "That ought to be perfect for you," said the re-

porter with the loud suit. "You're bound to do well with them because they're so fond of you."

The reporter was needling Carter about the well-known fact that he is not popular with a number of the men who used to be his gubernatorial colleagues, especially the other "New South" governors. Carter understood the needling and it provoked his only comment, delivered with a good-natured laugh: "Yeah, I'll do real well with fifty guys who each want to be President." On this the coffee klatch dispersed, and the participants adjourned to positions on their respective sides of the podium.

On another occasion, reporters traveling with Carter spotted a T-shirt in a souvenir shop, bought it, and presented it to the governor. The shirt was symbolic of Carter's Oregon primary night statement concerning Ted Kennedy and Hubert Humphrey. The T-shirt said, "KISS MY ASS" and carried the picture of a Democratic donkey.

Carter was working a group of well-wishers when someone, trying to make conversation, asked "How's Amy?" It was the sort of question that is usually responded to with a standard "Fine, just fine." But instead, Carter offered a candid glimpse of the problems of a family on campaigning.

"Amy cried the last time we left home," Carter said. "When she had school to go to, it was not so bad. But now she's at home all day without us [she was staying at the home of Carter's mother while her parents campaigned] and she misses us. It's hard for her."

Rosalynn Carter remembered the incident as well. "She just kind of cried," Mrs. Carter said. "It was very unusual. "She was two when Jimmy ran for governor and she's never done that. But that last Sunday that we left, she just kind of clung."

The incident was unsettling on both parents, and they decided that from then on, Carter's mother would come and stay in their home with Amy whenever Jimmy and Rosalynn had to go out campaigning.

"Rhode Island—that was a mistake," said Frank Church's former press secretary, Bill Hall. "He should have

spent more time in Rhode Island." As it was, Frank Church
spent just enough time in Rhode Island to louse up what
was already a too-late campaign. Church had hoped to
campaign long enough in Rhode Island to continue his
impressive streak of wins over Jimmy Carter to four out of
four. But as it turned out, Church campaigned just long
enough in Rhode Island to come down with an ear infection and strep throat, which proved the beginning of his
undoing in Ohio.

After tasting defeat for the first time in Rhode Island,
Church flew to California, where he attempted to campaign despite his illness. He wound up the worse for it,
spending two days in bed in California instead of shaking
hands at factory gates and shopping centers.

Finally, Church got his campaign in gear on Friday and
headed toward a commitment in Toledo, Ohio. The heavily Democratic, heavily organized, heavily patriotic, decidedly Polish-American Fourth Ward of Toledo had
turned out in large numbers to sit on the wooden bleacher
seats of a high school football field and listen to the oratory of men who wanted to be their President. Mo Udall had
sent word that he could not make it, but Jimmy Carter and
Frank Church were expected, and that was enough to bring
more than 2,000 people to the Fourth Ward Rally on this
warm, summery evening.

Jimmy Carter arrived promptly—so promptly, in fact,
that the crowd was just filing in when he got there. So
Carter worked the entrance, which enabled him to shake
hands with most everyone who was filing into the bleacher
area. A high school band was playing, and high school
twirlers were twirling, and there was a festive air to the
rally when Carter finally began to speak, some twenty
minutes after he had arrived and before the crowd had
finished filing in.

Carter gave his old, standard stump speech, the one he
had been giving throughout most of the campaign, the one
which essentially answered the question, "Jimmy Who?"

Carter had finished, given a farewell wave, and left amid
warm applause, and as the masters of ceremony looked
nervously around, it was apparent that Frank Church was
nowhere in sight. So local politicians got up to do some
impromptu speech-making, killing time by talking at length
in an overly patriotic and decidedly dreary fashion. Reporters mostly took the occasion to leave; a few stayed and

interviewed people in the bleachers. Most of the people interviewed seemed to take the line expressed by Bob and Geneva Watson. He is a Jeep plant worker and he said they were "Pretty much sure that we're going to vote for Carter" and his wife nodded her assent.

It was one hour later that Frank Church and his tiny traveling entourage swooped into the football field area. There had been a problem making connections in Chicago. In a remarkable show of political spirit, about half of the 2,000 people had stayed to hear the man who had served for years on the Senate Foreign Relations Committee and who had just headed the headline-making Senate investigation of the Central Intelligence Agency. Frank Church had been hurrying—racing—to make it to Toledo's Fourth Ward, and the knowledge that he was so late had not left him in the best of moods. Yet as soon as he hit the field and got within sight of the crowd, Frank Church exploded into an enthusiastic—no, it was actually ecstatic—grin, laughing and waving as if this was the most fun he had ever had, campaigning an hour late with the remnants of strep throat and an ear infection. Church hit the field at about the 30-yard line and moved briskly around left end, picking up speed and smiling and waving all the while as he crossed the field from sideline to sideline, then turned upfield and picked up 20 yards before being stopped by the speaker's stand. At his side (as always), matching him pace for pace (as always), was Church's wife, Bethine, who functions variously as the senator's adviser, answer-prompter, security guard, and mother. (She has been known to answer questions for him in interviews and take the onion off his sandwiches. She is also an enthusiastic political running mate who works a crowd along a fence as energetically as her husband. She calls him "Frostie.")

Frank Church was a little out of breath, and probably a little thirsty (a dab of white formed at the left corner of his mouth as he began to speak and it remained there throughout his talk); but he was an orator of impressive talents. He had a good and simple speech, and he pounded it home eloquently. He had a hard-hitting view of what to do about unemployment and biting attacks on Gerald Ford and Ronald Reagan for having turned their Republican race into a jingoistic debate on the Panama Canal.

When he finished, Church left the stand for a return dash across the field, once again smiling and waving as he went. Bethine had remained back to greet a few well-wishers, apparently assuming her husband had done the same; when she turned and saw him departing, she moved out like a pulling guard—albeit a dark-haired and pleasant-looking pulling guard—elbowing her way through the trailing band of people and a couple of security men until she caught up with her husband and fell into stride, and smiled and waved immediately to his right.

Frank Church had made a big impression with the some 1,000 who had stayed behind to hear what he had to say. "Now I don't know," Bob Watson said as Church was finishing his speech. "That fellow Church was really something." Said his wife, Geneva: "He's a better speaker [than Carter] but what got us is that he spoke to the issues we wanted to hear." Her husband nodded and added: "We're back to undecided."

Had he started earlier and stumped the state hard, Frank Church might have made an impact in Ohio; he was that good on the stump. But there was too little time remaining between Friday night and election day in Ohio, and, as it turned out, Church would not even have much of the time that was left.

On Saturday, as Church was working a shopping center in a Cleveland suburb, he received word that there had been a disaster back home in Idaho. The newly constructed $55 million Teton River Dam had crumbled, releasing a torrent of water that swept through 400,000 acres, bringing death and destruction to at least a half dozen communities.

Church cut short his campaigning and prepared to gather his belongings to depart. He cancelled plans to appear with the other Democratic candidates on ABC's "Issues and Answers" Sunday. Meanwhile, aides rushed to charter a thirty-three-seat, propeller-driven plane for a midnight flight west.

But even that plan wound up wrecked. Late that night, an airport baggage truck somehow ran amok—it was unmanned, the Church staff was told—and smashed into a propeller of the plane Church had just chartered. The plane was grounded, and Church was delayed.

Church, clearly haggard, moved to make the most of his time while aides tried to find another plane. He decided to videotape the interview for "'Issues and Answers" so it could be used Sunday, while the others appeared live; at least he would get on the air. He went to a local television station shortly after 1:00 A.M. and taped the interview. (When it was televised on Sunday morning, while the other candidates looked relatively fresh and vigorous, Church looked like a man who was answering questions at 1:00 A.M. after a night on the town, a few rounds with Muhammad Ali, and perhaps an invasion of Normandy.)

At 2:00 A.M., Church received word that his aides had secured two small Lear jets, each carrying six passengers, for Church and his wife and secret service agents and a few news media representatives.

At 5:00 A.M., the Lear jets left Cleveland, flying 1,850 miles to Pocatello, Idaho, in four hours. From there, Church and other state dignitaries flew over the dam and flood area, viewed the damage, and conferred briefly on how the matter should be handled by government authorities. That done, Church and his party turned right around and headed back to Cleveland.

It was 7:00 P.M. Sunday when the candidate and his small entourage entered the lobby of the Hollenden House in downtown Cleveland. There were puffy pouches under each of Frank Church's eyes, his face was ashen, and as he moved wearily toward the elevator he said to no one in particular, "Show me where my bed is."

He received no directions, but instead he received a request—demand, really—from an inebriated woman in the lobby who wanted an autograph and who got his attention by calling out: "Senator or congressman or whatever you are!"

Church, by now a pushover, signed her piece of paper, telling her softly: "You had it right the first time."

There were those who thought that Church went into Ohio not so much because he thought he could win, but because he figured it could help Carter win, and that Carter might then be more receptive to picking Church to run as his Vice President. The Church people were all quick to dismiss this line of speculation. But Bill Hall, Church's former press secretary, believes that the Idaho senator had become somewhat tired and frustrated after serving twenty years in the Senate. (Church's wife used to kid him about having opposed the war in Vietnam for ten years without

being able to stop it.) Was the Vice Presidency on
Church's mind all along? "I think so," Hall said. "He
seriously went after the Presidency but he thought he
might get the Vice Presidency out of it."

THE RESULTS: . . . *In Ohio, Carter swept to an overwhelming victory. He won 52.2 percent of the vote, compared to Udall's 21.0 and Church's 13.9. Carter came
away with 119 delegates—more than he had expected.*

On the night of the election, Frank Church dined at a
seafood restaurant in Cleveland. Church, who had repeatedly called himself the tortoise of the campaign and
Carter the hare, ordered turtle soup. Then he realized what
he had done. "My God," he said, "I feel like a cannibal."

*In New Jersey, the Humphrey/Brown "two-headed
monster" won; its offically designated uncommitted ticket
picked up 82 delegates to Carter's 25 and Udall's 1.*

The New Jersey ballot was so complex that it is quite
possible that it did not promote, in all instances, a true reflection of the will of the people. Consider Essex County.
There were some black precincts in which George Wallace received more votes than Jimmy Carter, despite the
fact that Carter had drawn very well among blacks throughout the campaign. Perhaps the blacks of Essex County
really were for George Wallace. But more likely, it was
that the ballot was so constructed that Wallace headed the
list of candidates—he had the place that was often the
regular Democratic Party line—and "they just went
straight across that voting line," said one Carter man.

*In California, Brown scored big, as expected. He won
59.0 percent of the vote, which brought him 204 delegates.
Carter's 20.5 percent earned him 67, which was less than
he had expected. Church got 7.4 percent and Udall 5.0,
giving them 7 and 2 delegates, respectively.*

"We were a little slow on the uptake—at least I was,"
Mickey Kantor said about the Brown campaign. "Four or
five days before the election I *still* thought that if we won
in New Jersey and won big in California the same day,
we'd be in okay shape and would have a chance at the
nomination. Here I was, I kept talking to the Udall peo-

ple—Mark Shields and Paul Tully—and they kept telling us Ohio was going to be close, and so we went into June eighth feeling good. Shows you what we knew!"

Morris Udall. He brought class to the Democratic primaries in 1976. He was hard-hitting in his attacks on Carter—in Ohio his television ads featured a jack-in-the-box poking ridicule at Carter's positions on issues. But he was always, in defeat (after defeat after defeat), a man of wit and gentle disposition. Because he had lost so often by so little, he chose for his theme song, near the end, "Second-Hand Rose," inviting people to call him Second-Place Mo. And when reporters presented him with a rubber chicken, he took one look at it and said: "Is this campaign a turkey?" Yet losing was serious and painful to him; and when he finally returned to Washington winless after the last of the primaries and was greeted by a genuine surprise gathering of enthusiastic supporters, Mo Udall broke down and cried.

The next day, June 9, George Wallace, Richard Daley, and Henry Jackson padded the Carter delegate count with their endorsements and made it clear—Jimmy Carter would be the Democratic nominee for President of the United States.

"Skill and luck," Pat Caddell would say later, "—they're both key parts of the political process. And in 1976 we had the best of both."

From 1972, when Jerry Rafshoon outlined the image and he and Hamilton Jordan both outlined the strategy, the Carter men made the right calculations. They were right in figuring that the country was ready to accept a southerner, if he was a sophisticated and nonracist alternative to George Wallace. They were right in figuring that Carter had to make a big initial splash outside the South —in Iowa and New Hampshire—and then show in Florida that he could take the South away from Wallace. They were right in seeing early that Pennsylvania would be their big casino, their chance to annihilate Scoop Jackson, when even Jackson did not see it coming until it was too late. ("What we were counting on," said Jackson man Ben Wattenberg, "was that we'd get the wind in our media sails after a big New York win. Then the reporters would all look at Scoop Jackson's worm farm and Jackson's peanut farm and Jackson's faith-healing sister.") And they were right in figuring that they could capture the nomination with a big win in Ohio, even if Carter was defeated in New Jersey and soundly whipped in California. All that was skill.

But the nomination could not have been won on skill alone. That was Caddell's other point. For even while Jimmy Carter and his men were doing so many things right, the nomination might well have gone elsewhere. . . .

If Jackson had run in New Hampshire, thus splitting the center-right vote with Carter, giving Udall the early victory and never letting Carter get off to his fast start.

If Udall and Bayh had campaigned in Florida, splitting the liberal and black vote with Carter and allowing Wallace to win, showing that Carter was not as strong in the South as he had been saying.

If Udall had been willing, right away, to spend $25,000 on television ads—instead of being off the air entirely during the last crucial weekend in Wisconsin, where he had been making such big gains and wound up just short of defeating Carter.

If Jackson had seen Pennsylvania early on as his big confrontation with Carter, and had planned and organized and spent there accordingly.

If Hubert Humphrey had made a real run early, instead of just sitting on Capitol Hill assessing and reassessing and re-reassessing.

If the liberals had gotten behind one man from the start, rather than siphoning votes from each other.

Ifs. It might have been different. But it wasn't.

For the last several weeks of the campaign, Jimmy Carter looked tired—bone tired. The lines of his face became pronounced, his skin faintly splotchy, his fragile-fair complexion marred by occasional pinkish patches. And the skin of his neck hung in loose excess.

Now Jimmy Carter was on his way to his last speech of the primary campaign, a talk at a shopping center in Cherry Hill, New Jersey. A Secret Service agent was driving the car and Carter was seated—slumped, really—in the right rear seat, where the Secret Service insists that the people it protects sit. Jody Powell and Greg Schneiders were in the car.

"I was there for your first speech," said Powell. "So I'm going to be here for the last."

Carter talked about the last sixteen months of campaigning. He had been in 110 cities and towns. He had been told that he made 2,050 speeches. Schneiders estimated that Carter had averaged 800 miles a day. Carter talked about how hard it all had been.

"If I had two more months to go, I probably could," he said. "But because it's near the end, I'm getting run down." He was looking forward to the end of the primary campaigning. Looking forward to a few days of rest and a few more days without speeches.

It had been a long sixteen months on the road. Carter, speaking very low to conserve his voice, shook his head and said: "If somebody told me right now that all I had to do was repeat what I'd just done for the last sixteen months and I'd have the White House—I'd tell him no."

July/Convention

It is 2:30 A.M. and out of the blackness of the night sky a small twin-engine plane floats in over the tall Georgia pines and bounces to a stop on a grass airstrip outside Plains that is used in the daytime by cropdusters. The door swings open and out steps a tall, familiar figure. Senator Edmund Muskie, one of the most famous members of the Democratic Party establishment, has come to call. More than that, actually; Senator Muskie has come hurrying —anxiously—to a job interview.

There was a time, just a few months before, when Jimmy Carter had a tough time getting his calls returned by the pillars of the Democratic Party. But that was 1,505 delegates ago, and now leading Democrats across the country are struggling to get calls through to this man who holds no public office, who is just a former governor now residing in Plains, Georgia. They want to offer their services and they want to offer advice and, mainly, they want to make sure they are on the in.

One of the main pieces of business on Jimmy Carter's mind in the days that followed June 9 was the selection of a vice-presidential running mate. He had instituted an elaborate procedure that included lengthy questionnaires on financial and medical histories, preliminary interviews by Carter's closest adviser, Charles Kirbo, detailed background investigations, and finally, for the finalists, a personal job interview with Carter.

Muskie was the first to be summoned for an interview. Carter had tried twice to reach the senator at a fishing camp in Maine on Saturday, July 3, and it was late when Muskie finally got the second message and returned the call and learned he and his wife, Jane, were being invited to come to Plains.

On Sunday, the fourth of July, the Muskies got themselves to the nearest airport and began a series of commercial airline flights that brought them to Atlanta's sprawling airport at about midnight. Carter's youngest son, Chip, had been sent to meet the Muskies, and he escorted them to the small twin-engined craft that carried the party to their predawn arrival in Plains.

Ed Muskie, who had been the party's vice-presidential candidate on the 1968 Humphrey ticket and who had unsuccessfully sought the presidential nomination in his own right in 1972, looks solemn and haggard as he steps out of the plane and walks across the soggy airstrip to a waiting car. He is driven a few miles to Carter's home, where he and Jane are to be house guests. There Carter and the travel-worn Muskie sit and talk for another hour before finally calling it a night at 3:30 A.M.

9:00 A.M. Carter cheerfully taps on the door of the guest bedroom, signaling it is time for the job interview to begin. For three hours the two men confer. Muskie is not too pleased with the fact that close to half the time is spent with Carter asking him for assessments about other men on his list: Senators Frank Church of Idaho, John Glenn of Ohio, Walter Mondale of Minnesota, Henry Jackson of Washington, Adlai Stevenson of Illinois, and Congressman Peter Rodino of New Jersey.

Reporters have gathered outside the Carter home. They have been told that the two men will emerge from the talks and hold a press conference on the front lawn. Instead, Muskie and Carter emerge and head for the center of the town, where Carter takes Muskie on a handshaking tour of Main Street and his depot headquarters. As they cross the tracks, Muskie's moccasin-style shoe catches on a rail and gets left behind. Everybody stops. The towering six-foot-four Muskie leans on the compact five-foot-nine Carter, retrieves his shoe, and the walk continues. Finally they drive to the airstrip where, beside the small plane, Carter and Muskie tell reporters that they have had meaningful discussions and discovered that they had no serious differences and that Carter intends to give new and broader meaning to the job of Vice President. And Muskie, the first of the establishment to be summoned to the Court of Jimmy the First, departs.

Carter's vice-presidential selection process was complex. In all, more than seventy people were involved before

Carter made up his mind. In late May, Carter's staff had compiled a list of two dozen names. Unknown to Carter, Pat Caddell and Hamilton Jordan then selected fourteen of the names and ran a poll. The results showed that none of the fourteen would significantly help or hurt a Carter ticket. Among those ultimately considered by Carter, Church and Muskie and Glenn finished near the top in name recognition. Mondale finished near the bottom, with only 30 percent recognizing the name.

June 12. Carter was handed the results of the poll. He then began to confer personally, usually by phone, with a number of influential people—"distinguished Americans," his staff called them. He eventually talked to about forty leaders of politics, business, labor, and at least two journalists (who were apparently willing to depart from the role of observers even though it meant they had become partisan advisers).

June 17. While vacationing on Sea Island, Georgia, Carter and Charles Kirbo began to trim the list. Carter concluded that since he was from outside Washington, his running mate ought to be from within the Washington establishment. Thus governors and mayors were eliminated. When Carter and Kirbo were done, Muskie was not on the list.

June 22. Kirbo met with James Rowe, Jr., long-time adviser of Democratic presidents and the man President Johnson chose to screen Humphrey's background before he was picked as Johnson's 1964 running mate. Together they drew up questionnaires on financial and medical matters—questionnaires designed to avoid the debacles of Spiro Agnew and Thomas Eagleton.

June 28. Kirbo went to Washington. He conferred with those on the list, interviewing each and handing each a set of questionnaires. Only one person interviewed, Senator Abraham Ribicoff of Connecticut, asked that his name not be considered. While in Washington, Kirbo talked with Muskie—but as one of the "distinguished Americans" who ought to be consulted, not as a potential Vice President. He asked Muskie about other candidates and learned in the process that Muskie himself wanted to be considered and that Muskie was, in fact, upset that he had not been on Carter's list. Kirbo later conferred with Carter by phone and eventually delivered questionnaires to Muskie as well.

July 2. Kirbo conferred in Plains with Carter about his interviews with the possible running mates. The list of potentials was cut to seven. Carter had come out of the primaries leaning toward Frank Church as his choice. Church had run strong campaigns in the West, where Carter had been weak; he had run what Carter viewed as fair and honorable campaigns; he was considered a liberal but he represented a rather conservative state; and he had extensive foreign affairs experience. But a number of the "distinguished Americans" did not rate Church as highly as they rated other possible candidates.

Kirbo, meanwhile, the slow-talking Deep South lawyer whose opinion was so highly valued by Carter, had thought Scoop Jackson would make a good Vice President. Others in the party—and in the Carter camp—argued that Jackson was too hardline and conservative on foreign affairs and defense matters; they talked about the political realities and about how the liberals would feel like outcasts and would not work for a Carter-Jackson ticket. All of this was thought to have an effect on Kirbo's thinking. Meanwhile, Kirbo came away from his Washington interview of Ohio's John Glenn very much impressed by the former military officer/astronaut who had ridden his Mercury space capsule to hero status and eventually to a U.S. Senate seat. Carter began to lean favorably toward Glenn.

July 3. Carter chose to speak first with Muskie, who was by now on his list of seven, and invited him to Plains.

July 8. Morning. Walter Mondale's turn. The senator and his wife, Joan, arrived at the small airport at Americus, Georgia. The car sent by Carter to meet Mondale had not yet arrived. "Do you suppose he is trying to tell me something?" Mondale asked reporters at planeside. Eventually, the escort arrived and the Mondales drove to Carter's home in Plains. Carter had always figured that Mondale was too liberal for him. Yet they hit it off very well during their three hours of discussion. Carter felt the views expressed by Mondale were very similar to his own—on the issue of busing, where Carter had thought Mondale would be too far to the left, Mondale said he favored an approach similar to that taken in Atlanta. They seemed to mesh on a variety of domestic and foreign issues. Carter was also impressed that Mondale had apparently thought out what he was going to say so that he could present his positions in a crisp and straightforward way. Moreover, the two men found that they liked each other personally —a fact which perhaps surprised each of them. They emerged from the Carter house and conducted a press conference in a rarefied atmosphere of easy banter and joviality, and then strolled among the residents and the tourists in downtown Plains.

July 8. Afternoon. John Glenn arrived for his interview. Their talk was concluded in less than two hours. They walked out to Carter's front lawn for a press conference that will be remembered for swarms of gnats and bees that hovered nearby and for Carter's petulance. Carter responded angrily when a television reporter asked if the questions could be delayed "a few seconds" until his cameraman was ready. "Do you want to come up here and run this press conference?" Carter snapped. "Do you want to take over?"

Glenn was a popular figure from a pivotal midwestern state. In part due to Kirbo's report, Carter had gone into the Glenn meeting expecting to be impressed. He left the meeting feeling somewhat down. "Jimmy commented that Glenn had certainly been well prepared," said one person close to Carter, "but that Glenn had gone into such detail that it was a little hard to sit there and listen to it all."

The two men parted without taking the stroll through town.

The Democratic Party convened in New York City.

> Come you busted city slickers,
> Better take it on the chin,
> Father Knick has lost his knickers,
> Give it back to the Indians.

Rogers and Hart offered that message to New Yorkers in 1939, in their musical *Too Many Girls*.

FORD TO CITY: DROP DEAD

President Ford offered that message to New Yorkers— embellished in the inimical style of the *New York Daily News* headline writers—in 1976, in his hardline handling of the financially crippled city's efforts to stave off bankruptcy. The Ford position provided ample fodder for gleeful Democrats in July, as they convened for what promised to be a convention unlike any of the stormy and divided times the party has had at more recent quadrennial gatherings.

There was no bitter fight over the presidential nomination. There was no bitter fight over the party platform. There was no bitter fight over the convention rules or over the delegate credentials. In short, there was no way the television viewers at home could be sure, at a glance, that they were watching a real Democratic National Convention. It was, in fact, not a convention at all; it was a coronation. The George McGoverns were there and so were the Richard Daleys; the Jesse Jacksons and the George Wallaces.

Jimmy Carter and his entourage swept into New York on Saturday, July 10, and the candidate took up headquarters on the twenty-first floor of the Americana Hotel. In the week that followed, the nation's eyes and ears and minds would be focused, through the miracles of network television, on the red-white-and-blue convention hall inside Madison Square Garden, where a week of oratory and pageantry was being performed. But the true place of power that week was the twenty-first floor of the Americana—in the pale, powder-blue corridor and the individual rooms, and mainly behind the big, polished, wooden double doors of the Americana suite where Jimmy Carter had established residence.

"Governor Carter's Suite. . . . Governor Carter's Suite. . . . Governor Carter's Suite. . . . Governor Carter's Suite. . . ." A bank of receptionists had been set up in a room off the corridor, politely answering telephone calls coming in through the convention and hotel switchboards and taking messages that Carter would never see. "Every important political person and a lot of those you never heard of are trying to get through to Jimmy now," said one staff member. "You wouldn't believe it."

Carter did not return any of these phone calls. Instead, Greg Schneiders or Pat Caddell would stop by the switchboard on a regular, alternating basis and collect the messages. They would see to it that the calls were returned the same day by a high-ranking member of the Carter staff (not just a volunteer), and pertinent information was then passed on, if absolutely necessary, to Carter.

(Separate telephone lines were installed in Carter's suite. These phone numbers were given out to only a handful of people—perhaps ten—including Democratic National Committee Chairman Robert Strauss.)

Carter's official inaccessibility kicked a sizable burden over to senior members of the Carter staff, especially Hamilton Jordan, his campaign director. Failing to get through to Carter personally, most of the Democratic dignitaries would try to score with Jordan. And this in turn placed a large burden on Jordan's administrative assistant, Caroline Wellons, who months before had mastered the art of maintaining unflappable cool and magnolia politeness in the most hectic of pressure circumstances. (Wellons was always Jordan's administrative assistant; but because she was a woman, she found herself often being called Jordan's "secretary"—and the problem with that was that many of the heavy politicos who called wanted to speak to someone who had more clout than just a secretary; they wanted to speak to someone like an administrative assistant, and it was hard for them to realize that few people in the Carter organization had more influence with Hamilton Jordan than did Wellons. "I wish you *were* a secretary," Jordan once mock-fumed at Wellons, who like most administrative assistants had neither typing nor shorthand skills. "Then I wouldn't have to do all my own typing.")

The twenty-first floor. Elevators did not stop there. Access was gained by going to the twentieth floor, which was also staff headquarters, and then being screened and gaining clearance to walk around a guard-post table and walk up a bare concrete stairwell to the twenty-first. Members of the Carter entourage had been issued a variety of color-coded passes. But only a few of those were good for entry to the twenty-first floor.

The twenty-first floor. For all its aura of elite, it was not a very palatial place. There were Secret Service agents guarding doors and passageways; there was also a guy strolling the corridor bare-chested. There was a procession of dignitaries who were being granted appointments with the near-nominee; there was also a man with a grocery bag filled with six-packs, returning from a nighttime mercy mission for his friends.

Security was vigilant. When Hamilton Jordan arrived in New York, the Manhattan-based security operatives did not recognize him and would not permit him to enter his own offices or room until one of the assistants came down to vouch for the boss. So too with Jody Powell. He arrived credentialless and was permitted entry only when his wife, Nan, who had arrived ahead of time and had her proper pass, came down and assured security personnel that she would see to it that her husband behaved properly.

Security was fast. Pat Caddell, who can organize complex polling operations but has trouble with the monotonies of life, somehow managed to lose his color-coded credentials somewhere between the door of his room on the twenty-first floor and the bottom of the stairwell on the twentieth. Within an hour, security experts had changed the locks on Caddell's door, lest the credentials had fallen into the wrong hands.

And consider the case of the man with the bag full of beer. A middle-aged-looking woman with blond hair was staffing the checkpoint at the table on the twentieth floor and she had heard all of the lines before—a score of gate-crashers (some of them highly placed) had to be turned away at the checkpoint every hour. So she was understandably wary—but inexplicably rude—when the man came with the six-packs, just as Jody Powell had asked him to, so the Carter hierarchy could sit around and sip beer and watch the convention that night. The man with the beer told her that he was expected by Powell on the twenty-first floor and asked her to phone up and check with him. The woman instead lied: "Mister Powell's not here. He's at the convention hall." The man with the bag said he knew better. The woman made a telephone call and reported back: "You can leave the beer but you can't go upstairs yourself." The man with the bag said he was a friend of Powell's and Powell had invited him to come up too. Finally the woman agreed to make the proper phone call to Powell; she was told that indeed the beer man was to be escorted upstairs to see Powell and only then did she relent, unsmiling.

To the Democratic heavies and hangers-on down below, the twenty-first floor seemed to be the essential place to be, the citadel of what C. Wright Mills would have recognized as "The Power Elite." But those on the twenty-

first floor saw little mystique. "Access to the twenty-first
floor was sort of like sex," Greg Schneiders observed. "It
didn't seem very important except to the people who didn't
have it."

🏴 🏴 🏴

Among those who were granted audiences with Carter
on the twenty-first floor were delegations of women,
Spanish-speaking Americans, and prominent blacks. When
the Latins came in, Carter did a little talking in Spanish.
When the blacks came in, he spoke to them in plain English. The black delegation pushed two basic points: (1)
they wanted Carter to keep Basil Patterson as vice chairman of the Democratic National Committee—Carter indicated that he would; and (2) they were unhappy that
Carter had not at least considered Los Angeles Mayor
Thomas Bradley, a black, among the finalists for Vice
President. Carter said that he had concluded that he
wanted a man from Washington D.C., and that because
of this he had exluded all governors and mayors. Jesse
Jackson, one of the blacks, said, according to others in
the room, something to the effect that he had not expected that Carter would wind up picking Bradley, "but it
would have made all of us proud to see a black man get
off the airplane in Plains, Georgia." The line of rea-
soning left Carter somewhat stunned and he said so. Carter told them that he had not wanted to act out a charade,
that it would not have been honest to make it appear that
the black mayor had a chance when in fact he did not
because he had no Washington experience.

🏴 🏴 🏴

The only suspense at the Democratic convention was
the anticipation as to who Carter would choose as his
running mate. In his Americana suit, Carter interviewed
the four other Washington-based "finalists," although they
were largely, by that time, pro forma interviews. There
was Frank Church, who had once led Carter's list, but who
had gradually slipped in part because of the reservations
of some of the "distinguished Americans" and in part because Carter and his staff were turned off by people who
had been lobbying hard for Church behind the scenes—

among them Carter's finance chairman, Morris Dees. There was Senator Adlai Stevenson, who was considered too colorless, but who was being considered largely because he was Mayor Richard Daley's man (he was known by some politicians as "Dick Daley's pet rock"). There was Scoop Jackson, who had fought Carter and lost and had come out in support of Carter when he needed it; but Jackson was considered too conservative to be included on the Carter ticket. And there was Congressman Peter Rodino, who promptly took himself out of consideration by telling Carter he feared that a recurrence of glaucoma would make it difficult for him to campaign. Rodino asked Carter to keep the matter confidential; but at a press conference the next day, a reporter asked Carter a question and the former governor acknowledged that one of the seven finalists had indeed asked that his name be withdrawn from the list. Carter left the conference with reporters pursuing him to the elevator asking him to supply the name. Carter stepped into the elevator. "Maybe Jody will have something for you later," he said as the door closed leaving the reporters outside. Up in his suite on the twenty-first floor, Carter located Rodino by phone. He explained what he had let slip and said that he would like to supply the name, since he had gone that far already —if Rodino did not object. It had gone too far to stop. Rodino consented.

From the day he arrived in Manhattan, Carter had been getting hints that some of the party's leaders— principally Robert Strauss—would like to see him choose Muskie. Muskie would help him with the Catholics and people of European ethnic origins, where polls were showing Carter was weak; also, Muskie's extensive knowledge of the federal bureaucracy and budget problems would prove useful.

But in the last days before Carter was to make his selection, the vice-presidential finalists were all being careful so as not to make it appear that they were doing anything overt to try to campaign for the job. All they wanted to do was to drop out of sight and keep their names and faces out of the newspapers for a couple of days—lest Carter think someone was trying to mount a public relations pressure campaign. Television networks and some newspapers, meanwhile, tried to keep watch over the activities of the frontrunners.

Among those who tried to live a low-key existence was Muskie. *Newsday* Washington correspondent Myron S. Waldman was keeping track of Muskie, and he filed this report to his editors:

On his way to his Gotham Hotel headquarters . . . Muskie told a reporter he intended to go to a museum with his wife, Jane, but didn't know which one. He added that he did not much care for modern art. About half an hour later, his press secretary told reporters that Muskie had decided not to reveal where he was going.

Reporters walked out of the hotel and hired two taxis to wait with meters running. The sight of reporters and a television truck caused pedestrians to stop. As the crowd gathered, the doorman came out. He was nervous. "Please clear the sidewalk," he said.

A television crew began to film the crowd it had helped to create. This brought more pedestrians to a halt. A policeman arrived to control the crowd. The excitement among reporters grew. Would Muskie go to the museum or not?

Soon Muskie and his wife emerged. The crowd cheered. No, he would not tell a reporter where he was going. The reporter and his colleagues raced for the cabs. Muskie got into a station wagon. The ABC television truck pulled out. And the chase began.

Up 56th Street and left on Madison Avenue the parade proceeded, cabbies cursing, running red lights and defying buses whose drivers tried to cut into Muskie's reluctant entourage. A technician leaned out of the ABC truck and filmed the fleeing station wagon. Finally, at Madison and 75th, the station wagon stopped in front of the Whitney Museum. "You're spoiling our fun," Mrs. Muskie complained.

Inside, the Muskies, tailed by television cameras and reporters, immediately began the tour of the exhibit, "Two Hundred Years of American Sculpture," conducted by Peterson Sims, curator of the museum's permanent collection. Sims, a young red-bearded man in a gray sweater and ascot, led the Muskies through the modern section first.

He showed them crushed auto parts. He showed them bricks. He showed them a Martinson's coffee can filled with paint brushes. "That's like your Hole In One Award," Mrs. Muskie said to her husband.

Someone mentioned that the exhibit had gotten a bad review. "I've never read a review as mean as that," Sims said. "Have you read any of mine?" Muskie asked.

Later, the Muskies toured primitives and older sculptures crafted in a style of realism, among them a statue of a beast in which was hidden a device which, when activated, expressed a single point of view.

"Interesting," Muskie said when asked afterwards how he felt about modern art now. "I enjoyed that animal who stuck his tongue out at us. His instincts were similar to mine."

🏴 🏴 🏴

The drama of the Democratic National Convention had come down to this: Muskie or Mondale. Carter had narrowed the field down to the two senators. Carter had been leaning away from Glenn since they had talked in Plains —there was concern on the Carter staff about Glenn's use of income tax shelters; and there was some concern that a ticket that would feature two former military officers would provoke criticism. "That ticket didn't sound quite right," joked a Carter confidant. "Carter-Glenn sounds like a middle-income housing development."

There were powerful forces urging Muskie and powerful reasons to back up their views, primarily the Catholic ethnic balance he would bring, shoring up Carter where he was weakest among Democratic voters. But Peter Rodino had told Carter forcefully on Monday that he did not need to put a Catholic on the ticket to appeal to the Catholic and ethnic vote—as long as he had prominent Catholics campaigning for the ticket. Rodino said he would campaign for Carter regardless. Carter was also concerned about Muskie's legendary hair-trigger temper, and by reports that he was at times unnecessarily harsh on his staff.

"It was down to whether Jimmy should be safe and go
with Muskie or politically bold and go with Mondale," one
Carter aide said. "The chemistry with Mondale had been
very good and, like Jimmy, he would be a whole new face
on the national scene. That cut it for him, I guess."

July 15. As he had promised, Carter telephoned those
he did not pick on Thursday morning to let them know
the decision had gone against them. This was, in one instance, a difficult thing to do.

Jimmy Carter's personal assistant, Greg Schneiders,
reached for the phone at 8:40 A.M. and dialed the New
York Sheraton Hotel.

He asked for the room number John Glenn's staff had
provided. Carter had to break the news to Glenn that he
had chosen another to be his vice-presidential running
mate.

The number rang. No answer.

Schneiders explained to the hotel operator that "Governor Carter needs to talk to Senator Glenn right away.
Is there another number where we can reach the
senator?"

"We're not allowed to give out that information," the
operator replied.

She agreed to ring the other number herself, however.
But the number was busy. Schneiders waited. She tried
again. Still busy.

Schneiders explained that this was a very important
call that Jimmy Carter was making to John Glenn and
could she please break in on the busy line? Glenn would
want very much to speak with Carter, Schneiders told her.
No, she said, hotel policy.

Schneiders asked her to please send someone upstairs
to tell Glenn to hang up the phone. The New York Sheraton operator refused.

Five minutes later, Glenn's phone was free, Schneiders
got the call through and put Carter on the line, and
Carter told Glenn the news he did not really want to
hear.

Carter also called Fritz Mondale.

"Did I wake you up?" Carter asked. "Would you like
to run with me?"

Carter had won his nomination. He had picked his running mate. That night he would stand before the convention (and before America and the world) and deliver the most important speech he had ever made, before the largest audience he had ever faced. But before that, Carter had some friends to thank. So shortly after announcing his selection of Mondale, he walked across the street to the City Squire Hotel to the Georgia delegation's caucus. There, in a room crowded with more that 200 people, Carter offered emotional words of thanks. At one point, his eyes filled with tears and his voice broke as he spoke to the people of his state.

"When I announced and began to campaign for the highest elective office, perhaps in the world, nineteen months ago, not many people thought I had a chance, but a lot of you thought I had a chance [cheers].

"There were a lot of times when I was lonely. There were a lot of times when there was a great deal of doubt. We had some serious setbacks, and I made some mistakes, but I never had a feeling of loneliness or withdrawal or isolation or abandonment from the people of Georgia.

"For about eight months, I was by myself. But, later, when the going really got tough, you just can't imagine how it made me feel to get off a small airplane in an isolated airport and see some of you, standing there—" his voice broke completely; he was on the verge of tears, but did not cry—"with signs waving back and forth in the snow and to see the expressions of friendship and support for me. I could not have carried New Hampshire, which was a close election, without you, and I could not have carried Florida, which was a close election, without you. I could not have carried Wisconsin, which was a close election, without you.

"The strength of our political effort has been the closeness between me personally and voters around the country. Women in the shoe factories and textile mills. And men driving trucks and making electronics equipment and working on farms and cutting hair and waitresses in restaurants. To a substantial degree they felt they could have confidence in me and that I was close to them. And there wasn't any powerful political figure that stood between them and, possibly, the next President. And I'll never shake that intensely personal relationship, because I want to be sure that when I am in the White House the American people feel: that's my President."

📰   📰   📰

Congressman Andrew Young, the bright, forceful Atlantan who was once a deputy of Martin Luther King, Jr., and who had been an early Carter supporter, also spoke before the Georgia delegation.

"Back in January, 1975, when Jimmy Carter announced he was running for President, I was there at the Hyatt Regency in Atlanta and I introduced Jimmy. Last week, when I was starting to get my notes together for the seconding speech [which Young gave for Carter at the convention], I thought it might be interesting to hear what I had said about Jimmy way back in the beginning. So I called my friend Aubrey Morris at [radio station] WSB in Atlanta, and I said, 'Aubrey, could I listen to your tape of that press conference?' Well, he laughed and he said to me, 'Andy, we didn't keep that tape because we didn't think Carter was going anywhere.'"

📰   📰   📰

Back in his suite on the twenty-first floor of the Americana, Carter had little to do except rehearse his speech for that night. For that he needed mostly privacy. Carter walked into the grand-scale living room, shut the large wooden double doors behind him, and then for good measure he slid some furniture over against the doors, building a barricade that would assure against unwanted interruption. There, in fortified privacy, Carter rehearsed a speech that had been put together through more than a month of painstaking drafting.

On July 2, Patrick Anderson had arrived in Plains with the first draft. Carter read the text that night and the next day, Saturday, he told his speechwriter he wanted to write a draft that would be his own. He asked Anderson to telephone people around the country and get them to make suggestions, offer ideas, even contribute a few paragraphs or an overall theme. Talk to some young people, Carter said. Talk to some bright people. Carter was torn between two concepts: since this was the most important speech of his life to date, he wanted it to be truly his; yet he also wanted a wide range of ideas to work with.

That afternoon, Anderson sat in the study of Carter's home and began working the telephone.

He called Washington and spoke to Henry Owen, who had been the head of planning in the State Department under Dean Rusk and was now at the Brookings Institution.

He called New York and spoke to Theodore Sorenson who had been a speechwriter for John Kennedy and who has been credited with having written the inaugural address line: "Ask not what your country can do for you; ask what you can do for your country."

He called Vermont and spoke to Olin Robison, president of Middlebury College.

He called Boston and spoke to Patrick Caddell, public opinion analyst and all-purpose adviser to Carter. And he spoke once more with Stuart Eizenstat, Carter's issues adviser.

Throughout the Fourth of July festivities, Anderson worked out of the study at Carter's house, set back among the trees at 1 Woodland Drive. From time to time, Anderson would type the suggested phrases, passages, and themes, and forward them to Carter.

The following Friday, several days after Anderson handed Carter the last of the outside opinions, Carter presented his speechwriter and Jody Powell with a draft— twenty-five pages written by Carter in longhand on a yellow legal pad. He had incorporated some of the suggestions and portions of the original Anderson draft, but the work, several Carter aides later said, was now very much a Jimmy Carter production. (The yellow legal pad. It was the instrument on which Richard Nixon wrote his speeches affirming Vietnam and denying Watergate. Said one Carter adviser: "Not even Nixon can ruin the yellow legal pad.")

Carter asked Powell and Anderson for their criticisms of the work. The two men had some. Carter flew to the convention in New York and Anderson began working on a third draft, based on Carter's version plus talks with Caddell, Eizenstat, and Adam Walinsky, who had written for Robert Kennedy, and Ted VanDyk, who had written for Hubert Humphrey. At 6:00 P.M. Sunday,

Carter asked for the latest draft. At 9:00 P.M. Sunday, he got it.

Carter worked on the draft Monday night. Tuesday at 5:00 P.M., he met with Powell, Caddell, Rafshoon, Anderson, and a few others in his suite on the twenty-first floor at the Americana Hotel. They went over a typewritten draft of the speech, line by line.

Carter and his men had carefully worked a number of lines into the speech that would appeal to the Catholic and ethnic voters. "Ours is the party that welcomed generations of immigrants—the Jews, the Irish, the Italians [Carter pronounced it "eye-talians"], the Poles, and all others—enlisted them into its ranks, and fought the political battles that helped bring them into the American mainstream—and they have shaped the character of our party."

Also: "We *can* have an America that encourages and takes pride in our ethnic diversity, our religious diversity, and our cultural diversity. . . ."

And there was a passage which hailed America's immigrants as "the best and the bravest." During a drafting session, one Carter adviser took issue with the phrase. It was not historically accurate, he insisted, "They just were not often the best and the bravest."

Carter looked up and offered a crisp reply: "Well, *you* go tell Pete Rodino that his father was the worst."

The phrase stayed.

   🇺🇸 🇺🇸 🇺🇸

The drafting process of this major political speech had itself been heavy on politics. Representatives and advocates of specific blocs and interest groups had been urging —even demanding—that Carter include words of praise for this group or that. Before it was over, drafts had been shown to people who had written for two generations of leading Democrats—writers for John Kennedy, Robert Kennedy, Lyndon Johnson, Hubert Humphrey. "They kept saying Jimmy's going to blow it, that there should be more of this and less of that," recalled one Carter man. "But they were looking for a JFK-type speech, and this was not JFK, it was Jimmy Carter."

The final speech wound up with one passage that was purely the product of Kennedy-man Theodore Sorenson.

"It is time for America to move and to speak, not with boasting and belligerence, but with a quiet strength—to depend in world affairs not merely on the size of an arsenal but on the nobility of ideas—and to govern at home not by confusion and crisis, but with grace and imagination and common sense."

But the speech was, in the end, Jimmy Carter. Among the passages he penned in longhand and retained throughout the drafting process were these trademarks of his own populist appeal:

"We should make our major investments in people, not in buildings and weapons. The poor, the weak, the aged, the afflicted must be treated with respect and compassion and with love."

And a flat, no-frills statement on jail reform: "I see no reason why big-shot crooks should go free while the poor ones go to jail."

July 15. Night. This is a Democratic National Convention like none other in the party's modern history. A Democratic convention without warfare. Without bitterness. Without rancor. Without division. Without a liberal-conservative split or a North-South split. Without one side going home in bitterness determined to sit on its hands until after November.

This is the convention where the Deep South is welcomed back to the party. Welcomed back after it had captured it. But it is more. It is also the convention where the Democratic liberals and conservatives decided to stand together and cheer together, regardless of the ideology or sloganeering that had prompted the applause.

Nowhere was the new Democratic unity more obvious than in the first seat, right, of the Illinois delegation. This was the seat of the chairman of the Illinois delegation, the man who came back, Richard J. Daley, mayor and still boss.

🏳️ 🏳️ 🏳️

It is 9:25 P.M. and the convention is awaiting the arrival of Jimmy Carter. A couple of Chicago toughs—bodyguards for the boss—lock arms around the mayor's aisle chair, so a reporter cannot get near to ask a question. Daley has asked for a glass of water and he is clearing his throat and wetting the dryness that has settled in his mouth. "Jesus, you picked a helluva rotten time to want to do an interview," says the bodyguard in the brown suit. "He's not going to do it. Not now."

Somebody has just passed word to the mayor that the first thing Jimmy Carter will do upon entering the Garden is walk up the aisle and shake Daley's hand. It will be a symbolic gesture that the past is buried and that the mayor who was unceremoniously thrown out of the Illinois delegation by the liberals who ran things in 1972 is back again in good graces and great power.

It will also be a gesture of appreciation, for after all, Richard Daley had helped Carter capture the nomination —once he became convinced that Carter was a winner. (Scene: the Illinois delegation caucus. Daley asks his delegation to make its backing of Daley unanimous. A Jerry Brown delegate speaks up. "No, I will not make it unanimous," the delegate says. Daley is quick to reply: "Then we will make it unanimous without you." Such is the politics of Mayor Daley.)

"It's a great satisfaction for the mayor to come back and prove he was right," says William Lee, president of the AFL-CIO in Chicago and probably Daley's oldest friend in the Illinois delegation.

"Mayor Daley never was gone really," says Adeline P. Keane, who has taken the delegate seat of her husband Chicago Alderman Thomas Keane, the Daley ally who would be there himself except for the fact that he is now in jail on a conflict-of-interest charge.

"The Mayor's never been down," says Senator Richard J. Daley, Jr., who refers to his father by his father's title. "He never looks back. He figures 'That's life.' He's been building toward his present position since 1928, when he went to his first convention."

A couple of other reporters have come over to the Illinois delegation. One is Dan Rather of CBS, who was reporting at the Chicago convention in 1968 when Daley's police rioted and smashed demonstrators—the hectic convention where television caught Daley making an obscene gesture at a speaker who was denouncing the police tactics. Now, from midway in the Illinois delegation, a man in a very white sportcoat says to a man in a very white suit, "that Rather's got a helluva lot of nerve showing up at the Illinois delegation. Let him go stand with the kookies."

Carter arrives at the hall. Daley clears his throat and

straightens his jacket. But Carter, led by his security men, turns left instead of right and heads straight for the podium instead of straight for Daley. Daley leans over to his candidate for governor, Michael J. Howlett, and shrugs. "Life is full of surprises," Daley says, and he begins to applaud the party's nominee, pounding his hands so hard that the wattles beneath his jowls commence to quiver.

⬛ ⬛ ⬛

As Carter made his way to the microphone, reporters in the press grandstand areas flanking the podium began rereading the advance text of the speech text provided to them by Carter aides. What they did not know was that there were a couple of passages that were in Carter's own text that were not included in the texts prepared for the reporters. These were the few light touches that had been submitted by two Hollywood comedy writers—Jack Kaplan who used to work for Jerry Rafshoon's ad agency; and his associate, John Barrett—who had been flown in to bring a few smiles to the Carter epic. "We left them out of the press texts because it would look, well, too corny to have them in," a Carter assistant explained.

Kaplan and Barrett had presented their comedy offerings to Carter in short memos, hand printed in capital letters on a yellow legal pad. For all the drafting and consulting that went into the speech, for all the efforts of all the highly regarded political speechwriters, it was a memo by the two Hollywood writers that produced the most famous, most frequently quoted passage of Jimmy Carter's nomination speech of 1976. The memo, from Kaplan and Barrett to Carter, came complete with parenthetical cues and stage directions.

(AFTER THANK YOUs JIMMY TURNS TO AUDIENCE AND SAYS:) HELLO, I'M JIMMY CARTER. (LAUGH) AND I'M RUNNING FOR PRESIDENT OF THE UNITED STATES. (APPLAUSE).

BOOK TWO

August/Midsummer's
Nice Dream

Carter 66 percent. Ford 27 percent.

Carter 68 percent, Reagan 26 percent.

Suddenly, Jimmy Carter was the champion of the poll vault. Catapulted by the euphoria of the Democratic convention, Carter quickly soared to a lead that Louis Harris called "one of the most substantial ever recorded."

That was in mid-July. Less than two weeks later on August 1 George Gallup weighed in with figures almost as overpowering.

Carter 62 percent, Ford 29 percent.

Carter 64 percent, Reagan 27 percent.

Jimmy Carter had doubled his preconvention lead over his Republican rivals. In two weeks, the Republican Party would be convening in Kansas City to choose a presidential nominee: either President Gerald Ford or former California governor Ronald Reagan. But it hardly seemed to matter. For in those hot and heady days of early August Carter's advisers were sitting in Georgia ostensibly planning for victory but in fact thinking landslide.

A 33-point lead is a powerfully seductive force in campaign politics, and in the month of August Carter himself seemed to succumb. He went into what his aides later would refer to as his "Presidential Period." He acted less like a candidate and more like a man who had already been elected. Busloads of advisers on economic, foreign, and domestic policies began to arrive in Plains as the Democratic nominee began a lengthy and thorough period of consultation. When he wasn't involved in detailed policy consultation, he was binding wounds and healing divisions among liberals, moderates, and conservatives. This was the time when Ralph Nader stayed overnight at the Carter house and joined in with the candidate, his staff, and the press corps in a softball game. (Eventually

244

the candidate even brought actor Robert Redford in and consulted him on environmental matters.) For weeks after the Nader visit, Phil Wise, Carter campaign coordinator for the southern states, received angry reports from politicians in his area who were furious over what seemed to be a newly formed alliance between the candidate they were backing and the consumer advocate they detested.

Throughout the months of June, July, and August— the months of big margins in the polls—there was one voice of caution and concern in the Carter camp. It belonged to Patrick Caddell.

"I'm not sure that Jimmy will win the election this fall," Caddell said at one point in midsummer. But most of his colleagues on the Carter staff would just nod and feign concern. "You've got to understand Pat," explained another senior aide who is fond of Caddell. "He's a congenital pessimist. It's his job. He's just not happy unless he's unhappy. And he's not at peace unless he's frantic."

It is a fact that throughout a campaign season, Pat Caddell lives on black coffee and cigarettes and quick meals grabbed usually around midnight. His eyes, through a campaign, are surrounded by concentric dark circles. His frame fills to well-rounded proportions; it becomes permanently welded at the ear to a telephone and at the right hand to a ball-point pen, and the pen is set into perpetual motion across a legal pad well before January and it does not stop until the first Tuesday in November; and that is good because it is the only exercise he gets.

It is also a fact that Pat Caddell was right. He based his early warnings on polls.

🏴 🏴 🏴

July 22, 1976

Memorandum

To: Carter Campaign
From: Cambridge Survey Research [Caddell's company]
Re: The Unenthusiastic Carter Vote

. . . At this point roughly a third of all Carter voters in [Illinois, Washington, Florida, Iowa, the South, the Deep South, and the Farm Belt] describe themselves as not very enthusiastic at all about their choice of

Jimmy Carter. In fact, to emphasize the large pool of
unenthusiastic Carter voters it should be pointed out
that there is no state or area yet in which a majority
of all registered voters (not merely Carter voters) is
very enthusiastic or even somewhat enthusiastic
about Jimmy Carter.

To be sure, an even larger proportion of unenthusiastic voters is found among Ford voters, and if only
voters who were very enthusiastic or somewhat enthusiastic about their candidate were to vote, Jimmy
Carter would do better than if all voters, regardless
of their degree of enthusiasm, voted. However, it must
be kept in mind that it is likely that a voter who is
unenthusiastic about an incumbent is more likely to
actually turn out and vote for his choice than is a
voter who is unenthusiastic about a challenger.

When Carter voters are separated by religion the
least enthusiastic group are the Jewish voters.
Roughly half of all Jewish Carter voters are as yet
unenthusiastic about their choice at this time. Catholic Carter voters in these areas are less enthusiastic
than Protestant Carter voters, but it should also be
noted that Catholic Ford voters are even less enthusiastic about their candidate.

Ideologically the unenthusiasm in the North is
among liberals and in the South among conservatives.
In both regions the unenthusiastic voter is two to
three times as likely as the enthusiastic voter to find
Jimmy Carter ambiguous (vague, two-faced, too political, etc.) on the open-ended question "What do
you dislike about Jimmy Carter?" In addition outside
the South 10–20% of the not very enthusiastic
Carter voters would vote for Eugene McCarthy if he
were on the ballot.

Another poll heightened Caddell's concern. It showed
inordinate problems on the Democratic homefront: women,
youths, Catholics, Jews, and many who called themselves
liberals. Democrats usually build up margins of 25 percent
or more in these categories, and yet Carter was edging
President Ford by just 3, 4, or 5 percent.

"If I didn't know you were a Democrat," Caddell told Carter, "I'd never be able to tell it from these results."

And in August, Carter pollsters found Carter voters defecting right before their eyes. This was during a series of lengthy interviews in which pollsters asked people a series of open-ended questions about how Carter would handle various issues. A number of people who identified themselves as likely Carter voters at the outset of the interviews were saying near the end that actually they weren't sure how they were going to vote, after all. "I mean, they were defecting right in the middle of the interviewing," Caddell said. "That's frightening. That is the classic example of a soft vote."

Caddell got Carter and Jordan to study the lengthy survey results. But in the brand-new, plush offices of the Carter-Mondale headquarters—they had moved uptown to a sparkling high-rise on Atlanta's Peachtree Drive—the thing that kept emotions high was the staff squabbling over who was getting the offices with windows and who was getting the offices with doors. When it came to the campaign ahead, the Carter-Mondale people were confident.

"We still had that big euphoria factor to contend with," Caddell said. "It was because of those damn public surveys that kept showing us so far ahead. A lot of that was very soft. I mean, it just didn't make sense—here was Carter with a massive lead when matched up against an incumbent President, but then Ford also had a 55 percent favorable rating on how he was doing his job. Also, Ford had less voter support—even with this high favorable rating —than George McGovern had at any point in the Gallup Poll in 1972.

"It just didn't make sense."

≋   ≋   ≋

August 3. Jimmy Carter was keeping a promise. He had told the people of New Hampshire during the primary that he would return if he won the Democratic nomination.

Carter decided that he would make the strength of the American family a campaign theme, and he had speechwriter Patrick Anderson draft a suitable, high-toned speech for the noontime, outdoor rally at Manchester, New Hampshire.

Carter arrived at the noontime rally, and the prepared text of the American family speech was distributed to the press corps. But the nominee added a little introduction: he lashed out at what he called the "Nixon-Ford administration" and accused it of governing by "vetoes and not vision . . . scandal and not stability . . . rhetoric and not reason. . . ."

Then, at a fundraiser at the Wayfarer Inn, Carter ad-libbed a warning that the Republicans would soon be unleashing "an almost unprecedented, vicious, personal attack against me."

Predictably, the news of the day, as carried by the networks and the press, centered on Carter's highly charged, superpartisan attack and accusation. The American family message was lost. The candidate was dismayed by the lack of attention that was paid to his statement of high family principles, and so were some of his advisers. Others in the Carter hierarchy knew that Carter had scooped himself.

The problem Carter had in Manchester, New Hampshire, would continue to plague him in the months to come. He would step on his own news story by ad-libbing a comment in a speech or answering a question carelessly. Time after time, he would become frustrated upon learning that he had made news—but not the sort of news he had set out to make.

"It started the first trip he made to New Hampshire before Labor Day," one of Carter's closest advisers, his wife, Rosalynn, said much later. "He had a speech on the family. And then at a reception he said something about the Republicans attacking him very personally. Nobody ever knew that Jimmy made a speech on the family. And it was a good speech. He was really worried about it."

Memorandum

Personal and Confidential

To: Jimmy Carter
From: Hamilton Jordan

. . . The Tone of the Campaign

I thought that the tone of your remarks last week in New York [was] highly partisan and un-Presidential.

I feel that you should re-examine the manner in which you publicly discuss Ford's relationship with Richard Nixon.

The American people perceive Gerald Ford as being an honest, well-intentioned man who inherited a job bigger than he can handle. They see many of the same attractive personal qualities in you, but have made the tentative judgment that you are more capable of leading the country than Ford.

I do not worry in the weeks and months ahead that we can clearly demonstrate that you are a better qualified person to lead the country and manage the government. I do worry that our campaign rhetoric might undermine the favorable personal image you have with the American voters. Any statements which are perceived to be—directly or indirectly—by the American people as being personal attacks on Gerald Ford will hurt us and help him.

I feel strongly that you should discontinue using the phrase "Nixon-Ford Administration." I believe that the Republican Party generally and Gerald Ford specifically can be held responsible for many of the problems facing our country today. The American people are ready to hold them accountable at the polls in November for the past eight years, but the phrase "Nixon-Ford Administration" suggests a very conscious effort on your part to equate Ford, the man, with Nixon, the man. This does not and will not wash with the American people and I believe that it will be generally interpreted as a personal attack on the integrity of Gerald Ford.

When I watched you say that on the news recently, it sounded harsh and out of character for you. It certainly did not sound like a man who wanted to put Watergate behind us and unite the country.

🏴 🏴 🏴

August was a time of minor gaffes:

There was the Wallace gaffe. In an interview, Carter was trying to emphasize that Republican John Connally had slipped badly in the polls. Connally is ranked so low, he said, that only George Wallace is rated below him. Carter then had to apologize to Wallace.

There was the Bush gaffe. In a speech in Atlanta, Carter had accused the Republican administration of using top government jobs as "dumping grounds for unsuccessful candidates." Whom was Carter talking about? Carter aides mistakenly handed reporters a confidential staff memo. It cited George Bush, director of the Central Intelligence Agency, as an example. The timing was unfortunate since Bush was arriving in Plains the next day to give Carter an intelligence briefing. "It was a serious mistake on some staff member's part," Carter said, praising Bush's capabilities as CIA director.

There was the grain gaffe. In a speech at the Iowa State Fair, Carter said flatly that he would stop embargoes on grain exports "once and for all." But later he was asked by a reporter whether he would permit grain exports if the United States were struck by natural disaster and faced the threat of hunger. Carter could have refused to deal on such hypothetical grounds. Instead, he said that perhaps he had been "too strong" in his statement; obviously, embargoes might be needed in the unlikely event of a natural disaster. The stories the next day dealt with Carter backing off his no-embargoes pledge. And, handed this ammunition, the Republicans fired salvos about how Carter was flip-flopping on issues.

And there was the meeting with the bishops.

August 31, Washington, D.C. Jimmy Carter and six Roman Catholic bishops are seated in a circle in a meeting room at the Mayflower Hotel. Carter has been the target of small numbers of antiabortion, right-to-life picketers ever since Iowa; they grew in number as he grew in stature as a political reality in 1976. But polls have consistently shown that a majority of Catholics back the U.S. Supreme Court view which has permitted abortion, rather than the official Catholic church position, which opposes abortion, in any form, at any time, for any reason. Still, polls are also showing that Jimmy Carter has a problem with Catholic voters.

Carter has reason to believe the meeting with the bishops will be a good one. Mondale had talked with Bishop

James S. Rausch (of Washington, D.C.). The bishop had said a meeting with Carter would be productive, and Mondale had agreed. Mondale had passed the word to Carter through an aide. The aide passed the message to Carter along with his own advice: Don't do it; you can't say anything to the bishops that will please them, it will only artificially keep the issue alive. Carter opted for the Mondale view. So now Carter was sitting in the Mayflower Hotel, in a room full of bishops.

In that meeting room, Carter plans to build an "intimate personal relationship" with the Catholic prelates. That is, after all, his strong suit. He touches early on abortion, telling the bishops that while he does not support the proposed constitutional amendments prohibiting abortion, he does personally oppose abortion. He says the government should do nothing to encourage abortion. He disavows the Democratic Party's own plank, saying it appears to discourage citizens from trying to get an antiabortion amendment to the Constitution enacted. He pledges that he will not actively oppose people who are trying to enact antiabortion amendments.

Then he launches into what he hopes will be the "intimate personal relationship" clincher—a discussion of how he and the bishops agree on a wide range of social issues. The cities . . . housing . . . health. Most of all, Carter is trying to create a friendly, cooperative atmosphere. But, seated in the circle, it is Archbishop Joseph L. Bernardin of Cincinnati who sets the tone. After Carter gives his extemporaneous talk, the archbishop *reads* his own statement, prepared in advance. He says that until the bishops and Carter get the abortion issue resolved, there is no point in discussing anything else. He goes on to repeat the church's official, unalterable opposition to abortion, and to state that the church feels it is up to the government to step in and prevent abortions.

Carter's strategy has unraveled. A bishop asks if Carter means that he would not favor any form of constitutional amendment restricting abortion. Bernardin adds that the church has had many lawyers working on the issue and that they say there are many possible forms that an amendment could take.

Carter says that he can't comment on an amendment without seeing the way it is worded. Perhaps the church will have some wording to suggest, he says. Bernardin says that the church (which has lobbied vigorously against abortion) is not in that business.

Carter says he won't flatly oppose all possible amendments; he says someone may just come up with some sort of wording that he could endorse. The bishops listen politely.

The meeting adjourns. Carter shakes hands with the bishops, tells them he appreciated the opportunity to meet with them and exchange views. And—in a magnificently inadvertent choice of words—he says he hopes his relationship with the bishops "will grow after this embryonic start."

Carter walks out of the room and enters a room next door. "I think it went rather well, don't you?" he asks an aide.

"No," the aide says.

While Carter is inside posing for pictures with the bishops, Archbishop Bernardin is outside telling reporters that he is "disappointed" in what Carter had to say. Bernardin adds: "Governor Carter did tell us that if acceptable language could be found, he would support a constitutional amendment."

Was Carter signaling a change in his abortion position? Reporters press for clarification. Later, Carter attempts to set things straight. No, he tells reporters, he has not changed his position. There have been two antiabortion amendments proposed to date, and he opposes both. He knows of no other acceptable antiabortion amendment, and he cannot imagine one. He just meant to tell the bishops that he didn't want to rule out something which he had never seen or heard of.

What had happened, clearly, was that Carter had again tried too hard to please. He had not changed his position, but he had bent it to its supple limits. A close Carter aide well versed in Georgia politics once remarked, "In a sense, Jimmy's not much different in the way he runs now than when he was running for state legislator. He still places heavy emphasis on pleasing the people who are in the room with him at that moment." But now Jimmy Carter was running for President; it would never again be just bishops or farmers or factory workers or teachers in the room with him. The whole country would be in the room with him every time.

Carter had gone into the meeting with the bishops

hoping to score points and boost his Catholic vote. But the session produced only two types of news:

1. Some accounts focused on the archbishop's statement that he was "disappointed" with Carter's position.

2. Others were built around a theme of how Carter's position on the abortion issue was once again fuzzy.

On August 3, Carter slid into the backseat of a Secret Service sedan alongside Greg Schneiders and set out from his home for a quick trip to New Hampshire. The drive to the airport in Albany took about a half hour. On the way, Carter reached over and handed Schneiders a copy of a book that Caddell had prepared. It was a lengthy, detailed analysis of Ford's strengths and Reagan's strengths, matched up with various vice-presidential candidates, compared to Carter and Mondale, broken down into categories for every conceivable group and region. "Tell me what you think," Carter said.

As the car neared the airport, Schneiders handed the book back to Carter. The candidate looked a little surprised. "Finished already?" he asked.

"Yes, but I only read the Ford stuff," Schneiders confessed. "That's the only part I felt I had to read. If Kansas City shows that I'm wrong, then I'll have to go back and read Reagan."

Carter smiled. "I only read the Ford section, too."

August/Kansas City

Socrates and Soapsuds and Chimpanzee and Trailblazer and Volunteer—all the President's men—were far from confident. They moved through the corridors and caucus rooms of sweltering Kansas City, communicating with each other by code name through an elaborate radio communications network. They were wheedling and cajoling and scratching and scrounging, trying to lure uncommitted delegates to the fold and at the same time hold their own delegates who were already committed to Tarzan, their code name for the President of the United States.

It was not supposed to be like this. It was supposed to be a glorious ceremonial reaffirmation at Kansas City: the Republican Party convening in the heartland of America to formally bestow the Republican presidential nomination upon a Republican President who very much wanted to answer the call. All that had to be done first, or so it seemed back in the previous autumn, was dispose of this rather annoying challenge from a man they viewed as an aged onetime movie actor who boasted only a fringe of support, galvanized around his predilection for right-wing bromides.

Ronald Reagan had started with a stumble, proposing back in September 1975 his $90-billion plan, which was a proposal to cut federal spending by transferring $90 billion in social programs to the states. When pressed for details, Reagan men had come forth with examples of programs that in fact could not be transferred and other sorts of misinformation. There seemed to be no good explanation for how they had arrived at the $90-billion figure, and the only lasting impression from the effort was that it seemed that Reagan and his issues advisers did not know what they were talking about. This was the kickoff of the Ronald Reagan campaign. And over at 1600 Pennsylvania Avenue, the President's men were indeed shaking. With mirth.

But Reagan had recruited some highly able outside talent. People like John Sears, who had shown masterful political skill in the Nixon campaign of 1968 and who was now Reagan's campaign manager; David Keene, young, bright, savvy, and a man who could practice politics and still retain a sharp sense of humor; and Martin Anderson, one of the brightest conservative thinkers in the issues side of politics, who was brought in to bail out the former California governor after the $90-billion debacle.

There was one more factor. Star quality. Reagan had it. He would walk into an airport without fanfare late at night, and heads would turn and the word would spread and soon he would be signing autographs. It was not like this for any of the other would-be presidents in the primary campaigns of 1976, not Jackson nor Udall, nor Bayh, nor Church. And certainly not Jimmy Carter.

Three weeks before the New Hampshire primary, John Michel, Ford's New Hampshire campaign director, had sat red-eyed and frustrated. The White House had told him it was unlikely that Ford would be in the state to campaign. "I'll tell you, those guys in Washington are not living in the real world," he told Patrick J. Sloyan of *Newsday*. "I was down there in December, and I told them that Ronald Reagan was running one helluva campaign up here. I wanted help and some money. I couldn't even get some literature with Ford's picture on it to pass out. They just didn't believe they had a fight on their hands."

New Hampshire. Ford eventually did make two campaign swings through the state, and he won by a bare 1,587 votes. A switch of just 794 votes would have made the difference. News media accounts told of a President Ford victory. But for all practical purposes, it was not. New Hampshire had shown, most of all, that Ronald Reagan could take on an incumbent President and run him dead even. The lesson of New Hampshire was that the outcome of the Republican nomination fight was, clearly, unclear.

Florida. Reagan was believed to have an early edge as the President's campaign wallowed in discord. But the Ford men brought in Californian Bill Roberts, who put the state organization together. On March 2, Ford had a clearcut victory, winning 53 percent of the vote.

FORD'S FLORIDA VICTORY SEEMS TO ASSURE HIM OF GOP NOMINATION, *The Wall Street Journal* headline declared. Ford had won New Hampshire and Florida, and two uncontested primaries in Vermont and Massachusetts in between. As Reagan campaigned through Illinois, the thing he was asked most was: Are you going to withdraw from the race? The second-most-asked question was: When?

Illinois. Ford won decisively. White House chief of staff Richard Cheney was saying that Reagan's challenge had probably been the best thing that could have happened to Ford, because it showed that he could win outside his Grand Rapids, Michigan, congressional district—something he had never done. Reagan made Ford into a bona fide winner.

North Carolina. Reagan was so tired of being asked when he was pulling out that he made himself scarce to reporters. His campaign was in such bad shape that his operatives had stopped their efforts to get on ballots in areas like southern Ohio, where the primary would not be until June. It seemed a costly exercise in futility. North Carolina loomed as the crusher. March 23. North Carolina was counting its votes, but Reagan, who was sick of the questions and the concession statements, was not sticking around. He was in the air, flying home, when the results came in. Reagan won, 52.4 percent to 45.8 percent. The Californian was caught so unprepared that, upon landing, he could do little more for a victory statement than say no comment.

Texas. The Ford people were making a big effort. The President was stumping, and altogether the Ford campaign was spending $1 million—one-tenth of its entire primary budget—on Texas. But if North Carolina was a stinging jab, then Texas was a haymaker. Reagan carried every district and came away with 100 delegates to Ford's zero. "That was the crusher," Dick Cheney would later say. "We got zapped."

Indiana, Georgia, and Alabama went to Reagan three days later. Nebraska went the following Tuesday. It was clear that Reagan would be in until the end.

        ▨   ▨   ▨

From the outside, once the primaries were over, it appeared that Reagan was just a handful of votes behind

Ford, that nobody had a 1,130 majority of the delegates, and that the pool of about 140 uncommitted delegates was the key.

But from the inside, where John Sears was sitting, it appeared increasingly that Reagan was going to fall short. Not only did their chances of dipping significantly into the pool of uncommitted delegates seem slim, but they were suffering defections from their own ranks. Something had to be done to shake things up. So it was that Sears sold Reagan, champion of the conservative cause, on the plan to tap Pennyslvania's liberal Republican senator, Richard S. Schweiker, as his vice-presidential running mate— and to announce it prior to the convention. Sears and Reagan hoped they could thus win some moderate delegates while still holding their conservative base.

The move stunned the Grand Old Party. Conservatives cried that they had been sold out. Some bolted from the Reagan camp; Mississippi's Clarke Reed, leader of the state's bloc of 30 uncommitted delegate votes, was the most prominent of the defectors to Ford. Reagan gains came later; one here, one there. The Schweiker ploy was called a gamble. But a gamble takes place only when a person is truly risking something in the hopes of scoring a big win. And as Reagan strategist David Keene later observed, "We had nothing to lose."

The Schweiker ploy seemed to be causing more commotion than motion. The Reagan forces were still trailing, perhaps a little more now, and yet the Ford forces did not have the nomination firmly clinched. And this led Sears to come up with another plan. The plan was called, for short, 16-C. And it was on the vote on 16-C that the nomination would be won.

Rule 16-C was Reagan's last strategic move. The Reagan forces were proposing a change in the convention rules to force Ford to disclose the name of his vice-presidential choice before the nomination vote. The convention has a right to know, was the Reagan rallying cry. But really it was one last bid to shake things up, to cause Ford to make a choice that would perhaps alienate some of his supporters—perhaps, just perhaps, spark a few defections to the Reagan side.

Socrates was Thomas Korologos, and Volunteer was William Timmons from Tennessee. They had been congressional liaison men for Richard Nixon's White House; now they were back, trying to help Ford lock up the nomination. On Tuesday, at 6:00 P.M., they met with Soapsuds, who was Bryce Harlow, respected adviser to Presidents Eisenhower and Nixon, and now a lobbyist for Proctor and Gamble. They counted their votes. They needed 1,130 to stop the 16-C ploy. "We could only count 1,125," said Socrates. He passed the word to Chimpanzee, Ford's chief of staff, Richard Cheney.

Hidden in a listening post in a loft above the Kemper Arena, a Ford operative was monitoring his radio and waiting to relay commands from Volunteer. But the radio was silent. It had been silent for some time, in fact. The operative was fidgety; all of this modern electronics communication equipment was at his command, yet he could only wait for it to tell him what to do, and it was silent. Finally, Bill Tucker, a Ford floor whip, entered the listening post, breathless from his long climb from the convention floor. "You don't even have this damn radio turned on!" Tucker told the operator. "Oh, God."

The roll call was about to begin when the hot line rang beside Volunteer. The Maryland delegation was calling. One of their men was missing; he was outside the hall and couldn't find his pass so he could not get back in. Every vote counted; a Ford aide was dispatched to rescue the stranded delegate. Roll call. It was going to be close. Florida passed; so did Mississippi. And at the end of the first calling of the roll, neither side had a majority.

Florida was called for a second time: 28 yes, 38 no. The Ford command trailer behind the arena erupted in hoots and hollers and applause. Reagan had been beaten back on 16-C. By the time Mississippi waded in with its full 30 votes for the Ford position, the aides in the Ford trailer were breaking out the Coors and drinking toasts.

Meanwhile, a horde of camera people, photographers, and reporters had surrounded the Reagan trailer, waiting to ask Sears what this meant for the nomination vote the next night. Rawhide—that was the Ford team's code word for Reagan—called his campaign chief. "Is there any help you need?" Reagan asked Sears. The strategist glanced out at the waiting pack.

"Well, if you could get a tractor and pull this trailer out of here, it would be helpful," Sears said. Sears knew then what would happen the following night.

🏴   🏴   🏴

Wednesday night. Kemper Arena was New Year's Eve, the Mardi Gras, Carnival, and a Bicentennial Fourth of July. It was Reagan banners and Reagan Frisbees and Reagan confetti, and mainly it was Reagan horns, shrill, blasting, deafening air horns. This was the demonstration following the formal placing of Ronald Reagan's name into nomination. But it was more. It was a celebration of an effort that had at least been the most formidable challenge to a sitting President in modern history. The Reagan campaign had taken the staid, structured Grand Old Party and turned it into tough, bloody, exciting theater.

The Reagan demonstration had been officially scheduled for fifteen minutes. But it went on. And on. And on. The noise shattered Kemper Arena for about an hour, while the Ford people fumed, unable to turn it off. Away from the floor, Lyn Nofziger, Reagan's paunchy, perpetually rumpled convention floor manager, confessed. "Yes, it was me," he said. Nofziger had kept the demonstration going deliberately; he wanted to keep Reagan on television through prime time, pushing the inevitable Ford nomination back until Middle America had gone to bed. He had wanted, at least, one more pound of flesh. He got it.

🏴   🏴   🏴

Early Wednesday afternoon, in the wake of the crucial vote on 16-C the night before, John Sears talked with Ford operative F. Clifton White. The two camps had agreed back in June that the winner of the nomination would go to the hotel of the loser as soon as the balloting was over, to demonstrate party unity. Now it was agreed that after the balloting, Cheney would call Sears in the Reagan trailer to set up the meeting. According to Ford and Reagan officials, the Reagan camp made two requirements: (1) that the meeting be strictly between the two political leaders and no one else; and (2) that Ford would not offer the vice presidency to Reagan. Word of the requirements was carried back to Cheney; Cheney conferred with Ford and sent word back to the Reagan men that the requirements would be adhered to.

At 12:30 A.M. Thursday morning, the convention nominated Ford by a vote of 1,187 to Reagan's 1,070. Cheney, in the President's suite at the modern Crown Center Hotel, called Sears. The Reagan man reiterated the two requirements. The President and his advisers assumed that Reagan did not want to be in the position of turning down the President's call to serve as his running mate and that he did not want the job. Ford, for his part, did not want to run with Reagan; the scars of the long nomination fight, where Reagan took Ford to the wire and demonstrated the President's lack of political clout, were still deep.

Ford drove to the Alameda Plaza Hotel, Reagan headquarters, accompanied by Cheney and Harlow. The two leaders met upstairs, alone, while the Ford and Reagan aides milled about and made uncomfortable small talk. In the meeting, the two men were cordial but reserved toward each other. They talked about the campaign they had just endured. They exchanged ideas about what issues seemed to be bothering Americans and what campaign appeals seemed to work best. Then Ford said he would like to get Reagan's reaction to several people he was considering for Vice President. He said Rockefeller had definitely taken himself out of the running. Ford then mentioned several names, among them Charles Percy, Elliot Richardson, John Connally, Howard Baker, Robert Dole. Reagan was generally complimentary about all of those Ford mentioned except Richardson. He told the President he did not think the Reaganites within the GOP would accept the selection of Richardson, the moderate from Massachusetts. Reagan was a bit more complimentary about Dole than he was about others; Dole had earlier asked Reagan, through an intermediary, to put in a good word for him with the President.

At 3:15 A.M., back at the Crown Center, Ford summoned nine top advisers to his eighteenth-floor conference room. A Vice President had to be chosen. For all of the weeks before, Ford had not indicated his preference to any of his advisers. Not even to Cheney, his chief of staff, the man who helped him put together his procedure for choosing a running mate.

In the conference room seated at Ford's left was Vice President Nelson Rockefeller, who had been eased out of the 1976 picture because he was seen as a liberal millstone to the Ford effort. Others around the table included old friends and political associates from his kitchen cabinet: Senator Robert Griffin (R-Mich.), Melvin Laird, and Bryce Harlow. There was the influential Texas conservative Senator John Tower. There were White House staff men Richard Cheney, his chief of staff, and John Marsh, his counselor. And there were campaign staff men Stuart Spencer, his top strategist, and Robert Teeter, his pollster. Most prominent among the missing was Ford's campaign manager, Rogers Morton, who had not been invited.

It had been a long, hard, emotion-draining day for the President and his men. They had been up early, counting votes and politicking delegates, making sure there would be no slips and that the nomination would not be blown by some last-minute oversight. They had worked right up to the convention balloting that night. There had been time for congratulations and brief toasts and partying, but now Ford and his close advisers were gathered for very serious business.

Starting at 3:15 A.M., they waded through the names under consideration for the vice presidency. Some sipped Scotch as they talked; some smoked.

The tension and emotion that had filled Kemper Arena earlier that night was a subject of concern to the Ford men. The convention was volatile, unpredictable. Would it balk at anyone Ford picked and insist on drafting Reagan instead? Was there a danger of a bitter floor fight? A runaway convention, out of control of even the President?

This, they agreed, could be catastrophic. They remember how the divisiveness of the Democratic Convention of 1968 had crippled Hubert Humphrey at the start of his campaign. A main concern now, the advisers agreed, was that the vice-presidential nominee should not be someone who would cause the Reagan people to bolt.

They started with two dozen names, and within two hours they had narrowed it down to four:

● Senator Howard Baker of Tennessee, a Republican star of the Senate Watergate hearings;

● William D. Ruckelshaus, once interim head of the

FBI, and former deputy attorney general who became a Watergate hero when he was fired by Richard Nixon in the Saturday Night Massacre;

• Anne Armstrong of Texas, former White House counselor under Nixon, former chairwoman of the Republican National Committee, and now U.S. ambassador to Great Britain.

• Senator Robert Dole of Kansas, former congressman and former chairman of the Republican National Committee.

Each had supporters within the President's inner circle.

Teeter was especially high on Ruckelshaus. Others, among them Cheney, looked upon Ruckelshaus as clearly the most liberal of the four. Teeter felt that Ruckelshaus was a Watergate hero who had made his reputation nationally for refusing Richard Nixon's order to fire Archibald Cox as Watergate special prosecutor.

He had domestic experience as the head of the Environmental Protection Agency. And despite his popularity with liberals due to Watergate, he was viewed basically as a middle-of-the-road to conservative Republican. Also, Ruckelshaus was a Catholic—and Jimmy Carter had problems in winning support among Catholics. But Ruckelshaus had never won a statewide election in Indiana; his only attempt had been an unsuccessful challenge of Senator Birch Bayh in 1968. And there was the fear that he would be too liberal for the Reaganites.

Stuart Spencer strongly recommended Anne Armstrong. Most in the room agreed that she was a person of very high quality. Perhaps she was indeed the most capable of the four. But there were facts of life to consider. Teeter had done a poll which indicated that the country was not yet ready for a woman Vice President. He had run trial heats with Ford and various running mates, The presence of a woman on the ticket cost Ford more votes than the presence of any other male Vice President. A number of people would vote for Ford with any male Vice President, but would then turn around and vote for Carter when a woman was paired as Ford's Vice President. Most of those interviewed who switched when a woman was placed beside Ford were, in fact, women themselves.

Howard Baker was probably the best known, nationally, of the four finalists. He also was a Watergate hero figure of sorts, having gained fame with his favorite question:

"What did the President know, and when did he know it?" He could, perhaps, defuse a possible problem for Ford, the Watergate residue that lingered and was compounded by Ford's pardoning of Richard Nixon.

Ford had never been especially close to Baker; yet Baker was widely viewed outside that conference room as the frontrunner for the vice presidency. He would be perceived as essentially a southerner, but the Ford men did not entertain much hope of capturing the South from Carter. In fact, Carter was so strong in Tennessee that it was highly questionable whether Baker could carry his own state for the ticket. So there seemed little geographic advantage to Baker.

(Reports had surfaced that Baker's wife once had an alcohol problem; but advisers in the room stressed that this did not figure in the final deliberations of the Ford men.)

Dole, of Kansas, could bring strength to the traditionally Republican Farm Belt, where Ford and his men recognized the President's policies had not always been popular. Dole was aggressive and articulate. He could carry the burden of the campaign offense while Ford emphasized his role as a President in the White House. Ford knew Dole and liked him; they were friends who had served together in the House of Representatives. And, mainly, Dole had good conservative credentials. He would go down well with the volatile Reaganites.

Throughout the session, Rockefeller spoke out often, offering pros and cons on many of the names and participating actively in the discussion. Tower and Harlow also offered frequent analyses. Laird and Griffin, in contrast, seemed more inclined to second what others were saying instead of staking out firm positions of their own. "They seemed to be interested in positioning themselves so they could come out later and let it be known that they were the ones who had urged the selection of whoever it was that Ford picked," said one of the advisers in the room.

The predawn hours of the morning droned by. Finally, at 5:00 A.M., bone-weary, the President and his advisers came to a firm conclusion: the ultimate decision ought to be made by rested, clearheaded people. "Why don't we sleep on it for a couple of hours?" someone suggested.

They adjourned and reconvened at 9:30 A.M., fresher but not really refreshed. The job had to be finished soon. The selection had to be made and announced in time for the delegates to get the word and for the speeches to be written, and for preparations to be made for the final convention session that night.

Once again, they reviewed the four finalists. They kept in mind the strategy Ford would probably employ in the fall. The Republican base would have to be in the Farm Belt: Nebraska, Kansas, Missouri, Iowa, North Dakota, South Dakota, Minnesota. Also the industrial midwestern states of Illinois, Michigan, Ohio, and Indiana. Baker was popular around the country in general, but Dole could certainly help most in the Farm Belt. Dole had gone to bat for the farmers against the Ford administration to oppose its embargo on grain sales to the Soviet Union, charging that Secretary of State Kissinger had meddled in domestic agricultural policy. Dole's comments were not popular in the White House then, but they were viewed with a bit more appreciation that night.

And Dole was viewed by all as a fighter. A man of wit, he had nonetheless assumed a tough-talk role in the past. When the Nixon White House was outraged at the *Washington Post*'s Watergate revelations, Dole was contacted, and he dutifully attacked the paper for "mudslinging" and printing "political garbage." But he went on to become critical of the operations of H. R. Haldeman and John Ehrlichman, and in 1973 he was fired as party chairman by Nixon—thus escaping the onrushing Watergate tidal wave.

Ford wanted his vice-presidential running mate to campaign long and hard this fall—often while Ford remained in the White House.

It was shortly after 10:00 A.M when Ford looked up and told the men around the table that he had made his choice: Dole. At 10:30 A.M., he called the Kansan's suite at the Muehlbach Hotel. "Would you like to be on the ticket?" Ford asked.

"Certainly," Dole replied.

Then Ford made calls to break the news to Baker and John Connally. A White House aide was dispatched to the Muehlbach to drive Dole and his wife to the Crown Center Hotel to meet with the President.

The aide jumped in his car and headed for the Crown Center garage door. It was locked by the Secret Service as a security precaution. He tried another. It was locked, too. Precious time was wasted before he finally escaped from the garage. The Ford aide raced to the Muehlbach, hurried to the designated floor, stopped in front of a door, and knocked. The door was opened by tall, silver-haired John Connally. The aide gulped. He looked at the room number. Wrong room. He mumbled apologies, found the right door, and the right vice-presidential hopeful. The Ford man chauffeured Robert Dole and his wife to their meeting with the President in the only car he had been able to find on such short notice, a compact, rented Pacer.

🏳️ 🏳️ 🏳️

President Ford delivered what was perhaps the best speech of his life on the platform at Kemper Arena Thursday night. His normally wooden delivery had been lifted to eloquence. He had prepared for this event with painstaking practice in front of television videotape machines and was coached by former actor Don Penny. Now, on the platform, Ford was giving the performance of his career. ". . . You at home, listening tonight—you are the people who pay the taxes and obey the laws. You are the people who make our system work. You are the people who make America what it is. It is from your ranks that I come, and on your side I stand. . . ."

Beneath the platform, in a special VIP holding room, the Vice President of the United States was shouting in fury. While the President was giving his speech, Nelson Rockefeller was blowing up at the President's chief of staff, Richard Cheney. He yelled an accusation that Cheney had been responsible for the fact that the microphone went out as Rockefeller was nominating Dole (it had been one more humiliation for Rockefeller). Rockefeller had been feuding with Donald Rumsfeld, Cheney's predecessor and mentor. Now he was apparently transferring his anger to Cheney, who, ironically, had often in private discussions cited Rockefeller as one of the public officials he most admired. Cheney looked stunned, and Rockefeller bellowed on. Now, the Vice President said, he was being asked to suffer one last indignity—the order in which the dignitaries were to walk out onto the platform following Ford's address had Dole going out first, then his family, and finally Rockefeller. This was too much. He would look like forgotten baggage. "I am still the Vice President of the United States of America!" Rockefeller thundered. Cheney quickly fixed the order so that Dole and Rockefeller walked out onto the platform side by side. The Vice President was appeased. And soon he was standing there before the entire country, on the platform with Ford and Dole and all the other Grand Old Party celebrities; standing there together, one big happy family.

THE RACE: *It is the Sunday after the Republican convention, and Pat Caddell is in New Jersey on business while his organization is running a new private poll for Carter. Caddell's assistant Dottie Lynch walks into Caddell's room—her face is ash-white, and Caddell wonders if she is well. She hands the pollster a slip of paper and says softly, "It looks like our lead is 8 or 9 points."*

Eight or 9 points. It had been 25 (Carter 57; Ford 32) just before the Republican convention, according to Gallup. The Grand Old Party affair had been high drama and good theater. Surely Ford could be expected to come away with a sizable boost in the polls. But this was far more than expected. Caddell reached for his security blanket, the telephone. He confers with his office in Cambridge, Massachusetts. There is some newer data, but it will not help much. It looks like Carter over Ford by a narrowed margin of 9 or 10 points.

Caddell calls Hamilton Jordan in Georgia. Jordan is stunned. (The next day, Gallup concludes a poll showing Carter in slightly better shape, leading Ford by 50 to 37, a margin of 13.)

The race has tightened with a rush. Later, Caddell figures the bad news might have been good, after all. "It did wonders for the Carter campaign," he says. "It brought everyone back from thinking about where their offices were going to be in the White House."

Blueprint/Carter

Jimmy Carter's strategy for the fall campaign was shaped through the months of summer. It was detailed in two memos written by Hamilton Jordan. The first was handed to the candidate in June, well before the Democratic convention. The second was handed him in early August, addressed to both Carter and Walter Mondale.

📧 📧 📧

I.

Confidential

Memorandum for Jimmy Carter

Your Image with the American People

Once a political image is fully developed, it is not easily changed or even modified. To create an impression on the American electorate, you have to penetrate the reluctant consciousness of a people who are alienated from their government and its leaders. Only by bombarding them with impressions over an extended period of time is an image created. But just as you lack control over the image that is created (Jimmy Carter is "fuzzy" on the issues), you have even greater difficulty changing those initial impressions in specific ways or refining them.

Because your rise politically this year has been so rapid and dramatic, I do not believe that your image is fully developed or has much depth. I believe that there is still time for wrong impressions to be corrected and certain strengths to be magnified. . . .

It is important that we carefully consider the image you project during the summer months.

Overexposed

I started worrying back in March that you were being overexposed. There were very few Tuesday nights and Wednesday mornings that you were not on television and all over the newspapers winning another primary. Toward the end of the primaries, I believe that some people just started to get tired of you and all of the "original" candidates and for that reason turned to "new faces" like Church and Brown.

As compared to Gerald Ford, you are still a "new face" and an "outsider." And I know nothing that will do more to fully restore these qualities to your image than for you to spend a lot of time at home with your family and friends while maintaining a low political profile. At the same time, it is likely that Ford and Reagan will occupy centerstage fighting for delegates and the nomination.

Electoral College Projections

Needed to Be Elected President: 270 Electoral Votes

I. *Southern States Carter Is Likely to Carry*

1.	Alabama	9
2.	Arkansas	6
3.	Georgia	12
4.	Kentucky	9
5.	Louisiana	10
6.	Mississippi	7
7.	North Carolina	13
8.	South Carolina	8
9.	Tennessee	10
10.	Virginia	12
		96

II. *Southern States Likely to Be Heavily Contested*

11.	Texas	26
12.	Florida	17
		43

III. *Important Border States Which Can Be Carried*

13.	Maryland	10
14.	Missouri	12
		22

IV. *States of High Democratic Performance/Likely to Vote Democratic*

15.	Massachusetts	14
16.	Wisconsin	11
17.	Minnesota	10
18.	District of Columbia	3
		38

V. *Critical Large/Industrial States*

19.	California	45
20.	New York	41
21.	Pennsylvania	27
22.	Illinois	26
23.	Ohio	25
24.	Michigan	21
25.	New Jersey	17
26.	Indiana	13
		215

Electoral Vote Analysis

I. Presume that Jimmy Carter is able and likely to win the electoral votes from the states in categories I, II, III, and IV.

I.	Southern/Likely to Carry	96
II.	Southern/Contested	43
III.	Important Border States	22
IV.	Probable Democratic States	38
		199

These electoral votes (199) represent 74% of the electoral votes that Carter will need to win the Presidency. Of the states included in this analysis, those in categories II and III are most likely to be seriously challenged by the Republican nominee. The states included in categories II and III—Texas, Florida, Missouri and Maryland —are states that we can win. If you assumed that we would lose these four states, we would still have 134 electoral votes from the Southern states we are likely to carry and the probable Democratic states. Those 134 electoral votes would represent 49% of the votes needed to win the Presidency.

II. Presume then that Carter is able to win the electoral votes of the states in categories I, II, III and IV giving him a base of 199 electoral votes on which to build. Consider the various options available to achieve the necessary votes to win a majority of the Electoral College.

Review the states in V—described as "Critical Large/Industrial States":

California	45
New York	41
Pennsylvania	27
Illinois	26
Ohio	25
Michigan	21
New Jersey	17
Indiana	13
	215

Presuming then that Carter carries states in I, II, III and IV, he will need 71 electoral votes to achieve a majority in the Electoral College. From the states above, he could get the 71 votes needed from any of the following combinations:

1. *Carry New York and California*

New York	41
California	45
	86

2. *Carry New York or California and One of the Three Large Industrial States*

New York	41
Pennsylvania	27
	68 (Technically, 3 votes short)

New York	41
Illinois	26
	67 (Technically, 4 votes short)

New York	41
Ohio	25
	66 (Technically, 5 votes short)

California	45
Pennsylvania	27
	72

California	45
Ohio	25
	70 (Technically, 1 vote short)

California	45
Michigan	21
	66 (Technically, 5 votes short)

3. *Lose New York and California, but Carry 3 or 4 Other Large States*

Pennsylvania	27
Illinois	26
Ohio	25
Michigan	21

3 of the above 4 = 71 plus electoral votes

Strategic Conclusions

The conclusions that can be drawn from these . . . analyses are quite simple:

1) The Southern states provide us a base of support that cannot be taken for granted or jeopardized.
2) The Republicans cannot win if they write off the South. Consequently, we have to assume that they will challenge us in the South. I believe that they will challenge us in those larger Southern and Border states that they view as contestable— Texas, Florida, Maryland, and Missouri.

3) I believe that we can win each of those four states that are likely to be contested.

4) A Southern or Western running mate might be selected by the Republican nominee to assist them in their challenge to us in the South.

5) Based on the analysis of Democratic potential in each state, we should not publicly concede a single state to the Republicans. This should be our public posture which will result in their having to worry and spend time and resources defending states that are likely to vote Republican.

6) If Ford is the nominee, you will have the same advantage over him that you had over many of your primary opponents—full time to devote to the campaign. This should result in our being able to spend some time campaigning in states that they will either write off or ignore because of size or lack of comparable time to spend campaigning.

7) We obviously can and must do well in the large industrial states.

8) Although the Southern states provide us with a rich base of support, it would be a mistake to appear to be overly dependent on the South for victory in November. It would be harmful nationally if we were perceived as having a "Southern strategy." The strength of the South in the electoral college is quite obvious to the media. But to the extent that regional bias exists in this country—and it does— there would be a negative reaction to a candidacy that was perceived as being a captive of the Southern states and/or people. Sad but true. Southern regional pride can be used to great advantage without unnecessarily alienating potential anti-Southern voters.

The General Election Campaign

Preface

For the first time in recent history of American politics, the Democratic Party will have the opportunity to conduct a well coordinated and integrated national campaign that mutually benefits the national ticket,

Congressional and gubernatorial candidates, legislative
and local candidates. The reason is that the party's
nominees will receive Federal monies and will not be
competing with state and local candidates for the same
dollars. To the contrary, the Presidential and Vice-
Presidential nominees will be able to help them raise
monies for use in their own campaign. This lack of
competition for the same dollars coupled with the
ability of the nominees to raise monies for Democratic
candidates should give the national ticket and party
the leverage it will need to insure an integrated national and state effort. . . .

It is my strong recommendation that Bob Lipshutz
continue as Treasurer of the campaign. The Budget
Director will report to him and Bob will maintain control over all expenditures, accounting and Federal reports. I do not know any person in the campaign who
has made a greater contribution to our success than
Bob Lipshutz. I do not know where we would be today
without him.

II.

Personal and Confidential

To: Jimmy Carter
      Walter Mondale
From: Hamilton Jordan

You will find in the following pages an analysis of
our present political posture and some strategic premises for the general election campaign.

Also, a formula which attempts to provide us a
framework for the allocation of our major resources.

We will begin soon to make commitments in terms of
the schedule, media and organization. Your comments,
criticisms and suggestions are needed.

Introduction

As we look ahead to the general election, it is important that we establish a framework and mechanism for
the allocation of our resources.

We had three long years to prepare and execute a strategy for winning the Democratic nomination. Our public campaign lasted two years. Our finances were limited only by our own ability to raise funds. We spent two hundred and fifty days on the road in 1975 and another one hundred and twenty-five in 1976. Most of this time was well spent—some was wasted. But, there was always enough time to make adjustments.

Yet, in the general election we are dealing with limited and finite resources.

We will have—at most—forty-five (45) campaign days between Labor Day and Election Day.

We will have $21.8 million to spend

When that time is gone and that money is spent, there will be no more.

Consequently, it is important that we develop a realistic and precise framework for allocating these finite resources that takes into account the major political considerations and our own strategy while providing us with an appropriate amount of flexibility.

Strategic Premises for the General Election

Before presenting the formula for the allocation of resources, it is necessary first to understand the strategic premises on which this formula was constructed.

These premises are basic to our total strategy. To the extent that there is a strong objection to the premises stated here, it should be presented and resolved so that the formula can be adjusted

They are:

1) *Our clear and single goal must be to simply win 270 electoral votes*. We cannot afford initially to become so enamoured with our own survey results and the prospects of a landslide that we lose sight of the 270 electoral votes we will need. To expand our limited resources trying to win 400 electoral votes, we could very easily fall short of the 270 we need to win the election.

2) *We should spend a small amount of time early in the campaign challenging Ford in states that are traditionally Republican states in a Presidential election.*

Ford lacks a base of support—there is not a region of the country nor a political grouping of states that he can count on in November. Consequently, he lacks the mathematical base on which to build a majority of the electoral votes. Without a base, he lacks a strategy. By making a trip early in the campaign into several traditionally Republican states, I believe that we can effectively put Ford on the defensive, making him spend time and money in states he should carry. Perhaps more importantly, we can prevent the Republicans from ever developing a clear strategy for winning.

3) *The Southern and Border states are our base of support that cannot be taken for granted or jeopardized —the only way we can lose in November is to have this base fragmented.* We need to spend early time campaigning in the South and several key border states. If our solid lead here holds, we can probably cut back on time here in October and simply "show the flag" regularly.

4) *We must resist tremendous pressures and always retain a high degree of flexibility in the allocation of our resources and the objectives of our strategy.* We must never forget that in 1968 in six weeks Hubert Humphrey closed twenty points on Richard Nixon and almost won the Presidency. We will probably not know until mid-October if the election is going to be close or if there is potential for a big victory. Either way, flexibility is critical and necessary and will be maintained at all costs.

5) *Jimmy Carter and Walter Mondale will play to their strengths.* As he heads the ticket, it obviously will be necessary for Carter to campaign in all areas of the country. However, Carter obviously will have to play the lead role in protecting our base in the South. Mondale should work areas of the country where he is stronger than Carter and work with certain groups and elements of the party that he has a special relationship with—liberals, labor unions, members of Congress, etc.

6) *If by mid-October we have a commanding lead and have the flexibility previously advocated, the goals and objectives of the campaign can be appropriately broadened.* If our projected lead in the Electoral College is commanding and our survey results solid in

mid-October, we can begin to spend an appropriate amount of time and resources trying to win the mandate we will need to bring real and meaningful change to this country.

Explanation of Formula Factors

The formula which is described and presented in the following pages takes into account three basic factors:
—the *size* of a state
—the *Democratic potential* of a state
—the *need* we have to mount an effective campaign

Size. As the objective is to win a majority of the votes in the Electoral College (270), it follows that the major consideration in allocating the compaign's resources is the relative size of each state. I have made the judgment in assigning numerical values to each factor that the *size* of the state is as important as the *Democratic potential* and *need* combined. Consequently, fifty percent (50%) of the points allocated in the formula are based on the relative size of each state. Using the total number of votes in the Electoral College as a mathematical base (538), I have assigned a single point in value (1) for each electoral vote a state has.

Democratic Potential. We must, of necessity, focus our resources first on those states that have the greatest Democratic potential and are most likely to vote Democratic if worked effectively. For that reason, twenty-five percent (25%) of the points assigned (280) are allocated based on the relative Democratic potential of each state.

Need. "Need" is best described as our judgment as to the relative amount of time, resources and energies that we should invest in a particular state. This is the most arbitrary of the factors considered and a rationalization is presented later in this section for the numerical values assigned each state. Factors considered in establishing the relative need are:
—Survey information from Pat Caddell
—strategic premises of the general election
—whether or not we campaigned in the state in the primaries

—how well or poorly we did in the state in the primaries
—other information which is presented
Approximately twenty-five percent (25%) of the points assigned (265) are assigned based on the relative *need* of the states.

Summary.

Size +	Democratic Potential +	Need =	Total Points
50% +	25%	+ 25% =	100%

OR

538 pts. + 280 pts. + 265 pts. = 1083 pts.

[Jordan then presented thirty-one pages of separate, detailed formulas allotting points to each state for size, Democratic potential, and need. He measured Democratic potential by assigning what he called "indicator" points for the number of elected Democratic members of Congress and state officials. He reduced the "need" to campaign in each state to numerical terms by dividing the states into four groups: states in Group A each received 9.8 points; Group B, 6.2; Group C, 3.5; Group D, 2.0. Then he put all of these totals into his original formula to determine the "percent of effort" the Carter campaign needed to devote to each state. (See Appendix III.)

[Next, Jordan arbitrarily assigned a numerical value to indicate what one day of campaigning by each of the Carter-Mondale celebrities would be worth. Jimmy Carter topped the list with a 7. Walter Mondale was worth a 5, Rosalynn Carter 4, Joan Mondale 3, Jack and Judy Carter 2, Chip and Caron Carter 2, Jeff and Annette Carter 2.

[Jordan multiplied these figures by the number of days each person would be out on the campaign, and wound up with what he called "total scheduling points." And he multiplied the total scheduling points for the campaign by the "percent of effort" that had already been calculated for each state, and wound up with a precise number of points for each state.

[It was then up to the schedulers to determine just how

to apportion the time of the various campaigners to equal the total points allotted to each state.]

Summary

As a result of this exercise, we can determine how much time should be spent in a particular state. For example, the state of Oregon earned 16 scheduling points. This might result in the following trips to that state:

1. Jimmy Carter spends ½ day there	3.5	points
2. Walter Mondale spends 1 day there	5.0	points
3. Joan Mondale spends ½ day there	1.5	points
4. Rosalynn Carter spends 1 day there	4.0	points
5. Jack and Judy spend 1 day there	2.0	points
	16.0	points

These five trips—spread over an eight-week period—would give the ticket good exposure in the state of Oregon.

Blueprint/Ford

> From the president's standpoint, the greatest staff problem is that of maintaining his contact with the world's reality that lies outside the White House walls . . . the concept that "even your best friends won't tell you" about unpleasant things applies with tremendous force to the president.
>
> —George E. Reedy, former press secretary to President Lyndon Johnson, in his book, *The Twilight of the Presidency.*

Presidents get out of touch. They become isolated. They learn of the world's reality through the people who work for them, which is to say that all too often they don't learn of it at all. When the truth is good, the White House is suddenly full of assistants who are eager to bring the news. When the truth is bad, inescapably bad, there are still loyal assistants who carry out their duty by getting the word to the President. But when the truth is distasteful, embarrassing—humiliating—to a President, all too often the word does not get to him at all. Presidential aides admit that this goes on frequently, and they say they are protecting the President; but mostly they are just protecting themselves from having to bring their boss the most painful of news. It is easier, by far, to alter reality. Thus dissents are softened, harsh judgments modified, stinging phrases toned down; by the time the view is presented to the President, it is not the view that the rest of the world is seeing. He has lost contact.

So it was that Woodrow Wilson was broken by his League of Nations dream; and Lyndon Johnson by his Vietnam War policies; and Richard Nixon by his Watergate lies. Three vastly different Presidents, with three vastly different problems, but they shared one basic thing: they were out of touch.

Gerald Ford went into the fall campaign with grave political problems. But he had no illusions, thanks to the truly gutsy efforts of a group of advisers. They saw it as their job to provide the President with their view of just what the problem was—which in an election year meant in large part just what it was that the public was seeing and thinking. Michael Duval, Jerry Jones, Foster Chanock, and Ford's campaign pollster, Robert Teeter, among others, working under the direction of Richard Cheney, combined to produce one of the most remarkable presidential memos ever prepared in a White House. It contained comments that could upset the President and comments that could disturb him—but they were comments that the President had every right to know.

It was the President's 1976 election strategy memo, 120 pages long, plus a bulky set of appendixes. It began by trying to make clear just how serious Ford's problems were —concluding, nevertheless, that Ford could still win. And it included a section that, mincing no words, told the President just what the public viewed as his strengths and shortcomings—and it was clear from the memo that the public perception of Ford's shortcomings was sizable, and that he did indeed have problems.

This was a proud and accomplished man who had graduated from the University of Michigan and Yale Law School (only three other U.S. Presidents had ever graduated from law schools); his staff told him in the memo that many citizens viewed him as "not smart" and that many questioned whether he was "competent or intelligent enough to be President."

This was a man who had steered the country through the aftermath of the disclosure of criminal activity at the highest levels of the Nixon administration; his staff told him he was viewed as "not-in-control of government" and a "puppet" of Secretary of State Henry Kissinger and other officials.

This was a man who had been elected to Congress every two years for a quarter of a century and had stumped annually to help his colleagues; his staff told him that his national approval rating "declined" when he campaigned, and that he was considered a "poor communicator—especially via television."

The 1976 strategy memo was a masterfully constructed document. It told this President, who would be putting everything on the line in the fall campaign, every last bit of bad news he was entitled to know. Yet it carried throughout the positive, uplifting threads of can-do optimism. The authors were men who fervently wanted the President to win the November election; they were *his* men. But they had no illusions about the task ahead and felt the President should have no illusions, either.

Ford had taken comfort in the heroic comeback of Harry Truman in 1948; his staff told him that he was no Harry Truman and that the two situations were not comparable; Truman's Democratic Party was embraced by a majority of the electorate, while Ford would start from a decidedly minority Republican base. The Ford men even made a trip to the Truman Library in Independence, Missouri, to get a copy of Clark Clifford's 1948 strategy memo to Truman to point up the differences between the two presidential campaigns.

The Ford memo proved to be remarkably accurate in pinpointing the areas where Carter was strong and the areas where Carter was vulnerable to attack. In the weeks ahead, Republicans went on to exploit the perceived Carter weaknesses outlined in the memo; and this proved a major factor in helping Ford close the gap. The memo was given to the President shortly before his nomination in Kansas City.

    ▦   ▦   ▦

Memorandum to the President

. . . As the following analysis shows, you face a unique challenge. No President has overcome the obstacles to election which you will following our Convention this August. For example, President Truman trailed Dewey in August 1948 by 11 points, whereas we expect to be trailing Carter by about 20 points after our Convention.

Of course, the Ford-Carter gap will begin to close (perhaps even before our Convention) on its own almost irrespective of what we do. However, although the point spread may close over time fairly easily down to a point where Carter is 5 to 10 points ahead, the remaining distance to victory will be very difficult.

Because you must come from behind, and are subject to many constraints, no strategy can be developed which allows for any substantial error.

We firmly believe that you can win in November. . . .

There are six points that we wish to emphasize at the beginning:

1. The Nation is at a crossroad. . . . *For many Americans who believe that unconstrained government is a threat to individual freedom, your election in November is a national imperative. For them and for us, the campaign is not simply a fight for power. We are fighting for principle. Your supporters welcome whatever discipline and hard work is necessary to win because they believe in you and because you stand for the principles they think are important.*

2. *If past is indeed prologue, you will lose on November 2nd*—because to win you must do what has never been done: close a gap of about 20 points in 73 days from the base of a minority party while spending approximately the same amount of money as your opponent.

3. You cannot overcome the Carter lead on your own no matter what you do. Of course, your "offensive" campaign is a crucial element, but *to win, Carter's position must be changed* by a strong attack launched by the Vice Presidential nominee and others.

4. *You are not now perceived as being a strong, decisive leader by anywhere near a majority of the American people.* Our campaign must change this perception, but it cannot unless some current problems such as in-house staff fighting are corrected.

5. You cannot possibly win without a highly disciplined and directionalized campaign. The first step is to develop and adopt a basic strategy. Once adopted, *your strategy must not be changed unless clearly justified by hard data.* If the strategy is not followed, or if it constantly changes, your campaign will become chaotic.

6. In preparing this memorandum, we have tried to be completely candid. We have viewed our strengths and weaknesses in the context of the election challenge. We recognize that a "weakness" in this context may be a "strength" in normal times. Thus, *this paper*

is not intended as criticism of anyone, but rather we have tried to present a hard, realistic analysis of the obstacles to your victory and how they can be overcome. *We firmly believe that you can win.*

Major Constraints

. . . The President's strategy must recognize and deal with the following constraints:

1. The Democratic Party enjoys a 43% to 21% advantage. A GOP candidate will always have difficulty closing a large gap on a Democratic opponent.

2. Campaign expenditures for both candidates will be the same. We no longer have the previous advantage of being able to outspend our opponent. This is a particular handicap when we are behind.

3. Given the dollar limitation, any dollar wasted cannot be recouped. Limited resources is a major restraint.

4. The GOP Convention is late; the Party will be divided after the nomination fights and will have little time to bind its wounds.

5. A Campaign designed to woo various voter blocs through extensive government programs and patronage is not in the cards in 1976.

    a. Budget dollars are not available to fund extensive new program initiatives.

    b. The broken promises of 1972 have made the buyable voter blocs wary of promises.

    c. The President's most basic philosophy has been to ask the people to sacrifice short-term benefits in return for long-term gains. Changing this philosophy now is too late:

      —to be credible to the recipients

      —to escape a media storm.

Definition of Problem

. . . Our election goal must be to win enough popular votes in enough States to get over 270 electoral votes. In broad terms, we have to close a nearly 3-to-2 gap in seventy-three days from the base of a minority party.

On the other hand, Carter's popularity is based almost exclusively on his awareness factor. His support is very thin and clearly vulnerable to deterioration. . . .

President Ford's perception must change and Carter's perception must change. In order to win, we must persuade over 15% (or about 10 million people) to change their opinions. *This will require very aggressive—media-oriented efforts. . . .*

Elements of the Perception Problem

In the following "perception" analysis, we have tried to capture the current perception of the President and Carter, using descriptions commonly used by those polled or interviewed by the press. We have attempted to use descriptions which may best reflect the perception held by the voter who is *not* a hard partisan for the President or Carter. In short, we believe that these are the perceptions of the people in the "middle." *These perceptions do not necessarily reflect your true character or style as President. They are a reflection of how the TV viewer and newspaper reader "sees" you.* We have presented this with the "bark" off because we must solve this perception problem in order to successfully communicate your leadership qualities. This obstacle must be overcome or there is no chance for victory.

Perception of Carter

Positive

- A winner who has "it." A man with real personal appeal; "I like him."
- A man with strong spiritual and moral values; an honest man of character.
- A family man.
- A man who cares about the common man and his problems.
- A new kind of politician who is against the corrupt Washington system and will not lie.
- A man concerned about government efficiency and dedicated to making the government work better.

- A man who seems to deal with and resolve issues in a non-controversial way.
- He is seen as an economic liberal and a social conservative.
- He is a man with quiet strength; he will not let the politicians run over him. He is in control and will run the country with authority.
- Seen as responsible Democrat—not a maverick; not extreme.

Negative

- An arrogant man.
- A man who wears his religion on his sleeve; he is self-righteous. Lacks humility.
- A man who tries to be all things to all men; we don't know where he stands on the issues.
- A man about whom we don't know enough; we really don't know who he is as a person.
- A Southerner.
- May not be experienced enough to be President. . . .

Perception of the President

Positive

- I like him; he is a good man who tried hard. I hope he succeeds.
- He is safe and will do the right thing.
- He came in under horrible circumstances and the situation in the country has gotten better under him.
- An honest man who will try to do the right thing; he has restored honesty in government.
- He will keep the activists from taking over and springing another Great Society on us.

Negative

- Not decisive.
- Not really on top of the job.
- Doesn't seem to have a clear view of where he is

going and why; doesn't seem to understand our problems or have solutions for them.

- Spends too much time on politics, too worried about election, doesn't seem to spend enough time on the people's business, too much of an old politician.
- Seen as part of the old-time, do-nothing Washington establishment.
- He is politically expedient; he seems inconsistent —swings one way and then another.
- Not strong enough to lay Reagan away; does this reflect on his abilities?
- Not in control of government. HAK and others seem to be able to control him; he is their puppet. He doesn't seem to want to use his power and authority.
- Makes errors, may not be smart enough to do the job.
- Fights with Congress while problems remain unsolved.
- Boring; not exciting.
- Appointed by Nixon; whom he pardoned.

Conclusions on Perception of the President

One positive thing is that we are not working against a hard, anti-President Ford feeling. Even the disapproval in the Gallup (although high) is not firm. There is not a hard, *negative* feeling. It is just that not enough voters have a strong, *positive* feeling about the Ford personality and character.

There is one disturbing factor beginning to show up in Bob Teeter's latest data. Some of those polled are beginning to raise the question of whether the President is considered smart enough for the job.

Also, he apparently has lost a great deal of his perception of being open. This has contributed to the President's decline. This is linked to the President being perceived as becoming more political (especially when he goes on the attack in a partisan, strident manner). This is why the primary campaigns have really hurt the President's national standings.

Also, there is a clear public perception that no one

is in control of this Administration—no one at the White House, in the campaign, or anywhere. This is a major negative.

The following are some specific conclusions on the perception problem:

- Many do not see the President as a leader—they perceive that he has:
  —Limited vision
  —No will to control his Administration
  —No compassion
- He also looks like a loser to many:
  —Can't lay Reagan away
  —Many errors by the campaign and White House staff
  —Seems befuddled in the face of campaign and Congressional challenges
  —Doesn't seem to be able to get anything done
- After a promising start, he is coming to be seen as just another politician.
- To some, he doesn't seem good enough to be President:
  —Indecisive
  —Reactive
  —Not smart

Causes for Poor Perception

- The struggle with Reagan.
- Overexposure on political matters, transparent campaigning techniques.
- Inability to communicate a vision of what life in America should be, and a well-articulated, logical program to get us there.
- Inability to articulate goals and programs effectively.
- Serious White House, Administration and PFC organization and personnel problems.
  —Not bringing strength of incumbency to battle.
  —Press considers speeches too poor to report seriously.
  —Error rate is high; poor execution by campaign and government officials.
  —Lack of team play. No control over prima don-

nas. In-house bickering among staff receives extensive attention of the press.

It is important to consider the perceived strengths and weaknesses of the candidates, along with their perceived reasons in the context of what is real. The following is an attempt to briefly identify the key actual strengths and weaknesses of Jimmy Carter.

Carter's Actual Strengths and Weaknesses

Strengths

- He is bright, intelligent and disciplined.
- His strategy is on target with the mood of the electorate, and he plays the strategy effectively (vision, character, morality, spirituality).
- A good political mind, good instincts. He's "new" —not from Washington.
- A good, well-knit organization which executes effectively. So far, does not leak. Low error rate.
- A favorable public perception, on characteristics and issues important to the voters. By avoiding specifics, his actual positions appear to be *conservative on social issues and liberal on economic issues.*
- He has united the Democratic Party, which will work on his behalf.
- He promises change, that he has solutions to the problems.
- He is subtle; he can send political signals with a light touch. These signals don't seem political.
- His religious background.

Weaknesses

- Overly ambitious, which may make him devious.
- Personal makeup is not in tune with public perception. He appears to be vindictive, arrogant, egotistical, bull-headed.
- Position on issues is to the left of a rightward moving electorate—Humphrey-Hawkins, and many others.

- He has the support of the Democratic Party which brought us our current problem of a big, unresponsive federal government; he will either have to defend the Congress, or Party, or reject it—either of which will give him problems.
- He is inexperienced.
- He is a "winner" only because he has had weak opponents thus far.

President Ford's Actual Strengths

- His decency and honesty.
- His record; the country is in good shape.
- His experience and understanding of the issues—he has done the job and handled the Office.
- The power of the incumbency; he is the President. People will have to want to kick him out.
- People have empathy with him.
- His family.
- His personal makeup; he isn't vindictive, mean or an egomaniac. He can listen to others, take advice. In short, he is human.

Weaknesses Which Are Persistently Attributed to the President*

- Does not think in terms of vision and quality of life, and articulate these.
- Seems unwilling to take charge and discipline his Administration and campaign, even when it is in his interest; is a poor organizer.
- Is a poor communicator—especially via television.
- Decisions often lack political subtlety—both sides are angered.
- Administration decision process is often incapable of bold, rapid action; in seeking the "safe" course, we often miss opportunities when timing is critical.

---

* *(Author's footnote)* Ford's advisers apparently were unable to bring themselves to follow their own style and entitle this section "President Ford's Actual Weaknesses." Yet, this was clearly what they were getting at.

SUMMARY CHART

Ford/Carter Perception—National Survey

FORD

Positive: Honest and decent — But primaries raise problem of political honesty

Question: Intelligence — Is he competent or intelligent enough to be President? Is he sensitive to how all this relates to average individual?

Negative: Leadership — Weak, indecisive, lacks vision

CARTER

Positive: Religious, ethical, conservative, regular Democrat — He supports traditional American values—he has a conservative life style. He's a Democrat, but not an extremist.

Question: Deceitful — Is he some kind of fanatic who might be dangerous?

Negative: Inexperienced, lacks record of accomplishment and is vague and not specfic — Is he up to the job? We don't know enough about him. Why is he avoiding clear expression of issues?

Targets of Opportunity

As a general proposition, there is a base vote for each candidate in a two-way Presidential election, consisting of:

    35 percent for GOP
    40 percent for Democrats

The election is thus decided by the 25 percent "swing vote" made up of Republican and Democratic defectors, the independents and ticket splitters.

Our Base		Swing States		His Base	
Nebraska	5	Alaska	3	Georgia	12
Kansas	7	California	45	Minnesota	10
Vermont	3	Connecticut	8	D.C.	3
Idaho	4	Delaware	3	Alabama	9
N. Dakota	3	*Florida	17	Arkansas	6
Utah	4	Illinois	26	Louisiana	10
Wyoming	3	Kentucky	9	Mississippi	7
Arizona	6	Maryland	10	S. Carolina	8
S. Dakota	4	Michigan	21	Mass.	14
Oklahoma	8	Missouri	12	Rhode Island	4
Indiana	13	Montana	4	Hawaii	4
Colorado	7	Nevada	3		87
N.H.	4	N.J.	17		
Maine	4	N. Mexico	4		
Iowa	8	*New York	41		
	83	*N.C.	13		
		Ohio	25		
		Oregon	6		
		Pa.	27		
		Tenn.	10		
		*Texas	26		
		*Va.	12		
		Wash.	9		
		*W. Va.	6		
		Wisc.	11		
			368		

---

* State cannot be categorized properly due to insufficient data.

Swing Constituency in Key States

. . . In very general terms, the target constituency in the suburbs for the President is the upper blue collar and white collar workers, often from a family which has risen in mobility in the last generation. These are independent minded voters, many of whom are Catholic. In addition, there is a weakness in Carter's support among Catholics and also among Jews. The upwardly mobile Catholics are a group becoming more independent and conservative, and they represent the key to victory in the northern industrial states where they are from 25–48% of the voters.

Campaign Goals for Swing Vote (Independent and Ticket Splitters)

A. *General Goals*

1. Cause the swing voter to reevaluate the President. This will take an "attention getter" (such as a good acceptance speech) so that people will reevaluate their assumptions about the President's personal characteristics and once again begin to listen to what he has to say.
2. Develop a major and highly disciplined attack on the perception of Carter. We must close the gap between Carter's perception and his actual weaknesses. He must be seen as:
   * An unknown. A man whose thirst for power dominates. Who doesn't know why he wants the Presidency or what he will do with it.
   * Inexperienced.
   * Arrogant—(deceitful).
   * Devious and highly partisan (a function of uncontrolled ambition).
   * As one who uses religion for political purposes; an evangelic.
   * As liberal, well to the left of center and . . . the old-line Democratic majority.
   * Carter's campaign must be linked (in the public's mind) to Nixon's '68 and '72 cam-

paigns—very slick, media-oriented. A candidate that takes positions based on polls—not principles.

Description of Strategy

Strategy Basics (Cross-Cutting Concepts)

A. The President's campaign must be highly disciplined.
- The President must establish iron-clad control over Administration and campaign officials. For the period from the time of implementation of this plan until the election, every higher visibility action of Administration and campaign officials must be cleared at the White House. Administration prima donnas must subvert their personal ambitions to the objective of getting the President elected.
- The President must take specific actions to demonstrate that he is a capable and competent leader.

B. The President's campaign must be television oriented. We must change the perception of literally millions of voters, and this can only be done through the mass media with the principal emphasis on television. This is true for coverage of the President and media advertising.

Strategy Specifics (Actions Aimed at Specific Objectives)

A. Establish leadership qualities:
- Avoid self-deprecating remarks (Ford not a Lincoln) and acts (being photographed with a cowboy hat).
- Carefully plan, prepare and execute *all* on-camera appearances. The President should be seen on television as in control, decisive, open and candid. Prep time (15–30 minutes) should be built into the President's schedule (with Bill Carruthers) immediately preceding on-camera events. For example, the President should re-

294 RUNNING FOR PRESIDENT

hearse his Acceptance Speech (before departing for Kansas City), using a teleprompter and
video tape.

- Use ads and advocates to compare the President's personal characteristics and experience
with Carter's.

- The President must not go on the attack personally (not only because it results in a negative
voter reaction) because the country does not
want strident, divisive tactics. The country is
coming together (as we saw over the 4th of
July weekend) and part of this healing process
is a rejection of politicians who are perceived to
be aggressive attackers.

B. Show that the President has taken control of his
Administration and campaign and is on the road
to victory.

- Instill a new discipline in the President's White
House and campaign staff.
- Control prima donnas in Administration.
- Announce that the President will not campaign
by relying on hoopla for TV, but rather will use
this Bicentennial election year to improve the
Presidential electoral process by focusing on
issues.
NOTE: We should plan for a major campaign
swing for the last two weeks, possibly including
the use of a train.
- Hold open the option of challenging Carter to
a series of debates.

C. In order to ensure that every single action by the
President between the time the strategy is adopted
and the election is reviewed to determine its impact on the strategy, a *Review Group* should be
established. This group should have three functions:

First, to assess every proposed Presidential action (from scheduling to positions on issues)
along with the actions of every key Administration and campaign official, to determine how
that action impacts on the strategy objectives.
Each target group will be indexed and given

a specific weight so that all actions can be judged in terms of how they impact each target group/State and a "net assessment" can be rendered.

Second, the group should act as a political crisis management group which can meet on less than an hour's notice, at any time, to advise the President on how to react to opportunities or attacks as they develop.

Third, synchronize Presidential activity, campaign advertising, press plans . . . and the Attack Plan. This group should be viewed as "personal to the President," that is, it should not appear in any organization chart, and it should receive no publicity. Its membership should be kept very small (five or six) and the campaign and Administration "superstars" should not be part of it on a permanent basis because of their lack of availability. Obviously, the President will often want to consult with one or more of his top officials, but he should also have the advice of the Review Group separately.

The Review Group should be one step removed from the pressures of *running* the day-to-day White House/campaign activities. This should enable them to maintain perspective, thus avoiding such errors as the "Schweiker blunder."*

---

* *(Author's footnote)* Ford White House officials say that the "Review Group" was never actually created. Chief of Staff Richard Cheney said that he often exercised, on an informal basis, the functions outlined in the strategy memo for the "Review Group," and that the President did as well. "We just did not want to superimpose a layer of people in the White House to judge formally all Carter and agency actions," Cheney said. "And frankly, it violated my sensibilities." During discussions of scheduling and matters concerning specific issues, Cheney would take note of aspects that could have political repercussions and later call them to the attention of the President. And when he conferred with the top officials of the campaign committee, Cheney said, he would make them aware of upcoming governmental developments that could affect the campaign.

Timing of government actions and announcements was occasionally

Budget

The budget should be developed by the PFC, reviewed by the Advisory Group and approved by the President.
The following relative priorities are suggested:

           40%—Advertising
           25%—Carter/Mondale attack
           15%—Presidential events
           15%—PFC activities
            5%—Vice President (plus funds for
                "attack")

National Campaign Projections

Media (Including Campaign '76)	$10,000,000
Presidential Travel	500,000
Vice Presidential Travel	1,450,000
Advocates Travel	500,000
Polls	800,000
National Headquarters (Including Special Groups)	3,000,000
Closing Costs	250,000
Reserve	2,800,000
States	2,500,000
Total	$21,800,000

Attack and Carter's Reaction

1. *Background*
   Carter's popularity is based primarily on his perceived credibility, but it is very soft. The voter's

---

based on campaign considerations, Cheney acknowledged; for example, the President put off until after the election his proposal that statehood should be considered for Puerto Rico, even though an advisory committee had directed him to make his recommendation by the end of October. But more often, the effect of campaign considerations on the governmental actions concerned the degree of emphasis, visibility, and personal identification that the President desired concerning a specific announcement. On some occasions, the President personally made the announcement; on other occasions, the White House made the announcement; and on still others, the agency involved made the announcement.

perception of Carter can be substantially changed.
Our basic objective should be to change the perception of Carter:
—move him to the left on social issues and away
  from traditional American values;
—identify him as a partisan Democrat; and
—show that he is devious and arrogant, driven by
  personal ambition in ruthless pursuit of power.
We cannot wait much longer before launching the
Carter attack—he is building a very substantial
lead and is beginning to look like FDR in the polls.
 . . . But the attack in the South must be on
issues. We should not attack him *personally* there
since this would cause a backlash of regional
pride. It must be a respectful disagreement on a
high plane. (An example of how *not* to attack
Carter is Senator Dole's line on *Face the Nation*
[7/18]: "He is Southern-friend McGovern.")

Carter's choice of Mondale can be viewed as a potentially serious mistake which opens his ticket to
attack as being liberal, especially on social issues.
There are two obvious possible motives for the choice
of Mondale and both present interesting attack opportunities:
1) Carter could be going for the big mandate by
   trying to win as many States as possible; or
2) He could be very worried about the third party
   threat by McCarthy.

Finally, we should try to characterize Carter's campaign as a mirror image of Nixon's '68 and '72 campaigns. The following similarities should be pointed
out:
• A candidate who tries to be all things to all
  people.
• Avoids specifics on issues (RN—'68 campaign).
• Driven by personal ambition—harsh and manipu-
  lative.
• Secretive and surrounded by a protective and
  fiercely loyal staff. (One problem we face is the
  fact that in general the press likes the Carter

298 RUNNING FOR PRESIDENT

staff. This may well change as he adds people and pressures increase.)

Interlude: The Plans

The Carter blueprint and the Ford blueprint were very different in tone and style. Yet they wound up with strikingly similar analyses.

The Carter plan discussed the fall campaign in terms of whether Carter would win in a close contest or win in a landslide. The Ford plan hoped for a narrow come-from-behind victory, at best. But strategists in both camps agreed, in their separate memos to the candidates, about where the battle would be fought. They cited the same battleground states: New York, New Jersey, Pennsylvania, Ohio, Illinois, Michigan, California. The Carter memo added Indiana to these seven; the Ford memo added Texas.

And they both came down to the same basic conclusion. Ford could not really hope to win unless he carried at least five of the big eight. He would need five, plus a smaller swing state or two; six out of eight to be safe.

Each camp added something to the literature of presidential politicking. On the Carter side, Jordan introduced a unique, detailed application of new math to old politics. He put the Carter politics of building warm personal relationships into nonpopulist terms of higher mathematics. This gave the Carter-Mondale operation a good foundation for making early scheduling decisions. The concept is flawed only when taken as a final authority on the allocation of the candidate's time. For built into the complex series of formulas is the assumption that personal appearances in a state by the candidate and his people are the best way to win the voters of a given state. This is not necessarily true in a general election. In a state primary campaign, it is usually crucial for a candidate to politick in the state—it is the only sure way of getting political exposure there. But in a general election, a candidate has other means of influence. He can, perhaps, do more to capture urban ethnic votes in Cleveland by getting good national television exposure while handshaking in ethnic communities of Pittsburgh or Milwaukee than he can by campaigning through shopping centers in the rural, small-town Protestant Ohio countryside.

On the Ford side, pollster Robert Teeter added to the presidential campaign arsenal a tool known as the "perceptual map." The perceptual map looks like a graph and illustrates visually what a politician has to do politically to get elected. What it does is plot, with clusters of dots, the positions of the voters on basic philosophic issues—and at the same time, it plots the positions of politicians, as perceived by the voters.

Teeter and his associates asked eligible voters a series of questions dealing with economic and social matters, having people express their feelings to each question on a scale of one to ten (which corresponded to liberal-conservative philosophies). Based on these answers, a person's economic philosophy could be plotted along a horizontal scale—the far left being the most liberal, the far right the most conservative. This horizontal "economic" index, Teeter found, also indicated party preference: Democrats were left of center, Republicans right.

Then the Teeter pollsters would ask the same people a series of questions dealing with defense and foreign policy and national security matters. (The Teeter poll called these Traditional American Values.) These would be plotted on a vertical scale, the bottom being the most liberal, the top being the most conservative.

Plot the two ratings (horizontal and vertical) on a graph, and a single dot can be made to correspond to a person's basic philosophic position.

The voters were then asked to rate the candidates in a similar manner. The result was surprising. People rated Carter slightly to the left of center (toward the liberal side) on social-economic matters and just above the center (toward the conservative side) on national security matters—which put him right in the center of the greatest number of dots signifying where voters saw themselves. Ford was seen as just to the right on the social-economic line. But the Ford pollster was startled to find that people perceived that Ford was just to the *liberal* side (below the center) on the national security (Traditional American Values) scale. In other words, he was viewed as being more liberal than Carter in that context.

Thus, throughout the fall campaign, the Ford strategists saw their job as being twofold: (1) to move Ford, as perceived by the public, up and to the left—that is, to show him as being more conservative on national security matters and more liberal on social-economic matters; and (2) to move Carter, as perceived by the public, down—to make him appear more liberal on national security (Traditional American Value) matters.

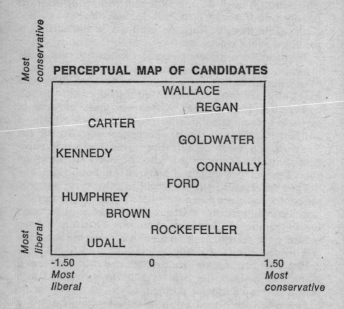

PERCEPTUAL MAP OF CANDIDATES

Most conservative

WALLACE

REGAN

CARTER

GOLDWATER

KENNEDY

CONNALLY

FORD

HUMPHREY

BROWN

ROCKEFELLER

Most liberal

UDALL

-1.50   0   1.50
Most liberal   _Most conservative_

This was one of the underlying assumptions of the Ford strategy memo—that it would not be enough to position Ford perfectly on each issue: it would be up to the Ford camp to shift the public view of Carter as well. The Ford memo devoted significant attention to altering the public perception of Carter. The Carter memo did not spend nearly so much time on the matter of Gerald Ford.

One Last Huddle

Just before Labor Day, Jimmy Carter summoned his brain trust to Miss Lillian's Pond House, which is just down the dirt road that runs into the highway. Walter Mondale was there, and so was his top aide, Richard

Moe, plus the Carter regulars, Hamilton Jordan, Jody Powell, Greg Schneiders, Jerry Rafshoon, Pat Caddell, Charles Kirbo, Robert Lipshutz, Tim Kraft, Rick Hutcheson, Stu Eizenstat. Carter sat next to the fireplace. The formal kickoff of the fall campaign was just hours away.

"I haven't heard the first thing about what our approach is going to be," Carter said at one point, according to others in the room. "What are our themes going to be?"

The meeting had been called to review the overall campaign ahead. But it is most memorable because the candidate and his advisers discussed—for the first time in any formal way—just what it was that Carter ought to be saying in the campaign.

Leadership: Carter has it, Ford doesn't. Competence: Carter has it, Ford doesn't. The economy: the Republicans have messed it up; inflation is soaring, and so is unemployment. That is the way the Carter people saw it, and that is the way they believed, based on their polling, that the public would see it.

But the meeting made it clear that the Carter advisers had been negligent in one crucial area. From early June, when it became clear that Carter would be the Democratic nominee, to early September, when he was to formally hit the campaign trail, the advisers had not given detailed thought to just how Carter ought to translate basic themes to the public. Just what should he say and when should he say it?

"There was a real vacuum there," Hamilton Jordan later conceded. "Jimmy really developed a lot of the themes himself in the primaries. And nobody really focused on it the way we should have."

September/Kickoff

September 6.

Plains is asleep. The headlights of the sedan play across the wooded front lawn of the Carter home as the car eases down the driveway and turns right on Woodland Drive. It is 6:33 A.M., Labor Day. The sun has yet to rise. Jimmy Carter is off and running for President.

The motorcade that is the Carter car, a Secret Service support car, and two press-pool cars moves silently through the deserted town. Only one light is shining in predawn Plains; it is on the large sign above the bank of stores on Main Street, the red, white, and blue sign that reads: CARTER FOR PRESIDENT. The motorcade heads toward Warm Springs. Carter is forgoing the traditional Labor Day rally in Detroit's Cadillac Square, where Democrats have become accustomed to kicking off their fall presidential campaigns, in favor of Franklin Delano Roosevelt's "Little White House." The candidate and his staff decided early that it makes more sense to start the fall campaign in Jimmy Carter's Georgia rather than Jerry Ford's Michigan.

It is 8:30 A.M. when Carter rolls into Warm Springs, and at this early hour the streets are lined with several thousand Carter supporters who are being stirred to partisan highs by a blaring drum-and-bugle corps. The car moves up the tree-lined path of the thermal spa vacation home where Roosevelt died in 1945, and the crowd that jams the picturesque grounds cheers as the candidate climbs onto the famous front porch to begin his campaign.

It is a scene beautifully staged. Hillside resort, rich in symbolism; early-morning sun; carefully assembled guests. James Roosevelt and Franklin D. Roosevelt, Jr., are there. So is Graham Jackson, the black accordionist who was an FDR favorite and who was pictured weeping in a

famous photograph at the time of the President's death.
And so are a number of patients in wheelchairs, brought
there because FDR was himself crippled and because
Carter intends to talk a bit about improving the life of the
handicapped. It is a perfect setting for a candidate who is
seeking to restructure the old Roosevelt coalition of big-
city Democrats and southern Democrats.

With his private polls showing a number of traditional
Democrats still having doubts about him, Carter wraps
himself securely in the blanket of his Democratic ante-
cedents.

He draws a striking parallel in discussing Roosevelt.
"His opponent in 1932 was an incumbent president, a
decent and well-intentioned man who sincerely believed
that there was nothing our government could or should do
to attack the terrible economic and social ills of our nation; he was leading a Republican Party which lacked the
strength and vision to bring us out of those dark days."

He quotes the sign on Harry Truman's desk: "The buck
stops here." And he adds, "Now no one seems to be in
charge. No one is responsible. Every time another ship
runs aground—CIA, FBI, Panama, unemployment, defi-
cits, welfare, inflation, Medicaid—the captain hides in his
stateroom while the crew argues about who is to blame."

Leadership. It is to be a major theme of the Carter
campaign. Another will be the economy. "Under Johnson
and Kennedy, the inflation rate was 2%. . . . Unfortunately, under this Republican administration the inflation
rate has averaged more than 6%. When President Johnson
went out of office unemployment was less than 4%. . . .
Under this Republican administration the unemployment
rate has been the highest since the Hoover depression."

Patrick Anderson had written a draft of the Warm
Springs speech, but the final product was largely Carter's
own effort. "He used only some of what I wrote," Anderson said. One of the purely Carter lines comes near the
end of the speech: "I owe special interests nothing. I owe
the people everything."

The line evokes strong applause. It is to become
a trademark of Carter's standard stump speech. It pro-
vides a fitting climax to a speech that is well-written,
well-delivered, and well-received. The crowd cheers enthusiastically as Carter steps off the portico when the
address is done. And Graham Jackson, the black

accordionist, begins playing "Happy Days Are Here Again," and all that is missing is Jim Farley and Fala.

🏳️ 🏳️ 🏳️

It is still fairly early into Labor Day when the Carter entourage arrives at the Darlington 500, the 500-mile stock-car classic in South Carolina. Carter has always been big on stock-car racing, and this had been viewed by the candidate and his advisers as a natural second stop on this kickoff day. Big crowd, big splash, a folksy-country-populist sort of thing that will certainly be different. But as the Carter plane touches down near the Darlington track, the candidate's men are privately concerned. They are concerned because they have won themselves a new shadow—Bob Dole—and they just aren't sure how the event will turn out.

Several days before the race, Carter operatives had heard that South Carolina's archconservative senator, Strom Thurmond, the Democrat-Dixiecrat-turned-Republican, had been putting pressure on Barney Wallace, who owns the Darlington track, to get Dole in along with Carter. The Carter advance people heard that indeed Dole was coming. Greg Schneiders passed the word to Carter, and Carter said that he did not want to go if Dole was going to be there. Carter advance people passed this message to Wallace, who was by then in a bind because he did not want to say no to either politician.

Schneiders then called Wallace, and an unusual bit of political bargaining was set in motion. Wallace had figured that Carter and Dole would ride around the track once together in the lead car before the start of the race. Schneiders countered that they could let Dole ride in the lead car, and Carter would then ride farther back in the pace car (which goes around immediately ahead of the racing cars)—but that Carter would then get to go around the track twice, while Dole circled just once. Finally it was agreed that Carter would be in the lead car and Dole would ride back in the pace car and each would circle just once, and then both would go into the VIP booth to watch the race.

On Labor Day, the grandstand is filled with spectators —an estimated 70,000 people have come for a day at the races, Darlington style. The track infield is clogged with

trailers and campers and spectators. In the middle of
them is a fellow from Columbia, South Carolina, named
Billy Johnston. He is sipping beer with a group of friends,
and he is talking about Carter. "I don't like him too much,
not too much at all," Johnston says. "You know, I just
think he's too liberal. He was like that as governor, and I
expect that he will be like that as President. He's talking
about things like amnesty, and I think he'll just want to
spend a lot of money." Johnston's friends nod. Suddenly
the grandstand erupts. It is not just a cheer, it is a roar,
and it grows louder and louder. Jimmy Carter, perched
on the back seat of a cream-colored Cadillac convertible,
is circling the track grinning and waving. Johnston and
his friends are cheering as loudly as anyone. Why? "He's
a southerner, isn't he?" Johnston says, struggling to applaud
and not spill his beer. Dole arrives five cars back, in a
brown Cadillac, and he is greeted by tepid applause, a
scattering of boos, and mostly just silence.

After circling, Dole moves, as planned, to the VIP
booth. But Carter officials—without telling track officials
—have scheduled their man to do a handshaking in the
pits; Carter works the mechanics down where all the
crowd can see, while Dole sits obviously in the VIP booth.
Then Carter heads over to the grandstand to mingle with
the crowd. The Secret Service is angry now; many in the
crowd have been there partying and drinking beer for a
day or so, and the agents are naturally worried about an
incident. Schneiders and campaign trip director Jim King
run ahead to scout the crowd for some average-looking,
noninebriated Americans, and soon Carter is watching the
race with them.

Darlington is a Carter coup.

The Warm Springs-Darlington high faded fast. On the
second day of the formal campaign, Carter and his entourage plunged into a series of events that wound up as
minor campaign calamities, and for the next several days
the Carter effort was distinctly down.

September 7.

New York. The candidate was scheduled to do a high-
visibility media number that is standard in any Gotham

campaign. He was going to work a subway stop; he would do it in the morning, and the nightly news would be alive with Carter and the big-city people. It would be a nice complement to the Georgia rural and Carolina stock-car settings of the day before. It would represent the other vital part of that Roosevelt coalition of the South and the urban North. That was the plan.

Carter was taken to the subway stop at Columbus Circle in Manhattan. He arrived at 7:40 A.M. and was immediately surrounded by the Manhattan paparazzi, which is even more aggressive than the national paparazzi, which was there, too. No people were exiting, so Carter walked downstairs; the media mob moved aggressively with him, pushing and shoving and jockeying for position, and Carter reached the station below and stood there, in the eye of the hurricane. Still no people. Carter walked to his right, then to his left. But the only hands around to shake were holding cameras or microphones or notepads and pens.

"Can't we find any real people?" Carter asked Kevin Gorman, a tall, moustached, but clean-cut press assistant. Gorman shrugged. There were very few subway riders to be seen, and those who were there had a difficult time shoving their way past the media for the privilege of shaking the hand of the man who wanted very much to shake their hand.

Off to the side, Congressman Edward Koch shook his head. "I don't know why they chose this station—anybody who knows anything about New York knows this is not really a commuter stop. Especially not this early in the morning. They might start arriving here later (just before offices are to open), but nobody leaves for work from here. He should have been up at Eighty-sixth Street."

This first event of the day was a disaster, but it was not the candidate's fault. Carter had been victimized by sloppy advance work; his staff took him to a poorly selected subway stop, and then it did not make adequate arrangements to accommodate both press coverage and the candidate's needs.

Next stop was Brooklyn College. Carter was forced to abandon his prepared text because there was no lectern and his microphone was not working. Carter once again attacked Ford, as he paraphrased the headline writers, for having told New York to "drop dead." He hit heavily on issues of city and neighborhood decay, but he also discussed his position on amnesty, Lieutenant Calley, Vietnam, and FBI director Clarence Kelley, who had permitted FBI carpenters to construct $335 worth of valences in his Washington apartment.

Carter said the FBI director should "set an example" in fighting crime, and he added, "The director of the FBI ought to be purer than Caesar's wife." This naturally led reporters to ask the obvious question of Carter as he left the college: Would he fire Kelley? "Knowing what I know now, yes, I would have to fire him," Carter said. And this —not the statements on city and neighborhood issues —is what the news stories focus on in most newspapers, radio and television coverage. Again Carter had stepped on his own story; the news he made was not the news he wanted to make. It frustrated the candidate, and it frustrated his advisers.

"We talked to him about that," Rosalynn Carter said later. "He'd say, 'They ask me questions; I am just going to answer them.' And I talked to him about it but he just thought it was better to do it that way. I didn't.

"What I tried to get him to do was not answer the questions. People walk up to you and stick a microphone in your face at the airport or something like that—don't answer them. Do your thing and leave. But he didn't do it. He never would listen to us about that.

"What Jimmy tried to do—what I think he really tried to do—was to be open and honest with the reporters if they asked a question, like if you are going to fire Clarence Kelley. Instead of saying "I don't know"—he tried to say what he was going to do. But—it didn't work."

The Brooklyn College event was over, but the day's disasters continued. Carter scheduled to meet with a community-action coalition in Philadelphia to discuss various urban neighborhood problems. The meeting was to take place in the rectory of Our Lady of Pompeii Roman Catholic Church. But once again, the Catholic church hierarchy injected itself into the political campaign. According to the sponsoring group, the Coalition of Organizations for Action: "The archdiocese of Philadelphia has informed the pastor of Our Lady of Pompeii that if a community meeting is held with Gov. Carter on Catholic property, then the abortion issue must be on the agenda."

The sponsoring group wanted to hear Carter discuss

other issues. So the site was switched from the Catholic church to the Lutheran Church of St. Simeon, where the church made no attempt to dictate the agenda. The switch further embarrassed the Carter camp, however; it prompted reporters to question why the shift was made, and heightened the impression that Carter was held in low esteem by the Catholic church.

Due to the questioning, Carter felt called upon to bring up the abortion issue himself at the community coalition group's meeting. And later, Jody Powell commented, "We think the real problem with the abortion issue is not on the issue of abortion itself, but on how Jimmy handles it. We know that this fuzziness thing is hurting him and we don't want to be fuzzy on the issues, not even in the Catholic communities. But if we don't handle it properly, it could become a problem for us."

It was late and the candidate and his staff were on edge when their entourage neared the Hilton Inn in Scranton, where they would stay overnight. It had been a horrible day. But soon it would be over, and there would be a chance to put things back together the next day.

A large crowd was waiting outside the hotel, and they were exuberant, for a change. Carter sized them up as friendly and strode into their midst. But half the crowd was, in fact, protesters. Antiabortion protesters. They swarmed around the candidate, shouting slogans and waving their placards in his face. The advance team had not seen to it that barriers were in place to permit the candidate to walk into the hotel through the crowd. They were a classy crowd of protesters; some carried signs showing a huge Jimmy Carter sporting a huge grin, with a fetus clenched between his grinning teeth; others showed garbage cans with babies in them. As the protesters closed in, the candidate and his staff were jostled and shoved. Carter hopped on a station wagon tailgate, as if intending to make a speech. But he saw that there was both a friendly crowd and a hostile crowd, and so he jumped back down and went inside the hotel. The reporters went to the press room to file stories. They found plenty of coffee—the Carter campaign had a thing about getting reporters coffee—but no typewriters and no phones. The staff and press corps headed wearily toward their rooms; there were only two elevators—one was reserved for Carter, and the other was barely running. The Carter entourage settled in for a needed night's sleep. In the park across the street, the antiabortion people had taken up all-night chanting, burning candles and at times singing "God Bless America."

Tomorrow had to be better.

🏴 🏴 🏴

Carter, his staff, and the press corps awoke before dawn the next day and stepped into morning showers that gushed a cold brown liquid in place of warm, clear water. "I know the Carter people promised us coffee in the morning," said columnist Robert Novak. "But I didn't know it would be coming out of the shower head."

At 6:55 A.M., Carter was in place at a gate of the Haddon Bookbinding Factory, awaiting a shift change so he could shake hands with workers. But somehow the advance people had gotten this wrong, too. Very few people showed up, and those that did show couldn't get through the barricades to shake Carter's hand.

Next was a round-table discussion between Carter and unemployed people that had been set up in a hotel. It was to highlight one of the things Carter does best: talk informally, understandingly, with ordinary people, especially down-on-their-luck people. It was the classic media event: a panel show with no audience except Carter's traveling press. The candidate and the unemployed people sat around a table, but the sound system was not working; television microphones were picking up nothing. At one point, Greg Schneiders walked into the room and said to a reporter, "When is it going to start?" "SSSHHHH," came the response from reporters straining, with little success, to hear. "It's going on now."

Also, it turned out that one of the panel of unemployed people was in fact a Carter volunteer, and that others of the "unemployed" in fact had jobs.

🏴 🏴 🏴

Throughout the first week, Carter's private polls were showing him weak in the Catholic, and especially ethnic, neighborhoods of the big cities. His schedulers took him into seven ethnic neighborhoods by the end of the first week. The first couple of days were marred by snafus and

unforeseen events that overshadowed Carter's major ethnic effort.

But on Pittsburgh's Polish Hill, everything fell into
place. It happened Wednesday on the steep slope of
Brereton Street. Television cameras were in place as
Carter paused outside the Immaculate Heart of Mary
Church while local parochial-school students clustered
around him. He pulled on a red-and-white "Polish Power"
T-shirt. And then, as the cameras rolled, he bowed his
head so the Reverend John Jendzura could kiss him on
both cheeks. Peck. Peck. Carter beamed.

🇺🇸   🇺🇸   🇺🇸

Wednesday afternoon, Carter took time out from his
Catholic/ethnic schedule to deliver a speech on Middle
East policy to the B'nai B'rith Convention in Washington,
D.C. "I find it unacceptable that we have in effect condoned the effort of some Arab countries to tell American businesses that in order to trade with one country or
company, they must observe certain restrictions based on
race or religion," Carter said. "These so-called 'Arab boycotts' violate our standards of freedom and morality. . . .
Moreover, according to a recent House subcommittee report, the Department of Commerce has shut its eyes to the
boycott by failing to collect information on alleged of-
fenses, and failing to carry out a firm policy against the
boycott. If I become President, all laws concerning these
boycotts will be vigorously enforced."

Campaign rosters are filled with well-meaning people
who write memos to the candidate offering crucial information and advice. Every campaign needs someone to
limit the flow of paper to the candidate. In the Carter
campaign, the task fell to Greg Schneiders.

To: Governor Carter

From: Greg

STAFF MEMOS SCREENED (In the future whenever I
withhold a memo . . . I will list it so that you can be
aware of its existence and can request to see it if
you like.)

1. 50 pages of bio on the Jewish leaders you will meet. . . .
2. Covering memo and proposed statement from Conservationists for Carter on the importance of home gardening.

September 9.

Chicago is under attack. Jimmy Carter is on the Michigan Avenue bridge, crossing the Chicago River at night, and suddenly the sky is ablaze with the rockets' red glare and bombs bursting in air, and Mayor Richard Daley, riding in the car at Carter's side, is beaming. It is his show. The Cook County Democratic Organization is conducting its quadrennial torchlight parade, a mile-long spectacular of fireworks and machine patriotism. Thousands of families, many of them patronage families, line the streets, waving placards bearing the salute of this ward or that, and all of the signs look as though they were printed on the same press. Every ten feet, a party worker loyally holds a blazing torch.

This is Richard J. Daley's powerful elixir. Usually the parade and rally are held late in the campaign, designed to generate a climactic bit of enthusiasm. But this year, Daley's handpicked candidate for governor is Michael Howlett, a man of ample avoirdupois—it sags from his chin and rolls over his beltline, and it combines with his pasty complexion and gray hair, close-clipped, to give him the bearing and countenance of a machine ward regular. The Democratic candidate for governor appears headed for a sizable defeat, and Carter is trying to sail through Illinois knowing that he is navigating with a dropped anchor. It is because things are going so poorly that the mayor's torchlight parade and rally have been moved up early. The time for elixir is now.

The Richard J. Daley Grand Fireworks and Torchlight Parade moves majestically through the streets of Chicago. Carter, Daley, and Senator Adlai Stevenson, Jr., are in the front car. Howlett is in a car farther back. (Chicago newspapers took note of this in the days to come, and there were suggestions that Carter had not wanted to be associated closely with Howlett. But the Carter men say that the displacement of Howlett was Daley's doing. The

Carter camp had decided early on that it would support Howlett regardless of his expected poor showing. Carter officials say that before the parade, Greg Schneiders checked with Bill Daley, the mayor's son, and asked if he wanted Howlett to ride in the Carter car, too. Bill Daley said no, the Carter men say, and when Schneiders reiterated that it was okay with Carter, the younger Daley reportedly replied, "No, that's the way the mayor wants it.")

The parade pulls to a stop in front of the Medinah Temple, a monument of Arabian architecture that tonight is decorated with banners proclaiming that Ukrainians and Croatians and Slovenes and each of Chicago's fifty wards love Carter.

Inside, there are speeches. Howlett, his mind apparently on his Republican opponent, Jim Thompson, lets fly with a blast that unfortunately coincides with what the Republicans have been saying about Carter.

Inexplicably mentioning no names, Howlett warns about a man who "sounds like a Democrat when he talks to labor unions, a Republican when he talks to businessmen and an independent when he talks to independents." And in case that is not enough, he adds, "We can't afford a rookie at the head of our government, because rookies make mistakes." The Carter people cringe.

Exit Howlett. Enter Daley. The mayor lavishes praise, one by one, on each candidate on the 1976 county ticket. After he has gotten to "Sid Olsen, the fighting Viking," who is running for recorder of deeds, he trumpets, "We have the best candidates and you are the best organization —and that's why we're going to win this election in 1977, our Bicentennial year!"

It has been a mind-numbing night, this evening of politics, Chicago-style. And perhaps this explains what happens when Jimmy Carter begins to speak. Clearly, he has a specific point in mind: apparently he is going to talk, in his standard rally speech, about the importance of preventive health care. But even his own staff members are startled when Carter—with no warning—suddenly starts shouting out the names of childhood diseases.

"Whooping cough!

"Cholera!

"Typhus!

"Typhoid!

"Diphtheria!

"Polio!

"They tried to immunize me against those diseases," Carter says, harkening back to his rural south Georgia childhood, "and quite often they succeeded."

🏴 🏴 🏴

Memorandum

To: Governor Carter
From: Pat Caddell
Re: Last Week's Poll Results
Date: 11 September 1976

1. *The Results.* With the exception of New Jersey and Florida, the leads in all major states were less than 10 points, and in most cases the margins were a razor thin few points. Illinois was quite poor, for reasons I will discuss. By the way, once again we run much, much better with men than with women, in these large states. As we saw in the national surveys, voters under 35 years old are a constant disappointment. In most cases we lead this group by only narrow margins. First, the results:

	Carter	Ford	Undecided	Might not vote
California	44%	41	9	6
Texas	48	41	10	1
Florida	51	39	8	1
Illinois	39	48	12	2
Michigan	42	47	8	3
Ohio	45	43	10	2
Pennsylvania	45	41	12	2
New Jersey	49	34	14	4
New York	46	40	11	3

Post Labor Day

	Carter	Ford	Undecided	Might not vote
Wisconsin	46	42	9	3
Indiana	43	42	11	4

In all the pre-Labor Day states two important points stand out. First, the Catholic situation is serious. In most of the industrial states we barely carry the Catholic vote, and in Illinois, Michigan, and California we are actually losing that segment. Our leads are held because of the excellent showing (for a Democrat) with Protestants. It appears that the Catholic problem is more severe in the industrial urban areas, and that our margin with Catholics grows as you move from those urban industrial states (Texas, Florida). These results truly magnify the Catholic problem beyond what the National poll would indicate.

Second, the regional pattern is duplicated in our geographic results. We barely carry urban Democratic areas such as Pittsburgh, Cleveland, Toledo, and the Bay Area of California, and our margins are far below expectation in others, such as Philadelphia, Detroit, and Chicago. The only reason we carry most of these states is because of our showing in normally Republican areas; running near even in Central Dutch Pennsylvania, Cincinnati, and San Diego. *If we expanded our margin to even a respectable Democratic showing in the urban Catholic centers, then all these key states could be held by wide margins. . . .*

II. Individual States. . . . Illinois—This state is in serious trouble. We show the state being lost by nine points. A University of Chicago survey shows us losing 44% to 41% with the patterns the same, except a slight improvement in the suburbs and with Protestants. The truth is we are probably losing by five or six points. We are losing Catholics by 11 points— 48% to 37%! We are being murdered in the suburbs of Cook County and Chicago by almost 63% to 25%, while Howlett gets 12% at the moment! Our margin in the City is only 20 points, 51% to 31%, and we are losing Rockford-Peoria by 20 points, while carrying Southern Illinois by three points. One-fourth of the Democrats defect and we lose Independents by 20 points, 54% to 34%.

The problem is two-fold: Daley and Howlett. Both are very unpopular. Our close attachment to Daley is death in the Republican-Independent suburbs, and has almost destroyed our anti-establishment image.

In Illinois a plurality *disagree* that we represent new leadership and a plurality agree it would be a risk to elect Carter President—unheard of results for us anywhere in the country. Howlett is being beaten better than two to one, our favorable rating stands at 48%, and Ford is popular here. . . .

The Catholics. Below is the break-down of vote by religion in the various states.

| | Catholics | | | Protestants | | |
	Carter	Ford	Undecided	Carter	Ford	Undecided
California	40%	47	11	45	41	11
Texas	52	38	10	45	44	10
Florida	55	36	6	49	43	8
Illinois	37	48	11	38	49	12
Michigan	44	47	8	41	49	7
Ohio	47	41	10	43	45	10
Pennsylvania	49	34	13	35	51	11
New Jersey	44	38	14	49	32	16
New York	43	43	12	38	50	10
Post Labor Day						
Wisconsin	51	32	13	42	50	7
Indiana	55	31	13	39	46	16

. . . Just for the record note that only 40% of Catholics favor a constitutional amendment on abortion and that Catholics, regardless of their position on the amendment, rate abortion as an area where the President can do the least. . . .

A few interesting figures. Carter lost 4% overall in favorability post N.Y.C. to post K.C., but with Catholics dropped 9%. Ford gained eight points in positive job rating with Catholics in the period, but only 2% overall.

September 17.

Carter sat down for an early-morning interview with the Associated Press and wound up being pressed about his plans for tax reform. His imprecise handling of a tax question in Boston had hurt him during the early primaries; and now his imprecise handling of another question was going to cause him some rough going in the early stages of the fall campaign.

Carter explained his tax-reform intentions by saying: "The overall effect would be to shift a substantial increase toward those who have the higher incomes and reduce the income [tax] on the lower-income and middle-income taxpayers."

Q: "What do you mean when you say shift the burden?"

A: "That means people who have a higher income would pay more taxes at a certain level."

Q: "In dollar figures, what are you thinking of as higher?"

A: "I don't know. I would take the mean or median level of income and anything above that would be higher and anything below that would be lower."

Q: "The median family income today is somewhere around $12,000. Somebody earning $15,000 a year is not what people commonly think of as rich. . . ."

A: "I understand. I can't answer that question because I haven't gone into it. I don't know how to write the tax code now in specific terms. It is just not possible to do that on a campaign trail. But I am committed to do it and I have already talked to congressional leaders in the House and the Senate about the need and have found an agreement among them. As far as telling you specifically what the tax code would be, there is no way I can do that."

Q: "You are saying that you would like voters to make you President and you are not able to say what the impact might be of this very major change you are talking about. How would you respond to that?"

A: "It hasn't created a problem for me as far as I have been able to detect."

Carter detected that he had a problem about his income-tax intentions within hours. The Associated Press story moved out on the wires, complete with lengthy sections of transcript from the interview. There was Carter raising the specter that people earning above the "mean or median level"—which, the reporter pointed out to him, meant roughly $12,000—would have to pay higher taxes. Actually, Carter did not mean to imply that taxes would be raised for families with an income in this relatively low range; but he had not been precise.

Carter was further victimized by a horrendous error on the original Associated Press transcript. The words "and middle-income" were omitted from his statement about his desire to "reduce the income [tax] on the lower-income *and middle-income* taxpayers."

The wire service eventually flashed an "urgent" correction. But the Republicans—eventually including Ford himself—chose to ignore the correction when quoting and attacking Carter's intentions concerning income-tax reform.

Later Greg Schneiders remarked, "It's a mistake to have a candidate do long interviews, particularly tough interviews, early in the morning. His answers were not very good, but the questions were horrible. At another time, Carter would have caught the fallacy of their questions. . . . He would have explained himself better."

Schneiders is a low-key, thoughtful man. But tucked into his comments was the bitterness that the top echelon of the Carter campaign—beginning with Carter—had begun to feel about the press. They were becoming particularly upset about the television networks and their coverage; but the newspapers, wire services, and news magazines did not escape their increasing ire. It would, in a matter of days, become the consuming outlet of frustration of the candidate and his advisers.

THE RACE: *Carter's margins in his southern base states continue to be substantial. But the race is narrowing in the large industrial states that both camps view as the battleground. And suddenly Eugene McCarthy is looming larger than life. Eugene McCarthy, a gray eminence from a decade past. He is running again. In 1968, as a Democratic senator from Minnesota, McCarthy ran with a purpose—he took on President Johnson and made the Vietnam War the issue at a time when other more glittering names were too timid to tackle the party leader. But in 1976, as a former senator, McCarthy seems a purpose-*

less man—diffident, no longer a Democrat, just a former national political figure who had run before and who insists on running again even though he knows he cannot win and seems not to care who does.

As the races tighten in the large battleground states, the few votes that independent candidate McCarthy can siphon from Carter are magnified in importance. Two percentage points in these big states could be the difference between victory or defeat. The Carter officials look to court action to keep McCarthy off the ballots.

September/Rose Garden Strategy

On September 6, when Jimmy Carter was in Warm Springs and Darlington and Norfolk, President Ford was in the Oval Office.

On September 7, when Jimmy Carter was in New York and Groton and Philadelphia and Scranton, President Ford was in the Rose Garden. (He was inviting reporters to watch him as he signed a disaster bill. Later, he called reporters out to the garden again to watch him sign a child day-care bill that was merely a newer version of one he had vetoed earlier.)

On September 8, when Jimmy Carter was in Pittsburgh and Washington and Cleveland and Columbus, President Ford was on the White House lawn. (He was jabbing at Carter's comments about FBI director Clarence Kelley and fielding questions on other matters, including abortion.)

On September 9, while Jimmy Carter was in Carbondale and Springfield and Peoria and Chicago and Milwaukee, President Ford was in the White House press briefing room. (He was making a statement on the death of China's Mao Tse-tung; and he was back in his office, signing the New Hampshire–Vermont Interstate Sewage bill; and he was receiving the ambassador of Guinea; and he was making a speech at a Washington hotel.)

President Ford, in his own way, was also off and running in Campaign '76. The President was running a carefully planned Rose Garden strategy that had its origins in a memorandum prepared back in June.

Sensitive/No Distribution

June 11, 1976

Memorandum For: Dick Cheney
From: Mike Duval/Foster Chanock
Subject: "No Campaign" Strategy

Overview

The best strategy for the President to win in November—given the circumstances laid out below—may be for him to announce after the Republican Convention that he will not actively campaign for the Presidency. He would "turn back" Federal matching funds to the Treasury, offer to debate Carter on a series of substantive issues, and go back to work as President with no campaign activities whatsoever.

An alternative is to announce a highly truncated campaign schedule.

Reasons for Adopting This Strategy

This high-risk strategy would be adopted only if it appeared to be the best way of winning the November election. This might be the appropriate judgment *if the following conditions* [exist] *after the President's nomination in August:*

- The President is trailing Carter in the national polls by 15 points or more.
- The national polls show that Ford is closing the Carter lead, but the projection is that this will reverse later in the fall, with Carter again widening his lead.
- It is likely that there will be a major defection of Republican voters (primarily disenchanted Reagan supporters) to Carter. This condition would be met if the current *New York Times* survey (which shows a Republican defection of 35% to Carter) continues to hold.
- The Democratic Party and organized labor have pulled together strongly behind Carter, thereby

giving him an extensive "grass roots" organization in all States.
- The polls continue to show that issues are not a
decisive campaign factor. The voters continue
to react to personality traits and themes.

If such a situation exists, and if the President can
realistically calculate his odds as less than 40%
chance of winning, then the "no campaign" strategy
should be considered.

The Strategy

Under this strategy, the President would announce,
sometime in late August or early September, that he
will not actively campaign for the Presidency. The
President would state that (all or most of) his matching funds will be "turned back" to the Treasury, and
that he will spend his time working as President.

The White House Press Office would put out a carefully reasoned set of "ground rules" which would
cover the Vice Presidential campaigning and other
technical problems. The President would make it clear
that, to the extent he would travel around the country
on "official" business, the cost of this travel would be
well under what he would be spending anyway under
the election campaign law. This kind of analysis is
necessary to avoid the charge that the President is
using this simply as a ploy to get around the campaign
financing law.

All Presidential activities, trips, etc., would have to
be carefully worked out to be official and not raise any
question of campaigning. Obviously, there would be
some travel and, in the case of crowd situations, we
would have to be careful that we took no action to
raise crowds or otherwise exploit him politically, that
would not be taken in an off-election year.

The President would announce that he will hold
one (or more) press conferences a week with local/
State press augmenting the White House Press Corps.
This will enable the press to get the President's views
on campaign issues.

The President would offer to meet Carter for a

series of four nationally televised debates on foreign policy, national defense, economic policy and domestic policy.

The Result of the Strategy

Although it's difficult, of course, to quantify what this strategy could produce, I think it's fair to assume that at least the following would occur.

- The President would show a marked increase in the polls (some of which would be natural anyway at that time of the year) and this would be generally characterized by the press as public endorsement of his decision.
- There would spring up throughout the country hundreds of independently run and financed "Ford for President" organizations by citizens who want to help the campaign but have no national organization to turn to. This should not be underestimated, because it could be a truly remarkable phenomenon of individual efforts to help elect the President.
- The Republican National Committee would initially complain about this on the grounds that the President would not be available to campaign for other GOP candidates but, in the end, I think they would support the decision. To the extent that the President did increase in the polls as a result of this decision, it will help all Republican candidates. Also, the RNC could devote all resources to the other candidates.
- The President would have a great deal of time to devote to Presidential duties, which could have a very beneficial impact on his election chances. Presidential appearances could be strategically targeted to highlight desired themes through Administration action.
- Although the press would be initially confused and very skeptical and distrusting of this decision, they would nevertheless have to report the President's actions as being Presidential. This could result in a very favorable contrast

between Ford as President and his rival as a campaigner.

- This is likely to produce serious problems for Carter. His entire strategy will be predicated on a Ford campaign, and I suspect he would not know how to react to such an announcement. To the extent the polls do shift in favor of Ford, he would really have no alternative strategy available to him. This might well result in cracks in his organization, and mistakes.
- This strategy will recast the campaign away from personality and theme to issues and substance.

Carter has successfully campaigned for over five months without being pinned down on most issues. The press has tended to treat him as a phenomenon rather than as a candidate under scrutiny. There is no reason to believe that we will [be] substantially more successful at pinning him down than his opponents have been.

This leaves us in a personality contest. Both Carter and the President are perceived as honest and sincere men of integrity. Carter's advantage is in his campaign style, anti-Washington stance, and being the nominee of a larger, grass-roots party. Given the constraints on time and spending, we cannot defeat Carter in a beauty contest. Therefore, we must steer the campaign back to the issues, even though the American public does not really care about them at a substantive level of detail.

We can steer the campaign onto the issues and prove the President's desire and superior ability to be President by challenging Carter to a series of four debates in the month of October. One debate is risky and less likely to really focus on issues. Thus, the President can challenge Carter to debates on domestic affairs, the economy, national defense and foreign policy. In this situation, we can maximize the advantage of incumbency, since the President is far more knowledgeable, experienced and balanced than Carter. To be fair, we can make the challenge September 1 and offer any briefings or information over the month that Carter would like to have. If he accepts, he acknowledges ignorance; if he declines, arrogance.

If he declines, the President can schedule four, fifteen minute unilateral policy speeches, thereby re-packaging his policy positions and underscoring Carter's fuzziness.

This is likely to go a long way towards neutralizing the anti-government attack on the President. This strategy is so unconventional that the "establishment" based attack just will not work.

▬ ▨ ▨ ▨

Interlude: Summer Camp Counseling

Vail, Colorado. Nelson Rockefeller was out of uniform. He wore a gray summer suit and a dark tie as he sat in the chalet set up against the mountains in this place that was a ski resort by winter and now a Republican strategy summit by summer. President Ford set the sartorial tone for the meeting with a light-blue gold shirt beneath a dark sweater. Bob Dole, John Connally, Rogers Morton, Dick Cheney, Jim Baker, and Stuart Spencer had all gotten the message and dressed casually. They sat around a hickory fire in the August days that followed the GOP convention, planning strategy for the fall campaign.

Actually, most of the detail work was done in morning sessions over in the Scott House, where the Cheney family stayed, attended by all of the strategists and advisers but not the luminaries such as the President, Dole, Rocke-feller, or Connally. Plans laid out in the strategy book were reviewed and approved. The Rose Garden strategy was perfected, and battle plans were mapped.

As the President and his men saw it, the race would focus most closely on eight big states: California, Michigan, Illinois, New Jersey, New York, Pennsylvania, Ohio, and Texas. Ford needed five of the big eight to win, they figured. If he got five, plus his Republican base states in the Farm Belt and the Rockies, and a couple of the smaller swing states, he would win. Five out of eight. It became the real goal of the Ford campaign. It was time for leisurely unwinding after the Kansas City scare; a time of tranquillity. The only tense moment for the Ford strategists came when one of Cheney's daughters placed a coiled wooden rattlesnake beside the door, causing all the President's men a moment of panic as they entered the home one afternoon.

Over in the President's chalet, the leaders of the Grand Old Party pondered the big picture. They talked about how to best lure the ticket-splitting swing vote to the Ford line. How to appeal to the new generation of suburban homeowners, upper-salary-level blue-collar workers and lower-salary-level white-collar workers, better read and more upwardly mobile than their parents, many of them Catholic.

At one point, Connally suggested that in view of the mammoth financial and social problems of the cities, it just might be that the cities can't be saved, that perhaps they'll just have to be allowed to collapse, with new centers being built elsewhere to take their place. One participant recalls Connally suggesting that there was plenty of room in the sparsely populated West for the unemployed thousands of the crowded cities of the East.

It was in Vail that Ford announced that James Baker, a forty-six-year-old Houston lawyer and chief convention delegate hunter, would become his national campaign chairman, replacing Rogers C. B. Morton, the affable, snow-thatched mountain of a man who had long been a friend of Ford's since their days together as congressmen. Morton had upset White House and campaign officials at various times with careless comments, such as his statement after one primary defeat that he was "not going to rearrange the deck chairs on the *Titanic.*" The move came suddenly, as far as reporters covering the Vail summer camp were concerned—MORTON OUSTED, the headlines said—and Morton did not appreciate the ungentle nature of his treatment by the Ford men. At one point in the Vail meetings at the President's chalet, he passed a note to Rockefeller, which the Vice President carelessly left behind. The note said that Morton's removal as chairman had been handled very badly from his perspective, and that he would appreciate anything that the Vice President could do to help. There was, apparently, little that Rockefeller could do.

September/The First Debate

September 23. The campaigns of 1976 converged on Philadelphia for what both camps viewed as probably the most important night of the year so far. Gerald Ford and Jimmy Carter would meet in the first presidential debate since the famed 1960 contests between John F. Kennedy and Richard Nixon. Both the Ford and Carter people figured their candidate had much to gain.

For Ford, the debates had been viewed as the cornerstone of a come-from-behind strategy. The President's advisers saw the debates as a chance for the President to dispel the notions that he was not intelligent and not capable of running the government and leading the country. Ford, the advisers knew, had mastered the complexities of the federal budget; he had held forth brilliantly (but also boringly) in a series of budget briefings before reporters and local officials in New England and Florida during the primary campaigns. The debates would be a chance for the President to demonstrate competence and poise. He was not a good stump campaigner, in the eyes of his advisers. The debate in Philadelphia was, to the Ford strategists, the true kickoff of the President's campaign.

For Carter, the debates were a chance to show, most of all, that this still relatively unknown man from Georgia could be presidential. The debates were a chance for him to demonstrate that he was not fuzzy on the issues. They were a chance for him to show that he had done more in 1976 than just grinning and winning; he could show that he was well acquainted with the issues facing the country. They were also a chance for the public to see the two candidates side by side, and the Carter camp was convinced that Ford would suffer by the comparison.

Style, both camps had come to believe, was probably more important than substance. In fact, in the debate, style perhaps *was* substance. Histories of the 1960 debates were studied by Ford and Carter strategists. They knew that people who had heard the first debate on radio generally thought Nixon had won, but people who saw it on television gave the debate to Kennedy. Carter had the Kennedy look—the cool, the blur, the shag. He could speak to people with warmth and compassion. He was bright, and he could think on his feet. He could handle himself, his advisers figured, and Ford would be plodding, stiff, wooden. In Plains, Carter did not actually rehearse for the debates; he just went off by himself and studied briefing books compiled by his issues staff and advisers.

Ford rehearsed. He studied his briefing books, and then several of his top aides came into the Oval Office and fired questions at him as he practiced handling tough questions and thorny issues in as informative and yet relaxed a manner as he could muster.

The first debate of the campaign was to be held in the historic Walnut Street Theatre, just three blocks from Independence Hall. (In the last century, one of the theater's original managers had bequeathed his own skull to the management upon his death and proceeded to appear for years after his demise, as was his last wish, in the role of Yorick in *Hamlet*.) Late in the afternoon, the lobby bar of the Benjamin Franklin Hotel wound up as the scene of an unusual cocktail conference. Jody Powell was there, and sitting at a table with him were his two Ford counterparts, White House press secretary Ron Nessen and President Ford Committee press secretary William Greener. The Ford and Carter men joked amicably. Greener suggested a trade: let the Carter and Ford camps swap advance copies of their schedules. "We get them anyway through various contacts," Greener said, "and so do you." Powell knew that Ford was not planning to go anywhere and that a swap would mainly enable Bob Dole to shadow Carter around the country that much more often. "We'll see," Powell said, making a mental note to be sure to forget the suggestion.

In the afternoon, Carter walked from the Benjamin Franklin Hotel to the nearby theater to familiarize himself with the setup. He carried over his shoulder a suitbag (it was a trademark of his; he carried his own bag everywhere throughout the campaign). Naturally a reporter asked him what was in the bag. "This is my Superman cape and overalls," Carter said.

🏁　　🏁　　🏁

Greg Schneiders walked his boss into his theater dressing room, said good luck, and as Carter walked toward the stage, Schneiders bolted out the theater door. Quickly he walked toward South Tenth Street, taking care to stretch his stride so as to avoid the piles of droppings that polka-dotted the streets, courtesy of the horses that carried Philadelphia's finest as they guarded the city's two important visitors.

Schneiders removed his staff pin and his tie and walked into the working-class Locust Bar. Let the other aides watch the debate from their VIP seats, Schneiders figured; he wanted to see how real people took to the Carter and Ford efforts. Schneiders ordered a Budweiser.

Moderator Edwin Newman introduced the three reporters who would be asking the questions: Frank Reynolds of ABC, James Gannon of *The Wall Street Journal,* and Elizabeth Drew of *The New Yorker* magazine. He addressed a few welcoming remarks to "Governor Carter" and "President Ford."

"Dammit, it's not supposed to be President," Schneiders mumbled, reaching for a beer. "That was one of the things we were insisting on in the negotiations. It was just supposed to be Mr. Ford and Mr. Carter." The Carter people had also insisted on arrangements so that the two men would not be standing side by side—they did not want obvious comparison made of President Ford's several inches of height advantage over Carter. Schneiders went to a pay phone in the rear of the bar and telephoned the Carter aides viewing from backstage. No, he was told, the Carter forces had yielded on that point, and titles were okayed. Schneiders returned to his bar stool and beer.

The first debate was on domestic policy—a concession to the Carter people who had felt that, what with unemployment soaring and the country experiencing economic woes, this would be Carter's strong suit. The first question was tailored to his strength: just how would Carter achieve a reduction in unemployment, which he had said was a top priority?

On the television screen, it was clear that Jimmy Carter was nervous. He started his answer softly, tentatively, talking about strong leadership in the White House but not looking at all like a pillar of strength. There was nothing Kennedyesque about Carter so far except his hair: from the forehead down, he looked like a south Georgia boy who had been asked to debate the President of the United States. "We will never have an end to the inflationary spiral, and we will never have a balanced budget, until we get our people back to work," he said, but the words read more forcefully than they were delivered. Carter suggested channeling federal research and development funds into areas where jobs could be created; he talked about spurring housing programs. This was to have been his big hit answer; yet his comments wandered.

Nick the bartender turned his back on the set. Aaaahhh . . . ," he said, frowning. Schneiders stared at the picture, unsmiling. There were eleven customers in the Locust Bar, and all of them had stopped their conversations to watch the debate.

Ford, in rebuttal, was critical of any suggestion that jobs should be created by additional federal spending.

Ford was asked about taxes. He called for a $28-billion tax cut, with 75 percent of it to go to individuals and 25 percent to business. But, he said, Congress would then have to hold the line on spending.

"He's no dummy," said a man in a blue shirt sitting four seats to Schneiders's right. His friend replied, "Well, he's sure as hell dull."

Carter responded. "Well, Mr. Ford, of course, is changing considerably his previous philosophy. The present tax structure is a disgrace to this country. It is a welfare program for the rich. . . ." He was still speaking tentatively, but his message was strong. Two sentences later, though, he betrayed his nervousness and talked about the "Great Depression of the 1940s."

Schneiders winced.

Replying to another question, Carter said that if necessary he would defer implementation of new programs to have a balanced budget by 1981. He said, however, that if unemployment went down to 4 or 4.5 percent from its current 7.9 percent, $60 billion would be generated in new federal revenue, this could go toward new programs, he said. "There is not going to be any $60-billion dividend." Ford responded. He said if there were any such surplus, the money should be used to give a break to taxpayers, not to finance new programs.

Ford, when asked, was forced to defend his pardon of Richard Nixon for his Watergate crimes and to reiterate his opposition to pardons for Vietnam War draft evaders. Carter restated his advocacy of a pardon for draft evaders but then passed up an opportunity to attack Ford for pardoning Nixon.

Carter got stronger when asked about reorganizing the federal government. He held forth on the "bureaucratic mess" in Washington. Later, Ford misstated Carter's tax-reform intentions, saying that he told the Associated Press he would "raise taxes on those in the . . . middle-income brackets or higher." Carter called Ford to task for misquoting him and, gaining strength as the debate wore on, he firmly attacked Ford.

"Mr. Ford, so far as I know, except for avoiding another Watergate, has not accomplished one single major program for this country. And there has been a constant squabbling between the President and Congress. And that is not the way this country ought to be run."

Schneiders was smiling now. "He's cooking," Schneiders said.

Just when Carter had found a new source of inner power, the ABC network audio facilities lost theirs. At 10:53 P.M., the historic debate was suddenly plunged into coast-to-coast silence. The two candidates could do nothing but stand or sit and wait. They looked at each other and at the reporters and at the audience.

Throughout the debate, the mostly blue-collar clientele in the Locust Bar had watched quietly. Now they were talking all around Schneiders, and they were saying generally that Ford was doing better than they had expected. Carter? Well, they weren't so sure about him now.

Schneiders turned to the man on his right. "Who won?" he asked. The man smiled. "The Phillies"—he paused for laughter—"naw, really, I hate to say it, but I think the Republican won, you know?" Others nodded.

At 11:18 P.M., after a delay of twenty-five minutes, the sound came back on, Carter finished his response to the last question, and the two candidates delivered their closing remarks.

Schneiders left the bar quickly, put on his staff pin and tie, maneuvered his way around the streets laden with

horsepies, and slipped back into the Walnut Street Theatre dressing room just after Carter had gotten there. Carter aides were slapping their candidate on the back and
shaking his hand and telling him he had been great.
Schneiders knew better. No, he told one of the other advisers, Carter had not won. Maybe it was even. At best.

🏳️ 🏳️ 🏳️

THE RACE: *Ford pollster Robert Teeter measured the
debate by having a sampling of people watch on television,
each of them with a rheostat knob at hand. They were in-
structed to turn it to the right when something was said
that made them feel favorably disposed toward Ford, and
to the left for Carter. The degree to which the knob was
turned would measure the intensity of feeling. The results,
plotted on a graph with a continuing zigzag line that
moved throughout the debate, showed Ford clearly out-
scoring Carter.*

*Taxes and tax cuts, Carter's record as governor, and
Carter's spending plans all were way over to the pro-Ford
right side of the graph.*

*Carter scored rather well a half hour into the debate
with his statements about a bureaucratic mess, and scored
about the same a half hour later with a comment on tax
reform. That was about it for Carter. Carter scored mildly
in his closing statement, and Ford scored much better in
his.*

*The debate, according to the Teeter test, went clearly
to Ford. Various subsequent, independent surveys gave an
edge to the President as well.*

September/The Playboy Connection

Word spread rapidly through the train.

Jimmy Carter was stumping Harry Truman-style, whistle-stopping from New York to New Jersey to Pennsylvania on the *Democratic Special*. He was out at each stop, talking about tax reform and leadership and trust. But on board, reporters were talking about sex. Sex and Jimmy Carter and *Playboy* magazine.

Jimmy Carter had done an interview for *Playboy* magazine. Press releases from *Playboy* containing the complete text of the interview had just hit the newspaper home offices. He had talked about how he had "looked on a lot of women with lust." He had said he had "committed adultery in my heart many times." He had talked about not condemning someone who leaves his wife and "shacks up with somebody out of wedlock." He had talked about someone who "screws a whole bunch of women."

And just for good measure, in the last breath of a ten-page interview, Carter (who needed to carry Texas) had defamed Lyndon Johnson. He had linked Johnson and Nixon, accusing both of "lying, cheating and distorting the truth."

Carter advisers were stunned. "What in hell is going on?" one of them asked. "Has this whole thing gone mad?"

It had.

Months earlier, at the urging of Jody Powell and other advisers, Carter had agreed to sit for a series of interviews with Robert Scheer, a free-lance writer commissioned by *Playboy*. (*Playboy* editor Barry Golson also sat in on the final session.)

For a presidential candidate to do a *Playboy* interview was startling. But the end product could have been even more startling than it turned out to be. For Rosalynn Carter, at the urging of her husband and his staff, also submitted to a *Playboy* interview. By her own recollection, Mrs. Carter was interviewed for almost an hour by *Playboy*'s representative, Scheer.

"Jody got me to talk with him," Mrs. Carter recalled. ". . . But when you are talking to someone like that who does not understand at all what religion is—no conception of what it is—you want to say, 'Listen, this is what it means; it is not anything ugly; it is not anything that people cannot understand if they don't want to. It's like this—' And this is what Jimmy was doing at the end when he said those things. He was through and he said, 'I am going to explain it to you once and for all.' And he used his own language that that young man would understand. You know, I even felt like talking to him that way myself. When he kept questioning me about homosexuality, I said, 'I told you everything I was going to say about it.' And I know how Jimmy felt. And I didn't blame him a bit."

Throughout the controversy that followed the *Playboy* article, Mrs. Carter was called upon a number of times to answer questions about whether she thought it was proper for her husband to give the interview in *Playboy*. She defended her husband always—in the latter days of the campaign she even appeared jointly with him in an effort to boost Carter's relatively low standing among women voters. But throughout, she wondered if *Playboy* was going to publish her interview as well. *Playboy* editor Barry Golson said Scheer interviewed Mrs. Carter only to gather background information for his interview and article concerning her husband.

As the Carter advisers saw it, *Playboy* readers were probably favorably disposed toward voting for Carter, but they were also probably a little uneasy about him. A long, low-key, thoughtful discourse by Carter in *Playboy* ought to put them at ease, the advisers figured. Many of the country's notable figures had already done *Playboy* interviews, among them: California governor Jerry Brown; the retired chief of naval operations, Admiral Elmo Zumwalt; Walter Cronkite; and Ford's own treasury secretary William Simon. So Carter could say he was in good company.

For more than nine pages in the magazine, the interview with Carter proved to be thoughtful, philosophical, and thoroughly unmemorable—just as Powell had anticipated. But then, one-third of the way through the last page, the magazine carried an italicized editor's note explaining the circumstances of what was to follow. A routine, uncomplicated question touched off a stream of conscious discourse that would significantly alter the shape of the presidential campaign. This is how it appeared in *Playboy*:

(At the final session, which took place in the living room of Carter's home in Plains, the allotted time was up. A press aide indicated that there were other appointments for which Carter was already late, and the aide opened the front door while amenities were exchanged. As the interviewer and the PLAYBOY *editor stood at the door, recording equipment in their arms, a final, seemingly casual question was tossed off. Carter then delivered a long, softly spoken monolog that grew in intensity as he made his final points. One of the journalists signaled to Carter that they were still tapping, to which Carter nodded his assent.)*

PLAYBOY: Do you feel you've reassured people with this interview, people who are uneasy about your religious beliefs, who wonder if you're going to make a rigid, unbending President?

CARTER: I don't know if you've been to Sunday school here yet; some of the press has attended. I teach there about every three or four weeks. It's getting to be a real problem because we don't have room to put everybody now when I teach. I don't know if we're going to have to issue passes or what. It almost destroys the worship aspect of it. But we had a good class last Sunday. It's a good way to learn what I believe and what the Baptists believe.

One thing the Baptists believe in is complete autonomy. I don't accept any domination of my life by the Baptist Church, none. Every Baptist church is individual and autonomous. We don't accept domination of our church from the Southern Baptist Convention. The reason the Baptist Church was formed in this country was because of our beliefs in absolute and total separation of church and state. These basic tenets make us almost unique. We don't believe in any hierarchy in church. We don't have bishops. Any officers chosen by the church are defined as servants, not bosses. They're supposed to do the dirty work, make sure the church is clean and painted and that sort of thing. So it's a very good, democratic structure.

When my sons were small, we went to church and they went, too. But when they got old enough to make their own decisions, they decided when to go and they varied in their devoutness. Amy really looks forward to going to church, because she gets to see all her cousins at Sunday school. I never knew anything except going to church. My wife and I were born and raised in innocent times. The normal thing to do was to go to church.

What Christ taught about most was pride, that one person should never think he was any better than anybody else. One of the most vivid stories Christ told in one of his parables was about two people who went into a church. One was an official of the church, a Pharisee, and he said, "Lord, I thank you that I'm not like all other people. I keep all your commandments, I give a tenth of everything I own. I'm here to give thanks for making me more acceptable in your sight." The other guy was despised by the nation, and he went in, prostrated himself on the floor and said, "Lord, have mercy on me, a sinner. I'm not worthy to lift my eyes to heaven." Christ asked the disciples which of the two had justified his life. The answer was obviously the one who was humble.

The thing that's drummed into us all the time is not to be proud, not to be better than anyone else, not to look down on people but to make ourselves acceptable in God's eyes through our own actions and recognize the simple truth that we're saved by grace. It's just a free gift through faith in Christ. This gives us a mechanism by which we can relate permanently to God. I'm not speaking for other people, but it gives me a sense of peace and equanimity and assurance.

I try not to commit a deliberate sin. I recognize that I'm going to do it anyhow, because I'm human and I'm tempted. And Christ said, "I tell you that anyone who looks on a woman with lust has in his heart already committed adultery."

I've looked on a lot of women with lust. I've com-

mitted adultery in my heart many times. This is
something that God recognizes I will do—and I have
done it—and God forgives me for it. But that doesn't
mean that I condemn someone who not only looks on
a woman with lust but who leaves his wife and shacks
up with somebody out of wedlock.

Christ says, Don't consider yourself better than
someone else because one guy screws a whole bunch
of women while the other guy is loyal to his wife. The
guy who's loyal to his wife ought not be condescend-
ing or proud because of the relative degree of sinfulness. One thing that Paul Tillich said was that religion
is a search for the truth about man's existence and his
relationship with God and his fellow man; and that
once you stop searching and think you've got it made
—at that point, you lose your religion. Constant reas-
sessment, searching in one's heart—it gives me a feeling of confidence.

I don't inject these beliefs in my answers to your
secular questions.

(*Carter clenched his fist and gestured sharply.*)

But I don't think I would *ever* take on the same
frame of mind that Nixon or Johnson did—lying,
cheating and distorting the truth. Not taking into consideration my hope for my strength of character, I
think that my religious beliefs alone would prevent
that from happening to me. I have that confidence. I
hope it's justified.

Carter deputy press secretary Rex Granum had sat in
on the interview. "I told Jody about what Jimmy had said
there at the end," Granum recalled. "I emphasized the
lust quotes, but not so much the Johnson thing. But I guess
I didn't make a big enough deal over any of it. After all,
we always figured we'd have a chance to approve the
quotes. Scheer promised us that. In fact, Scheer kept telling us how when Jerry Brown was interviewed, the Brown
staff got to re-write so much of the stuff, and that we'd
have the same chance, and so on."

Scheer says he did make several telephone efforts to
reach Powell in order to let the Carter people look over
the transcript. The Carter people insist that the effort was,

at best, perfunctory; they say Scheer must have realized that the final quotes would not have been approved had the Carter staff been able to review the transcript.

Regardless, Carter's quotes appeared in full in the magazine. And the result was devastating to the Carter campaign.

"*Playboy* killed us," Pat Caddell said. "The story broke on Monday. On Tuesday night, our polling showed that we were falling. We went from 9 or 10 points ahead to about even. And by Wednesday night, we had fallen behind! We were trailing Ford for one night. I don't think there was ever any decline that was so rapid, except perhaps what happened to McGovern because of the Eagleton thing" (George McGovern's 1972 decline after it was disclosed that his vice-presidential running mate, Thomas Eagleton, had received psychiatric shock treatments).

Carter began to come back by Thursday—anticipation of that night's presidential debate, Caddell believes, plus the natural resurgence after the initial *Playboy* shock. And even though Carter did not win the debate, at least it took the immediate attention away from the *Playboy* quotes.

Caddell surveys showed that the *Playboy* article had two lasting effects on the Carter campaign. It hurt Carter with the women's vote, where he was already suffering, and it led more people to believe that it would be risky to have Carter as President.

     ▰   ▰   ▰

"The *Playboy* interview was a mistake," Carter said later in an interview. "Had we been more knowledgeable, we would not have put that much faith in what they said about our being able to go over the text and so forth. It's over with, but I think it really hurt us. It demonstrated a confirmation of Ford's proposal to the American people that I was not quite to be trusted—that I was not what I was supposed to be, and that in some ways I was misleading the American voters.

". . . Some people have never read the *Playboy* article, never seen the nude pictures, never seen what I said. [To them] it was a sign of an absence of good judgment. And it created doubt about my basic character—how can this deeply religious person who professes to be moral associate himself with this magazine?"

But most of all, the problem was not that Carter talked to the *Playboy* people; the problem was what he said to them. He, and he alone, turned an uneventful philosophical discussion into an epic of titillation, true confessions, and political blunder.

🏴 🏴 🏴

Johnson Country. On the day after the debate, Jimmy Carter touched down in the land of the late President he had defamed. Carter had already issued an apology to Lady Bird Johnson from Plains, Georgia; but the wire services were carrying stories quoting her as saying she was still "distressed, hurt and perplexed." As *Peanut One* was touching down, Democratic Party Chairman Robert Strauss, a Texan close to the Johnson family, shook his head. "We're down now," he said sadly. "There's no doubt about it. We're down. We're still ahead, but we're down. This campaign hasn't had a break—and it's due for one."

But there would be no break that day. Carter stepped out of *Peanut One* and into a press conference on the tarmac of the Houston airport. An apology was again clearly in order. But for some reason—a mystery to even his closest aides—Carter chose his words so as to make it appear that he was really blaming other people (such as editors at *Playboy*) for inserting comments attacking Lyndon Johnson at the end of the *Playboy* piece. He seemed to indicate that someone had misrepresented his views. Speaking before the Texas reporters, cameras, and microphones, he seemed to be talking not about his own comments, made of his own volition, in response to a question from *Playboy*. Instead, he said:

". . . After the interview was over, there was a summary made that unfortunately equated what I had said about President Johnson and President Nixon. . . . I'm very sorry that misrepresentation of what I feel about President Johnson caused Mrs. Johnson any discomfort or embarrassment. For that I am truly sorry. . . . I realize that if you read it, it says that after the final completion of the interview.

"My reference to Johnson was about the misleading of the American people. The lying and cheating part referred to President Nixon. And the unfortunate juxtaposition of these two names in the *Playboy* article grossly misrepresents the way I feel about him. The only culpability or blame that I placed on Johnson [earlier] in my interview was the fact that during the Vietnamese War, under Presidents Kennedy, Johnson and Nixon, the American people were not involved in an accurate understanding of what circumstances were in Vietnam. . . . But I have no criticism of President Johnson except that the American people were excluded."

Reporters traveling with Carter were stunned. The candidate who had promised never to lie or make a misleading statement had appeared to be carefully misleading reporters at his Texas press conference. "He's the one who said all that stuff, not *Playboy's* editors," one newsman said to Jody Powell, who was standing near the fringes of the press conference. "Yes, he said it," Powell agreed. Minutes later, he talked with Carter, and Carter then acknowledged to a few reporters, "That was my analysis and unfortunate juxtaposition of the two names. It was a mistake, and I have apologized . . . I thought the interview was over. . . ."

Carter had excellent public appearances in Houston and Dallas that day. His speeches were strong and effective, his crowds were friendly. But much of the attention of the Carter press corps had been drawn away from the appearance by the startling way in which he explained the *Playboy*/Johnson debacle.

Jody Powell was fuming. As *Peanut One* carried the Carter campaign toward an overnight stop in San Diego, all of the frustrations that had been building within the thirty-three-year-old press secretary suddenly surfaced. Reporters in the back of the plane were going around saying that now Carter had tried to mislead. Distort. And for the press secretary who had served Carter with dedication for years, it was too much.

Powell was not without some justification. The Carter campaign had been victimized in the past by some bad stories (it happens in every campaign). It had been frustrated in the past by some accurate stories that dwelled on the candidates' gaffes and offhand remarks in answer to questions, instead of on what Powell felt should have been the substantive news of the day.

Now Powell, fuming, went back to the press section of *Peanut One* and started picking fights. He defended the way Carter handled the Johnson matter, and bristled at the suggestion that Carter had tried to mislead or deceive.

"You guys are operating on a double standard and I'm damn well sick and tired of it," Powell said at one point, interjecting himself into a conversation between a reporter and another staff member. "Everything Jimmy does is examined under a microscope and picked apart and Ford sits there hiding in the White House and gets off scot-free. We've tried to run an open campaign and look what we get. Why don't you go after Ford and smoke him out and make him answer questions? . . . Let me tell you right now, we don't have to do it this way anymore. We can run a closed operation too. We can cut off your access to the candidate."

        ▨   ▨   ▨

(Days later, up front in Carter's personal section of the plane, Patrick Anderson was chatting with Jody Powell. "When you get into the White House . . . ," Anderson began. But Powell, embittered after weeks of wrangling with reporters, interrupted, "I'm not going to be in the White House. I don't want to put up with those assholes back there." And he jerked his thumb toward the press section in the rear.)

        ▨   ▨   ▨

"One surprise to me," Carter said in an interview later, "was the difficulty of running against an incumbent. The fact that I would be treated as a candidate and he would be treated as a President . . . by the news media was something that we did not anticipate."

Carter tried to make it home to Plains for the weekends, and there, along with resting, he would view videotapes of television news shows. "It was absolutely shocking, the difference in my coverage and Ford's coverage," Carter said. "And I honestly thought that it was seriously hurting our campaign. And as I have said many times

I never have felt that the news media treated me unfairly—and I was fair game with all of you, and if I made a mistake, jump on it and so forth. But to see President Ford impervious to that kind of cross-examination and scrutiny and intense personal criticism made me look very bad in contrast to him on the evening news, which is a major opinion shaper.

"... We were considering at one point sending either Jody or Jerry Rafshoon or Charles Kirbo or perhaps myself to meet with the executive officers of the three networks." But that, he said, was never done.

Carter, in his *Playboy* interview, had observed at one point that "the national news media have absolutely no interest in issues at all . . . the traveling press have zero interest in any issues unless it's a matter of making a mistake. What they're looking for is a 47 second argument between me and another candidate or something like that. There's nobody in the back of this plane who would ask an issue question unless he thought he could trick me into some crazy statement."

In fact, covering Jimmy Carter was not an easy thing. He was not softer on issues or more vague on issues than any other candidates in this or any other year; he was about the same as the rest. He did give some speeches devoted to specific issues: farm policy, economic policy, Middle East policy, small business administration, nuclear proliferation, women's rights, senior citizens, health care. But most of the time, he gave his standard stump speech (which did contain general positions on a number of issues). And when he was asked questions by reporters seeking to break new ground in one issue area or another, the answer would usually be a recitation of his position almost word for word as it was contained in his stump speech or one of his issue speeches. So for reporters as well as the candidate the question of how to deal with issues in the campaign was a problem.

It was also a problem for Stuart Eizenstat. The tall, slim, Ivy-looking Atlantan was Carter's chief issues adviser, and those who talked to him were impressed by the depth of his knowledge in a wide variety of issues, domestic and foreign. Like Powell and Jordan and so many of the Carter hierarchy, Eizenstat was in his early thirties. But unlike the others, he alone among the upper echelon pushed hard—and usually unsuccessfully—

for Carter to speak out more on issues, to give more speeches devoted to explaining in depth his stand on an issue.

By the end of the campaign, Eizenstat would be riding the plane fuming in his own right—but his frustration, unlike Powell's, would be the lack of issue-oriented speeches. "People want to know these things," he would say. "The homeowners want to know as much as they can about what Jimmy has in store for them. Dammit, I wish I could get them to understand." But the view that predominated was once expressed by Hamilton Jordan at a meeting with several other advisers: "I don't care if we ever have another issues speech. Let's stick to the themes—competence, leadership, idealism, get the country moving again."

Among those who agreed with the Carter camp that President Ford was getting an easy ride in September was Ford's own chief of staff, Richard Cheney. "Let's face it," he said, "we played to television's problems. We knew that their measure of fair treatment was equal time. So we would go out in the Rose Garden and say nothing—just sign a bill—and we'd get the coverage. Issues did not dominate this campaign. Now, people can blame television for that, but we're no more virtuous than they are in that sense. We played it that way."

Richard Cheney is a candid man.

When the Carter entourage arrived at the Royal Inn Hotel, overlooking the San Diego harbor, Powell went straight to Carter's room. The candidate sat on the bed, his hands folded in front of him; the press secretary paced back and forth across the motel carpet. They discussed, once again, Houston.

"If you go back and look at exactly what you said," Powell recalls having told Carter, "if the press conference had ended right there, then you'd be subject to people trying to get all over your ass about deliberately misleading the press. I don't know why you said it that way—I think you tried to say too much when a short answer would have done it. Nothing can be done about the sort of scrutiny you're under [from the press]. But you've got to be very careful not to give them opportunities to jump all over you.

"My feeling . . . [about what the reporters are saying] is: Who are they to judge why you said what you said initially? It goes beyond the bounds of propriety for the press to jump on you when you've clarified it."

Carter interrupted. "What should we do about it?" he asked.

Powell responded: "I don't know—maybe a sit-down-and-let's-have-it-all-out sort of thing."

Carter: "When?"

Powell: "I don't know."

Carter: "How about tonight?"

Quietly, word was passed. Lower-level Carter aides fanned out. "The governor wants to see you upstairs." Perhaps a dozen reporters—all from the print media—were to be asked. A couple could not be reached; they had already left for dinner.

One by one, the reporters walked into a suite furnished like a living room. Schneiders and Powell were there. Have a seat. There was cold beer. Then Carter walked in, shirtsleeves rolled up; he pulled a narrow coffee table over to the wall and sat down, straddling the table, cowboy-like.

Carter spoke softly. He said he recognized that there were some problems that had come to a head and he wanted to talk with the reporters about them. He said he wanted the meeting to be off the record. The reporters glanced at each other. Nobody wanted to permit himself to be used, but, on the other hand, it did not seem right to cut Carter off in mid-thought and walk out. For a moment, those in the room were very unsure.*

Carter continued. No one took notes, but the essence

---

* Here the telling of the story becomes awkward, because I was one of the reporters in the room. But because Carter has since referred in a public press conference at the Plains depot to comments that I made in that room, I feel it is all right to put those remarks in context.

of his opening remarks was that he realized that some problems had arisen between the reporters and himself and his staff, problems arising out of the Houston airport press conference and problems concerning campaign coverage in general. Carter said that, after all, we were all in the campaign together, and he was sure we only wanted what was best for our country, and he'd asked us up to the room to see what advice we could give for how relations between the candidate, his staff, and the press could be improved.

Now the atmosphere seemed clearly awkward. One reporter interrupted to say that he did not think it was his place to be giving *advice* to Carter—or to Ford, for that matter. But that Carter did have a right to know what it was the reporter heard and saw that led him to write the story as it appeared. He said he would stay and discuss those matters, but not give advice.

Carter simply nodded and said he understood, and the meeting went on. Some present read Carter back the direct quotes of what he had said in Houston, and he emphasized that he had not at all tried to mislead the Texans in his choice of wording. From there, he talked about his frustrations concerning press coverage and how the news stories seemed too often not to focus on what he felt ought to be the news. And a couple of those present pointed out to him that at times it was his gaffes or carelessly worded statements that took the play away from his own planned events. Powell, speaking in a friendly tone, repeated his threat to make Carter less accessible if coverage did not change. Reporters said that Carter should do what he thought best for his campaign— whether it meant to be accessible or inaccessible—and that the reporters should do their jobs as they saw fit, either way. The meeting—an extraordinary session in campaign politics—was conducted on a basically frank but cordial note, and it ended after about an hour in the same vein. In the weeks to come, Carter was, in fact, less accessible to the traveling press corps. He still gave a large number of interviews, but the emphasis was on local interviews with local reporters at every stop.

October 1. Jimmy Carter is fifty-two today, and between Portland (Maine) and Nashville and Pittsburgh he has managed to acquire seven birthday cakes and one close call. The close call came in Nashville, when someone showed up with a special birthday gift—a bronzelike plaster-of-paris bust of Jimmy Carter fixed with a thoroughly hideous grin. The person-bearing-bust moved up the aisle at a rally in an airport hangar and was just about to force Carter to have his picture taken with the monstrosity when Greg Schneiders pivoted, cut to his left, sprinted up the stairs two at a time, and intercepted the bust person with less than a second to spare. Up at the podium, the birthday person looked relieved.

On the flight to Pittsburgh, a Carter aide radios ahead to have five straw hats waiting for the Carter entourage at the hotel. The skimmers are at the Airport Hilton when the Carter entourage arrives. A small party is thrown, staff and press only. Rosalynn Carter has flown in; she wanted to help her husband celebrate. So do five reporters. To the tune of "Heart of My Heart," Carter is serenaded in a bouncy, upbeat tempo by the journalistic quintet, occasionally leering and waving their straw skimmers as they sing:

Lust in my heart, how I love adultery
Lust in my heart, it's my theology
When I was young, at the Plains First Baptist Church. .
I would preach and sermonize
But oh how I would fantasize

Oh, Lust in my heart, who cares if it's a sin. .
    (it has never been)
Leching's a noble art
It's OK if you shack up
'Cause I won't get my back up
I've got mine
I've got lust in my heart.

Carter and his wife smile as the reporters launch into the second chorus:

Lust in my heart, oh it's bad politic'ly
Lust in my heart, but it brings publicity.
When I grew up and ran for president

A bunch of women I did screw
But in my head, so no one knew.

Oh, Lust in my heart,
I said I'd never lie,
    ('bout my roving eye)
I should have played it smart
But I'm no gay deceiver
I'm a Christian eager beaver
As Playboy *said, I've got lust in my heart.*

Carter laughs and comes up afterward to thank the
reporters; he appears to have enjoyed it. Mrs. Carter
smiles and follows her husband to the front, but some
think she did not enjoy the lyrics as much as her husband
did.

There is small talk, and then Carter asks if any of
the reporters have heard about the big news of the day:
the Earl Butz quote. The reporters have. John Wesley
Dean III, of Watergate fame, had ridden back to Washington from the Republican convention on a plane carrying, among others, Ford's agriculture secretary, Earl Butz.
Later, writing in *Rolling Stone,* Dean quoted Butz as
having uttered, in the presence of others, including singer
Pat Boone, a truly vulgar racial slur.

Carter says he has not heard exactly what it was that
Butz said. A reporter tells him just as Mrs. Carter joins
the group. The Butz quote, the reporter is saying, was
that there are only three things that blacks like: "tight
pussy, loose shoes, and a warm place to shit." Mrs.
Carter immediately pivots and strikes up a conversation
with the person on the other side of her, giving no indication that she has even caught the drift of the conversation.

Carter, meanwhile, just shakes his head. "Awful,"
he says.

The Butz case proves to be one more headache for
Ford. He stalls instead of asking for Butz's immediate
resignation. Eventually, as should have been clear to
the White House, the pressure of public outrage forces
Butz to resign. By delaying intead of acting, Ford has
infuriated black Americans.

THE RACE: *Playboy and the Philadelphia debate have knocked the polls into disarray. Harris comes in on debate night with a Carter lead of 7. Gallup is in a period of flux. his September 24-27 poll published following the first debate shows Carter with an 8-point bulge: Carter, 50; Ford, 42; McCarthy, 4; undecided, 4. (The Gallup Poll situation is even more complex than that. It turns out that the accurate Gallup figures for the September 24-27 poll showed Carter with a larger lead than Gallup had made public at that time. Carter really had an 11-point lead [Carter, 51; Ford, 40] instead of having slipped to 8. Figures from the South and urban areas— both pro-Carter categories—were often late in coming in, Gallup spokesman James Shriver says, and not all of them were included in the figures published at the time. "We rushed and didn't have a chance to polish them up," Shriver says. Thus, it turns out, Gallup erroneously made Carter's decline seem worse than it was. And in an election where many voters were not strongly committed to either candidate, this might have damaged Carter by making his problems appear worse than they were.)*

Gallup's poll the next week is a shocker. Gallup says the Carter lead has collapsed to a precious 2. But by the time Gallup gets his poll to the newspapers, the second presidential debate has been held and the 2 percent margin is declared obsolete on the day it is printed nationwide.

October/The Second Debate

The second debate, Jimmy Carter had promised, would be different. He had been nervous in the first debate, he said. He had been a little awed by the fact that he was standing there beside the man who was the President of the United States. He had been too timid. Too reserved. He had perspired.

It was typical of Jimmy Carter that he discussed these very private feelings in public—just the day after the first debate, in fact. He did not feign bravado; he did not strive for macho. He was just a man debating the President in front of millions of people, and he had gotten nervous, so he said so. And he said the second debate, in the Palace of Fine Arts, located in the shadow of the Golden Gate Bridge in San Francisco, would be different.

This time, Carter rehearsed. For one hour in his suite at the Sheraton Palace Hotel—"a depressing little suite," one of his aides called it—Carter submitted to question-and-answer drilling with a couple of his advisers.

On the day of the debate, October 6, Carter rested at the home of Walter Shorenstein, a wealthy San Francisco developer. There, the man from Plains lunched on lox and bagels with Greg Schneiders. The young administrative assistant deliberately did not mention the debate; he did not want to add to the pressure his boss was feeling. But he did want to help Carter get into the necessary frame of mind. So he brought up the matter of past Presidents and said that he really did not feel a special reverence for past Presidents. "I just don't think that reverence is felt anymore," Schneiders said. "I don't remember Truman, but I do remember Eisenhower, and I didn't feel a special reverence for him. [Schneiders was twelve in Eisenhower's last year in office.] And I certainly didn't feel a special reverence for any of the more recent Presidents."

Carter interrupted. "I felt it for Roosevelt."

Schneiders went on "I think the recent Presidents have diminished it. Remember the feelings in the South toward Kennedy—it's hard to remember the feelings of hatred some southerners felt for Kennedy. Remember Johnson and Nixon. And the jokes about Ford."

Carter arrived at the ornate theater first, shortly before the 6:30 P.M. starting time for the debate. He stepped out of his car, stepped over several television cables, waved to a small crowd clustered outside, and entered the side theater door. Ford arrived a couple of minutes later; his car stopped a couple of yards to the rear of where Carter's had been. There, a special low ramp had been built—red on the sides and topped with non-skid grooved rubber matting; it stood about three inches high, just enough to get the President over the cables. Ford walked across the ramp, waved to the crowd, and entered via the same door.

The clock in the Yacht Harbor Club is trimmed in green neon and advertises Belfast Sparkling Water. A United Seed Company calendar graces the wall. The pool table off to the side remained the center of activity throughout moderator Pauline Frederick's opening remarks. But the game abruptly stopped when Max Frankel of *The New York Times* asked the first question, and the players joined the nine people already seated at the bar, watching the television set.

As in the first debate, Carter had wanted to answer second. As in the first debate, his aide Barry Jagoda won the flip of the coin, and by his agreement that meant his boss had to go first.

"Our country is not strong anymore," Carter was saying. "We are not respected anymore. We can only be strong overseas if we are strong at home. And when I become President, I will not only be strong in those areas but also in defense. . . ."

"Geez," said one of the pool players. "Did he ever change his tune." Over near the end of the bar, near the television set, Greg Schneiders (minus staff pin and tie but plus a cigar) grimaced.

". . . We have become fearful to compete with the Soviet Union on an equal basis," Carter went on. "We talk about détente. The Soviet Union knows what they want in détente, and they have been getting it."

Gary, the ex-Green Beret tending bar, nodded. "He's going to take care of his GIs—you watch," he said. Schneiders smiled and took a George Burns drag on his cigar. "This one is going to be more bloody than the last one," he said.

Ford, too, was taking more to the offense. "Governor Carter again is talking in broad generalities," he said in the first words he spoke in the second debate. The tone was set. Ford went on to say, "Mr. Carter has indicated he would look with sympathy to a Communist government in [Italy]. I think that would destroy the integrity and strength of NATO, and I am totally opposed to it."

Carter was quick to hit back. "Mr. Ford unfortunately made a statement that is not true. I never advocated a Communist government for Italy. That would be ridiculous for anyone to do who wanted to be President of this country. I think this is an instance of deliberate distortion. . . ."

Ford had said Carter once advocated in November 1975 cutting the defense budget by $15 billion, and that a few months later he began talking about cuts of $8 or $9 billion, and more recently $5 to $7 billion. Carter retorted, "I have never advocated any cuts of $15 billion in a defense budget." But as a matter of fact, newspaper clippings in Savannah and Los Angeles show that Carter, in those earliest days of his campaign effort, did entertain the possibility of defense cuts as high as $15 billion; but throughout 1976, Carter had stuck to the $5 to $7 billion figure as the one he thought attainable.

Prompted by thorough questioning from Frankel, Henry L. Trewhitt of the *Baltimore Sun,* and Richard Valeriani of NBC, the candidates moved through SALT (Strategic Arms Limitation Talks) negotiations, defense spending, and policies in Asia, Europe, Africa, the Middle East, and the question of the Panama Canal.

"Every time we have made a serious mistake in foreign affairs, it has been because the American people have been excluded from the process," Carter said. The problem, he said, was secrecy. He promised to renew FDR's fireside chats.

Carter accused Ford of using the defense budget for a "football" by inflating it whenever he was feeling political heat from the right wing: when he fired James Schlesinger as defense secretary, when he was struggling in the Texas Republican primary, and at the time of the GOP convention in Kansas City.

"Jesus," said a man at the bar in a blue work shirt, his expression and nod showing approval of Carter's tactic.

"He's zinging it to him this time," said one of the pool players.

"He's got his shit together," said Gary, the Green Beret.

Schneiders agreed with the bartender. "Everyone always says nobody wins these debates. Well, we'll see what they say this time."

Just then, Frankel asked a rather lengthy question about whether the Soviets had perhaps gotten the better of the United States in foreign affairs despite some setbacks in the Middle East.

Ford began predictably and safely. "I believe we have negotiated with the Soviet Union since I have been President from a position of strength. And let me cite several examples. . . ." From there, Ford started by reciting details of nuclear arms negotiation statistics, and then—without meaning to—dropped a bomb on his own campaign.

Ford: ". . . Now, what has been accomplished by the Helsinki agreement? Number one, we have an agreement where they notify us and we notify them of any military maneuvers that are to be undertaken. They have done it in both cases where they have done so. There is no Soviet domination of Eastern Europe, and there never will be under the Ford Administration."

Frankel: "Did I understand you to say, sir, that the Russians are not using Eastern Europe as their own sphere of influence and occupying most of the countries there and making sure with their troops that it is a Communist Zone whereas on our side of the line the Italians and French are still flirting with possible Communism?"

Ford: "I don't believe, Mr. Frankel, that the Yugoslavians consider themselves dominated by the Soviet Union. I don't believe the Rumanians consider themselves

dominated by the Soviet Union. I don't believe that the
Poles consider themselves dominated by the Soviet Union.
Each of those countries is independent, autonomous. It
has its own territorial integrity and the United States does
not concede that those countries are under the domination
of the Soviet Union. As a matter of fact, I visited Poland,
Yugoslavia and Rumania to make certain that the people
of those countries understand that the President of the
United States and the people of the United States are
dedicated to their independence, their autonomy and their
freedom."

Moderator: "Governor Carter, may we have your
responses?"

Carter was slow on the uptake. But eventually he got
around to focusing attention on Ford's blunder. ". . . I
would like to see Mr. Ford convince the Polish-Americans
and the Czech-Americans and Hungarian-Americans in
this country that those countries don't live under the
domination and supervision of the Soviet Union behind
the Iron Curtain."

Schneiders was grinning and puffing at the same time.
"I love it," he said. "If only the first one had gone like
this."

Down at the other end of the bar, a man said, "Poland's not dominated? That's the strongest comment Ford
has made—and he's all wrong!"

Carter had captured the Yacht Harbor Bar. This time,
when Schneiders returned to the theater, he would have
glad tidings to report.

The debate went on for an hour more, with Carter
blasting Ford for yielding to Arab pressure and permit-
ting the Arabs to boycott American firms that did business
with Israel or had American Jews in their management
and with Ford speaking in great detail once again about
SALT negotiations and defending his decision to use the
military to rescue the crew of the freighter *Mayaguez*
when it was seized by Cambodia's Communist government.

But for all practical purposes, the debate was over.
Foreign policy experts generally thought Ford handled
himself well in defending America's foreign policy. But
the Eastern Europe comments proved a political blunder.

The problem on the Eastern Europe question was that
Ford had overrehearsed. He had gone into the debate

primed to counter a question that was never asked. Ford and his advisers had expected that he would be asked about a position that had been expressed privately by a State Department official, but which had been leaked to the press and had become a political embarrassment to the President. The State Department official, counselor Helmut Sonnenfeldt, had taken the position that the United States should, in its planning, concede the obvious *military* reality that Eastern Europe is under the military domination of the Soviet Union. Sonnenfeldt's view was that this ought to be conceded since the United States obviously did not intend to take any military action to counter an internal action within Eastern Europe by the Soviets. Sonnenfeldt also believed that the United States ought to continue *political* efforts to encourage greater independence for Eastern Europe, even while conceding this obvious military fact of life.

The leaking of Sonnenfeldt's view of the military reality brought Ford political problems from his party's right wing. He had gone into the debate rehearsed to try to ease this political pressure by emphasizing that he did not intend to concede Eastern Europe to the Soviet Union. But once on camera, Ford went too far.

Ford pollster Robert Teeter's panel of viewers, equipped with rheostat measuring devices, gave the debate clearly to Carter. The Democratic candidate scored well with his promise of a fireside chat, for attacking Ford for selling weapons to Iran, and for criticizing Henry Kissinger and Ford's handling of the Panama Canal negotiations, the Arab boycott, and the Vietnam missing-in-action cases. Ford scored best with his slap at Carter for being sympathetic to Italian Communists, for his Mayaguez defense, and for promising to provide Congress with information on the Arab boycott that had previously been withheld by his administration. But his Eastern Europe comments wound up on the Carter plus side of the chart—and, in fact, even his own closing remarks were recorded as a plus for his opponent.

Hamilton Jordan was giddy. "He did it!" Jordan said, whooping like a Georgia linebacker who had just fallen on a fumble to win the Gator Bowl. "Jimmy cleaned his clock!" After the first debate, Jordan had gone around claiming victory to reporters, even though he did not believe his own words. "But this time is different. Jimmy won it. And that Eastern Europe thing—I can't believe Ford said it. The issue will haunt Ford in the days to come," Jordan said, laughing. "You can depend on it!"

A reporter told Jordan he doubted that. The Ford officials are just about to hold a briefing, he said. Surely the President will have his men clear it up quickly; surely they'll come out and say the President misspoke (Presidents somehow never make mistakes, they just misspeak), and the affair will turn out to be a one-day, one-shot issue that will soon be forgotten.

"We'll see," Jordan said, still laughing.

🏴 🏴 🏴

The President's advisers walked into the Holiday Inn on Van Ness Street to brief the press after the debate. Michael Duval suggested that they stop and think their Eastern Europe problem through. Don't worry, Cheney said; he was prepared. General Brent Scowcroft, assistant to the President for national security, added that he, too, could handle it. Duval let it drop.

PRESS CONFERENCE
THE HOLIDAY INN

9:15 P.M. PDT

CHENEY: "We would be happy to respond to any questions you might have by way of obvious focus on the debates tonight."

Q: "Are there Soviet troops in Poland?"

SCOWCROFT: "Yes."

Q: "How many would you say?"

SCOWCROFT: "Offhand, I don't recall. There are four divisions. I am not sure, but a substantial number."

Q: "Do you think that would imply some Soviet dominance to Poland?"

SCOWCROFT: "I think what the President was trying to say is that we do not recognize Soviet dominance of Europe and that he took his trip to Eastern Europe—to

Poland, to Rumania, to Yugoslavia—to demonstrate, to symbolize their independence, and their freedom of maneuver."

Q: "Do you think he succeeded in saying what you just said he said? He said Poland was free at one point during that answer."

CHENEY: "I think the point, Lou, was the President was focusing on the fact we want separate independent relationships with each of those nations, and that was the purpose of his travels. I think you would get a similar statement, I would assume, from some of those governments and that his policy of his Administration is that we are interested in separate, independent autonomous relationships with governments like Yugoslavia, Rumania, and Poland."

Q: "Did he misspeak himself? Is that what you are saying?"

CHENEY: "I would have to go back and check the transcript, Bob, but I think you have to look at it within the context of the allegation that was made, that somehow this Administration recognizes or has sanctioned the charge or wants a relationship based on the assumption of dominance and we don't assume that. We want a separate independent relationship with each of those countries."

Q: "But he did misspeak himself. That is fair enough to say, isn't it?"

SCOWCROFT: "I think you have to look at the transcript."

Q: "We got his quote."

SCOWCROFT: "That is clearly what he was getting at."

Q: "He said the U.S. does not concede Eastern Europe itself independent under the domination of the Soviet Union."

SCOWCROFT: "He does not concede the domination of Eastern Europe. That is what he took the trip for—to demonstrate, to symbolize the independence of those countries. He did not concede. . . ."

Not one of the President's men had gone to the President to warn him just how serious the problem could be. No one had urged that he clarify his statement. After the debate, Ford just went to his residence feeling all was

well, and his aides went to the press conference and discovered all was not.

The President left San Francisco the next morning at
dawn and headed south. A speech was scheduled at the
University of Southern California. On board *Air Force
One*, his aides were by then aware that they had a problem. They suggested that Ford admit that he had not
spoken clearly on the Eastern Europe matter and that he
state that of course Eastern Europe is dominated by the
Soviets. Ford was stubborn. He flatly refused.

Instead, standing in front of USC students carrying
signs—including one that read: "Ford Frees Poles; Carter
Wins Polls"—the President dug in, barricading himself
with protective diplomatic nuance. He stressed in his
speech that what he was saying in San Francisco was that
he did not *concede* that Soviets dominated Poland. The
United States, he said, "has never conceded and never will
concede" Soviet domination of Eastern Europe.

A student shouted out, "Make up your mind, Jerry."
And the audience laughed.

The President issued a written statement about how he
had long admired the Polish people. But that didn't help.
His advisers told him again that he was only perpetuating
the problem. He must state what everyone in America
knows is the truth: he must admit that, indeed, Eastern
Europe is dominated by the Soviets. The advisers were
relieved when Ford, at last, agreed.

His chance came the next morning at a question-and-
answer breakfast with a group of mostly admiring San
Fernando businessmen. In answer to a question, Ford
said:

"It has been alleged by some that I was not as precise
as I should have been the other day. But let me explain
what I really meant. I was in Poland a year ago and I had
the opportunity to talk with a number of citizens of Poland
and believe me, they are strong people." He then added:
"They don't believe that they are going to be forever
dominated, *if they are,* by the Soviet Union."

If they are. Over near the wall, Ford's campaign press
secretary, William Greener, a popular and understanding
spokesman, looked as if he had just sat on the golden
spike. His eyes widened, his ever-florid face reddened.
The problem, he knew, had not been abated.

If they are. Why did the President toss that phrase in? "Sheer stubbornness," one White House adviser guessed. Another offered this explanation: "The President is a stubborn man, but he is really like a gyroscope. If you push him suddenly over one way, his immediate reaction is to pop right back to where he was originally. But if you gently nudge him in the right direction, he'll bend, all right."

Next stop was Glendale, where Ford was featured speaker at ceremonies honoring the family that founded the community, the Verdugo family. Ford opened by saying how pleased he was to be at the "Vertigo festival." (*Vertigo,* according to dictionary definition, is a disordered condition in which a person or his surroundings seem to be whirling about.) As he spoke, his assistants were circulating in the press area, attempting to tone down the ongoing gaffe. "Hell, yes," Cheney said, "he knows Eastern Europe is dominated by the Soviet Union." Reporters quoted Ford's breakfast comment back, and Cheney, surprised, said he would check the transcript.

Seeing that the problem remained, Cheney called Ford's personal assistant, Terry O'Donnell, and asked him to bring the President to a holding room at the festival.

There, Cheney laid it on the line. The problem would not go away, he told the President, until Ford—personally—made it clear that he recognized that Soviet military troops were stationed in Poland and that the Soviets did indeed dominate the region. Ford agreed. He told his aide to have a group of reporters assembled and he would tell them in a few minutes. Ford left to greet some local dignitaries and then returned to the room.

As Ford was about to go out and concede the obvious to the reporters, Cheney, still concerned, asked his boss if he was sure about just how he wanted to phrase his comment. Ford whirled, his face hardened in anger, his eyes blazing fury, and pointed a finger in Cheney's face and said loudly: "Poland is *not* dominated by the Soviet Union!" Then, as Cheney was frozen in shock and panic, he saw the President drop his arm and break out in that familiar easy grin and begin to laugh heartily; and he realized that in this end of the worst week of his campaign, a week of personal flubbing and frustration, the President was able to enjoy playing a joke on his embattled aide, poking fun at himself in the process.

Ford turned and left the room still laughing, and told reporters in the parking lot:

"Perhaps I could have been more precise in what I said concerning the Soviet domination of Poland. I recognize that there are, in Poland, Soviet divisions. It is a tragedy. . . . I hope in the future the Poles will be able to find another solution. . . . I trust that my observations will put an end to this misunderstanding. It was a misunderstanding. Maybe I did not make myself clear."

Four days later, in an effort to further pacify America's ethnic communities, Ford met for forty-five minutes with leaders of Eastern European ethnic organizations. He said he recognized Soviet military domination of Eastern Europe. "The original mistake was mine," he said. "I did not express myself clearly. I admit it."

Thus what should have been a quick fluff-and-fix-it situation was finally put to rest, but not until the President had gone through days of difficulty and frustration over the most implausible of predicaments: Gerald Ford, a lifetime American Legion Republican, had somehow wound up seeming softer on communism than his Democratic opponent.

🏴 🏴 🏴

It had not been a good period for Ford. In addition to making life difficult for himself, the President—who brought honesty to the White House after Richard Nixon's Watergate scandal—found himself involved in an investigation by the still-functioning Watergate special prosecutor's office.

On September 26, Nicholas M. Horrock of *The New York Times* had reported that the Watergate special prosecutor's office was investigating whether funds from two maritime unions had been covertly paid to Ford when he was a congressman by having the money laundered through two Republican political committees in Kent County (Grand Rapids), Michigan. The investigation, according to the report, centered on a period of ten years beginning in 1964.

Then, the day after the debate, Jerry Landauer and Christopher A. Evans of *The Wall Street Journal* reported that, according to a thirteen-page Internal Revenue Service audit of Ford's personal and campaign finances, Ford had gotten along in 1972 on just five dollars a week in pocket money. Meals and travel expenses were frequently paid for by political or private-interest groups who were entertaining him or whom he was addressing.

Carter, meanwhile, roared out of the San Francisco debate sounding a new hard line.

He jumped on Ford's Eastern Europe comments. "Apparently, when Mr. Ford went to Poland, as happened to George Romney [in 1968], he was brainwashed," Carter said in Albuquerque. (He was referring to the then Michigan governor's admission, which crippled his 1968 effort in the GOP primary race, that he had been "brainwashed" by American officials in Vietnam.)

He raised questions about Ford's honesty, stating that Ford ought to publicly discuss the charges that had been made against him. "Mr. Ford is in hiding," Carter said in Albuquerque, "he comes out of the Rose Garden, memorizes a 90-second speech, and goes back into hiding." At one point he added with indignation: "Mr. Ford has not been willing to expose himself to the public" (His audience tittered.)

And Ford aides said the President exploded in rage when he was told that at one point Carter told a crowd that it was time for Ford to tell Americans "the truth, the whole truth, and nothing but the truth."

On October 14, Watergate Special Prosecutor Charles R. Ruff issued a statement saying that an investigation had uncovered no evidence to corroborate an allegation that Ford had mishandled campaign funds during his years as a congressman.

Ford called a press conference—his first full-scale televised press conference since February. "The thing that means more to me than my desire for public office is my personal reputation for integrity. . . . For too many days this campaign has been mired in questions that have little bearing upon the future of this nation. The people of this country deserve better than that." Ford said that he hoped that the special prosecutor's announcement "will elevate the Presidential campaign to a level befitting the American people and the American political tradition."

A few minutes later, Ford took issue with Carter's debate statements about America's strength, accusing his opponent of "slandering the good name of the United States."

THE RACE: *The polls are going in opposite directions, but they wind up not far apart. Harris shows Carter continuing a slow, steady slide: he was ahead by 7 after the first debate, then by 4 on October 11, and now, on October 20, it is Carter by 3—Carter, 45; Ford, 42; McCarthy, 5.*

Gallup, who had Carter ahead by just 2 as of October 4, has the Democrat moving back up to a 6-point lead on October 11 and keeping his 6-point margin as of October 18—Carter, 47; Ford, 41; McCarthy, 2.

"Jimmy had hit his stride by the last week of September," Caddell says, "but then after the second debate he got strident. Ford was a major casualty of the debate, but so was Jimmy—he knocked himself off his stride and changed his tone." The public was just not going to believe Ford was dishonest, Caddell says. The President's reputation for being an honest guy was that strong.

Interlude: Probes

One day in October, the FBI appeared at the Washington headquarters of the President Ford Committee. The agents of the Federal Bureau of Investigation were investigating allegations of possible criminal wrongdoing by the President and his campaign officials.

Specifically, the Justice Department had been told by an informant that the President Ford Committee had not reimbursed the government for expenses incurred back in the summer when the President hosted several receptions in the White House for wavering Republican delegates, an effort to use the majesty and mansion of the office to line up convention delegate support. Quietly, at the order of Attorney General Edward Levi, the FBI began investigating for possible misuse of government funds, especially the use of government funds for political purposes.

For Ford campaign chairman James Baker, the next ten days were personal and political hell. "I kept thinking back to the Nixon campaign people and Watergate," he said. "We had taken special care to make sure that every single expense had been reimbursed. With 1972 in mind, we were going to be especially careful. We'd checked it all out in advance with the Federal Election Commission and gotten their clearance. We'd had all of the counsels, for the committee and the White House, put all the clearances in writing. But now we had to go back and dig out all the receipts and everything and we couldn't afford to have anything get lost.

"And all the time we were really sweating it. For ten days we were digging out receipts. What if anything got out? What if a story appeared that we were under investigation? People would think, oh yes, another Watergate. None of it ever got out. But if it had, it could have been disaster."

In the end, all of the documentation proved in order, and the FBI agents finally closed their investigation and left. An FBI spokesman confirmed that the investigation took place and that the report was transferred back to the attorney general. No action was taken, and the case was closed.

But the incident, plus the Watergate special prosecutor's fall campaign investigation involving the President, left Baker deeply concerned about possible abuses of power. "There has got to be some prosecutorial restraint —or else we can have a real perversion of the political process," Baker said. "Perhaps we ought to say that during the eight weeks preceding a presidential election there can be no investigation of a presidential candidate. Perhaps we ought to just say that if evidence of wrongdoing is brought in there will be an investigation—right after the election. If there isn't some sort of restraint, a candidate's reputation can be tarnished—and the political process perverted—just by a news story about the fact that an investigation is taking place, even if the allegation later proves unfounded. And that would be a damn shame."

Martin Price is a free-lance investigative reporter. He spent much of the fall digging into the personal affairs and business dealings of Jimmy Carter. He also spent the

month of October on the payroll of the President Ford
Committee.

As Price recalls it, he was hired "to do both administrative and investigative work." As campaign chairman
James Baker recalls it, Price was hired "initially for
some sort of special projects category . . . as a trouble-
shooter," but that Price was "taken off when I learned
what he was doing—he was checking into the records of
the financing of the Carter peanut operation." As campaign
press secretary William Greener recalls it, Price was not
taken off the payroll, but was paid "to guarantee that he
would *stop* investigating Carter and that the tone of the
campaign would be kept the way Jim Baker wanted it."

Federal Election Commission records show that the
President Ford Committee paid Price on two occasions:
on October 19 he received $1,000, and on October 31—
just two days before the end of the campaign—he received $1,181.80.

Price, who writes for the right-wing Liberty Lobby,
originally became connected with the Ford campaign
through Greener. The press secretary said that Price contacted him and expressed an interest in investigating Carter. He asked Greener for leads, the press secretary said,
and Greener told him he had heard that Carter once received a loan from the Small Business Administration for
his peanut enterprise.

Price began investigating. He came up with several
items, and each was reviewed by the President Ford Committee's legal counsel. Then the information was passed on
to Baker and others. "I had the stuff and they refused
to use it," Price said. "They just made a political decision . . . the factions were split as to whether it should
be used or not."

Said Baker: "He was on the payroll before I knew
what he was doing. I pulled him off that [investigation]
because the downside of what he was doing would have
been worse than the upside. In the light of 1972—Watergate—it would have smacked of dirty tricks."

From that point on, the Ford Committee says it paid
Price specifically *not* to investigate Carter. "We felt the
only way to guarantee that he would not investigate Carter anymore was to pay him a salary and order him
not to investigate him," Greener said. Price spent his last
weeks of the campaign officially sitting by himself, think-

ing up sample questions and answers for Ford to use in preparation for his debates and preparing some position papers on matters including the Trilateral Commission, on which Carter once served.

But if the President Ford Committee was really paying Price to guarantee that he would not put out Carter scandal material, the Ford men did not get their money's worth. For while he was being paid by the Ford Committee, Martin Price fed United Press International information on the financing of Carter's peanut business that became a story that was carried across the country on October 23. The UPI story said that Carter and his mother had gotten an SBA loan for $175,000 in 1962 for their peanut warehouse business. It said Carter had been granted deferrals in his loan-payment schedule in 1966 (the year he first ran for governor) and 1970 (the year Carter won the governorship). The 1970 deferral was due to "weather conditions," the severe drought that hit the Georgia peanut fields, the story said.

The story, which carried the byline of Leonard Curry, contained a sentence which said: "UPI was told about the matter by a source friendly to President Ford." That source, Curry said in an interview, was Martin Price, who, he knew, had ties to the right wing. Curry said that Price had contacted Grant Dillman, the UPI bureau chief in Washington, and had given him the information, and that Dillman had then told Curry to write the story. Curry said that he was unaware, however, that Price was being paid by the Ford Committee.

But while UPI may not be happy to know that its informant was secretly a Ford Committee staff member, Price is not happy with the way his job turned out, either. "This election was given away!" Price said. "I mean those Ford people wouldn't use the stuff I got. It was the cleanest campaign I'd ever seen. It was a debacle!"

🏴 🏴 🏴

On October 11, sex became a part of the issues of Campaign '76.

Sex entered the campaign, courtesy of syndicated columnist Jack Anderson, while most Americans were sipping their first cup of coffee that day. Anderson devoted his spot on the ABC television show "Good Morning,

America" to a disclosure that a member of the President Ford Committee had been feeding his column allegations —which proved false upon Anderson's checking— about sexual misconduct involving Jimmy Carter.

Ford Committee press secretary Greener denied that any committee staff member was spreading such smut stories, and he said if he ever found out that anyone was, that staff member would be fired immediately.

But apparently there was indeed a Ford Committee staff member circulating the tales of sex, and the Ford campaign person was in fact a member of Greener's staff. James G. Wieghart, respected Washington Bureau chief of the *New York Daily News*, said that a Ford Committee staff member who worked under Greener gave his newspaper information similar to that which Anderson broadcast. He said his newspaper checked the facts and found them false, and thus ran no story. But Wieghart said that his newspaper's source contacted him after Greener's denial and pleaded that he keep the identity of his source confidential. Wieghart agreed. He will not reveal the name of the aide who tried to get him to print a story about sex and Jimmy Carter.

October/The Decline

Memorandum

To: Carter Campaign
From: Pat Caddell
Re: Latest survey data
Date: 16 October 1976

The Decline

. . . In the 14 small states that we have surveyed and the two large states, it is clear we are on the decline. Ford has been gaining steadily since the beginning of the week and we seem to be dropping off. . . . The decline is evident in the West, the Border States, and even in the South. . . .

In the South we find the margins have become precarious in South Carolina, Mississippi, and Kentucky. We now trail slightly in Oklahoma, although we're still slightly ahead with likely voters. We trail in Virginia and Louisiana. . . .

The situation in Texas is one of greatest concern. Now we are showing Chicanos and blacks at the lowest possible voting percentage (18). Were they to reach their normal voting level (24), we would probably have a five to six point lead in Texas. However we also show slippage in East Texas. . . .

Groups

1. In the surveys we seem to find several disturbing patterns. We are beginning to see middle income Independents swing away once again. We are also seeing liberal as well as conservative defection. . . .

365

. . . Vice-President. Walter Mondale has a positive/ negative rating of 44%/27%, while Dole's rating is 36%/35%. Dole's negative has been rising, and if our newer survey figures indicate that his debate was as bad as it seems we might want to develop an attack issue against Dole. In any event we ought to continue to raise the fact that it is the Ford/Dole ticket versus the Carter/Mondale ticket.

What Is to Be Done

1. The tide must be turned. We cannot continue to have this decline for another week or ten days, or we run the risk of falling behind. It seems even at the moment that this would be a close election. Ford's greatest weakness is not Ford personally, it is that Ford is bad on the economy and that Ford is a do-nothing-president. We need to go back to the themes that we used prior to the Second Debate when we stressed our opposition in aggressive *issue* terms rather than aggressive *personal* terms. More than anything else we need to undertake this kind of aggressive issues attack.

▨   ▨   ▨

October 18. Hamilton Jordan was down, very down. The Carter brain trust had gathered in the office of treasurer Robert Lipshutz in the modern high-rise Carter-Mondale headquarters on Peachtree Drive, and Jordan sat glumly. No one there had ever seen the normally affable Jordan so depressed.

"We couldn't jar him out of it," recalled Tim Kraft, the moustachioed director of field operations who had been recruited to head up the initial Iowa effort. "He'd always been the buoyant force. Back in Iowa when we didn't have a chance and we didn't have any money or anything —he'd close every conversation with something like, 'Okay, we're going to win!' But all that was gone from him."

Jordan had just read Caddell's poll. The South seemed to be crumbling. The South, which had to be Carter's solid core—his whole campaign strategy was based on a strong South—was slipping away. "When I saw that southern base jeopardized," Jordan recalled, "I knew we were in a helluva mess."

Jordan read Caddell's figures and accepted them. "At the rate it's going, it might be gone," Jordan said. "I don't know if we can. . . ."

Jody Powell, when also told of the figures, accepted them. Charles Kirbo did not. Maybe, he said, they were wrong. Maybe it was an aberration in the polling. Mondale, who'd been appearing before good crowds, called Jordan and was told about the figures. "I think Caddell's gone crazy," he said. But Mondale's chief aide, Richard Moe, told his boss that the last person who judged a campaign's success by the size and enthusiasm of his crowds was George McGovern (just before he went down to a landslide defeat in 1972).

Finally Caddell spoke up to Kirbo. "Look," he said, "when the numbers were good for us, nobody ever questioned them. Now they're bad. But this is just the way they are."

The third and final presidential debate was just a few days away. Some new television commercials needed to be written. Powell decided he could be of more use writing TV spots than riding *Peanut One*. The press secretary and the other advisers decided not to tell Carter just how bad things looked. No sense in upsetting him with the debate just around the corner. Powell called Carter and told him simply that he was not going on the road for a while, that there were some things that needed to be done. Carter did not ask for details. He just asked Powell for some suggestions on things he ought to be saying from the stump, and he took a few notes. Again, Carter made it a point not to press Powell for details on what was happening back at headquarters. But Powell knew his boss's mind well. He hung up the phone and rejoined the group. "Jimmy knows," he said.

Powell and Caddell and Rafshoon spent the night in the nearby offices of Gerald Rafshoon Advertising Inc., writing new commercials. Caddell had not slept for forty-eight hours. Powell had the flu.

They produced several spots aimed at doing away with

the campaign hoopla and trying instead to simply re-assure voters about Carter.

CARTER: *For the past two years I've traveled this country and talked about things that concern people most. I've talked about one thing more than any other, and that's mismanagement. Sometimes it's hard to put your finger on it, but it's felt in the things that matter most in the quality of our lives. It makes hard work useless, because it wastes our taxes, it eliminates the possibility of a decent savings account. It wipes out the dream of a home by making mortgage money too tight. It makes a decent education impossible. This is one real source of our government's failings, mismanagement. We talked about this problem when I became governor of Georgia, and we beat it. We cut waste and inefficiency, and even left a surplus of $116 million dollars. Now I'm not saying it's going to be easy to do in Washington, but we can't afford not to try. We didn't become a great country by giving up. Together we can make the effort.*

Let's get started.

Rafshoon had already written special spots for airing in the South. "They were blatant—waving the bloody rebel flag," Caddell said. "And they were very effective."

ANNOUNCER: *On November 2, the South is being re-admitted to the Union. If that sounds strange, maybe a southerner can understand. Only a southerner can understand years of coarse, anti-southern jokes and unfair comparison. Only a southerner can understand what it means to be a political whipping-boy. But, then only a southerner can understand what Jimmy Carter as President can mean. It's like this: November 2 is the most important day in our region's history. Are you going to let it pass without having your say? Are you going to let the Washington politicians keep one of our own out of the White House? Not if this man can help it.*

CARTER: *We love our country. We love our government. We don't want anything selfish out of government, we just want to be treated fairly. And we want a right to make our own decisions.*

ANNOUNCER: *The South has always been the conscience*

of America—maybe they'll start listening to us now. Vote for Jimmy Carter on November 2.

Caddell flew with Carter from New York to Newport News, Virginia, to Williamsburg, scene of the final debate. Aboard *Peanut One,* Caddell said, he urged Carter to criticize Ford's pardon of Richard Nixon for his crimes connected with the Watergate scandal. "I told him it is our strongest weapon and we ought to use it," Caddell said. "But he said, 'If we can win without it, I don't want to do it. It will spill blood all over the place. It will rip our country apart.' " Caddell did not press the issue.

October/The Third Debate

Memorandum

To: Carter Campaign
From: Pat Caddell
Re: Latest thoughts and findings
Date: 20 October 1976

. . . the decline observed over last weekend has been across the board with the expected impact in the big states. There are no indications in the latter states that the decline is at this moment on-going . . . the race is a stable but close election. How long the situation will remain calm is unclear.

In many cases, the decline in the Carter vote has only partially reflected a rise in the Ford vote. In many cases the bulk of the movement has been to undecideds—a strange phenomenon this late in an election. At the moment we find Carter ahead in New York by a close margin, ahead slightly in Pennsylvania, probably several points ahead in Texas in real terms, a couple ahead in Illinois, and essentially even in Ohio, New Jersey, and California.

The movement with women is evident in all the big states. Were the election solely among men, Carter would win in a landslide. It is in state after state that the vote of women has declined. Below are the margin differences in the big states by sex.

	Men	Women	Difference
Illinois	+6	−11	17 points
Michigan	+1	−12	13 points
New York	+11	—	11 points
New Jersey	+5	−5	10 points

California	+4	—3	7 points
Texas	+4	—3	7 points
Ohio	+1	—	1 point

After extensive cross analysis, we find that the women are by and large (1) middle-age, to only a lesser extent younger (2) middle-income, $10–20,000 (3) most important mostly non-working (at home in daytime) and (4) Catholic women. We are losing non-working women in Illinois by —21 points, Ohio by —7 points, New Jersey by —25, Texas by —7, New York by —3, and California by —13 points.

Why

. . . our questions show women view Carter less able than do men, Ford more able. . . . Also, they rank Ford's ability on foreign affairs as a more important factor. In reviewing the questions on the candidates, we find that on the question "Jimmy Carter would be a risk as President because we don't know what he would do," which in late September was rejected by 12 points, it is now only rejected by 2 points—with men continuing to reject the statement and women now agreeing with the statement.

. . . *on the crucial economic issue women are more negative on the economy and yet favor Ford.* This explains in part why the economy is not cutting for us the way it should.

Given women's attitudes on the economy and other issues, it seems clear that if Carter overcame his image problems, we could blow the election wide open.

It would also appear, given the rise of "risk" for Carter, that the Ford negative campaign is having an impact, particularly on women.

Other Trouble Signs

1. *Favorable/unfavorable*—On personal rating questions Carter is averaging 51% favorable and 41% negative ratings. Ford is averaging 58% favorable and 37% negative. In every big state his favorable/unfavorable rating exceeds that of Carter.

2. *Young people & liberals*—Carter is still running
low among 26–35 year olds. In every big state Carter
loses just under 30% of the liberals to Ford. This
erosion with liberals if reduced in half would secure
for Carter all the big states surveyed.

Vice-Presidential Findings

We are finding that Dole now has a negative rating
and Mondale quite a positive rating. In addition in
Illinois, Ohio, New York, and New Jersey we found
pluralities of voters agreeing with the statement "Bob
Dole is not qualified to be President and that worries
me." This is clearly a plus point and we should find
ways of hitting this ourselves and with others quickly.
Dole is a lever (1) to compare candidate judgment
(2) move liberals and young (3) move floating Democrats ("Democrats started World War II"—a statement
he repeated Monday!) and (4) scare women voters.
This could be a real ace in the hole.

Georgia Record

Ford is hurting us with these attacks on Carter's
record in Georgia.

Women. As far as the Carter strategists were concerned,
that is what the third and final debate of 1976 was all
about. Winning the hearts and minds and, mainly, votes
of those women who were over the age of thirty, who were
housewives, and who were disenchanted with Jimmy
Carter in such large numbers that his once-sure election
was now in doubt.

Fortified by the analyses of Pat Caddell, the Carter advisers set out, in preparing for the third debate in Colonial
Williamsburg, Virginia, to come up with a game plan that
would appeal most of all to women voters.

Women viewed Carter as a risk, Caddell said. Carter
would have to be reassuring. He would ease off his hard
attack line of the second debate. He would quit playing
games with Ford's title; he would not insist on calling his

adversary "Mr.," it would be "President" Ford in the third
debate. He would try to find a tactful, low-key way of
working the negative aspects of Bob Dole into the debate.
He would be a real gentleman.

One thing remained as Carter and his advisers arrived
in Williamsburg on October 22. They had to find a good
way of dealing with the *Playboy* interview. That, they felt,
just heightened Carter's problems with women voters. It
had never been dealt with adequately.

Carter, Charles Kirbo, and Jody Powell spent part of
the afternoon going over various ways that the *Playboy*
matter could be handled. They adjourned after having
discussed several options, none seeming very satisfactory.
Later, in the lobby of the Williamsburg Lodge, where the
staff and the press were staying, Kirbo spotted Powell and
Caddell and beckoned to them. "There's another approach
you might want to pass on to Jimmy if you get the
chance," Kirbo said in his understated, deferential way.
He then laid out what Caddell and Powell saw was precisely the right approach. Later, Carter would look for a
way to inject the topic into an answer in the debate in the
Phi Beta Kappa Hall on the William and Mary College
campus at Williamsburg.

🏳️ 🏳️ 🏳️

"Two hundred years ago," moderator Barbara Walters
was saying on the television screen, "five William and
Mary students met at nearby Raleigh Tavern to form Phi
Beta Kappa. . . ." Just down the road from her microphone at the Phi Beta Kappa Hall, in a tavern called The
Cave, a group of students had gathered, and in their midst
was the twenty-nine-year-old Greg Schneiders, without the
staff pin and without the tie but with the cigar and with
the Bud.

The mostly blue-collar crowds in the Locust Bar in
Philadelphia and the Yacht Harbor Bar in San Francisco
had watched the debates attentively; all conversations—
and even the pool games—had stopped during the hour
and a half that the candidates were engaged in verbal
combat. Not so with the college crowd in The Cave. These
William and Mary students talked throughout the entire
debate; they talked loudly, indifferent to the piece of history that was happening right before them. There were

about forty students in The Cave; about fifteen actually paid attention to what was happening on the television screen, brought to them live and in color from their own campus auditorium just a block away.

Interrogating the two candidates were syndicated columnist Joseph Kraft, *Washington Post* editorial writer Robert Maynard, and *Los Angeles Times* Washington Bureau chief Jack Nelson. The noise of students talking was so great in The Cave that it was hard to hear Maynard's question, which was about voter apathy. The campaign, Maynard said to Carter, had digressed from important issues to "allegations of blunders, brainwashing, and fixations on lust in *Playboy*. What responsibility do you accept for the low level of this campaign for the nation's highest office?"

The question fit perfectly into Carter's woo-women strategy. First he talked about the fact that people had been disillusioned by the "aftermath of Vietnam, Cambodia, Watergate and the CIA, people have felt that they have been betrayed by public officials." It sounded like part of his standard stump speech. But from there he went on to discuss the *Playboy* piece.

"I have to admit that in the heat of the campaign—I have been in 30 primaries, I have been campaigning for 23 months—and I have made many mistakes. And I think this is part of being a human being. I have to think the campaign has been an open one. The *Playboy* thing, I don't know how to deal with it exactly. . . ." (In fact, by then he knew exactly how to deal with it—low-key, apologetic, human, coming on like every mother's son who had ever misbehaved but deserved a second chance.) ". . . I agreed to give the interview to *Playboy*. Other people have done it who are notable—Governor Jerry Brown or Walter Cronkite, Albert Schweitzer, Mr. Ford's own secretary, Mr. Simon. Many other people, but they weren't running for President.

"In retrospect, from hindsight, I would not have given that interview. . . . If I should ever decide in the future to discuss my deep Christian beliefs and condemnation and sinfulness, I will use another forum besides *Playboy*. I will say this, I am doing the best I can to get away from that. During the next ten days the American people will not see the Carter campaign running television advertisements or newspaper advertisements based on a personal

attack on President Ford's character. I believe the opposite is true with President Ford's campaign and I hope
that we can leave those issues in these next ten days about
personalities and mistakes of the past—we have both
made some mistakes—and talk about unemployment, inflation, housing, education, taxation, government organization, stripping away of secrecy and the things that are
crucial to the American people.

"I regret these things in my own long campaign that
have been mistaken, but I am trying to do away with
those the last ten days."

There were no over-thirty housewives in the college
crowd in The Cave, so Schneiders turned to the man next
to him and asked what he thought of the answer. The
man, middle-aged, looking like a professor, and wearing
a Carter button, explained to Schneiders that he was
somewhat prejudiced because he was connected with the
local Carter effort but that he thought it was great. Just
the right tone. "Think so?" Schneiders asked. "Seemed a
little low-key to me." No, the man said, just right.

Nelson of the *Los Angeles Times*, an investigative reporter for years, asked Ford to talk in detail about his
role in trying to limit one of the original Watergate investigations, a probe by the House Banking and Currency
Committee. Whom had Ford talked to? Anyone in the
White House? And would Ford be willing to open up the
White House tapes from that Nixon period for examina-
tion?

Ford went through a lengthy recitation of how he did
not recall having talked to any White House people about
the matter; and the tapes, he said, were in the jurisdiction
of the court. He said he had only stepped in to curb the
committee activity at the request of Republicans on
the committee, and he recited the details of how he had
been investigated and been given "a clean bill of health"
by various congressional and law-enforcement bodies.

It was Carter's turn for rebuttal.

Moderator: Governor Carter, your response.

Carter: I don't have any response.

The move, stark and simple, caught the theater and
viewing audience by surprise. It appeared to be a gentlemanly thing, not attacking an opponent who was clearly
on vulnerable ground. But that, too, was part of the
Caddell analysis: the public just will not believe evil of

Ford, so there's no point in trying to attack him in a morality play.

The debate moved on. Carter, when asked, defended his past statement that he would not go to war in Yugoslavia even if Soviet troops were sent into the country. He said he would never go to war unless America's security was directly threatened, and that it would not be in this case. Ford said: ". . . I firmly believe . . . that it is unwise for a President to signal in advance what options he might exercise if any international problem arose."

Gun control was raised. "Oh, no," Schneiders said. "This is a no-win issue for us." Carter reiterated his view that handguns, but not long guns, should be registered. Ford said registration would not decrease the crime rate.

Carter deftly turned a question about whether his non-federal background would hamper his ability to run the government into a chance to softly jab at Bob Dole. He said that in the only major decision he had had to make so far, he had chosen Mondale as his running mate—because he was "the best person qualified to be President if something should happen to me." He said he had never heard Ford make such a claim about Dole. And after Ford had responded, Carter still had not. Ford said Dole was "fully qualified to be President" and later said that Dole would do an "outstanding job as President." "We're still waiting to hear it, Jerry," said one student in The Cave. Another said: "Come on, he said it close enough for anyone to be satisfied."

Near the end of the debate, Joseph Kraft asked Ford about the low growth and high unemployment rates of the economy, and asked if it were not really a "rotten record." Ford said he "violently" disagreed, and talked in rosy terms about his administration's economic record. Carter, in response, said: "Well, with all due respect to President Ford, I think he ought to be ashamed of making that statement because we—" Schneiders put his fist to his forehead. "Jesus! A few minutes to go, and he's going to get tough again!" But Carter softened the rhetoric by tossing in a lot of statistics, concluding at the end that Ford's economic record was "a very serious indictment of this administration, probably the worst one of all."

Around the bar at The Cave, opinion was mixed. Some thought Carter won, some thought Ford won, some were undecided, and many were not paying attention. But

Schneiders felt good as he left. Because the debate was not targeted on audiences like the students in The Cave. It was aimed at the housewives; and the administrative assistant felt his boss had been, by and large, on target.

≋   ≋   ≋

The President took to the stump. The Rose Garden strategy had served its purpose, allowing Ford to emphasize his image as a competent and working leader of the nation, allowing his committee to conserve precious campaign funds, and—just as important—frustrating the Democratic opposition.

But in October, the President made his big campaign moves. One move was aimed at solidifying his slipping base in the midwestern Farm Belt—he scheduled a speech on agricultural policy at Iowa State University. Another was a time-tested media winner—his own whistle-stop day, sweeping the length of Illinois in a train named the *Honest Abe.*

October 15. Thousands of students cheered as the President came to the microphone at Iowa State. Ford spoke: "It is great to be in Ohio—Iowa State!" First the students were stunned, and then they laughed at the President's mistake, and Ford could do little but laugh, too. "You know we Michiganders have Ohio State on our mind," he said, recovering nicely. He went on to offer a football metaphor of sorts. "You score a lot of touchdowns. I congratulate you, but we are going to score a lot of touchdowns for the United States of America in the next four years!"

Ford followed with twenty-three minutes of agricultural policy. But days later, Ford's chief of staff, Richard Cheney, and his press secretary, Ron Nessen, complained angrily in separate interviews that the television networks had highlighted the President's geographic miscue but ignored his statements on the issue of agriculture. Their criticism of the television coverage was an echo of the complaints of Jody Powell and Greg Schneiders—and Jimmy Carter himself—earlier in the campaign.

Ford and his wife celebrated their wedding anniversary that night in their suite in the Sheraton in Joliet, Illinois, by watching the televised vice-presidential debate between Walter Mondale and Bob Dole. Both vice-presidential candidates had appeared nervous at first, but Mondale seemed to recover as the debate went on, and Dole did not. Normally a bright and witty man, Dole's attempts at humorous put-downs seemed forced and fell flat. And his charge that 1.6 million Americans were killed and wounded in "Democratic wars" in this century was painful even to staunchly patriotic Republican listeners.

The next day, Ford set out on his whistle-stop from Joliet to Pontiac to Bloomington to Lincoln to Springfield to Carlinville to Alton. It was a day aimed at putting Illinois, a key state, in the Ford column.

At his first stop, Ford told the crowd how pleased he and Betty were to spend their anniversary in Joliet, *Indiana.*

At his third stop, in Lincoln, he stood on the rear platform of the train and opened with a greeting: "Hi, everybody. It is great to be in Pontiac!" (Stunned silence.) "I have just been corrected—Bloomington!" (Doubly stunned silence.) "—and Lincoln!" (Laughter and a scattering of mock applause.)

At his sixth stop, Ford jabbed at Carter's plans for defense cuts. He noted that Theodore Roosevelt had once said: "Walk softly and carry a big stick," but Ford said that Carter wanted to "speak loudly and carry a flyspotter! . . . er, flystopper! . . . flyspot . . . [he paused] flyswatter!"

Fluffs and flubs became a part of the Ford style on the stump. It had been apparent well before he had become President, when he had said in Boston one day that he would never forget Paul Revere's historic words about the signal from the Old North Church: "One if by day and two if by night." It had been apparent early in his presidency, when he rose at a formal White House dinner honoring President Anwar Sadat of Egypt and proposed a toast to President Sadat and his people of "Israel."

It had been apparent during the campaign in Iowa and Illinois, and it was apparent on several occasions in California: like the time in San Diego when he introduced the celebrities attending his rally and, waving at the Serendipity Singers, called into the microphone ". . . the Ser-a-binity Singers!"; the time in Pasadena when he introduced the Republican candidate for senator, Dr. S. I. Hayakawa, as "Dr. Haya-kama." The fluffs troubled a number of people on the Ford staff, but one White House aide tried to find a ray of sunshine after the Haya-kama goof. "It was better than what he called Hayakawa in a private meeting," the aide said. "He called him 'Hiawatha' the first time."

There were times when the light moments of the Ford campaign were not of the President's accidental making. At the San Diego rally, when Ford spotted a man in a huge chicken head (an advertisement for local radio station KGB), he shouted into the microphone: "The chicken —I love it!" And James Naughton of *The New York Times* heard destiny's call. He approached the chicken man on the spot and handed him $100 in exchange for the costume that seemed a green-and-red kin to "Sesame Street's" Big Bird. Then, the next day, as Ford was holding an airport press conference in Portland, slowly from the center of the crowd of reporters in front of the President surfaced a huge chicken; higher and higher it rose, until the large feathered creature was towering over the other reporters who were dutifully recording the President's words for the readers of *The New York Times*. Ford continued with his press conference, pretending not to notice. But later Ford joked with Naughton about the incident. (Naughton eventually tried to submit the huge chicken head on his expense account, under the notation: "Chicken for the President," but *Times* accountants disallowed the entry.)

While the presidential flubs and poultry feathers brought an added light touch to the October campaign, the President and his advisers nevertheless were well aware that they faced heavy going. Their response was to get tough.

During the whistle-stop through Illinois, Ford deliberately distorted Carter's position on defense spending. Early in 1975—well before the 1976 campaign had gotten started in earnest—Carter had said on two occasions (in Savannah and a few days later in Los Angeles) that he thought the defense budget could be cut by $15 billion. After talking with defense experts, Carter drastically scaled back his projections, and he campaigned throughout 1975 by talking about cutting defense spending by $5 to $7 billion. This in itself drew a clear distinction between Ford's present spending level and the one Carter was advocating. But Ford—on four occasions during the Illinois whistle-stop alone—tried to make his audiences think that Carter was advocating $15 billion in defense cuts, even though he knew very well Carter had talked about a much lower figure throughout the 1976 campaign.

"Jimmy Carter wants to cut the federal budget for the Defense Department by $15 billion," Ford told the audience in Bloomington. "I don't think that is the way to keep America number one."

In Carlinville, Ford said: "Jimmy Carter, on two occasions, has said if he became President he would cut the defense budget by $15 billion. . . ." In Springfield and Lincoln, he similarly clouded Carter's true position. And at each stop, he accused Carter of "slandering" America because of his statements on national defense. Just as Carter's misleading statements in defending his *Playboy* interview at the Houston press conference were the ethical low point of his campaign, these train station comments were Ford's. The President, caught up in the tumult of the campaign, did not add to the respect of his office as he whistle-stopped through Illinois on the *Honest Abe.*

The President Ford Committee, which did not have to pay for daily travel expenses back when Ford did his campaigning between the Oval Office and the Rose Garden, had millions to spend on advertising during the last weeks. One of the most effective of the Ford television ads run in the last few weeks was a man-in-the-street interview segment. What made the ad unique was that the men—and women—were standing on streets in Atlanta. And, one by one, in their Georgia drawls, they said that while they wanted a Georgian as President someday, they did not want Carter in 1976. They criticized Carter's record as governor and wound up saying in the Ford commercials that they were going to vote for Ford. This negative-style ad, the creation of John Deardourff and Douglas Bailey, made its point effectively.

"Hi. I usually don't get involved in politics. But for me, this year is too tough a year just to stand around and not do anything."

Joe Garagiola. Catcher; St. Louis Cardinals, Chicago Cubs, Pittsburgh Pirates, New York Giants. Lifetime batting average .257. Sportscaster. Television personality.

Garagiola is a middle-aged, middle-America guy. Ordinary is shtick to Joe Garagiola. His words are light on syllables; his pretense is no pretense. Joe Garagiola turned out to be the secret weapon of the Ford campaign. He was chosen to serve as moderator and Mr. Interlocutor for one of the most unusual political television efforts in presidential campaigning. He was Johnny-and-Merv-and-Dinah combined in a talk-show setup with the President as guest star and videotapes of the President campaigning in action that very day as the showpiece. Six Ford specials at about $60,000 each, localized for the major media markets, which corresponded to the major battleground states. The total effort cost about $1 million.

The Joe and Jerry Show, brainchild of John Deardourff and produced and directed under tight daily deadline pressure by Ford's television specialist Bill Carruthers, proved to be a media bonanza. Garagiola was personable and just-folks, making no pretense at knowing anything about the issues of the presidency; he was a perfect foil and counterpoint for the wooden style of Ford; and his mere presence made Ford look all the more competent and intelligent. The questions were fed and the answers anticipated. Yet the overall package managed to be effective without being slick.

Garagiola: Watergate really tore us up. We didn't know who to believe. The question is now: What is the difference between the Nixon administration and the Ford administration?

Ford: Well, there's one fundamental difference. Under President Ford, there's not an imperial White House, which means no pomp. There's no ceremony. There's no dictatorial authority. We've tried to run the White House as a people's house, where individuals have an opportunity to come in individually or in groups and express to me their views and recommendations.

Jack Ford was a regular on the show. So was former Democratic Congresswoman Edith Green of Oregon, who was heading a Democrats for Ford effort. Under questioning from Garagiola, they, too, would say nice things about the President. The half hour would go fast, moving back and forth between videotape shots and talk-show interviewing, politicking mixed with laughs and small talk.

"I know nothing about defense," Garagiola said. "I know nothing about nuclear power. I just know one thing: I'm a Jerry Ford fan."

October 27. Jimmy Carter was napping aboard *Peanut One*, the blue curtain pulled closed across the bunk bed that was specially built along the right windows in the first-class compartment area. Six feet away, Jody Powell, Greg Schneiders, and Pat Anderson were seated around the table where Carter usually worked on short hops such as this New York–to–Pittsburgh run.

The three advisers felt that the candidate was tired and that his stump speeches for the last couple of days had been rambling and listless. He needed some new, fresh prepared material for the Kennedy-Lawrence Dinner in Pittsburgh that night. The aides agreed on a three-part outline. Past, Present, Future. (1) Carter had traveled America for twenty-two months and had seen the problems caused by years of poor leadership; (2) but Carter had also seen America's strength and courage and optimism; (3) close with a variation of the "I see an America . . ." ending to the convention acceptance speech.

Anderson went to the rear of the plane; the electric typewriters were not working. So he wrote part of the speech standing up, using a portable typewriter balanced on a countertop. He wrote part of it on the bus from the airport to the hotel. And he finished writing in his hotel room.

". . . I see a new spirit in America. I see a national pride restored. I see a revival of patriotism. I see an outpouring of volunteerism. I see young Americans who don't drop out, but help out, as they did in the early 1960s, before we were divided by war and scandal. . . ."

Anderson picked up the new speech material and walked out to find Carter's room. Down at the far end of the corridor he saw a Secret Service agent standing guard. He walked to the door, knocked, and entered.

There, in the small hotel room, was the Democratic presidential nominee, clad in jockey shorts and a T-shirt, stretched out across the bed—lying not lengthwise, but widthwise. The candidate was exhausted. He had flopped down on the bed, and he was too tired to move. Carter took the text and, without stirring, dropped it on the floor beside the bed, directly under where his head hung over the side. He read silently, moving only to reach down with one hand and turn a page.

The speechwriter sat in a chair nearby, eating strawberries out of a basket that the hotel management had provided. Anderson watched as Carter read. This was Campaign '76, he thought. People think of a presidential campaign as a huge juggernaut, a rush of bands and balloons and speeches and motorcades, but what it finally comes down to is an exhausted man stretched out on beds in places like Pittsburgh, bearing the burden of decisions and feeling the ultimate pressure of win or lose.

Carter made one suggestion, and Anderson took the text to have it typed on the special, large-point speech typewriter. "Thank you very much, Pat," Carter said in a voice barely more than a whisper as Anderson walked out the door.

Two hours later, candidate Carter—showered, smiling, refreshed—delivered the speech forcefully before a large dinner audience, moving in and out of the prepared text, adding ideas of his own as he went along.

October 30. It is 10:30 P.M. when Carter and Greg Schneiders enter Carter's suite at the Sheraton Dallas. It has been a grueling day: St. Louis, Tulsa, New Orleans, McAllen (Texas), San Antonio. Rosalynn Carter is in the suite, waiting for her husband. The Carters go into the bedroom while Schneiders stays in the living room to do some work.

Schneiders pulls a list from his pocket and calls into the bedroom: "Governor, I've got a list of phone calls for you to do."

Carter answers with sarcasm. "Oh, thanks a lot. Well, Rosalynn has already got some people she wants me to meet." Mrs. Carter interjects: "I couldn't get rid of them."

Schneiders walks in. "Who are they?"

Mrs. Carter: "I don't know. But one man says he is a prophet, and they came all the way from Israel so he can put his hands on Jimmy's head so he can win."

Carter says he does not want to see anybody, but his wife has already promised the Israelis, so Carter relents. Schneiders goes upstairs to the room where the Israelis are waiting. There he finds the Jewish prophet, his wife, and public-relations man. The prophet seems much smaller than his wife, and she does the talking. They would like a laying-on-of-the-hands session with Carter tonight, followed by a long discussion with the Democratic presidential nominee. Their fall-back position is to lay on hands tonight and have the discussion tomorrow.

"Here's what we'll do," Schneiders says. "You can see the governor for the laying-on-hands ceremony tonight. But there will be no other meeting. Not tonight, not tomorrow. His schedule is very tight."

"Picture?" asks the PR man.

"No picture," says Schneiders.

Schneiders brings the prophet, his wife, and his PR man downstairs and into the living room of Carter's suite. A Secret Service agent on duty there asks Schneiders: "What's going on?"

Schneiders replies: "I'm not sure. But stay in the room."

Carter and his wife enter from the bedroom. Introductions are brief. The Jewish prophet speaks: "We want to pray with you." He asks Carter to sit in a chair that is near a sofa. Carter sits. Then the prophet walks around behind the chair and places his hands on the head of the Democratic presidential nominee. The wife of the prophet kneels in front of Carter. Then the prophet begins to chant in Hebrew—first softly, then loudly, his eyes closed, his voice husky with emotion. He is rocking back and forth and chanting with fervor. For about three minutes the chanting and praying goes on as the Jewish prophet keeps his hands on the neatly coiffed hair of the candidate from Plains, Georgia. Jimmy Carter just sits there, not saying a word. The ceremony reaches its climax as the prophet drops to his knees beside his wife, and in front of Carter the Israeli couple chant, every ounce of strength being channeled into their praying and wailing. Over near the wall, the PR man stands by, beaming. Then the chanting stops, and the prophet and his wife stand. "God bless you, God bless you, God bless you," the wife, weak from the ordeal, whispers. "Now you will win." The prophet, the wife, and the PR man leave. Carter and Rosalynn retire to the bedroom. The Secret Service agent is biting down on his lower lip, his eyes rolled to the ceiling as he carefully examines the expanse of white plaster.

Another night on the campaign trail has come to a close.

≋   ≋   ≋

URGENT URGENT URGENT URGENT

By Mathew I. Quinn

Plains, Ga. (UPI)—The deacons of Jimmy Carter's Baptist Church cancelled Sunday's services rather than admit four blacks and waive a church ruling barring "all niggers and civil rights agitators."

The Rev. Bruce Edwards, who described the wording of the rule to reporters, said he had urged the deacons to allow the Rev. Clennon King of Albany, Ga., and three other blacks to attend the Sunday services.

He said the deacons refused at a meeting last Tuesday night.

"I advised them I felt the best policy would be accept Rev. King into our church," said Edwards, standing in front of the locked doors of Plains Baptist Church.

"The deacons agreed to enforce the 1965 resolution which bars all niggers and civil rights agitators," Edwards said. "I told them I was very uncomfortable with that resolution."

Later State Sen. Hugh Carter, Jimmy Carter's cousin and the clerk of the church, said the resolution actually referred to "colored people" and "negroes." But Edwards insisted the original resolution used the word "niggers." . . .

The minister said: "Governor Carter has worked to rescind that policy. It makes us look pretty bad."

Carter was campaigning in Texas and California Sunday. . . . UPI 10-31 01:34 PES

Reporters covering the Carter campaign found out about the incident at the Plains Baptist Church just before the candidate arrived to address a chicken box-lunch rally in Fort Worth attended by thousands. They tried to ask Carter for a comment as he was walking into the hall, but the candidate, in his low-key way, gave them the brush-off. A reporter went to Powell to ask him to get a reply. Powell looked harassed. "Fuck you," said the normally affable and easygoing spokesman. Minutes later, he came back to the reporter and apologized.

🇺🇸 🇺🇸 🇺🇸

10:30 P.M. Jimmy Carter had been asleep for about a half hour. He had gone straight to bed after arriving at the El Mirador Hotel in Sacramento, fatigued by a day that began with the Plains church crisis and carried through speeches at the box luncheon in Fort Worth and the TV rally in San Francisco and an evening rally in Sacramento; and fatigued by two years of virtual nonstop politicking. Tonight the candidate was exhausted. Quietly, Jody Powell walked into the sleeping candidate's room and stood by the bed. "Governor? Governor?"

The figure in the bed stirred. "Yeah?"

"Governor, I really hate to wake you, but I think you've got to talk to Andy and Ham." It was 1:30 A.M. back in Georgia, but Representative Andrew Young, once Martin Luther King's lieutenant and now a close adviser to Carter, had to tell Carter what he thought should be done about the unpleasantness at the Plains First Baptist Church. Carter needed to get Young's view on the matter. He reached for the phone. Young told him that he should not resign from the church over the incident; he should speak out firmly against any attempt to keep the church segregated, but he should not turn his back on his church; he should work for change from within.

Carter, clad only in jockey shorts, conducted this policy discussion without leaving the bed. He hung up the phone. Powell, sitting on top of a low wooden dresser, asked his boss if he wanted to talk about tomorrow's schedule, being as how he was up now, anyway. Carter nodded. The two agreed that there would have to be a press conference tomorrow. Carter came up with a way of explaining his position; he talked out a rationale: "I can't resign from the human race because there's discrimination; I can't resign as an American citizen because there's still discrimination; and I don't intend to resign from my own church because there's discrimination. I think my best approach is to stay within the church and to try to change the attitudes which I abhor. Now if it was a country club, I would quit . . . but this is not my church, it's God's church. . . ."

Powell was off his dresser perch now, pacing back and forth as he talked, but there was nothing more to say. He was beginning to have a sick, knotted feeling deep down. "Let's sleep on it," he told Carter. The candidate rolled over and went to sleep, and Powell quickly exited. But he did not sleep. He went to the bar—it was a very quiet place tonight—and he was sitting silently and drinking when CBS correspondent Ed Bradley walked in. "Hey, man, what's happened here?" asked Bradley, who had just arrived in town. "Looks like somebody died."

Soon Powell returned to his room. He lay awake.

The primaries; the convention; 62 percent to 29 percent; the bishops; Scranton; 50 percent to 42 percent; *Playboy;* 47 percent to 45 percent; the debates; Houston; 47 percent to 41 percent; overkill; the Plains church; the Ghiardelli fizzle.

4:00 A.M. Powell called his wife, Nan, back in Atlanta. "For the first time, I was really thinking that Jimmy may well lose the election. It was my low point. I was very depressed. I convinced myself that I was calling her because *she* was upset. But I know that wasn't true. In fact, I think I said to her that we might really blow this thing. It was a godawful night."

Jimmy Carter and his aides and the traveling press made a discovery at about the same time the next morning when they stepped into their morning showers. The El Mirador Hotel had no hot water. Just cold, very cold. The shock of a cold shower awakens a man but shrivels his spirit, and perhaps it was a suitably humble beginning for this final day of Jimmy Carter's years of running for President.

The morning press conference went as planned. Carter gave his rationale for why he would not resign from the

church, and the Carter aides in the party felt that he handled a bad situation well. Jody Powell, his eyes bloodshot
and sunk deeply into the gray mask of his face, looked
relieved. Meanwhile, Atlanta flew Martin Luther King's
widow, Coretta, out to Los Angeles for a grand symbolic
show of support for Carter. A formal statement from Mrs.
King was handed to reporters by Carter aides. To further
help the candidate, she agreed to be interviewed. Did she
think Carter should resign from the church? "I think when
it comes to a matter of conscience . . . on what is right,"
she said, "and given the kind of creative moral leadership
that Jimmy Carter has been giving in this campaign . . .
that Jimmy Carter, in mind of that kind of moral leadership should resign from the church if they do not accept
black members." Jody Powell looked pained.

Carter-Mondale. They stood together under a green
canopy and raised their arms high and waved through a
gentle rain of balloons. Five thousand people jammed into
the IMA Auditorium in Flint, Michigan, stood and
cheered. This was the last stop for Carter-Mondale '76, a
hastily scheduled rally in Gerald Ford's home state. The
Detroit News had shown in its most recent poll that the
President's lead in Michigan had dropped to a statistically
insignificant 1 percent. Maybe—just maybe—the Democratic strategists thought, they could take Ford's state out
from under him.

"What do you think of Walter Mondale?" Carter called
through the shouting and cheering and balloons.

"Yeeeeaaa!!" came the reply.

"What do you think of Robert Dole?"

"Boooooo!!"

And to the people of Flint, where unemployment hovered at about 8 percent—which meant 20,000 persons out
of work—Carter called: "We'll never meet our country's
needs until we put our people back to work!"

"Yeeeeeaaaaa!!!!!" The yelling and screaming and
stomping and clapping set the rafters vibrating in the IMA
Auditorium. Jimmy Carter strode through the din and out
a side door into the chill, damp, quiet of a rainy night.
Soon he was in the solitude of his car. And a few minutes
later, he was riding home on Peanut One.

Someone had thought to put an electric piano on board, where a row of seats had been. The members of the Carter staff and the Carter press gathered around as James Wooten of *The New York Times,* a white reporter from Alabama, and Ben Brown, a black staff member from Georgia, shared the keyboard for a sing-along. They broke out the beer and the drinks, and the candidate came back (he left his suit jacket up front), and there was a mock awards ceremony for best-this and best-that (it was a little like a reading of a high-school yearbook). And there were some jokes and some laughs and some cheers. And then it was hushed as Carter joined his staff and the press corps in singing "Amazing Grace" and "Auld Lang Syne."

He had started alone, almost a half-million miles ago. Now Jimmy Carter's ordeal was over.

THE RACE: *Carter's lead has vanished. The Gallup Poll gives Ford a 1-point margin it calls "not statistically significant." The race, says Gallup, is a "virtual tie." On polling from October 28 to 30, Gallup comes up with data that initially give Carter 48, Ford 44, McCarthy 2, others 1, and undecided 5. But when the sampling is screened to reflect anticipated voter turnout, the figures swing toward the President: Carter 46, Ford 47, McCarthy 2, others 1, undecided 4.*

Harris polls from October 29 to 31 and calls it plus-1 for Carter. He gives Carter 46, Ford 45, McCarthy 3.

November/Election

Pat Caddell is calculating, felt-tip pen flying over the top sheet of a yellow legal pad, in the election night Situation Room that has been set up on the fifteenth floor of Atlanta's modern, elegant Omni Hotel. The country had been blanketed in basically good weather throughout the day, and the Carter strategists had been hoping for a large turnout at the polls. Now Caddell knows they did not get it.

In a nation where Democrats outnumber Republicans by close to two to one according to voter-registration figures, a good turnout should mean a Democratic victory. A poor turnout could mean that normal Democratic voters did not care enough to vote. Carter, who learned about the problem of a soft vote as early as the Massachusetts primary, is concerned about that.

Caddell is nervous. Amid the steady drone of a television set in Room 1536, the Situation Room, he and his associate John Gorman, plus Lannie Elderkin and Debbie Thompson, are working the phones, gathering figures and analysis from people across the country as the election night vigil gets under way. Down the corner and around the bend, in the Capitol Suite, Room 1522, the candidate and his family and a few close friends and a few top aides are following the early returns on three color television sets.

Early election night television traditionally feeds an eager nation a lot of early figures that are too small to be significant, and a lot of interviews with people who are close to the candidates but have little to say. The result, usually, is a living-color blend of trivia and tedium. There are exceptions.

Viewers in the elite rooms of the Omni's fifteenth floor brighten considerably when one of the networks suddenly zeroes in on the beaming but florid countenance of Billy Carter. The fifteenth floor knows that Billy has been in-dulging generously in his favorite Blue Ribbon Pabsttime, and soon their secret is shared with an eager country.

Coast to coast, Billy is making an observation about journalists. "Ninety percent of the reporters . . . can't read or write, and they'd be on welfare if they weren't re-porters," Billy Carter observes somewhat thickly. "The other ten percent are okay."

The interviewer perseveres. What does the brother of the candidate think about the way the night is going? "I can't say what I think," he answers, "but I think terrible."

The interviewer is game for one more try. What does Billy Carter think life in Plains will be like if his brother wins? Billy pauses. "Frankly, I think it's gonna go straight to hell!"

By 10:00 P.M., returns are pouring into the Situation Room via telephone and television. Each candidate seems to be picking his basic base area. Carter is capturing the South, but Virginia is looking like Ford, and Mississippi seems in doubt.

Ford is taking most of the midwest Farm Belt; Carter may have a hope in Iowa. The Rockies are Ford's.

It is coming down, as the Carter camp and the Ford camp figured all along, to eight big states: New York, New Jersey, Pennsylvania, Ohio, Illinois, Michigan, Texas, and California. Ford is going for five out of eight, with a couple of smaller swing states; to be sure, he needs six.

Caddell is heavily into his yellow legal pad, cradling a phone between his right shoulder and ear as he calculates. He hangs up the phone, does some quick scribbling, and suddenly, at 11:20 P.M., slams his yellow pad down on a desktop.

"If we get New York, we've got it!" Caddell shouts to no one in particular. He bolts from his chair and races out of the Situation Room clutching his pad of notes. He half-runs down the hall, takes the turn to the left, and walks into the Capitol Suite. Jimmy Carter is sitting there in front of the three television sets, slumped down low in a brown velvetlike chair with chrome arms, his left foot resting on a coffee table that is so close to his chair that his leg is bent at a sharp angle, his knee is as high as his head.

"If New York is there, we'll have it," Caddell tells him, "that is, when the four from Hawaii come in, too." New York is the question mark; that plus the sure four from traditionally Democratic Hawaii will put Carter over the top, Caddell figures.

Carter smiles. "We'll shake hands on it when it's all in," he says softly. Rosalynn is standing nearby, her husband's blue suit coat draped over the shoulders of her lightweight green dress. Fifteen minutes later, she's out in the corridor talking with sons Jack and Chip. An acquaintance walks by and shakes her hand and asks how it's going.

"We just went over," she says. But her analysis is premature.

11:43 P.M. In the Situation Room, John Gorman hangs up a phone. "The three networks are saying we have New York, but they're not ready to call it on the air yet." Just then, one of the networks is talking about New York. With 70 percent of the returns in, it is Ford 51 percent, Carter 49. Stuart Eizenstat, Carter's chief issues adviser, is in the room. "Jee-sus Christ!" he says.

12:04 A.M. Caddell enters the Situation Room, holding a cigarette in his right hand and chewing the fingernails of his left. "The problem in New York is that the precincts that are out are mostly Manhattan," Caddell says. "They should be ours. So New York still looks good, and Hawaii will give it to us." He makes a phone call. "I've been told Illinois will be fine. There will be enough votes in Cook County to make it okay. Ohio's looking okay, too; we're doing well in the rural areas." John Gorman has been making some calls, too. "Yeah, but we got screwed on the west side of Cleveland—plus the blacks, they didn't vote, either. So I don't know about Ohio."

12:45 A.M. The networks call New York for Carter. In the Capitol Suite, Rosalynn jumps in the air and squeals; for the moment, she is more cheerleader than First Lady. Carter smiles and gets up to turn the volume louder. Somebody in the room yells out the candidate's favorite expletive: "Good deal!"

In the Situation Room, a cigarette is dangling, Bogart-style, from Caddell's lip. He accepts the handshake of congratulations without changing expression. "Yeah, thanks," he says, turning back to a sheaf of papers clutched in his left hand. "Now as soon as we get Hawaii, we've got 271." Hawaii will be no problem, someone in the room says; everybody knows it is Carter country. Charles Kirbo walks in on the celebration. "Well, I'm not sure yet," he says slowly. "Got to be sure, you know."

1:10 A.M. Carter is still slumped in a chair, but he is grinning broadly now as he talks into a white telephone that has him in contact with the governor of Pennsylvania, Milton Shapp. "I'm proud of him," Carter says. "We've got one more state to go." Soon he is talking to another Pennsylvania man, Philadelphia's controversial mayor Frank Rizzo, a former Nixon Democrat, and apparently the man Carter just told Shapp he was proud of. "You did it," Carter tells Rizzo. He is referring to Philadelphia's large turnout that has given Pennsylvania to Carter. "I'm really proud of you. You knew what you were talking about. . . ."

Rosalynn is down on one knee, leaning over the right side of Carter's low-backed chair. About twenty staff members, family, and a few friends are in the room, watching the three television sets in front of the candidate. Among those present is actor George Peppard, attired in a khaki leisure suit, who had been allowed in by a friendly staff member. Television cameramen are ushered in for a few moments of footage of the candidate, and Peppard, a skilled man in front of cameras, picks that precise moment to walk over to Rosalynn's side and lean in to say a few words to her, thus becoming a part of the right portion of the Carter picture; Peppard's lady friend has coincidentally come to rest just at Carter's left, squeezed in between the candidate and the Reverend Martin Luther King, Sr., gray-haired father of the slain civil rights hero.

Carter never takes his eyes off the television sets as he is talking to politicians on the phone. New York City Mayor Abraham Beame, Chicago Mayor Richard Daley, Senators Hubert Humphrey and Edward Kennedy, AFL-CIO chief George Meany, and the union's chief political lieutenant, Al Barkan. One television set shows the Ohio results, where Ford and Carter are neck and neck. The candidate watches silently. Then they show Democrat Howard Metzenbaum pulling ahead of his rival in the Ohio Senate race. The candidate brightens—"Right on, Metzenbaum!"—and then he slumps back to his unsmiling self. He looks at another television set. "Still three percentage points," he says, looking at the Ohio figures that show Carter 51, Ford 48, with 69 percent in.

1:20 A.M. Jody Powell whispers something to Carter. The candidate gets up out of his chair and walks into a bedroom where he confers briefly with a couple of aides. Soon he is back in his chair. "Looks like we've lost Hawaii," Jody Powell confides to another person in the room. Carter television adviser Barry Jagoda adds, "It's very serious." The Carter men are worried about a Republican challenge to the results in New York, and they are looking anxiously at the neck-and-neck battles in Iowa, Illinois, Michigan, and Ohio. Even Mississippi, which shows Carter 51, Ford 48, with 85 percent of the vote in, is not considered sure enough to bring cheer to the Carter camp.

"It's there, it's going to happen for us, we'll take one more state somewhere for sure," says Greg Schneiders. "But I'd just like to get it over with soon."

2:00 A.M. Two and a half hours after Rosalynn Carter had first exclaimed, "We just went over!" the Carter election night enclave on the fifteenth floor of the Omni Hotel was still a weary, worried place. In the next hour, the Carter people had little new to tell each other. The Situation Room looked like Crash Central, people sitting on the floor as well as on beds, chairs, and even a dresser. They were staff people, plus a couple of stewardesses from the United Airlines crew that ran *Peanut One*. They were all dressed for a big formal party, a victory party downstairs at the World Congress Center, where 25,000 had been waiting to celebrate. Now, women in long gowns and men in three-piece suits were sitting on the floor, waiting.

3:28 A.M. CBS declares Hawaii for Carter. The Situation Room erupts in cheers. Suddenly no one is sleepy.

3:30 A.M. NBC awards Mississippi to Carter.

3:31 A.M. NBC flashes a sign: "Carter Elected." Inside the Capitol Suite, the Carters, their family, advisers, and friends are hugging and kissing and cheering. "YA-HOO!!" "YIPEE!!" Rebel yells and cowboy yells echo through the Carter suite.

3:33 A.M. ABC also declares Carter elected. Somehow in the din of the Capitol Suite, someone hears a telephone ringing. Walter Mondale is calling. Carter talks with his new Vice President as family and friends keep coming up and hugging and kissing Rosalynn, and she keeps saying, "We did it! We did it!"

After ten minutes, Carter is on his feet, forcing his voice, weary after more than 3,000 presidential campaign speeches, to its highest decibel. "Why don't all of you go on down to the ballroom and let me think about what I'm going to say?" Carter shouts. Then his voice softens a bit. "All right?"

The guests and friends file out. Carter is standing over near the television sets when Jody Powell, who had laid back during all the congratulating of the past few minutes, approaches. They do not talk. They just stand there, a fifty-two-year-old man and a thirty-three-year-old man who had traveled thousands of miles together, often just the two of them, two low-key and rather shy men who had forced themselves for months to go into strange towns in Iowa and New Hampshire and walk up to people they didn't know and introduce themselves and explain that this was Jimmy Carter and that he used to be a governor in Georgia and that he was running for President.

Tears have filled Jody Powell's eyes. He starts to speak, his lips form words, but no sound comes out, and then the tears are running down his cheeks, and he and Carter embrace. They hold each other for about half a minute, and then they separate, still without speaking, and Powell moves on to tend to arrangements for the press, and Carter starts thinking about what he will say downstairs.

As he starts to walk toward his bedroom, Carter glances at one of the television sets and sees Walter Cronkite in the midst of an announcement. Perhaps CBS is joining NBC and ABC in declaring him the next President. Carter walks toward the set and bends forward, straining to hear.

"He can't admit it!" Carter exclaims. "Walter said that *Reuters* joined *UPI* in declaring me the winner!" Carter laughs and dismisses CBS and Cronkite with a wave of the hand. "Aahhh—talk!" And he walks into the bedroom.

▨   ▨   ▨

4:04 A.M. More than 25,000 had jammed into the World Congress Center during the peak of the election night excitement, but now, when Jimmy Carter of Georgia has finally been elected, less than 5,000 remain. They are clapping and cheering as the Carter family walks onto the stage while the band plays the local country-rock favorite, "Why Not the Best?"

Carter opens with praise for his opponent. "I want to congratulate the toughest and most formidable opponent that anyone could possibly have, President Gerald Ford. As I've said many times throughout this nation, he's a good, a decent man. . . . I pray that I can live up to your confidence and never disappoint you. . . . Are you proud of our nation? [The crowd: "Yes!"] Do you think we can help to unify it and bring it back together? ["Yes!"] Do you think we can put our people back to work? ["Yes!"] So do I. And I'll do the best I can."

📧   📧   📧

7:03 A.M. Jimmy Carter's car turns off the highway and heads toward the old wooden depot, still bright green and white, that has served in Plains as the symbolic headquarters of Carter for President. Several hundred people are waiting. They have been there all night, dancing in the streets and partying in celebration. But even the best of parties can wear thin by sunrise, and the crowd waiting in the damp morning chill in Plains looks both distinctly happy and haggard. They had to wait mostly because of the closeness of the election, since the outcome had not been certain until well into the morning. But they had also had to wait still longer because an Atlanta police officer had blithely led the Carter press and staff buses onto the wrong expressway, escorting them in the opposite direction from the Atlanta airport—while the next President of the United States, who never, in two years of campaigning, liked to be kept waiting, sat fuming inside his empty *Peanut One*, delayed a half hour on his takeoff for the Albany, Georgia, airport (which was just a half hour by car from Plains).

The crowd closes in to hug the hometown man and pound him on the back, enveloping him in a punishing display of affection. Finally he makes it onto the loading platform, where the microphone is waiting.

It is a very tired man who walks to the microphone to greet a very tired audience. He speaks softly, in a voice breaking with emotion. "I came all the way through— through twenty-two months—and I didn't get choked up until I"—he stops here and wipes a tear from the corner of his eye and continues—"until I turned the corner and saw you standing here. And I said, 'People who are that foolish, we couldn't get beat.' The others, all the others who ran for President, didn't have people helping them who would stay up all night in Plains, Georgia, just to welcome me back.

"I want to thank the band, first of all; you've been up all night. And the choir. It was a long night, but I guarantee you it's going to be worth it to all of us. . . .

"I had the best organization any candidate ever had. Had the best family any candidate ever had. Had the best home community any candidate ever had. Had the best supporters in my home state any candidate ever had. And the only reason we were close last night was because the candidate wasn't quite good enough as a campaigner. But I'll make up for that when I'm President. . . ."

       ▓   ▓   ▓

Upstairs in the White House, Betty Ford sat with her family on the morning after, watching the television screen that was showing Jimmy Carter at the Plains depot. "He doesn't know what he's gotten into," she said softly to her family.

The President had gone to bed at 3:15 A.M. Wednesday without appearing before reporters or before the large Ford crowd that had gathered at the Sheraton Park Hotel for what had been billed in advance as a victory party. The Fords had watched the returns through the night in the executive mansion, and when the President went to bed, press secretary Ron Nessen had tried to make the press corps believe that Ford still expected to win the election. Somehow. When he awoke at 8:30 A.M., it was clear beyond any doubt that he would not.

An early meeting was convened in Richard Cheney's office in the West Wing of the White House. The top echelon of Ford advisers attended. The results were reviewed. They showed the election was Carter's. There was one other alternative. The weekend before the election, Cheney had asked Michael Duval to prepare a memo, just as a precautionary measure, on how the election could be challenged. The twelve-page Duval memo, in a black loose-leaf notebook with a red stripe, outlined a procedure that would be followed to comply with the law, and also a procedure to create the appropriate public climate. It included a checklist of well-known and powerful people to contact; it would be vital, the memo said, to have such well-known national figures send telegrams requesting that the President challenge the results in order to assure that the public would accept such a move. It also suggested that the next step would be to appoint a prestigious blue-ribbon panel to serve, in essence, as a twenty-four-hour grand jury, to see if indeed there was probable cause for challenging the election. But most of all, the Duval memo warned, there must be a real, legitimate reason to challenge the results. And it cautioned that it might not be advisable to challenge the results if it would mean that the President might win an electoral-vote victory but not a popular-vote victory.

"We'd lost the popular vote by almost two million votes," Baker recalled. "And as we looked at it, we saw that we had won more states by narrow margins than we had lost by narrow margins. So we knew that a challenge would not be tasteful as far as the public was concerned, and it probably would not be successful, either." There would be no challenge. At 9:57 A.M., Richard Cheney, Stuart Spencer, Jack Marsh, and Robert Teeter walked into the Oval Office and told the President that there was no chance. A telegram conceding the election was drafted and sent to Carter. At 12:15 P.M., Ford, his wife, and their children appeared in the press room to publicly concede defeat.

Standing there on the low podium in front of the blue curtain, the President was a drained, spent man. Physically, he could not have campaigned for one more speech. His voice was gone, reduced to a barely audible rasp by his final campaign blitz. After ending his Rose Garden campaign according to plan in October, Ford had hit twenty-five cities in twenty-two days, an exhaustive schedule by his standards, although in the same twenty-two-day period Jimmy Carter had been to forty-two cities. The difference was that Carter had been at it for two years nonstop; he had learned to pace himself. Gerald Ford, fighting to catch up from far back, had done the only thing he could in those last days: he had gone all out. At the end, after winding up in Grand Rapids, he had nothing left. Not physically, not emotionally. He had

broken down weeping a couple of times as he addressed
the crowd in this town that he had represented in Congress
for a quarter of a century. He had led them in the singing
of the University of Michigan fight song, shouting the
words into the microphone again and again: "Hail to the
victors valiant/Hail to the conquering heroes/Hail! Hail!
To Michigan/The Champions of the West." Then he had
broken down weeping once again when at the Grand Rapids airport he saw a mural depicting his life.

Now he was standing there on the podium in the press
room, a man so spent that he could not read his own telegram conceding defeat. Betty Ford did that for him as he
stood behind her, biting his lip. Then the President and
his family stepped off the podium and—in a gesture of
quality and kindness on this painful day—walked out
among the reporters, shaking their hands and thanking
them for having traveled with them on their long journey.

When there were no hands left to shake, Ford turned
and, with some difficulty, moved through the reporters
who had gathered around him, and headed toward the
door. At one point he paused, and, in his rasping whisper,
he said somewhat sadly, "I never was a good broken-field
runner. I guess you all knew that."

Interlude: The Results

The contest between Jimmy Carter and Gerald Ford
had commanded more attention than enthusiasm. There
were 150 million Americans eligible to vote for President
in 1976, the red-white-and-blue year of the American
bicentennial. Just 54.4 percent of them voted, the lowest
election turnout since Truman edged Dewey in 1948.

Jimmy Carter's margin proved thin but sufficient. He
needed 270 electoral votes; he wound up with 297,
compared to Ford's 241. Out of almost 81.5 million votes
cast, Carter came away with a 1,680,974 plurality. It was
barely a majority, 50.1 percent to Ford's 48.0. Carter
pulled his narrow popular- and electoral-vote majority
together by carrying just 23 states plus the District of
Columbia; Ford carried 27.

It was almost as if the two candidates had, by gentleman's agreement, split the country in the geographic cen-

ter. Draw a line down the western borders of Minnesota, Missouri, Arkansas, and swing it a little to the left to include Texas. All the rest of the continent that stretches to the west was Ford's. Most of what lies to the east went to Carter.

Carter captured the South, halting the trend of more than a quarter of a century of Republican encroachment below the Mason-Dixon line. From Florida up to Maryland, west through the border states of Kentucky and Tennessee, and down to Louisiana, the South embraced the Democratic ticket headed by Carter of Georgia. Only Virginia voted for Ford. It was the best showing in the southern states by a Democratic presidential candidate since Franklin D. Roosevelt carried them all in 1944.

As the Carter strategists and Ford strategists had predicted in the summer, a handful of large states proved to be the battleground. Five of eight is what Ford had figured he needed. He came up just short. Ford carried four of the eight: New Jersey, Michigan, Illinois, and California. Carter won New York, Pennsylvania, Texas, and Ohio—carrying the latter by just 11,000 votes out of 4 million cast, a hairbreadth margin of just two-tenths of one percent.

At a glance, Carter appeared to have resurrected the traditional southern-northern-industrial coalition of states that was once the strength of the Democratic Party. But that is only part of the story. For Carter actually fashioned his victory in ways unlike those of his party predecessors.

The South. For generations since the Civil War, the South belonged to the Democrats. But this was, in fact, the white South; blacks in the South were mostly not registered to vote, and those who were often opted for the party of Lincoln, voting Republican. Voting rights efforts of the 1960s resulted in a substantial increase in the registration of blacks, and this larger, influential body of black voters began casting its ballots for the Democrats by a heavy majority. But as the black southern vote grew in size and moved toward the Democrats, the white southern vote began to shift away. In 1964, Barry Goldwater carried five southern states for the GOP; in 1968, third-party candidate George Wallace and Republican Richard

Nixon dominated the South; in 1972, Nixon swept the South for the Republicans.

But in 1976, the South once again belonged to the Democratic candidate. Blacks voted for Carter overwhelmingly; the CBS News survey of people leaving voting precincts showed that Carter won 83 percent of the black vote. But Carter's popularity with the blacks was not exceptionally high; Hubert Humphrey and George McGovern received similarly high proportions of the black vote in 1968 and 1972. Also, the black turnout in the South (and nationwide) in 1976 was about the same as in 1972, and had actually dropped below the 1968 level, according to the U.S. Census Bureau survey. (The survey reported that 45.7 percent of the voting-age black population in the South actually voted in 1976, compared with 47.8 percent in 1972 and 51.6 percent in 1968. In fact, black voter participation was virtually the same in 1976 as it was in 1964—before the passage of the Voting Rights Act—when 44.0 percent of the blacks in the South voted.)

The difference in the South in 1976, it appeared, was that Carter attracted increased numbers of whites, especially lower-income whites, while retaining the support of the blacks. A study of results in various heavily white, predominantly rural counties indicated that a new pattern had emerged. Voting in these areas in northern Alabama, the upper rim of South Carolina, the Piedmont area of North Carolina, the Florida panhandle, and middle Tennessee, was analyzed by Patrick Caddell.

In 1968, these heavily white areas of small farms and light textiles voted for Wallace, with Nixon second and Humphrey a distant third. In 1972, they were overwhelmingly for Nixon. Yet in 1976, they went strongly for Carter—usually 60 percent or more, and in some places over 70 percent.

Carter carried those low-income white areas of the South decisively while he was losing in urban areas such as Mobile, Birmingham, and Montgomery, Alabama; Pensacola, Florida; greater Charleston, South Carolina; and greater Richmond, Virginia. In the southern black belt areas (named for the soil, but also well populated by blacks as well as whites)—those areas along the coasts of the Carolinas, the Gulf area, and western Tennessee along the Mississippi River—Carter won just narrowly. He appeared to have lost among the whites while needing his heavy black vote to give him his narrow margin. In fact, it appeared that in at least one southern state, Mississippi, Carter lost the overall white vote decisively and needed his substantial majorities among the blacks to barely carry the state.

By putting together substantial support among the southern blacks and the lower-income southern whites, Carter appeared to come close to realizing the Populist dream of Georgian Thomas Watson in the 1880s. Watson envisioned a Populist movement based on a foundation of poor whites and poor blacks. There is evidence that, in the South, Carter came close to forging that Populist goal.

The election of Jimmy Carter of Georgia caused a swell of regional pride through the entire South; he was, after all, the first resident of the Deep South to be elected President since Zachary Taylor's pre-Civil War victory in 1848. Yet he owed his election to a combination of forces, blacks and whites, which for generations had not existed as a cohesive political force in the South. Much was written in the days following Carter's election about how the nation had matured to the point where it was now ready to elect and accept a southerner. That is true. But a greater truth is that it was the South which matured and accepted the nation. For years the only politicians put forward for the presidency by the Deep South were men of troglodyte appeal: Strom Thurmond as a Dixiecrat candidate in 1948, George Wallace as an American Party candidate in 1968. And in between, the Deep South sent men to national political prominence whose views were Old South segregationist, far more conservative than the vast majority of the national Democratic Party. But the South matured. It matured in the 1970s, as a newer and more moderate breed of Democrat was permitted to rise in the South, men like Carter and Reubin Askew in Florida, and Dale Bumpers in Arkansas, and others; and the South also matured as blacks were registered to vote.

In 1976, all of these factors came into play. Eventually, of course, northerners in New Hampshire and Illinois and Wisconsin and Pennsylvania and Ohio—in a triumph of political reason over regional prejudice—voted for a man from Georgia as the winner of their presidential primaries. But the South had to first put forth a twentieth-century moderate who could make both northern whites and

blacks feel comfortable about voting for him. And then
southern blacks and southern whites had to unite behind
him to give him his solid southern base which proved crucial to his victory.

The North. Carter's success in northern industrial states
was also accomplished with a significant change in the
traditional Democratic victory formula. For while Carter's
winning percentage in the urban areas remained generally consistent with that of Democratic candidates in
past presidential elections, the urban turnouts were generally lower. This meant that Carter came out of the urban
areas (often blue-collar and heavily Catholic) with a
margin of far fewer votes than he had sought.

"One of the more disappointing results of the election
has to be how poorly we ran in the large cities and counties," Caddell said. "Our percentages were the same as
Kennedy's and Humphrey's in the urban areas. But our
total numbers of votes were much lower—hundreds of
thousands lower—in many cities, and that hurt."

Carter made up the deficit caused by his disappointing
urban totals with surprisingly strong showings in the rural
precincts of the northern industrial states. Carter cut heavily into the normally heavy Republican vote in these rural
areas, greatly reducing Ford's margin of victory there.
CBS News figures gave Ford an edge of just 53 to 47 percent in rural areas (population less than 5,000). Also,
Carter's standing with women voters improved a bit in the
last days of the campaign. According to a Gallup postelec-
tion poll, he lost the female vote by a narrowed margin of
48 to 51, while scoring much better among male voters,
beating Ford 53 to 45.

One of Carter's urban problems was his relatively poor
showing among Catholics—a problem that had shown up
in Caddell's polling throughout the fall. The CBS figures
showed Carter winning just 54 percent of the Catholic vote
—which is about four points less than Democratic candidates were used to receiving in most presidential elections—even when the large Catholic vote won by Kennedy,
the only Catholic President, is not included in the calculations. This meant that Ford scored better with Catholic
voters than any Republican in modern history.

Carter trimmed the usual Republican margin among
Protestant voters. He won 46 percent, the CBS survey said,

compared to an average of 39 percent share of the Protestant vote—which is what Democratic candidates had been pulling since 1952. Carter turned out to be a strong favorite among Jewish voters, winning 68 percent of their votes.

One of Carter's major pluses in the urban areas was the fact that the rank and file of organized labor returned strongly to the party fold. Carter won 63 percent of the votes of union members, according to the CBS News survey —a vast improvement over the 46 percent won by George McGovern in 1972. Nonunion blue-collar workers voted 54 percent for Carter, the survey said, and the difference between the union member vote and the nonunion member vote is a strong testimonial to the influence of organized labor.

The case of Ohio illustrates Carter's difficulties and strengths in the industrialized North. Carter came out of Cleveland's Cayahoga County with a 93,037-vote plurality, compared to Kennedy's 1960 margin of 140,975 votes and Humphrey's 1968 margin of 124,749. Normally, Carter's margin would not have been enough for a Democrat to have even a hope of carrying Ohio. Humphrey, in fact, lost the state despite his much larger cushion in the Cleveland area. But Carter cut sizably into Ford's margin in small-town and rural Ohio, and he wound up with the narrowest of victories.

In the other states that were on the Carter and Ford Big Eight list of battlegrounds, the pattern was much the same. In Pennsylvania, Carter's margin in Pittsburgh was one-quarter of what Humphrey's was in 1968, his margin in Wilkes Barre-Scranton was just over half of Humphrey's, and even in Philadelphia he fell about 16,000 below the 1968 Democratic margin. But Carter did well in the rural areas, preserving the state for the Democrats.

In Illinois, Carter ran better than Democrats are expected to do downstate, but his margin from Chicago's Cook County was 27,000 below Humphrey's total and 125,000 below Kennedy's.

In California, Carter fell short of what his advisers had expected him to pull in the San Francisco Bay Area. This, Caddell believes, cost Carter an opportunity to carry the nation's most populous state.

In New York, Carter scored well in rural areas, and he also picked up surprising support in the suburbs, an area where his strategists had thought earlier that he lacked strength. Ford had anticipated heavy margins in the heavily populated suburbs of Long Island's Nassau and Suffolk counties, plus Westchester County. In Nassau County alone, Ford's advisers had hoped for a 100,000-vote margin, but wound up with just a quarter of that. The Ford officials were especially surprised by their poor showing on Long Island because the President had devoted his final weekend to the area, holding one huge rally each in Nassau and Suffolk. But the reason for Ford's poor showing in these suburbs may well have been the strong sympathy that voters in the area felt for the plight of New York City. A *Newsday* poll a year before the election should have been enough to warn the Ford strategists: it showed that 71 percent of the people in Nassau and Suffolk opposed Ford's handling of the New York City financial crisis, a figure that included 74 percent of the Island's independent voters and 60 percent of Ford's fellow Republicans. "We figured right at the end that we probably should have spent the time in Ohio instead of campaigning in New York," said one top Ford adviser. But by then the President had made a commitment to Rockefeller that he would make the New York appearances, and the large Nassau and Suffolk rallies had been planned.

The independent candidacy of Eugene McCarthy was defeated in New York not in the election precincts but in the courts. Legal action by the regular Democrats successfully blocked McCarthy from being on the New York ballot. But he was on the ballot in 28 states where problems of early petition deadlines and cumbersome rules for petition signatures did not prove prohibitive. And in three states, McCarthy appeared to have been responsible for the fact that their total of 18 electoral votes went to Ford instead of Carter. Ford won Oregon's 6 electoral votes by a margin of just 1,713 in the popular balloting; McCarthy drew 40,296 votes there. Maine's 4 electoral votes went to Ford because of his 4,041-vote plurality; McCarthy received 10,874 votes in Maine. Iowa's 8 electoral votes were won by Ford because of his margin of just 12,932; McCarthy received 20,051 votes in Iowa. Take these 18 electoral votes from Ford and give them to Carter, and the electoral margin would have broadened to Carter 315, Ford 223.

In Oklahoma, Ford captured 8 electoral votes by a plurality of just 13,266 out of more than a million votes cast; McCarthy drew 14,101 votes, but while it is safe to assume that a strong majority of the McCarthy votes would normally have been Democratic, it is not safe to say that virtually all of them would have been Carter's; Ford might have held on for a narrow victory in Oklahoma even if McCarthy had not been on the ballot.

Carter campaign officials had been concerned that McCarthy's presence on the ballot in Wisconsin might be enough to tip the state to Ford; in fact, the state had a history of going Republican in presidential races, anyway. Carter did not do as well in the liberal university area of Madison; but his strength in rural areas proved significant, and he won by a plurality of 35,245, even with McCarthy drawing 34,943.

While Carter officials could point to the McCarthy candidacy as a way of arguing that their victory over Ford could really be viewed as being larger than in fact it was, the Ford officials could find solace in numbers, too. Carter victories in Ohio (by 11,116) and Hawaii (by 7,372) were so close that a switch of just a few thousand in the two states would have meant a full term as President for Ford.

The race should not have been that close. Carter entered the fall campaign with a good-size lead over an opponent who was a member of the decidedly outnumbered Republican Party, who had never been elected to either the presidency or vice-presidency, and who was not a gifted campaigner.

Carter fell victim to a number of clearly avoidable gaffes. But just as important were the problems of the Carter road show. Carter lost control of the daily news stories that his touring campaign was trying to produce; the themes he was trying to sound often were not heard. "The road show was a problem," Greg Schneiders conceded after the election. "And for that you have to fault the people who were always along to give advice—which means, really, just Jody and me—and, to a degree, Jimmy himself. We didn't have clearly developed themes and we didn't always get the theme we were working on across to the public." One of the problems was that there was no senior, wise head—no veteran of a national campaign—riding along on *Peanut One* to merely observe and offer suggestions. Nixon, Humphrey, and McGovern all made use of such senior consultants. Carter, on at least one occasion, suggested that perhaps Charles Kirbo ought to make a campaign swing to observe and suggest; but Kirbo says he rejected the idea because "it would just be a waste of time."

Looking back, Carter recognizes a number of mistakes. "I made some mistakes during the campaign," he said in an interview after the election. ". . . I think the *Playboy* interview was a mistake, and there were others. . . . One of them was unavoidable, and that was the underestimation of the presidency and the difficulty of running against Ford. He had two advantages: One was that people felt that he had done the country a favor about correcting the Watergate tragedy, and Ford capitalized on that very wisely by saying, 'I've done a pretty good job. Now give me a chance with my own administration.' And the American people are fair and that is a fair proposition.

"And the other [advantage Ford had] is that his advertising campaign was designed to create doubt about me. Fear about the future if I was President, so the concern and doubt about me and the knowledge and awareness of what he was—a feeling of indebtedness toward him— was something that almost proved, well you know, a source of loss.

"That part was unavoidable and there wasn't anything we could do about that, I don't believe."

🏴 🏴 🏴

The accepted wisdom on the election of 1968 is that Hubert Humphrey was closing with such a rush that if the election had been held only a few days later, Humphrey would have won. In 1976, Ford also closed from far behind and finished just short. But it is not necessarily true that, given a few more days or a week, Ford would have been elected.

It is, in fact, possible that the final Gallup Poll pinpointed the situation as it stood on Saturday, October 30 (the day the survey was completed). That survey, when weighted to anticipate likely voting turnout, gave Ford a one-point lead. Perhaps Ford actually was ahead by the slim lead of a point just before the election. If so, it was Carter who gained in the final couple of days. A number of officials of both the Carter and Ford campaigns feel that from early summer on, the election campaign was largely a referendum on Jimmy Carter. Carter was off to such a large lead in the early polls that people were led to conclude that Carter was going to win; thus, people viewed the campaign mostly by making judgments on whether or not they were comfortable with Carter as President. Only in the last few days of the contest did the public really come to see that Ford, in fact, could win. And only then did people start asking themselves if they truly wanted Ford to be their President for four more years. The surveys of Caddell, among others, spotted a large drift away from Carter and toward "undecided" in the last week. And a CBS News/*New York Times* survey following the election showed that six out of every ten voters who made up their minds during the last few days of the campaign wound up voting for Carter. This alone could have been his margin of victory. It seems that in the first few months of the presidential campaign people were deciding on Jimmy Carter. And in the last few days they were deciding on Gerald Ford.

Looking back, Ford's pollster Robert Teeter viewed the President's Eastern Europe gaffe in the second debate as significant. "The Eastern Europe thing hurt us because it killed our momentum," Teeter said. "We had been climbing tremendously, and from then on, we sort of flattened out. Our campaign did succeed in answering the voters' questions [doubts] about the President's intelligence, but it never succeeded in answering fully their questions about his competence—and this, I think, is where the Eastern Europe situation hurt the most."

Just before the fall campaign began, Teeter's "perceptual-map" method showed that Carter was in a perfect spot—barely in the upper left quadrant of the square map, rated just a little to the left (liberal) of the center on economic/social issues and a little above the center (toward conservative) on Traditional American Values of defense and national security. This was just where the largest portion of the voting population placed itself. Ford, however, was slightly in the lower right quadrant—a little conservative on social/economic issues, and a little to the liberal side (below center) on the Traditional American Values scale.

At the end of the campaign, Teeter's new map showed,

Carter had moved downward to a more liberal position on the Traditional American Values scale; Ford had moved up and to the left—putting him closer to the center of the voting population. Closer, but not quite close enough.

Finale

The stage stretched out almost a football field in length,
dominating the east steps of the United States Capitol. Its
plywood sides, covered with one coat of white paint, glis-
tened under a very high, blue winter sky. Down Pennsylvania Avenue, a digital sign alternately reminded that it
was January 20 and that the temperature was 20 degrees.

There was, on the Capitol grounds, an air of almost
Super Bowl excitement. One hundred thousand persons
jammed into the area between the Capitol steps and the
Supreme Court, many with blankets and binoculars and
thermos bottles filled with liquid warmth. But the stage
itself was set for classical theater, a finale of Shakespear-
ean proportions, with all of the characters of the year-
long drama assembled on the same platform, winners and
losers and bit players who had performed early but had
long since moved on. Mo Udall. Scoop Jackson. Hubert
Humphrey. Birch Bayh. George Wallace. Edward Kennedy. Frank Church. Nelson Rockefeller. Robert Dole.
Walter Mondale.

At 11:40 A.M., a marine sergeant stationed at the top
of the stairs spotted a familiar figure coming down the
corridor and crisply lowered a red signal flag he was holding in his right hand. On cue, the band played "Hail to
the Chief" for Gerald Ford for the last time as he appeared on the stairs and walked down past the assembled
dignitaries to his front-row seat.

Ford acknowledged the crowd's applause. Then he
turned and spoke to Hubert Humphrey, who looked
gaunt and markedly aged, recovering as he was from a
major cancer operation. "Hello, Hubert," Ford said, admiring Humphrey's heavy coat and fur hat. "You look
great!" Turning to others he added, "He's the sharpest
dresser in the crowd." And then back to Humphrey, who
had wanted more than anything to be the guest of honor

at his own inauguration: "You and I have seen a lot of these." Humphrey, beaming, agreed.

The marine lowered the signal flag again, and this time the band launched into the "Navy Hymn" as Jimmy Carter came down the stairs. Ford would be President for only a few minutes more.

1600 Pennsylvania Avenue. The room was between masters.

It was almost noon, and the sun bouncing off the snow that covered the Rose Garden bathed the Oval Office in light. The room was quiet, empty. The pale-yellow rug had been freshly vacuumed and the pillows on the yellow couch freshly fluffed. The pale-yellow walls had been stripped of mementos, and the shelves cleared of knick-knacks and books. The desk had been emptied and cleaned and polished; it was bare except for a set of matching long-stemmed pens.

The desk, Nell Yates was thinking, that was the problem. The room seemed forbidding and cold, even in the bright sun. The problem was the desk. She left and returned with five books, two volumes of Woodrow Wilson's *Life and Letters* and three of the *Papers* of Alexander Hamilton. She placed the volumes between two bookends, near the front left-hand corner of the large wooden desk. "At least now it makes you want to come in and do some work," she thought.

From around the bend in the corridor, a television set could be heard. It was carrying the voice of a soft-speaking Georgian.

". . . do solemnly swear . . . that I will faithfully execute . . . the office of the President of the United States . . ."

Nell Yates did not stop to listen. She went back to her desk in the yellow room adjoining the Oval Office and sorted through some last-minute paperwork. She was more interested in making sure that everything would be just right for her new boss. After all, inaugurations were no big thing to Nell Yates. She had been working as secretary in the White House since Eisenhower.

"They were all very capable men," said Nell Yates, a slim, brown-haired woman who speaks softly and does not like publicity. "Each was different. But they were all good men, and working for them was very pleasant. I don't expect it will be any different now." The quote was not interesting; it revealed little; it was probably part of the reason that Presidents come and go but Nell Yates stays on. Change, to Nell Yates, is no big deal.

Change. It happens in the American system in a precise, well-ordered way, set forth in spare detail in the United States Constitution in 1787, and followed with reverential devotion.

Change. In normal times, in the American system, power is surrendered—even to political adversaries—amid a setting of ceremony and celebration. In tragic times, such as the death of a President, power is transferred in muted tones. But for the thirty-eighth President of the United States, power had come in an unprecedented and wrenching way. Gerald Ford had never sought the presidency, and no one had ever considered him for it in his quarter-century of service in the House of Representatives. But in time of scandal, a Vice President had resigned, and Ford was appointed as a safe choice to fill a midterm vacancy. Then a President had crumbled under another scandal, resigning rather than face certain impeachment and conviction. And suddenly the presidency was thrust upon a stunned Gerald Ford, and Gerald Ford was thrust upon a stunned nation.

On August 9, 1974, after taking the oath of office, President Ford had addressed the nation.

. . . I am acutely aware that you have not elected me as your President by your ballots. So I ask you to confirm me as your President with your prayers. And I hope that such prayers will also be the first of many.

If you have not chosen by secret ballot, neither have I gained office by any secret promises. I have not campaigned either for the presidency or the vice presidency. I have not subscribed to any partisan platform, I am indebted to no man and only to one woman—my dear wife—as I begin the most difficult job in the world.

I have not sought this enormous responsibility, but I will not shirk it.

. . . I believe that truth is the glue that holds government together, not only our government, but civilization itself. That bond, though strained, is unbroken at home

*and abroad. In all my public and private acts as
your President, I expect to follow my instincts of openness
and candor with full confidence that honesty is always
the best policy in the end.*

*My fellow Americans, our long national nightmare is
over.*

Truth is the glue. . . . Honesty is always the best
policy. . . . Ford's efforts at ringing rhetoric turned
out to be cliché, but the old words were suddenly warm,
and the man and his manner reassuring. In the days that
followed, a country that had been ripped apart by bitterly
unpopular war and mind-boggling scandal saw that it had
at the helm a good and decent man who was without
pretension and was just trying to do his best.

Two years later, in 1976, the war was over and the
scandal was history, and the country, by a narrow margin,
rejected Ford's efforts to win the presidency on his own.
He was not a commanding figure; he was not viewed as
a man of vision or imagination or strength. (Indeed,
several of Ford's top advisers admitted privately that he
would not be their first choice for President.) But for the
time he served—that time when the nation viewed its
leaders with distrust and doubt—Gerald Ford was perhaps the best man for the job.

The Capitol. President Carter stood before the crowd,
the dignitaries, the country. He acknowledged their applause. Then he began his inaugural address. "For myself and our nation, I want to thank my predecessor for
all he has done to heal our land." Humphrey jumped
to his feet and led an ovation that was the loudest and
longest of the day.

President Carter turned to former President Ford and
smiled. "God bless you, sir," Catrer said softly, "I'm proud
of you." Ford slowly got to his feet, and tears filled his
eyes. He shook Carter's hand and waved to the roaring
crowd.

Finally Carter continued.

His speech was short and unpretentious. He talked for
fifteen minutes of old values and collective strength.

"I have no new dream to set forth today, but rather

urge a fresh faith in the old dream," Carter said. "The American dream endures. . . . You have given me a great responsibility—to stay close to you, to be worthy of you and to exemplify what you are. Your strength can compensate for my weakness, and your wisdom can help to minimize my mistakes.

"Let us learn together and laugh together and work together and pray together, confident that in the end we will triumph together in the right."

Then it was over. There was applause, and the former President came over to shake the hand of the new President. So did Rockefeller. And Mondale. And then many others.

Carter disappeared inside the Capitol. But Ford lingered on the platform, saying good-byes. He was among the last to leave. He walked up the familiar flight of stairs of the Capitol in the company, appropriately, of one of his friends from his days in the House, Congressman John W. Wydler of New York. Soon Ford was gone. His marine helicopter lifted off from nearby Fort McNair and swooped low over the Capitol dome. He was on his way to play in Bing Crosby's tournament at Pebble Beach, California.

And Jimmy Carter was beginning his inaugural parade. He stepped out of his limousine and walked with his family sixteen blocks up Pennsylvania Avenue, smiling and waving on his way to the White House.

Appendixes

Appendix One

Memorandum

To: Jimmy Carter
From: Hamilton Jordan
August 4, 1974

Personal and Confidential

I think we have reached the stage in our efforts where we should pause to assess our progress to this point and take a hard and realistic look at the future. I have attempted in the following pages to review the major aspects of our effort and to set forth some realistic detailed plans for the next several months. . . .

Pre-announcement activities

We will need to develop a system of informing key individuals and certain groups either in advance of the actual announcement or simultaneous with it. For the purpose of discussion, I divide the individuals you should personally talk with and/or notify into several groups. First, there is that group of key individuals who are politically significant or who are potential entrepreneurs or friends of yours, and who will be flattered and possibly persuaded to support your candidacy because you have chosen to personally confide in them. . . .

The second group are politically significant people who you know and who are friendly to you but are *not* likely to respond to being told of your plans with a pledge of support. This includes leaders in major labor unions and politically active national organizations, certain newspaper and magazine publishers, certain Democratic members of Congress, some Democratic governors and key Democratic activists. . . . The people I am talking about in this group are Al Barkan, Mike Mansfield, Katharine Graham, Carl Albert, Joe Crangle, and others of this sort.

. . . The third group of people to be notified are the Democratic members of Congress, Democratic governors and mayors, state party chairmen, members of the Democratic National Committee, and key Democratic Party workers and activists. My suggestion here is that we send a high-quality, personalized mailing to these people that would arrive simultaneous with your announcement. The message would be positive . . . [concerning] your commitment to run anywhere against anybody and convincing in terms of analyzing your prospects for winning the party's nomination. This mailing would not ask for money, but would ask for their advice and/or their support. . . .

The fourth group are our Georgia friends and supporters. We have computer tapes with the names of 8,000 persons who have contributed to your campaign and/or the Democratic Party. . . .

The fifth group of people to be contacted are your key out-of-state friends who are not necessarily Democrats and not necessarily active in politics but have met you somewhere along the way and had a favorable contact or experience with you. This should be a personal mailing which asks for their help and financial support.

The last group of people to be contacted are the large number of out-of-state names that we have accumulated from the last four years. These range from a trooper who drove you several years ago in Ohio to a businessman who met you at a prayer breakfast in Oklahoma to a woman that met you at a Democratic meeting in New York. By late November, Steve and I estimate that you will have 13,000–15,000 names that fall into this broad and very general contact. They should receive a positive, friendly letter which asks for their help and money. . . .

Announcement statement

When you consider how jaded and cynical the members of the national press corps have become and think about all the clichés and doubletalk they are presently hearing from ambitious politicians, then possibly you can imagine the challenge you have to say something that is fresh, bold, and believable. I will not attempt to write your speech here—that is something that should evolve from you, Jody, Stu, and the issues group.

Outline pragmatic strategy for winning Democratic nomination

It is our hope that your being the first to announce will result in your receiving a disproportionate amount of press coverage initially. Your being covered on a continuing basis and being treated as a serious, viable candidate depends to a large extent on your being able to convince the working press that you can—in fact—win the Democratic nomination. Consequently . . . [emphasize that] you are totally committed to the race and will run against anyone anywhere. You will run against Wallace in the South, Kennedy in New England.

Time and place

I believe that we have generally agreed that you should announce your candidacy for the Presidency the week following the Charter Conference in Washington, D.C. It was tentatively agreed that we should pursue the possibility of the press club announcement at least to the point of determining if that is—in fact—one of our options. . . . On the same day or next day I believe that it is important that we have some function here in Georgia where you announce your plans to our friends in Georgia. It is terribly important that you "share" your announcement with the Georgia people to avoid [it] being said that Jimmy Carter has gone national and has forgotten his state and people. . . .

We should never forget that our early announcement is a tactical maneuver which will hopefully result in your receiving inordinate amounts of coverage and publicity.

Your schedule between now and December

. . . We would do well to keep the primary schedule uppermost in our minds—particularly in terms of your schedule in out-of-state trips. It doesn't make sense to worry about West Virginia and Oregon if you haven't first [done] some work in Illinois and Pennsylvania. . . .

Relationship with Strauss and the DNC

We are laboring under one handicap at present that is not particularly significant now, but it will become more significant with the passage of time and increasingly difficult to correct or overcome. We lack having a strong Carter supporter on the inside of the Party apparatus to keep generally informed and [who] can effectively advocate a point of view on important matters that is favorable to you.

. . . Almost every potential Democratic candidate has someone on the executive committee who is close to them except us. . . . At an appropriate time—right up to the 1974 election—you need to discuss your plans with Strauss anyway. I think you can make the argument to Strauss that you are entitled to have representation of those committees which make the major decisions which will impact on the nomination process —particularly in view of the fact that most of the other potential candidates already have supporters on the executive committee in the DNC. . . .

Application of the targeting concept to a national campaign

In our national campaign to win the Democratic nomination for President, there are three major factors to be considered—the relative *size* of the state and the delegation to the Democratic National Convention, the *sequence* of the primaries and the *sequence* of the delegate selection process in the non-primary states, and our own campaign *strategy*. . . .

Sequence

Primary states: Sequence or chronological order of the primaries is important for obvious reasons. Good or poor showings can have a profound and irrevocable impact on succeeding primaries and a campaign's ability to raise funds and recruit workers.

The press shows an exaggerated interest in the early primaries as they represent the first confrontation between candidates, their contrasting strategies and styles, which the press has been writing and speculating about for two years. We would do well to understand the very special and powerful role the press plays in interpreting the primary results for the rest of the nation. What is actually accomplished in [the] New Hampshire primary is less important than how the press interprets it for the nation. Handled properly, a defeat can be interpreted as a "holding action" and a victory as a mediocre showing. I remember the Mc-Carthy-McGovern campaign in '72 and '68 as "victories" when in fact they ran second to Muskie and Johnson.

Non-primary states: The sequence of the selection of delegates in the non-primary states is important, but more as a test of organizational ability than as a test of the candidates and their campaigns. The initial delegate selections will generate some news stories and will be important, but in the long run they will take a back seat to the coverage of the primaries and will be significant in relation to the number of delegates being selected and its impact on the delegate totals of the various candidates. . . .

Strategy

. . . The strategy outlined below is general and tentative. The real value of this exercise is to develop a system for testing this and other strategies.

a. Early primaries. The prospect of a crowded field coupled with the new proportional representation rule

does not permit much flexibility in the early primaries.
No serious candidate will have the luxury of picking or
choosing among the early primaries. To pursue such a
strategy would cost that candidate delegate votes and
increase the possibility of being lost in the crowd. I
think that we have to assume that everybody will be
running in the first five or six primaries.

A crowded field enhances the possibility of several
inconclusive primaries with four or five candidates
separated by only a few percentage points. Such a
muddled picture will not continue for long as the press
will begin to make "winners" of some and "losers" of
others. The intense press coverage which naturally
focuses on the early primaries plus the decent time in-
tervals which separate the March and mid-April primaries dictate a serious effort in all of the first five
primaries. Our "public" strategy would probably be
that Florida was the first and real test of the Carter
campaign and that New Hampshire would just be a
warm-up. In fact, a strong, surprise showing in New
Hampshire should be our goal which would have
tremendous impact on successive primaries.

Our minimal goal in these early primaries would be
to gain acceptance as a serious and viable candidate,
demonstrate that Wallace is vulnerable and that Carter
can appeal to the "Wallace" constituency, and show
through our campaign a contrasting style and appeal.
Our minimal goal would dictate at least a second-place
showing in New Hampshire and Florida and respectable showings in Wisconsin, Rhode Island, and Illinois.
Our national goals (which I think are highly attainable)
would be to win New Hampshire and/or Florida out-
right, make strong showings in the other three early
primary states and beat Wallace.

b. April and May primaries. The late April and early
May primaries will dictate difficult and strategic de-
ficiencies on the allocation of resources. Lack of funds
in time will restrict us from running a personal campaign in every state. Hopefully, good press in the early
primaries will have solved some of our name recognition and given Jimmy Carter some depth to his new
national image. Nonetheless, there will still be ten
primaries in two weeks. If, by this point, we have

knocked Wallace off in left field in a primary or two, we will be in strong position to raise funds and enter them all. The results of the first primaries are not likely to be conclusive, and we will be in a position of making some tough decisions that can win or lose a Democratic nomination.

Appendix Two

Remarks by Governer Carter at the
Martin Luther King, Jr. Hospital
Los Angeles, June 1, 1976

We are here today to honor a man with a dream.

We are here to honor a man who lived and died for the causes of human brotherhood.

Martin Luther King, Jr., was the conscience of his generation.

He was a doctor to a sick society.

He was a prophet of a new and better America.

He was a southerner, a black man, who in his too-short lift stood with Presidents and kings, and was honored around the world, but who never forgot the poor people, the oppressed people, who were his brothers and sisters and from whom he drew his strength.

He was the man, more than any other of his generation, who gazed upon the great wall of segregation and saw that it could be destroyed by the power of love.

I sometimes think that a southerner of my generation can most fully understand the meaning and the impact of Martin Luther King's life.

He and I grew up in the same South, he the son of a clergyman, I the son of a farmer. We both knew, from opposite sides, the invisible wall of racial segregation.

The official rule then was "separate but equal," but in truth we were neither—not separate, not equal.

When I was a boy, almost all my playmates were black. We worked in the fields together, and hunted and fished and swam together, but when it was time for church or for school, we went our separate ways, without really understanding why.

Our lives were dominated by unspoken, unwritten, but powerful rules, rules that were almost never challenged.

A few people challenged them, not in politics, but in the way they lived their lives. My mother was one of those people. She was a nurse. She would work twelve hours a day and then come home and care for her family and minister to the people of our little community, both black and white.

My mother knew no color line. Her black friends were just as welcome in her home as her white friends, a fact that shocked some people, sometimes even my father, who was very conventional in his views on race.

I left Georgia in 1943 and went off to the navy and by the time I returned home ten years later, the South and the nation had begun to change.

The change was slow and painful. After the Supreme Court outlawed school segregation, the wrong kind of politicians stirred up angry resistance, and little towns like mine were torn apart by fear and resentment.

Yet the change was coming. Across the South, courageous young black students demanded service at segregated lunch counters. And in the end they prevailed.

In Montgomery, a woman named Rosa Parks refused to move to the back of the bus, a young clergyman named Martin Luther King joined the protest, and a movement had found its leader.

In 1961, we had a new President, John Kennedy, who responded to the demands of the civil rights movement, and who used the power of his office to enforce court orders at the University of Alabama and the University of Mississippi, and who by the last year of his life was giving moral leadership in the struggle for equal rights.

In August of 1963 Martin Luther King stood on the steps of the Lincoln Memorial in Washington and told a quarter of a million people of his dream for America.

"I have a dream," he said. "I have a dream that one day on the red hills of Georgia, sons of former slaves and sons of former slaveowners will be able to sit down together at the table of brotherhood."

"I have a dream," he said, "that my four little children will one day live in a nation where they will not be judged by the color of their skin but by the content of their character. I have a dream."

And so the dream was born. The challenge was made. The rest was up to America.

Three months after Dr. King's speech, President Kennedy was dead, and we had a new President, a Texan, a man whom many black people distrusted. But soon Lyndon Johnson stood before the Congress of the United States and promised, "We shall overcome!"

Lyndon Johnson carried forward the dream of equality. He used his political genius to pass the voting rights bill, a bill that was the best thing that happened to the South in my lifetime. The voting rights act did not just guarantee the vote for black people. It liberated the South both black and white. It made it possible for the South to come out of the past and into the mainstream of American politics.

It made it possible for a southerner to stand before you this evening as a serious candidate for President of the United States.

But war came, and destroyed Lyndon Johnson's Great Society. Martin Luther King spoke out against the war. There were those who told him to keep silent, who told him he would undercut his prestige if he opposed the war, but he followed his conscience and spoke his mind.

Then in the spring of 1968 he went to Memphis to help the garbage workers get a decent wage, to help the men who did the dirtiest job for the lowest pay, and while he was there he was shot and killed.

But his dream lives on.

Perhaps some of you remember the night of Dr. King's death. Robert Kennedy was in Indianapolis, running for President, speaking before a black audience. At that point, on that awful night, Robert Kennedy was perhaps the only politician in America who could have spoken to black people and been listened to.

Let me tell you what he said.

He said, "What we need in the United States is not division, what we need in the United States is not hatred, what we need in the United States is not violence and lawlessness, but love and wisdom and compassion toward one another, and a feeling of justice toward those who still suffer within our country, whether they be white or whether they be black."

Those words are still true today.

We lost Martin Luther King.

We lost Robert Kennedy.

We lost the election that year to men who governed without love or laughter, to men who promised law and order and gave us crime and oppression.

But the dream lived on.

It could be slowed, but never stopped.

In Atlanta, a young man named Andrew Young, who had been Martin Luther King's strong right hand, was elected to the Congress of the United States.

All over America, black men and women were carrying the dream forward into politics.

In Georgia, when I was governor, we appointed black people to jobs and judgeships they had never held before, and one day we hung a portrait of Martin Luther King, Jr., in our state capitol.

There were protests, but they didn't matter. Inside our state capitol, Coretta King and Daddy King and Andy Young and I and hundreds of others joined hands and sang "We shall Overcome."

And we shall.

I stand before you, a candidate for President, a man whose life has been lifted, as yours have been, by the dream of Martin Luther King.

When I started to run for President, there were those who said I would fail, because I am from the South.

But I thought they were wrong. I thought the dream was taking hold.

And I ran for President throughout our nation.

We have won in the South, and we have won in the North, and now we come to the West and we ask your help.

For all our progress, we still live in a land held back by oppression and injustice.

The few who are rich and powerful still make the decisions, and the many who are poor and weak must suffer the consequences. If those in power make mistakes it is not they or their families who lose their jobs or go on welfare or lack medical care or go to jail.

We still have poverty in the midst of plenty.

We still have far to go. We must give our government back to our people. The road will not be easy.

But we still have the dream, Martin Luther King's dream and your dream and my dream. The America we long for is still out there, somewhere ahead of us, waiting for us to find her.

I see an America poised not only at the brink of a new century, but at the dawn of a new era of honest, compassionate, responsive government.

I see an American government that has turned away from scandals and corruption and cynicism and finally become as decent as our people.

I see an America with a tax system that does not steal from the poor and give to the rich.

I see an America with a job for every man and woman who can work, and a decent standard of living for those who cannot.

I see an America in which my child and your child and every child receives an education second to none in the world.

I see an American government that does not spy on its citizens or harass its citizens, but respects your dignity and your privacy and your right to be let alone.

I see an American foreign policy that is firm and consistent and generous, and that once again is a beacon for the hopes of the world.

I see an American President who does not govern by vetoes and negativism, but with vigor and vision and affirmative leadership, a President who is not isolated from our people, but feels their pain and shares their dreams and takes his strength from them.

I see an America in which Martin Luther King's dream is our national dream.

I see an America on the move again, united, its wounds healed, its head high, a diverse and vital nation, moving into its third century with confidence and competence and compassion, an America that lives up to the majesty of its Constitution and the simple decency of its people.

This is the America that I see, and that I am committed to as I run for President.

I ask your help.

You will always have mine.

Thank you.

Appendix Three

CARTER/MONDALE CAMPAIGN SCHEDULING FORMULA

Devised by Hamilton Jordan

| State | Democratic | | | | | | | | | Percent |
	Size		Potential	Need		Total	Total	÷	1083	=	of Effort
Alabama	9.0	+	4.5	3.5	=	17.0	17.0	÷	1083	=	1.5%
Alaska	3.0	+	2.2	2.0	=	7.2	7.2	÷	1083	=	.6%
Arizona	6.0	+	2.2	2.0	=	10.2	10.2	÷	1083	=	.9%
Arkansas	6.0	+	6.7	3.5	=	16.2	16.2	÷	1083	=	1.4%
California	45.0	+	9.0	9.8	=	63.8	63.8	÷	1083	=	5.9%
Colorado	7.0	+	6.7	6.2	=	19.9	19.9	÷	1083	=	1.8%
Connecticut	8.0	+	9.0	9.8	=	26.8	26.8	÷	1083	=	2.4%
Delaware	3.0	+	9.0	2.0	=	14.0	14.0	÷	1083	=	1.2%
Florida	17.0	+	6.7	6.2	=	29.9	29.9	÷	1083	=	2.7%
Georgia	12.0	+	4.5	2.0	=	18.5	18.5	÷	1083	=	1.7%
Hawaii	4.0	+	6.7	2.0	=	12.7	12.7	÷	1083	=	1.1%
Idaho	4.0	+	2.2	3.5	=	9.7	9.7	÷	1083	=	.8%

State	Size	+	Democratic Potential	+	Need	=	Total	Total	+	1083	=	Percent of Effort
Illinois	26.0	+	9.0	+	9.8	=	44.8	44.8	+	1083	=	4.1%
Indiana	13.0	+	4.5	+	9.8	=	27.3	27.3	+	1083	=	2.5%
Iowa	8.0	+	9.0	+	6.2	=	23.2	23.2	+	1083	=	2.1%
Kansas	7.0	+	2.2	+	2.0	=	11.2	11.2	+	1083	=	1.0%
Kentucky	9.0	+	9.0	+	3.5	=	21.5	21.5	+	1083	=	1.9%
Louisiana	10.0	+	4.5	+	3.5	=	18.0	18.0	+	1083	=	1.6%
Maine	4.0	+	2.2	+	3.5	=	9.7	9.7	+	1083	=	.8%
Maryland	10.0	+	4.5	+	9.8	=	24.3	24.3	+	1083	=	2.2%
Massachusetts	14.0	+	9.0	+	3.5	=	26.5	26.5	+	1083	=	2.4%
Michigan	21.0	+	6.7	+	9.8	=	37.5	37.5	+	1083	=	3.4%
Minnesota	10.0	+	9.0	+	2.0	=	21.0	21.0	+	1083	=	1.9%
Mississippi	7.0	+	4.5	+	3.5	=	15.0	15.0	+	1083	=	1.3%
Missouri	12.0	+	6.7	+	9.8	=	28.5	28.5	+	1083	=	2.6%
Montana	4.0	+	9.0	+	6.2	=	19.2	19.2	+	1083	=	1.8%
Nebraska	5.0	+	2.2	+	2.0	=	9.2	9.2	+	1083	=	.8%
Nevada	3.0	+	9.0	+	6.2	=	18.2	18.2	+	1083	=	1.6%
New Hampshire	4.0	+	2.2	+	3.5	=	9.7	9.7	+	1083	=	.8%
New Jersey	17.0	+	6.7	+	9.8	=	33.5	33.5	+	1083	=	3.0%
New Mexico	4.0	+	4.5	+	6.2	=	14.7	14.7	+	1083	=	1.3%
New York	41.0	+	4.5	+	9.8	=	55.3	55.3	+	1083	=	5.1%

State	Size		Democratic Potential		Need		Total		Total	÷	1083	=	Percent of Effort
North Carolina	13.0	+	2.2	+	3.5	=	18.7		18.7	÷	1083	=	1.7%
North Dakota	3.0	+	2.2	+	6.2	=	11.4		11.4	÷	1083	=	1.0%
Ohio	25.0	+	2.2	+	6.2	=	33.4		33.4	÷	1083	=	3.0%
Oklahoma	8.0	+	2.2	+	6.2	=	16.4		16.4	÷	1083	=	1.5%
Oregon	6.0	+	6.7	+	6.2	=	18.9		18.9	÷	1083	=	1.7%
Pennsylvania	27.0	+	6.7	+	6.2	=	39.9		39.9	÷	1083	=	3.6%
Rhode Island	4.0	+	9.0	+	2.0	=	15.0		15.0	÷	1083	=	1.3%
South Carolina	8.0	+	4.5	+	3.5	=	16.0		16.0	÷	1083	=	1.4%
South Dakota	4.0	+	6.7	+	2.0	=	12.7		12.7	÷	1083	=	1.1%
Tennessee	10.0	+	4.5	+	3.5	=	18.0		18.0	÷	1083	=	1.6%
Texas	26.0	+	4.5	+	6.2	=	36.7		36.7	÷	1083	=	3.3%
Utah	4.0	+	4.5	+	6.2	=	14.7		14.7	÷	1083	=	1.3%
Vermont	3.0	+	2.2	+	3.5	=	8.7		8.7	÷	1083	=	.8%
Virginia	12.0	+	2.2	+	3.5	=	17.7		17.7	÷	1083	=	1.6%
Washington	9.0	+	4.5	+	9.8	=	23.3		23.3	÷	1083	=	2.1%
West Virginia	6.0	+	6.7	+	3.5	=	16.2		16.2	÷	1083	=	1.4%
Wisconsin	11.0	+	9.0	+	9.8	=	29.8		29.8	÷	1083	=	2.7%
Wyoming	3.0	+	2.2	+	2.0	=	7.2		7.2	÷	1083	=	.6%
Dist. of Columbia	3.0	+	9.0	+	2.0	=	14.0		14.0	÷	1083	=	1.2%

SCHEDULING FORMULA

Candidate	Numerical Value Per Day of Campaigning		Campaign Days Planned		Individual Totals
Jimmy Carter	7	×	43	=	301
Walter Mondale	5	×	43	=	215
Rosalynn Carter	4	×	35	=	140
Joan Mondale	3	×	27	=	81
Jack and Judy Carter	2	×	35	=	70
Chip and Caron Carter	2	×	35	=	70
Jeff and Annette Carter	2	×	35	=	70

Total Scheduling Points 947

SCHEDULING POINTS PER STATE

State	Percent of Effort	X	Total Scheduling Points	=	Scheduling Points Earned
Alabama	1.5	×	947	=	14
Alaska	.6	×	947	=	6
Arizona	.9	×	947	=	9
Arkansas	1.4	×	947	=	13
California	5.9	×	947	=	56
Colorado	1.8	×	947	=	17
Connecticut	2.4	×	947	=	23
Delaware	1.2	×	947	=	11
Florida	2.7	×	947	=	26
Georgia	1.7	×	947	=	11
Hawaii	1.1	×	947	=	10
Idaho	.8	×	947	=	8
Illinois	4.1	×	947	=	39
Indiana	2.5	×	947	=	24
Iowa	2.1	×	947	=	20
Kansas	1.0	×	947	=	10
Kentucky	1.9	×	947	=	18
Louisiana	1.6	×	947	=	15
Maine	.8	×	947	=	8
Maryland	2.2	×	947	=	21
Massachusetts	2.4	×	947	=	23
Michigan	3.4	×	947	=	32
Minnesota	1.9	×	947	=	18
Mississippi	1.3	×	947	=	12
Missouri	2.6	×	947	=	25
Montana	1.8	×	947	=	17
Nebraska	.8	×	947	=	8
Nevada	1.6	×	947	=	15
New Hampshire	.8	×	947	=	8
New Jersey	3.0	×	947	=	28
New Mexico	1.3	×	947	=	12
New York	5.1	×	947	=	48
North Carolina	1.7	×	947	=	16
North Dakota	1.0	×	947	=	9
Ohio	3.0	×	947	=	28
Oklahoma	1.5	×	947	=	14
Oregon	1.7	×	947	=	16

SCHEDULING POINTS PER STATE

State	Percent of Effort	X	Total Scheduling Points	=	Scheduling Points Earned
Pennsylvania	3.6	×	947	=	34
Rhode Island	1.3	×	947	=	12
South Carolina	1.4	×	947	=	13
South Dakota	1.1	×	947	=	10
Tennessee	1.6	×	947	=	15
Texas	3.3	×	947	=	31
Utah	1.3	×	947	=	12
Vermont	.8	×	947	=	8
Virginia	1.6	×	947	=	15
Washington	2.1	×	947	=	20
West Virginia	1.4	×	947	=	13
Wisconsin	2.7	×	947	=	26
Wyoming	.6	×	947	=	6
Dist. of Columbia	1.2	×	947	=	11

Appendix Four

OFFICIAL 1976 PRESIDENTIAL VOTE

Total Popular Votes: 81,551,659
Carter's Plurality: 1,680,974

State	JIMMY CARTER (Democrat) Votes	%	GERALD R. FORD (Republican) Votes	%	OTHER Votes	%	Electoral Votes	Plurality	
Alabama	659,170	55.7	504,070	42.6	19,610	1.7	9	C	155,100
Alaska	44,055	35.7	71,555	57.9	7,935	6.4	3	F	27,500
Arizona	295,602	39.8	418,642	56.4	28,475	3.8	6	F	123,040
Arkansas	498,604	65.0	267,903	34.9	1,028	0.1	6	C	230,701
California	3,742,284	47.6	3,882,244	49.3	242,515	3.1	45	F	139,960
Colorado	460,801	42.5	584,456	54.0	37,709	3.5	7	F	123,655
Connecticut	647,895	46.9	719,261	52.1	14,370	1.0	8	F	71,366
Delaware	122,559	52.0	109,780	46.6	3,403	1.4	3	C	12,779
Dist. of Col.	137,818	81.6	27,873	16.5	3,139	1.9	3	C	109,945
Florida	1,636,000	51.9	1,469,531	46.6	45,100	1.4	17	C	166,469
Georgia	979,409	66.7	483,743	33.0	4,306	0.3	12	C	495,666
Hawaii	147,375	50.6	140,003	48.1	3,923	1.3	4	C	7,372
Idaho	126,549	36.8	204,151	59.3	13,387	3.9	4	F	77,602
Illinois	2,271,295	48.1	2,364,269	50.1	83,269	1.8	26	F	92,974
Indiana	1,014,714	45.7	1,185,958	53.4	21,690	1.0	13	F	171,244
Iowa	619,931	48.5	632,863	49.5	26,512	2.1	8	F	12,932
Kansas	430,421	44.9	502,752	52.5	24,672	2.6	7	F	72,331

State	JIMMY CARTER (Democrat)		GERALD R. FORD (Republican)		OTHER		Electoral Votes	Plurality	
	Votes	%	Votes	%	Votes	%			
Kentucky	615,717	52.8	531,852	45.6	19,573	1.7	9	C	83,865
Louisiana	661,365	51.7	587,446	46.0	29,628	2.3	10	C	73,919
Maine	232,279	48.1	236,320	48.9	14,610	3.0	4	F	4,041
Maryland	759,612	52.8	672,661	46.7	7,624	0.5	10	C	86,951
Massachusetts	1,429,475	56.1	1,030,276	40.4	87,807	3.4	14	C	399,199
Michigan	1,696,714	46.4	1,893,742	51.8	63,294	1.7	21	F	197,028
Minnesota	1,070,440	54.9	819,395	42.0	59,754	3.1	10	C	251,045
Mississippi	381,329	49.6	366,846	47.7	21,205	2.8	7	C	14,483
Missouri	998,387	51.1	927,443	47.5	27,770	1.4	12	C	70,944
Montana	149,259	45.4	173,703	52.8	5,772	1.8	4	F	24,444
Nebraska	233,293	38.4	359,219	59.2	14,237	2.3	5	F	125,926
Nevada	92,479	45.8	101,273	50.2	8,124	4.0	3	F	8,794
New Hampshire	147,645	43.5	185,935	54.7	6,047	1.8	4	F	38,290
New Jersey	1,444,653	47.9	1,509,688	50.1	60,131	2.0	17	F	65,035
New Mexico	201,148	48.3	211,419	50.7	4,023	1.0	4	F	10,271
New York	3,389,558	51.9	3,100,791	47.5	43,851	0.7	41	C	288,767
North Carolina	927,365	55.2	741,960	44.2	9,589	0.6	13	C	185,405
North Dakota	136,078	45.8	153,470	51.7	7,545	2.5	3	F	17,392
Ohio	2,011,621	48.9	2,000,505	48.7	99,747	2.4	25	C	11,116
Oklahoma	532,442	48.7	545,708	50.0	14,101	1.3	8	F	13,266
Oregon	490,407	47.6	492,120	47.8	47,306	4.6	6	F	1,713
Pennsylvania	2,328,677	50.4	2,205,604	47.7	86,506	1.9	27	C	123,073
Rhode Island	227,636	55.4	181,249	44.1	2,285	0.6	4	C	46,387
South Carolina	450,807	56.2	346,149	43.1	5,627	0.7	8	C	104,658
South Dakota	147,068	48.9	151,505	50.4	2,105	0.7	4	F	4,437
Tennessee	825,879	55.9	633,969	42.9	16,498	1.1	10	C	191,910

State	JIMMY CARTER (Democrat)		GERALD R. FORD (Republican)		OTHER		Electoral Votes	Plurality	
	Votes	%	Votes	%	Votes	%			
Texas	2,082,319	51.1	1,953,300	48.0	36,265	0.9	26	C	129,019
Utah	182,110	33.6	337,908	62.4	21,200	3.9	4	F	155,798
Vermont	78,789	42.8	100,387	54.6	4,726	2.6	3	F	21,598
Virginia	813,896	48.0	836,554	49.3	46,644	2.7	12	F	22,658
Washington	717,323	46.1	777,732	50.0	60,479	3.9	9	F	60,409
West Virginia	435,864	58.1	314,726	41.9			6	C	121,138
Wisconsin	1,040,232	49.4	1,004,987	47.8	58,956	2.8	11	C	35,245
Wyoming	62,239	39.8	92,717	59.3	1,387	0.9	3	F	30,478
Totals	40,828,587	50.1	39,147,613	48.0	1,575,459	1.9	538	C	1,680,974

NOTE: This chart is based on official results obtained from the states. The "other" vote listed after Carter and Ford is a combination of third party and scattered write-in votes.

Electoral Votes

Carter   297
Ford   241

This chart, excluding the electoral votes, was compiled and published by *Congressional Quarterly*, and is reprinted with the permission of Congressional Quarterly, Inc.

436

Appendix Five

Inaugural Address of President Jimmy Carter

Following His Swearing In as the 39th President of the United States. January 20, 1977

For myself and for our Nation, I want to thank my predecessor for all he has done to heal our land.

In this outward and physical ceremony, we attest once again to the inner and spiritual strength of our Nation. As my high school teacher, Miss Julia Coleman, used to say, "We must adjust to changing times and still hold to unchanging principles."

Here before me is the Bible used in the inauguration of our first President, in 1789, and I have just taken the oath of office on the Bible my mother gave me just a few years ago, opened to a timeless admonition from the ancient prophet Micah: "He hath showed thee, O man, what is good; and what doth the Lord require of thee, but to do justly, and to love mercy, and to walk humbly with thy god." (Micah 6:8)

This inauguration ceremony marks a new beginning, a new dedication within our government, and a new spirit among us all. A President may sense and proclaim that new spirit, but only a people can provide it.

Two centuries ago, our Nation's birth was a milestone in the long quest for freedom. But the bold and brilliant dream which excited the Founders of this Nation still awaits its consummation. I have no new dream to set forth today, but rather urge a fresh faith in the old dream.

Ours was the first society openly to define itself in terms of both spirituality and human liberty. It is that unique self-definition which has given us an exceptional appeal— but it also imposes on us a special obligation to take on those moral duties which, when assumed, seem invariably to be in our own best interests.

You have given me a great responsibility—to stay close to you, to be worthy of you, and to exemplify what you are. Let us create together a new national spirit of unity and trust. Your strength can compensate for my weakness, and your wisdom can help to minimize my mistakes.

Let us learn together and laugh together and work together and pray together, confident that in the end we will triumph together in the right.

The American dream endures. We must once again have full faith in our country—and in one another. I believe America can be better. We can be even stronger than before.

Let our recent mistakes bring a resurgent commitment to the basic principles of our Nation, for we know that if we despise our own government, we have no future. We recall in special times when we have stood briefly, but magnificently, united. In those times no prize was beyond our grasp.

But we cannot dwell upon remembered glory. We cannot afford to drift. We reject the prospect of failure or mediocrity or an inferior quality of life for any person. Our government must at the same time be both competent and compassionate.

We have already found a high degree of personal liberty, and we are now struggling to enhance equality of opportunity. Our commitment to human rights must be both absolute, our laws fair, our national beauty preserved; the powerful must not persecute the weak, and human dignity must be enhanced.

We have learned that *more* is not necessarily *better*, that even our great Nation has its recognized limits, and that we can neither answer all questions nor solve all problems. We cannot afford to do everything, nor can we afford to lack boldness as we meet the future. So together, in a spirit of individual sacrifice for the common good, we must simply do our best.

Our Nation can be strong abroad only if it is strong at home. And we know that the best way to enhance freedom in other lands is to demonstrate here that our democratic system is worthy of emulation.

To be true to ourselves, we must be true to others. We

will not behave in foreign places so as to violate our rules and standards here at home, for we know that the trust which our Nation earns is essential to our strength.

The world itself is now dominated by a new spirit. Peoples more numerous and more politically aware are craving, and now demanding, their place in the sun—not just for the benefit of their own physical condition, but for basic human rights.

The passion for freedom is on the rise. Tapping this new spirit, there can be no nobler nor more ambitious task for America to undertake on this day of a new beginning than to help shape a just and peaceful world that is truly humane.

We are a strong Nation, and we will maintain strength so sufficient that it need not be proven in combat—a quiet strength based not merely on the size of an arsenal, but on the nobility of ideas.

We will be ever vigilant and never vulnerable, and we will fight our wars against poverty, ignorance, and injustice, for those are the enemies against which our forces can be honorably marshalled.

We are a proudly idealistic Nation, but let no one confuse our idealism with weakness.

Because we are free, we can never be indifferent to the fate of freedom elsewhere. Our moral sense dictates a clearcut preference of those societies which share with us an abiding respect for individual human rights. We do not seek to intimidate, but it is clear that a world which others can dominate with impunity would be inhospitable to decency and a threat to the well-being of all people.

The world is still engaged in a massive armaments race designed to ensure continuing equivalent strength among potential adversaries. We pledge perseverance and wisdom in our efforts to limit the world's armaments to those necessary for each nation's own domestic safety. And we will move this year a step toward our ultimate goal—the elimination of all nuclear weapons from this Earth. We urge all other people to join us, for success can mean life instead of death.

Within us, the people of the United States, there is evident a serious and purposeful rekindling of confidence. And I join in the hope that when my time as your President has ended, people might say this about our Nation:

—that we had remembered the words of Micah and renewed our search for humility, mercy, and justice;

—that we had torn down the barriers that separated those of different race and region and religion and where there had been mistrust, built unity, with a respect for diversity;

—that we had found productive work for those able to perform it;

—that we had strengthened the American family, which is the basis of our society;

—that we had ensured respect for the law and equal treatment under the law, for the weak and the powerful, for the rich and the poor; and

—that we had enabled our people to be proud of their own government once again.

I would hope that the nations of the world might say that we had built a lasting peace, based not on weapons of war but on international policies which reflect our own most precious values.

These are not just my goals—and they will not be my accomplishments—but the affirmation of our Nation's continuing moral strength and our belief in an undiminished, ever-expanding American dream.

Thank you very much.

Index

DISTINGUISHED BIOGRAPHIES

_____ 80096 **AN AMERICAN LIFE: One Man's Road to Watergate, Jeb Stuart Magruder $1.95**

_____ 81656 **BLACKBERRY WINTER: My Earlier Years, Margaret Mead $2.75**

_____ 80432 **CONVERSATIONS WITH KENNEDY, Benjamin Bradlee $1.95**

_____ 80243 **DIARY OF A YOUNG GIRL, Anne Frank $1.75**

_____ 80077 **FDR'S LAST YEAR, Jim Bishop $2.45**

_____ 48132 **GOLDA: The Life of Israel's Prime Minister, Peggy Mann $1.25**

_____ 81216 **HARRY S. TRUMAN, Margaret Truman $2.50**

_____ 80845 **JOHNNY WE HARDLY KNEW YE, Kenneth O'Donnel and David Powers $2.25**

_____ 80332 **CRAZY SUNDAYS: F. Scott Fitzgerald in Hollywood, Aaron Latham $1.95**

_____ 80936 **PAPA, Gregory Hemingway, M.D. $1.75**

_____ 80712 **UNQUIET SOUL: A Biography of Charlotte Bronte, Margot Peters $2.75**

_____ 80932 **SYLVIA PLATH, Edward Butscher $2.50**

Available at bookstores everywhere, or order direct from the publisher.

DB 7-77

POCKET BOOKS
Department RK
1230 Avenue of the Americas
New York, N.Y. 10020

Please send me the books I have checked above. I am enclosing $_____ (please add 50¢ to cover postage and handling). Send check or money order—no cash or C.O.D.'s please.

NAME_____

ADDRESS_____

CITY_____STATE/ZIP_____

DB 7-77